Ethics in Sport

William J. Morgan, PhD
University of Tennessee

Klaus V. Meier, PhD
University of Western Ontario

Angela J. Schneider, PhD
University of Western Ontario

Editors

Human Kinetics

Library of Congress Cataloging-in-Publication Data

Ethics in sport / [edited by] William J. Morgan, Klaus V. Meier, Angela Schneider.
    p. cm.
  Includes index.
  ISBN 0-7360-3643-1
    1. Sports--Moral and ethical aspects--United States. 2. Sports--Social aspects--United
  States. I. Morgan, William John, 1948-   II. Meier, Klaus V., 1945-   III. Schneider,
  Angela, 1959-

  GV706.3 .E86 2001
  175--dc21

                                                                                00-046151

ISBN: 0-7360-3643-1

Acquisitions Editor: Linda Anne Bump; **Managing Editor:** Amy Stahl; **Assistant
Editor:** Derek Campbell; **Copyeditor:** Barbara Walsh; **Proofreaders:** Jim Burns and
Sarah Wiseman; **Indexer:** Betty Frizzéll; **Permission Manager:** Courtney Astle;
Graphic Designer: Fred Starbird; **Graphic Artist:** Denise Lowry; **Cover Designer:**
Keith Blomberg; **Printer:** Versa Press

Printed in the United States of America   10   9   8   7   6   5   4   3

Human Kinetics
Web site: www.HumanKinetics.com

United States: Human Kinetics, P.O. Box 5076, Champaign, IL 61825-5076
800-747-4457
e-mail: humank@hkusa.com

Canada: Human Kinetics, 475 Devonshire Road, Unit 100, Windsor, ON N8Y 2L5
800-465-7301 (in Canada only)
e-mail: orders@hkcanada.com

Europe: Human Kinetics, 107 Bradford Road, Stanningley
Leeds LS28 6AT, United Kingdom
+44 (0) 113 255 5665
e-mail: hk@hkeurope.com

Australia: Human Kinetics, 57A Price Avenue, Lower Mitcham, South Australia 5062
08 8277 1555
e-mail: liaw@hkaustralia.com

New Zealand: Human Kinetics, Division of Sports Distributors NZ Ltd.
P.O. Box 300 226 Albany, North Shore City, Auckland
0064 9 448 1207
e-mail: blairc@hknewz.com

Contents

Preface

Ethically speaking, the last few years have not been good ones for sport. Indeed, reading the sports pages these days is very much like reading the muckraking novels of the early part of this century that depicted in stark detail the moral imperfections of American life. The Latrell Sprewell choking incident; the Tyson-Holyfield ear-biting boxing debacle; the college baseball incident in which a Wichita State pitcher, on the apparent counsel of his pitching coach, threw a ball at an unsuspecting University of Evansville leadoff hitter while he was 30 feet from home plate taking practice swings, shattering his eye socket in three places; and the bribery scandal surrounding the awarding of the 2002 Winter Olympic Games to Salt Lake City come immediately to mind. To say that these discomfiting events do not inspire moral confidence in sport is to say the obvious.

But moral skepticism of this sort is not necessarily a bad thing. That is because having a keen sense of how the real world actually works, what the Oxford philosopher Isaiah Berlin called a "sense of reality," can have a salubrious effect on our moral inquiries. For one thing, it can help us see the folly of setting our moral expectations too high since sport is no more immune to corruption than politics, religion, or any other cultural endeavor. For another, it can help us see the folly of setting our moral sights too low since recognizing the base motives that often drive sports and their institutions reminds us never to let down our critical guard or to assume, without bothering to look first, that all is well with our sports and the throngs that follow them so intently.

On the other hand, a very real danger exists in making too much of the moral failings of sport, in becoming too preoccupied with its dark side. And that danger is that doing so will harden us against sport's moral possibilities, that we will develop a mind-numbing, self-defeating moral cynicism. If that happens, we will come to expect nothing of sport save its corruption, which reduces moral criticism of it to mere debunking. This type of cynicism is evident in two recent journalistic accounts that pick up on some of the moral shortcomings of sport just cited. In the first, David Remnick, the distinguished *New Yorker* critic, noted that bad apples like Sprewell were able to silence critics of their shaky character with their winning play, a fact, Remnick declared, that proves that, "Like it or not, goodness is a bonus, not a requirement, for playing ball" (July 5, 1999, p. 5). In the second, *New Republic* editorialist Jason Zengerle complained that the Olympics "have become a total sham" and concluded that they "are already so far gone that there's really only one surefire way to fix them: abolish them" (February 15, 1999, p. 6).

The problem here is not that Remnick's criticism of the moral shallowness of professional sports or Zengerle's criticism of the moral hypocrisy of the Olympics is off the mark; rather, the problem is both writers' dismissive tone. That tone suggests that we should simply write off sport for the morally flawed affair it essentially is, rather than submit it to more intense moral scrutiny. What distinguishes the latter from the former is that it is informed not only by a sense of reality but also by a sense of just what is so grating about, to take just the second example, the International Olympic Committee's actions: that the committee members regularly, even willfully, it seems, violate their own self-professed ideals. The Olympics are supposed to stand for something more than the accumulation of money; they are supposed to stand for things like peace and international goodwill achieved through friendly yet spirited competition. Take away these ideals, I submit, and the criticism of sport loses its critical point and moral edge.

The proper response to the present moral debilities of sport, then, is to submit them to the scalpel of moral reflection, not to dismiss them in a fit of moral outrage or defend them by burying our heads in the sand. And if we are going to be successful in plying that moral scalpel, we will need to be able to see sport both for what it really is and what it is capable of at its best. In other words, we will need both our wits (sense of reality) and our ideals if our moral probing of sport is to accomplish its objective.

It is with this dual sensibility in mind, then, that we have selected the essays that appear in this collection. We invite you to consider their merits, criticize their shortcomings, and join in the moral discussion of sport they provoke.

William J. Morgan
Klaus V. Meier
Angela J. Schneider

Introduction

Ethical inquiry deals with questions and issues of value, where value is understood in the sense of the goodness (rightness) and badness (wrongness) of our actions. Ethics is, therefore, a normative or prescriptive form of inquiry rather than a descriptive one since it is concerned more with how human agents *ought* to treat one another rather than with how in fact they *are* treating one another (though the latter is frequently what prompts our moral queries in the first place).

In particular, three central questions will be at issue in our ethical examination of sport. First, how should human agents treat one another (and, in the case of animal sports, other sentient beings) in sport settings? Second, how should they comport themselves individually and collectively in their pursuit of athletic excellence? And third, how should sport be morally evaluated from the larger standpoint of society (that is, in terms of its contributions to the common good)?

These three questions divide even more specifically into the five major parts of our present anthology. Part I focuses on the knotty issues of competition, fair play, cheating, and the place of winning in sport. Here the question of how we ought to treat one another in sport breaks down into the following sorts of questions: Is there a morally defensible account of competitive sport? What moral limitations do notions like being a good sport and fair play impose on winning? Morally speaking, what constitutes success and failure in competitive sport? Why should fair play be prized over cheating? These questions all bear in one way or another on the moral character and integrity of competitive sport and what it tells us about proper conduct within it.

Part II takes up the moral controversy swirling around athletes' use of performance-enhancing drugs. This issue, which dominates much of the present ethical discussion regarding sport, raises questions about the basic character of our humanness—what makes us the particular beings we are and what threatens our humanity; and about the nature and character of sports—what makes sports the particular practices they are and what threatens their integrity. This issue also raises some controversial questions concerning the pursuit of athletic excellence. The most obvious one is whether taking drugs to boost performance is morally permissible in the first place. As the essays in this section attest, the answer proves to be a contentious one that touches on issues of harm, paternalism, coercion, fairness, and the character of sport. Another question concerns forced urinalysis to detect the presence of either performance-enhancing or recreational drugs. Issues of privacy dominate here, such as whether athletes have a right to privacy that sports officials cannot abridge, and the proper referential authority of sports officials, who are not officers of the state.

Part III ventures into the terrain of gender equity and gender identity in sport. What makes the issue of gender equity such a thorny one is the apparent physiological advantages men enjoy over women in sport. This is troubling because the traditional accounts of sexual equality in the literature simply presume that men and women have equal potential to succeed in their chosen fields and that that potential in the case of women is hindered, wrongly and unnecessarily, by sexist practices that privilege men over women. So the matter of just how to ensure sexual equality in sport for women in light of physical differences proves complicated indeed. That is why discussions about how best to achieve such equality in sport, and about the moral soundness of remedies already proposed (e.g., Title IX) to garner equal opportunity for women in sport, occupy the attention of most of the essays in this part. But such questions do not dominate the equity issue entirely, and for good reason. For if the physical requirements of sports themselves put women at a disadvantage and make them appear inferior to men, then a reasonable question—and one asked by the authors in this section—is whether justice is better served in such instances by deemphasizing or even abolishing these male-privileged activities rather than seeking entry into them.

The second issue of gender identity is no less vexing, if for no other reason than it raises doubts about the ideal of gender equity itself. For even though women have made great strides in breaking down the barriers that have excluded or limited their participation in sport, they have hardly made a dent in the dominant masculine bias of sport. Sport, it is argued, continues to operate as a male bastion that privileges the male body and traditionally male forms of athletic conduct and excellence. The media, it is argued further, are important ideological accomplices in this regard, portraying women in ways that frustrate their efforts to forge a distinctive athletic identity.

So far we have been considering our moral obligations to our fellow human agents in our sporting endeavors. Part IV marks a new point of departure by asking after our moral responsibilities to animals in sport, to sentient beings that are often exploited, maimed, and even killed in the name of sport. The central questions here are whether animals have any moral interests (pain and suffering) or rights (to live their lives untrammeled by humans) that properly limit or outlaw their use in sport. Questions regarding the aims of animal sports (for example, hunting for subsistence or for pleasure), the prerogatives humans are allowed to take with animals, and whether human interests in certain cases properly trump those of animals also figure prominently in these discussions.

The authors of part V question whether sport is good for society, whether it makes some larger moral contribution to the common good. The main questions addressed here include the following: Are sports that place a premium on physical violence (for example, boxing) a threat to the moral fiber of society? Does sport teach any values that are vital to the moral flourishing of society? Ethically speaking, what are we to make of the great public admiration accorded athletic heroes? Does sport inculcate a sense of belonging and a basic equality of condition that encourage civic pride and national solidarity? When, if ever, is it appropriate to alter the conditions of sport competition on grounds of social justice (basic fairness) to accommodate the interests of disabled athletes? How much public support (subsidies and tax breaks) of sport is morally warranted? All of these questions require that we take the larger measure of sport and examine how it stacks up morally compared to all other elements of society. And as part of this larger examination, we may find ourselves asking an even more basic question: might we all be better off without sports?

I
PART

FAIR PLAY,
BEING A GOOD SPORT,
AND CHEATING:
AT WHAT PRICE VICTORY?

Moral problems arise in all areas of life, and we can transfer the methods we use to deal with them from one area to another. Applying general moral values to sport situations can be referred to as *ethics and sport*. For  instance, racism, sexism, and violence are general moral issues. They arise (and should be opposed) in business, education, the professions (e.g., medicine, law, etc.), and, of course, sport. One philosophical perspective may be to apply, with sensitivity, those general moral standards and requirements (e.g., universality, consistency, impartiality, etc.) to sporting situations. For example, if the general moral standard is "do no harm," and it is applied to issues of violence in sport, it will raise questions about the way in which we would make moral judgments about these issues. On general moral matters such as racism, sexism, violence, and so on, the mainstream philosophical literature is the primary source for the discussion in parts of this book.

Sport is interesting, however, in that it imposes its own set of moral standards and requirements on those who participate in it. Our shorthand

1

Discuss the
Distinction
between
Ethics in
Sport &
Ethics of Sport

2   Ethics in Sport

way of referring to these standards and requirements is to talk of "fair play" and "being a good sport." These internal moral requirements are important for at least two reasons. First, they mean that general moral standards are usually applied to sport after due consideration has been given to sport's moral character. Second, the vast majority of people participate in sport because they enjoy it; therefore, people often have a built-in motivation to act morally and play fairly. The person who loves sporting competition will want that competition to be fair, or else he or she will not consider it sporting at all.

The articles in part I of this book assist us in unpacking and analyzing the notion of a special realm of sport morality—ethics in sport. Typically this special realm of the morality of sport has been discussed under the heading "fair play."

Fair play has always been an applied concept. Many treatments of fair play were, and still are, motivated more by the desire to use sport to teach some set of positive values than by the goal of understanding the nature of the concept itself. In other words, often people simply do not make the distinction between ethics in sport and ethics and sport. Ethics in sport is about internal issues related to sport and ethical behaviour; ethics and sport is ethical issues that come into sport from other areas in society—fair play is about ethics in sport; racism is about ethics in general society, and it impinges into the sport community as well. It is generally agreed that sport teaches values, but the content of those values—indeed, whether the values are positive or negative—depends on how sport is played, taught, and practiced. Fair play is often the term used to capture the view that sport should teach positive social values, with the chosen values forming the content of the concept. With this view, fair play forms a subset of general moral or social values applied to, and taught through, sport and physical activity.

Part I of this book is a survey and analysis of the contemporary debate on fair play, being a good sport, and cheating. The articles map out and examine different philosophical treatments of these concepts. For example, the chapters explore the concept of fair play using a number of approaches:

- Fair play as a bag of virtues
- Fair play as play
- Sport as contest—fair play as fair contest
- Fair play as respect for rules
- Fair play as contract or agreement
- Fair play as respect for the game

Some authors argue that the notion of fair play has its grounding in the logic of sport itself—ethics in sport.

Typical Characters in Sport

The discussions in these chapters will help readers recognize typical characters in sport and make general assessments of those characters based on the concept of fair play as respect for the game. Some possibilities follow:

- The good sport
- The poor sport
- The gamesperson
- The cheat
- The spoilsport
- The trifler

The Good Sport

The good sport embodies a particular attitude with regard to sport participation. The good sport respects the game. Because of this attitude, the good sport is concerned with the well-played game and appreciates good play, whether it is his or her own or the opponent's. The good sport is gracious in both victory and defeat because he or she recognizes that opponents share the values and spirit of sport.

The good sport plays fairly, recognizing that this is the only way to have a well-played and satisfying game. The good sport tries to play at his or her best at all times. The good sport respects and supports not only the rules of the sport but the spirit of those rules as well.

The Poor Sport

The poor sport, while perhaps playing fairly, uses different standards to judge his or her own play and that of opponents. The poor sport tends not to take responsibility for his or her own poor play and does not credit opponents' good play. The poor sport takes too much credit for his or her own good play and is more concerned with his or her own performance than with the well-played game.

The poor sport may abandon fairness and turn to cheating. He or she might give up if the game is going badly; in such a case the poor sport might adopt the stance of the spoilsport.

The Gamesperson

The gamesperson embodies a particular attitude toward the rules of the game that is based on a primary concern with winning. The gamesperson plays to the letter, not the spirit, of the rules. The gamesperson considers anything permitted that is not explicitly forbidden and sees penalties as costs of doing business. In other words, the gamesperson weighs the cost of a penalty as he or she determines whether to break a given rule. The gamesperson accepts the "good" foul (a prohibited act performed with the expectation of a penalty) as part of the game (for example, a defender in soccer handling the ball to prevent a certain goal). The gamesperson may well be completely fair in that he or she expects the opponent to play in exactly the same way.

The Cheat

The cheat is unconcerned about fairness. The cheat will break the rules (often hoping that no one notices) when he or she thinks it is to his or her advantage. The cheat is concerned only with the score, not with playing the game. Some authors argue that when one deliberately breaks the rules one ceases to play the game—for the game is constituted by its rules.[1] The cheat, in fact, no longer plays, and thus can never actually win. So the cheat intentionally and deceptively violates the rules to gain an unfair advantage.

The Spoilsport

The spoilsport intentionally destroys the game for others. When children play, the spoilsport might insist that the game be played to his or her advantage or he or she will take the equipment and go home. With adults it happens in more subtle ways; the spoilsport subverts the purpose of the game, making it impossible for others to play. An example would be insisting on the application of a technical rule that prevents the game from going on.

The Trifler

The trifler does not care about the game and does not try to play. He or she may be on the field but makes no effort to perform the actions the game requires. This situation differs from one in which a player is unskilled in a particular game but at least is trying.

Though we all are happy to pay lip service to the idea of fair play, is there really any room for it at the highest levels of sport? At the elite amateur level, or even in professional sport, is fair play just for losers?

Sport Teaches Character

Sport teaches character because it is competitive, physical, and emotionally demanding, and it pushes people to their limits. But there is no guarantee that the character traits sport teaches are good ones. Our sport heroes are indeed role models—but some actions teach that what counts is not the game itself, but rather personal advantage. At this point in the debate the typical response is that fair play and being a good sport are all very well for amateur sport (presumably where the outcome doesn't really matter), but in professional sports, where what really counts (money) is on the line, then fair play and being a good sport are for losers.

Some of the authors in this part argue the contrary; they believe that fair play and being a good sport are indeed compatible with elite and professional sport. They argue that a game won by a trick is not truly won. They try to prove that even in professional sport, where sport is entertainment and a business, sporting integrity cannot be bought. Every level of sport is still subject to the rules, values, and conventions of sport and fair play.

Sport, as opposed to physical recreational activities, is about competition, but for sporting competition to work, it must be fair. When does trying to get ahead, trying to gain an edge over an opponent, shade into unfairness? Athletes can ask themselves a couple of simple questions. First, what if everyone does what you are doing? Does your competitive advantage disappear if both you and your opponent use the same strategy or trick? The essence of sporting competition is that it is open. You may be the first to develop a new technique or a new tactical move, but as soon as you use it, every competitor is then at liberty to try that technique and use it in competition. Second, if everyone does it, would that be good for the game? Would the play of the game concerned, or would the sport itself, be improved if everyone used the technique in competition? Fair competition requires that each player or team have access to the same techniques and tactics permitted by the rules. Good sport requires that competitors be able to show their skills and that, generally speaking, the player with the greatest skill, commitment, and creativity win.

Note

1. Butcher, R., Schneider, A., "Fair Play As Respect for the Game" in this volume.

1

CHAPTER

Sportsmanship As a Moral Category

James W. Keating

Sportsmanship, long and inexplicably ignored by philosophers and theologians, has always pretended to a certain moral relevancy, although its precise place among the moral virtues has been uncertain. In spite of this confusion, distinguished advocates have made some remarkable claims for sportsmanship as a moral category. Albert Camus, Nobel Prize winner for literature in 1957, said that it was from sports that he learned all that he knew about ethics.[1] Former President Hoover is quoted as saying: "Next to religion, the single greatest factor for good in the United States in recent years has been sport."[2] Dr. Robert C. Clothier, past president of Rutgers University, paraphrased the words of Andrew Fletcher and commented: "I care not who makes the laws or even writes the songs if the code of sportsmanship is sound, for it is that which controls conduct and governs the relationships between men."[3] Henry Steele Commager, professor of history at Columbia University, has argued that it was on the playing fields that Americans learned the lessons of courage and honor which distinguished them in time of war. Commager sums up: "In one way or another, this code of sportsmanship has deeply influenced our national destiny."[4] For Lyman Bryson, of Columbia University, sportsmanship was of extraordinary value:

Reprinted, by permission, from James W. Keating, 1964, "Sportsmanship as a moral category," *Ethics: An International Journal of Social, Political, and Legal Philosophy LXXV:* 25-35.

The doctrine of love is much too hard a doctrine to live by. But this is not to say that we have not made progress. It could be established, I think, that the next best thing to the rule of love is the rule of sportsmanship. . . . Some perspicacious historian will some day write a study of the age-old correlation between freedom and sportsmanship. We may then see the importance of sportsmanship as a form of enlightenment. This virtue, without which democracy is impossible and freedom uncertain, has not yet been taken seriously enough in education.[5]

Pope Pius XII, speaking of fair play which is widely regarded as an essential ingredient of sportsmanship, if not synonymous with it, has said:

From the birthplace of sport came also the proverbial phrase "fair play"; that knightly and courteous emulation which raises the spirit above meanness and deceit and dark subterfuges of vanity and vindictiveness and preserves it from the excesses of a closed and intransigent nationalism. Sport is the school of loyalty, of courage, of fortitude, of resolution and universal brotherhood.[6]

Charles W. Kennedy was a professor of English at Princeton University and chairman of its Board of Athletic Control. His small volume, *Sport and Sportsmanship,* remains to this day probably the most serious study of sportsmanship conducted in America. Kennedy's commitment to sportsmanship was not merely theoretical and scholarly. As chairman of Princeton's Board of Athletic Control, he severed athletic relations with Harvard when unsportsmanlike conduct marred the relationship.[7] For Kennedy it was not sufficient that sportsmanship characterize man's activities on the athletic field; it must permeate all of life.

When you pass out from the playing fields to the tasks of life, you will have the same responsibility resting upon you, in greater degree, of fighting in the same spirit for the cause you represent. You will meet bitter and sometimes unfair opposition. . . . You will meet defeat (but) you must not forget that the great victory of which you can never be robbed will be the ability to say, when the race is over and the struggle ended, that the flag you fought under was the shining flag of sportsmanship, never furled or hauled down and that, in victory or defeat, you never lost that contempt for a breach of sportsmanship which will prevent your stooping to it anywhere, anyhow, anytime.[8]

Similar eulogies by other distinguished men with no professional or financial interest in sport or athletics could be multiplied without difficulty, but perhaps the point has already been made. The claims for sportsmanship as a moral category deserve some investigation. It is surprising that the experts in moral theory, the philosopher and the theologian, have seen fit to ignore so substantial an area of human conduct as that occupied by sport and athletics.

Three interrelated problems will be considered in this study: (1) the source of the confusion which invariably accompanies a discussion of sportsmanship and the normal consequences resulting from this confusion; (2) the essence of genuine sportsmanship, or the conduct and attitude proper to sport, with special consideration being given to the dominant or pivotal virtues involved; (3) sportsmanship as applied to athletics—a derivative or analogous use of the term. Once again special attention will be directed to the basic or core virtues which characterize the conduct and attitude of the well-behaved athlete.

The Source of Confusion and Its Consequences

What is sportsmanship? William R. Reed, commissioner for the Big Ten Intercollegiate Conference, is most encouraging: "It [sportsmanship] is a word of exact and uncorrupted meaning in the English language, carrying with it an understandable and basic ethical norm. Henry C. Link in his book 'Rediscovery of Morals' says, 'Sportsmanship is probably the clearest and most popular expression of morals.'"[9] Would that this were the case. Reed, however, does not define sportsmanship or enumerate the provisions of its code, and the briefest investigation reveals that he is badly mistaken as to the clarity of the concept. The efforts of no less a champion of sportsmanship than Amos Alonzo Stagg presage the obscurities which lie ahead. In addition to a brilliant athletic career at Yale and forty years as head football coach at the University of Chicago, Stagg did a year of graduate work in Yale's Divinity School and would thus seem to have the ideal background of scholarly training in moral theory and vast practical experience to discuss the problem. Yet his treatment leaves much to be desired. He defined sportsmanship as "a delightful fragrance that people will carry with them in their relations with their fellow men."[10] In addition, he drew up separate codes of sportsmanship, or Ten Commandments of sport, for the coach and for the football player and held that both decalogues were applicable to the business world as well. The second, and by far the most unusual, commandment contained proscriptions seldom found in codes of sportsmanship. "Make your conduct a worthy example. Don't drink intoxicants; don't gamble; don't smoke; don't use smutty language; don't tell dirty stories;

don't associate with loose or silly women."[11] Stagg's position is undoubtedly an extreme one, but it calls attention to a tendency all too common among the champions of sportsmanship—the temptation to broaden the concept of sportsmanship until it becomes an all-embracing moral category, a unique road to moral salvation. As always, there is an opposite extreme. Sportsmanship, when not viewed as the pinnacle of moral perfection, can also be viewed as a moral minimum—one step this side of criminal behavior. "A four point program to improve sportsmanship at athletic events has been adopted by the Missouri State High School Activities Association."[12] The first and third provisions of bylaw No. 9 detail penalties for assaults or threats upon officials by players or fans. Such legislative action may be necessary and even admirable, but it is a serious error to confuse the curtailment of criminal activities of this sort with a positive promotion of sportsmanship.

What, then, is sportsmanship? Another approach is by way of the dictionary, everyday experience, and common-sense deductions. Sportsmanship is conduct becoming a sportsman. And who is a sportsman? One who is interested in or takes part in sport. And what is sport? Sport, Webster tells us, is "that which diverts and makes mirth"; it is an "amusement, recreation, pastime." Our problem, then, is to determine the conduct and attitude proper to this type of activity, and this can be done only after a more careful consideration of the nature of sport. Pleasant diversion? Recreation? Amusement? Pastime? Is this how one would describe the World Series, the Masters, the Davis Cup, the Rose Bowl, the Olympic Games, or a high-school basketball tournament? Do the "sport" pages of our newspapers detail the pleasant diversions and amusements of the citizenry, or are they preoccupied with national and international contests which capture the imaginations, the emotions, and the pocketbooks of millions of fans (i.e., fanatics)? It is precisely at this point that we come face to face with the basic problem which has distorted or vitiated most discussions of sportsmanship. Because the term "sport" has been loosely applied to radically different types of human behavior, because it is naïvely regarded as an apt description of (1) activity which seeks only pleasant diversion and, on the other hand, (2) of the agonistic struggle to demonstrate personal or group excellence, the determination of the conduct proper to a participant in "sport" becomes a sticky business indeed. Before proceeding with an analysis of sportsmanship as such, it is necessary to consider briefly an all-important distinction between sport and athletics.

Our dictionary definition of sport leans upon its root or etymological meaning. "Sport," we are told, is an abbreviation of the Middle English *desport* or *disport,* themselves derivatives of the Old French *desporter,* which literally meant to carry away from work. Following this lead, Webster and other lexicographers indicate that "diversion," "recreation," and "pastime" are essential to sport. It is "that which diverts and makes mirth; a pastime." While the dictionaries reflect some of the confusion and fuzziness with which contemporary thought shrouds the concept of athletics, they invariably stress an element which, while only accidentally associated with sport, is essential to athletics. This element is the prize, the *raison d'être* of athletics. Etymologically, the various English forms of the word "athlete" are derived from the Greek verb *athlein,* "to contend for a prize," or the noun *athlos,* "contest" or *athlon,* a prize awarded for the successful completion of the contest. An oblique insight into the nature of athletics is obtained when we realize that the word "agony" comes from the Greek *agonia*—a contest or a struggle for victory in the games. Thus we see that, historically and etymologically, sport and athletics have characterized radically different types of human activity, different not insofar as the game itself or the mechanics or rules are concerned, but different with regard to the attitude, preparation, and purpose of the participants. Man has probably always desired some release or diversion from the sad and serious side of life. This, of course, is a luxury, and it is only when a hostile environment is brought under close rein and economic factors provide a modicum of leisure that such desires can be gratified. In essence, sport is a kind of diversion which has for its direct and immediate end fun, pleasure, and delight and which is dominated by a spirit of moderation and generosity. Athletics, on the other hand, is essentially a competitive activity, which has for its end victory in the contest and which is characterized by a spirit of dedication, sacrifice, and intensity.

When this essential distinction between sport and athletics is ignored, as it invariably is, the temptation to make sportsmanship an all-embracing moral category becomes irresistible for most of its champions. In 1926 a national Sportsmanship Brotherhood was organized for the purpose of spreading the gospel of sportsmanship throughout all aspects of life, from childhood games to international events.[13] Its code consisted of eight rules:

1. Keep the rule.
2. Keep faith with your comrades.
3. Keep yourself fit.
4. Keep your temper.
5. Keep your play free from brutality.
6. Keep pride under in victory.
7. Keep stout heart in defeat.
8. Keep a sound soul and a clean mind in a healthy body.

The slogan adopted by the Brotherhood to accompany its code was "Not that you won or lost—but how you played the game." In giving vigorous editorial support to the Sportsmanship Brotherhood, the *New York Times* said:

> Take the sweet and the bitter as the sweet and bitter come and always "play the game." That is the legend of the true sportsmanship, whether on the ball field, the tennis court, the golf course, or at the desk or machine or throttle. "Play the game." That means truthfulness, courage, spartan endurance, self-control, self-respect, scorn of luxury, consideration one for another's opinions and rights, courtesy, and above all fairness. These are the fruits of the spirit of sportsmanship and in them . . . lies the best hope of social well-being.[14]

Dictionaries that have suggested the distinction between sport and athletics without explicitly emphasizing it have remained relatively free from this type of romantic incrustation and moral exaggeration in their treatment of sportsmanship. Beginning with nominal definitions of sportsmanship as the conduct becoming a sportsman and of the sportsman as one who participates in sport, they proceed, much more meaningfully, to characterize the sportsman by the kind of conduct expected of him. A sportsman is "a person who can take loss or defeat without complaint or victory without gloating and who treats his opponents with fairness, generosity and courtesy." In spite of the limitations of such a description, it at least avoids the inveterate temptation to make sportsmanship a moral catch-all.

The Essence of Genuine Sportsmanship

Sportsmanship is not merely an aggregate of moral qualities comprising a code of specialized behavior; it is also an attitude, a posture, a manner of interpreting what would otherwise be only a legal code. Yet the moral qualities believed to comprise the code have almost monopolized consideration and have proliferated to the point of depriving sportsmanship of any distinctiveness. Truthfulness, courage, spartan endurance, self-control, self-respect, scorn of luxury, consideration one for another's opinions and rights, courtesy, fairness, magnanimity, a high sense of honor, co-operation, generosity. The list seems interminable. While the conduct and attitude which are properly designated as sportsmanlike may reflect many of the above-mentioned qualities, they are not all equally basic or fundamental. A man may be law-abiding, a team player, well conditioned, courageous, humane, and the possessor of *sangfroid* without qualifying as a sportsman. On the other hand, he may certainly be categorized as a sportsman without possessing spartan endurance or a scorn of luxury. Our concern is not with those virtues which *might* be found in the sportsman. Nor is it with those virtues which *often* accompany the sportsman. Our concern is rather with those moral habits or qualities which are essential, which characterize the participant as a sportsman. Examination reveals that there are some that are pivotal and absolutely essential; others peripheral. On what grounds is such a conclusion reached? Through the employment of the principle that the nature of the activity determines the conduct and attitudes proper to it. Thus, to the extent that the conduct and attitudes of the participants contribute to the attainment of the goal of sport, to that extent they can be properly characterized as sportsmanlike. The primary purpose of sport is not to win the match, to catch the fish or kill the animal, but to derive pleasure from the attempt to do so and to afford pleasure to one's fellow participants in the process. Now it is clear that the combined presence of such laudable moral qualities as courage, self-control, co-operation, and a spirit of honor do not, in themselves, produce a supporting atmosphere. They may be found in both parties to a duel or in a civil war. But generosity and magnanimity are essential ingredients in the conduct and attitude properly described as sportsmanlike. They establish and maintain the unique social bond; they guarantee that the purpose of sport—the immediate pleasure of the participants—will not be sacrificed to other more selfish ends. All the prescriptions which make up the code of sportsmanship are derived from this single, basic, practical maxim: Always conduct yourself in such a manner that you will increase rather than detract from the pleasure to be found in the activity, both your own and that of your fellow participants. If there is disagreement as to what constitutes sportsmanlike behavior, then this disagreement stems from the application of the maxim rather than from the maxim itself. It is to be expected that there will be differences of opinion as to how the pleasurable nature of the activity can best be maximized.

The code governing pure sport is substantially different from a legalistic code in which lawyers and law courts are seen as a natural and healthy complement of the system. In fact, it is in direct comparison with such a system that the essence of sportsmanship can best be understood. In itself, sportsmanship is a spirit, an attitude, a manner or mode of interpreting an otherwise purely legal code. Its purpose is to protect and cultivate the festive mood proper to an activity whose primary purpose is pleasant diversion, amusement, joy. The sportsman adopts a cavalier attitude toward his personal rights under the code; he prefers to be magnanimous and self-sacrificing if, by such conduct, he contributes to the enjoyment of the game. The sportsman is not in search of legal justice; he prefers to be generous whenever generosity will contribute to the fun of the occasion. Never in search of ways to evade the rules, the sportsman acts only from unquestionable moral right.

Our insistence that sport seeks diversion, recreation, amusement does not imply that the sportsman is by nature a listless competitor. It is common practice for him, once the game is under way, to make a determined effort to win. Spirited competitor that he often is, however, his goal is joy in the activity itself and anything—any word, action, or attitude—which makes the game itself less enjoyable should be eliminated. He "fights" gallantly to win because experience has taught him that a determined effort to overcome the obstacles which his particular sport has constructed adds immeasurably to the enjoyment of the game. He would be cheating himself and robbing the other participants of intense pleasure if his efforts were only halfhearted. Yet there is an important sense in which sporting activity is not competitive but rather co-operative. Competition denotes the struggle of two parties for the same valued object or objective and implies that, to the extent that one of the parties is successful in the struggle, he gains exclusive or predominant possession of that object at the expense of his competitor. But the goal of sporting activity, being the mutual enjoyment of the participants, cannot even be understood in terms of exclusive possession by one of the parties. Its simulated competitive atmosphere camouflages what is at bottom a highly co-operative venture. Sport, then, is a co-operative endeavor to maximize pleasure or joy, the immediate pleasure or joy to be found in the activity itself. To so characterize sport is not to indulge in romantic exaggeration. It is indisputable that the spirit of selfishness is at a very low ebb in genuine sport. Gabriel Marcel's observation concerning the relationship of generosity to joy may even have a limited applicability here. "If generosity enjoys its own self it degenerates into complacent self-satisfaction. This enjoyment of self is not joy, for joy is not a satisfaction but an exaltation. It is only in so far as it is introverted that joy becomes enjoyment."[15] In comparison with sport, athletics emphasize self-satisfaction and enjoyment; sport is better understood in terms of generosity, exaltation, and joy.

Although there is no acknowledgment of the fact, the concern which has been shown for sportsmanship by most of its advocates has been almost exclusively directed to its derivative meaning—a code of conduct for athletes. To the extent that the Sportsmanship Brotherhood was concerned with athletics (and their code of conduct would indicate that was their main concern), their choice of a slogan seems singularly inappropriate. "Not that you won or lost—but how you played the game." Such a slogan can be accommodated in the world of sport, but even there the word "enjoyed" should be substituted for the word "played." Application of this slogan to athletics, on the other hand, would render such activity unintelligible, if not irrational.

"Sportsmanship" in Athletics

Careful analysis has revealed that sport, while speaking the language of competition and constantly appearing in its livery, is fundamentally a co-operative venture. The code of the sportsman, sportsmanship, is directed fundamentally to facilitating the co-operative effort and removing all possible barriers to its development. Mutual generosity is a most fertile soil for co-operative activity. When we move from sport to athletics, however, a drastic change takes place. Co-operation is no longer the goal. The objective of the athlete demands exclusive possession. Two cannot share in the same victory unless they are teammates, and, as a result, the problems of competition are immediately in evidence. "Sportsmanship," insofar as it connotes the behavior proper to the athlete, seeks to place certain basic limitations on the rigors of competition, just as continual efforts are being made to soften the impact of the competitive struggle in economics, politics, international relations, etc. But we must not lose sight of an important distinction. Competition in these real-life areas is condoned or encouraged to the extent that it is thought to contribute to the common good. It is not regarded as an end in itself but as the only or most practicable means to socially desirable ends. Friedrich A. Hayek, renowned economist and champion of competition in economics, supports this position:

> The liberal argument is in favor of making the best possible use of the forces of competition as a means of co-ordinating human efforts, not an argument for leaving things just as they are. It is based on the conviction that, where effective competition can be created, it is a better way of guiding individual efforts than any other. It does not deny, but even emphasizes, that, in order that competition should work beneficially, a carefully thought-out legal framework is required and that neither the existing nor the past legal rules are free from grave defects. Nor does it deny that, where it is impossible to create the conditions necessary to make competition effective, we must resort to other methods of guiding economic activity.[16]

A code which seeks to mitigate the full force of the competitive conflict can also be desirable in athletics. While an athlete is in essence a prizefighter, he seeks to demonstrate his excellence in a contest governed by rules which acknowledge human worth and dignity. He mistakes his purpose and insults his opponent if he views the contest as an occasion to display generosity and magnanimity. To the extent that sportsmanship in athletics is virtuous, its essence consists in the practice of fairness under most difficult conditions. Since the sportsman's primary objective is the joy of the moment, it is obvious from that very fact that he places no great emphasis on the importance of winning. It is easy for him to be modest in victory or gracious in defeat and to play fair at all times, these virtues being demonstrated under optimum conditions for their easy exercise. The strange paradox of sportsmanship as applied to athletics is that it asks the athlete, locked in a deadly serious and emotionally charged situation, to act outwardly as if he were engaged in some pleasant diversion. After an athlete has trained and sacrificed for weeks, after he has dreamed of victory and its fruits and literally exhausted himself physically and emotionally in its pursuit—after all this—to ask him to act with fairness in the contest, with modesty in victory, and an admirable composure in defeat is to demand a great deal, and, yet, this is the substance of the demand that "sportsmanship" makes upon the athlete.

For the athlete, being a good loser is demonstrating self-control in the face of adversity. A festive attitude is not called for; it is, in fact, often viewed as in bad taste. The purists or rigorists are of the opinion that a brief period of seclusion and mourning may be more appropriate. They know that, for the real competitor, defeat in an important contest seems heartbreaking and nerve-shattering. The athlete who can control himself in such circumstances demonstrates remarkable equanimity. To ask that he enter into the festive mood of the victory celebration is to request a Pagliacci-like performance. There is no need for phony or effusive displays of congratulations. A simple handshake demonstrates that no personal ill-will is involved. No alibis or complaints are offered. No childish excuses about the judgment of officials or the natural conditions. No temper tantrums. To be a good loser under his code, the athlete need not be exactly gracious in defeat, but he must at least "be a man" about it. This burden, metaphorically characterized as sportsmanship, bears heavily upon all athletes—amateur or professional. But there are added complications for the professional. Victories, superior performances, and high ratings are essential to financial success in professional athletics. Too frequent defeat will result in forced unemployment. It is easy, therefore, for a professional athlete to view his competitors with a jaundiced eye; to see them as men who seek to deprive him of his livelihood. Under these circumstances, to work daily and often intimately with one's competitors and to compete in circumstances which are highly charged with excitement and emotion, while still showing fairness and consideration, is evidence of an admirable degree of self-mastery.

Attempts have been made to identify sportsmanship with certain games which, it is contended, were the private preserve of the gentleman and, as a result, reflect his high code of honor.

> Bullying, cheating, "crabbing" were all too common in every form of sport. The present movement away from muckerism probably should be attributed in large measure to the growing popularity of golf and tennis. Baseball, boxing, and many of our common sports trace their origin to the common people who possessed no code of honor. On the other hand, golf and tennis, historically gentlemen's games, have come down to us so interwoven with a high code of honor that we have been forced to accept the code along with the game. . . . The effect of the golf code upon the attitude of the millions who play the game is reflected in all our sports.[17]

It is true that in England the terms "gentleman," "sportsman," and "amateur" were regarded as intimately interrelated. The contention that the common people, and consequently the games that were peculiarly theirs, had no comparable code of honor may be correct, but it awaits the careful documentation of some future social historian. One thing is certain, however, and that is that there is nothing in the nature of any game, considered in itself, that necessarily implies adherence to a moral code. Some games like golf and tennis in which the participants do their own officiating provide greater opportunity for the practice of honesty, but if a high code of honor surrounds the "gentleman's games," it is due principally to the general attitude of the gentleman toward life rather than to anything intrinsic to the game itself. The English gentleman was firmly committed to sport in the proper sense of that term and eschewed the specialization, the rigors of precontest preparation, the secret strategy sessions, and professional coaching which have come to be regarded as indispensable for the athlete. "The fact that a man is born into the society of gentlemen imposes upon him the duties and, to some extent, the ideas of his class. He is expected to have a broad education, catholic tastes, and a multiplicity of pursuits. He must not do anything for pecuniary gain; and it will be easily seen that he must not specialize. It is essentially the mark of the bourgeois' mind to specialize."[18] Moreover, "too much preparation is contrary to all English ethics, and secrecy in training is especially abhorrent. Remember that sport is a prerogative of gentlemen. And one of the ear-marks of a gentleman is that he resort to no trickery and that he plays every game with his cards on the table—the game of life as well as the game of football."[19]

It is the contestant's objective and not the game itself which becomes the chief determinant of the conduct and attitudes of the players. If we take tennis as an example and contrast the code of conduct employed by the sportsman with that of the athlete in the matter of officiating, the difference is obvious. The sportsman invariably gives his opponent the benefit of the doubt. Whenever he is not sure, he plays his opponent's shot as good even though he may suspect that it was out. The athlete, however, takes a different approach. Every bit as opposed to cheating as the sportsman, the athlete demands no compelling proof of error. If a shot seems to be out, even though he is not certain, the athlete calls it that way. He is satisfied that his opponent will do the same. He asks no quarter and gives none. As a result of this attitude and by comparison with the sportsman, the athlete will tend toward a legal interpretation of the rules.

The athletic contest is designed to serve a specific purpose—the objective and accurate determination of superior performance and, ultimately, of excellence. If this objective is to be accomplished, then the rules governing the contest must impose the same burdens upon each side. Both contestants must be equal before the law if the test is to have any validity, if the victory is to have any meaning. To the extent that one party to the contest gains a special advantage, unavailable to his opponent, through an unusual interpretation, application, or circumvention of the rules, then that advantage is unfair. The well-known phrase "sense of fair play" suggests much more than an adherence to the letter of the law. It implies that the spirit too must be observed. In the athletic contest there is a mutual recognition that the rules of the game are drawn up for the explicit purpose of aiding in the determination of an honorable victory. Any attempt to disregard or circumvent these rules must be viewed as a deliberate attempt to deprive the contest of its meaning. Fairness, then, is rooted in a type of equality before the law, which is absolutely necessary if victory in the contest is to have validity and meaning. Once, however, the necessary steps have been taken to make the contest a true test of respective abilities, the athlete's sole objective is to demonstrate marked superiority. Any suggestion that fair play obliges him to maintain equality in the contest ignores the very nature of athletics. "If our analysis of fair play has been correct, coaches who strive to produce superior teams violate a fundamental principle of sportsmanship by teaching their pupils, through example, that superiority is more greatly to be desired than is equality in sport. . . . But who today would expect a coach to give up clear superiority—a game won—by putting in enough substitutes to provide fair playing conditions for an opposing team?"[20] Thus understood, sportsmanship would ask the leopard to change its spots. It rules out, as illegitimate, the very objective of the athlete. Nothing shows more clearly the need for recognition of the distinction between sport and athletics.

Conclusion

In conclusion, we would like to summarize our answers to the three problems set down at the outset.

1. The source of the confusion which vitiates most discussion of sportsmanship is the unwarranted assumption that sport and athletics are so similar in nature that a single code of conduct and similar participant attitudes are applicable to both. Failing to take cognizance of the basic differences between sport and athletics, a futile attempt is made to outline a single code of behavior equally applicable to radically diverse activities. Not only is such an attempt, in the nature of things, doomed to failure but a consequence of this abortive effort is the proliferation of various moral virtues under the flag of sportsmanship, which, thus, loses all its distinctiveness. It is variously viewed as a straight road to moral perfection or an antidote to moral corruption.
2. The goal of genuine sport must be the principal determinant of the conduct and attitudes proper to sporting activity. Since its goal is pleasant diversion—the immediate joy to be derived in the activity itself—the pivotal or essential virtue in sportsmanship is generosity. All the other moral qualities that may also be in evidence are colored by this spirit of generosity. As a result of this spirit, a determined effort is made to avoid all unpleasantness and conflict and to cultivate, in their stead, an unselfish and co-operative effort to maximize the joy of the moment.
3. The essence of sportsmanship as applied to athletics can be determined by the application of the same principle. Honorable victory is the goal of the athlete and, as a result, the code of the athlete demands that nothing be done before, during, or after the contest to cheapen or otherwise detract from such a victory. Fairness or fair play, the pivotal virtue in athletics, emphasizes the need for an impartial and equal application of the rules if the victory is to signify, as it should, athletic excellence. Modesty in victory and a quiet composure in defeat testify to an admirable and extraordinary self-control and, in general, dignify and enhance the goal of the athlete.

Notes

1. *Resistance, Rebellion and Death* (New York: Alfred A. Knopf, Inc., 1961), p. 242.
2. In Frank Leahy, *Defensive Football* (New York: Prentice-Hall, Inc., 1951), p. 198.
3. "Sportsmanship in Its Relation to American Intercollegiate Athletics," *School and Society,* XLV (April 10, 1937), 506.
4. Henry Steele Commager, in *Scholastic,* XLIV (May 8-13, 1944), 7.
5. Lyman Bryson, *Science and Freedom* (New York: Columbia University Press, 1947), p. 130.
6. Pope Pius XII, *The Human Body* (Boston: Daughters of St. Paul, 1960).

7. "Athletic Relations between Harvard and Princeton," *School and Society,* XXIV (November 20, 1926), 631.

8. Charles W. Kennedy, *Sport and Sportsmanship* (Princeton, N.J.: Princeton University Press, 1931), pp. 58-59.

9. William R. Reed, "Big Time Athletics' Commitment to Education," *Journal of Health, Physical Education, and Recreation,* XXXIV (September, 1963), 30.

10. Quoted in J.B. Griswold, "You Don't Have To Be Born with It," *American Magazine,* CXII (November, 1931), 60.

11. *Ibid.,* p. 133.

12. "Sportsmanship," *School Activities,* XXXII (October, 1960), 38.

13. "A Sportsmanship Brotherhood," *Literary Digest,* LXXXVIII (March 27, 1926), 60-61.

14. *Ibid.,* pp. 60-61.

15. Gabriel Marcel, *The Mystery of Being, Vol. II: Faith and Reality* (Chicago: Henry Regnery Co., 1960), pp. 133-34.

16. Friedrich A. Hayek, *The Road to Serfdom* (Chicago: University of Chicago Press, 1944), p. 36.

17. J.F. Williams and W.W. Nixon, *The Athlete in the Making* (Philadelphia: W.B. Saunders, 1932), p. 153.

18. H.J. Whigham, "American Sport from an English Point of View," *Outlook,* XCIII (November, 1909), 740.

19. *Ibid.*

20. Frederick R. Rogers, *The Amateur Spirit in Scholastic Games and Sports* (Albany, N.Y.: C.F. Williams & Son, 1929), p. 78.

2
CHAPTER

Fair Play As Respect
for the Game

Robert Butcher and Angela Schneider

Despite the prevalence and intuitive force of the term *fair play*, its precise content is much debated. Most historical introductions to the idea trace its roots to 19th century British Public Schools and the "Muscular Christianity" movement that, in turn, claim roots in classical Greek sport. In the mid-19th century, the term did not need much in the way of detailed explanation. Because sport was the preserve of an homogeneous elite (i.e., moneyed, educated, aristocratic, leisured males), their shared values spilled over into their sporting practices. Any decently brought up young man simply knew that certain things were "not cricket." But things rapidly began to change. McIntosh, in *Fair Play: Ethics in Sport and Education* (15), quotes contemporary 1891 discussions around the introduction of the penalty kick in soccer:

> It is a standing insult to sportsmen to have to play under a rule which assumes that players intend to trip, hack, and push their opponents and to behave like cads of the most unscrupulous kind. I say that the lines marking the penalty area are a disgrace to the playing field of a public school. (15: p. 80)

The authors would like to thank the Canadian Centre for Ethics in Sport for funding the research for this article.

Reprinted, by permission, from R. Butcher and A. Schneider, 1998, "Fair play as respect for the game," *Journal of the Philosophy of Sport, XXV:* 1-22.

The reasoning behind the statement is interesting. A player might trip, hack, and push his opponent by accident or by design. If it occurred by accident, no penalty was required. No gentleman sportsman would ever intentionally consider such behavior. Sport was played by gentlemen, so either way, the penalty kick and penalty area were clearly unnecessary and insulting.

The democratization of sport, itself a good thing, admitted players from a far wider variety of backgrounds. Indeed, even women were permitted to participate in sport! The old certainties were no longer shared, and assumptions made in the offices and boardrooms of sport governing associations were sometimes not reflected in the practices of athletes. This broadening of the base of participation in sport was both positive and healthy, but it carried a price: What was once taken for granted had now to be explained, debated, and justified.

Fair play has always been an applied concept. Many treatments of fair play were, and still are, motivated more by the desire to use sport to teach some set of positive values, than by the goal of understanding the nature of the concept itself. It is generally agreed that sport teaches values, but the content of those values—indeed whether the values are good or ill—depends upon the way in which sport is played, taught, and practiced. *Fair play* is often the phrase used to capture the view that sport *should* be used to teach positive social values, with the chosen values forming the content of the concept. On this view, fair play forms a subset of general moral or social values applied to, and taught through, sport and physical activity.

We begin this paper with a survey and analysis of the contemporary debate on fair play. We will map out and examine five different philosophical treatments of fair play and show how they are each intellectually unsatisfying. The approaches we will examine may be summarized as follows: (a) fair play as a "bag of virtues"; (b) fair play as play; (c) sport as contest and fair play as fair contest; (d) fair play as respect for rules; and (e) fair play as contract or agreement.

We will then present our own positive approach. We will argue that seeing fair play as "respect for the game" provides both philosophical grounding and intellectual coherence while fitting neatly with general intuitions. We will argue that the notion of fair play has its grounding in the logic of sport itself. This approach has a number of advantages:

1. Sport forms the conceptual grounding for fair play;
2. Fair play is a conceptually coherent concept;
3. The motivation for acting fairly will thus be found in the activity (sport) itself; and
4. There is a logical framework for discussions of the fairness of particular practices.

Naturally, there are some drawbacks to this approach. Fair play does not turn out to be the sum total of morality, nor does it answer all questions about the applicability of general moral concepts to sporting situations. What it does provide, however, is a method for determining right conduct in sport which refers directly to sport itself and not to a set of external, culturally determined, and variable values. In the final section, we will summarize our conclusion on fair play as respect for the game.

The contemporary debates around fair play have focused on a number of related issues: (a) content of the concept—what fair play is; (b) grounding of the concept—how to justify the claim that some action is and is not fair; (c) definitions of cheating and sportspersonship; and (d) the moral status of rule-breaking and cheating. A discussion of the different methods of grounding the concept of fair play will be our route to an examination of the varied approaches to the other issues. By and large, the philosophical grounding adopted for fair play dictates what can then be said about the other issues.

Bag of Virtues

The bag-of-virtues approach takes a list of not necessarily related virtues, praiseworthy attributes, or behaviors and associates them with, or applies them to, sport. It is easy to see how this method is derived from research in the social sciences. Here the need is to operationally define measurable behaviors so that data can be collected and analyzed. For the purposes of social scientific research, *fair play* has been defined positively as handshaking with opponents, congratulating team-mates, or negatively, as penalty minutes, incidence of violence, or verbal intimidation.

An additional impetus to this approach comes from the desire to use sport to teach social values. On this model, sport is the vehicle by which a set of approved values can be efficiently delivered.

The most developed contemporary work, from this perspective, has been conducted by Bredemeier and Shields, whose 15 years of work is brought together in *Character Development and Physical Activity* (1). They propose four elements of character—compassion, fairness, sportspersonship, and integrity—that can be taught through properly structured sports programs (1: pp. 193-194). These elements of character are derived from their developmental model of moral reasoning, then applied to sporting situations.

A similar practical motivation lies behind Lumpkin, Stoll, and Beller's four fundamental moral values or principles that, when taken together, are proposed as the basis of a reasoning strategy for fair play behavior (13). They propose justice, honesty, responsibility, and beneficence as their four fundamentals. These are selected on the grounds that they can all be found in historical guides such as "the Bible, the Pali Cannon [*sic*], the Book of Koran, and most societal ethics" (13: p. 21). Fair play thus becomes the application of these general moral principles to sporting situations. Different theoretical (or cultural) models of morality thus generate different conceptions of fair play.

The drawbacks of this approach are apparent. While *justice* (or fairness) is common to both lists and *responsibility* and *honesty* could be collapsed into *integrity*, the lists while compatible, are not identical.[1] Different views of ethics as such translate into different characteristics as the foundations of fair play, and just as we have no good method of arbitrating between the competing claims of different moral systems, we have no corresponding way of adjudicating between rival claims concerning fair play. Similarly, it is always open to the relativist to claim that a culturally grounded conception of fair play is not relevant to the enterprise upon which he or she is embarked. In the world of international and inter-cultural relations, these difficulties also arise and depending on the task at hand, are either dealt with, glossed over, or avoided altogether. In sport, the situation is interestingly different. The very nature of a sporting contest requires that the participants be engaged in the *same* activity. If fair play can be grounded in sport itself, we have the ideal method for claiming the allegiance of all sportspeople.[2]

The bag-of-virtues approach is discussed, and consequently dismissed, by both Keating (8) and Feezell (5) (although neither of them recognize it as such an approach). It is dismissed, as argued above, because it offers no defensible method of deciding which characteristics or actions should fall within the relevant definitions and no method of arbitrating between competing claims. The approach that is the standard for philosophical writers has been, not surprisingly, a conceptual analytic approach that looks first to the nature of sport and seeks to generate from that nature the moral ideals of fair play and sportspersonship.

Before we turn to these other, sport-based analyses of fair play, it is worth pointing out the difficulties highlighted by Bredemeier and Shields (1), and Lumpkin et al. (13). Because sport is conducted by human beings, it falls within the realm of morality. That is, the general rules of moral life apply to sport. Sport and any action which occurs within sport is, thus, amenable to moral discussion and analysis. However, what would count as a violation of the moral order is determined both by the nature of sport itself and the agreement of the competitors to modify or suspend the scope of general moral rules.

The most obvious examples of the modification of normal moral rules comes in the area of violence. In everyday life, pushing, shoving and diving into people is generally prohibited. However, on the rugby field those actions are constitutive of the game. One could not play rugby without engaging in those activities. By agreeing to play rugby, one accepts that one will be subjected to and must inflict actions that would be both illegal and immoral in other contexts. So in rugby, a morally culpable act of violence might be a punch or a kick but not a crushing tackle. (And, of course, this is true even if the tackle causes more physical harm than the punch.) What is true of violence is also true in other areas. Various forms of deception are game related skills in most sports. As such, those acts (referred to as "strategic deception" by Pearson [18]) are not morally wrong. Lying about a line call in tennis, however, would be.

The observation that participation in sport modifies general moral rules raises two issues. The first issue concerns just what it is that one agrees to when one decides to participate in a sport. One certainly agrees to accept actions that are permissible within the rules of the game. One also agrees to accept accidents that are a foreseeable consequence of the game. What is less clear is whether one also agrees to accept actions which, while against the rules, are common practice in a given game. (We will look at this issue of agreement in more detail below.)

Second, we might, on moral grounds, wish to limit the possible content of the sorts of "agreements to compete" into which people can enter. Bare-knuckle boxing is currently banned in many countries (despite the argument that it is, in fact, safer than boxing with protective equipment because there is less brain damage, because the boxers cannot sustain as many blows to the head). That is, on moral grounds, we do not allow willing competitors to suspend the usual social rules against this form of violence to the extent bare-knuckle boxing would require. (Whether we should ban bare-knuckle boxing is, of course, subject to debate. The point to be made here is that the general requirements of morality can be brought to bear to limit actions in the realm of sport.)[3]

The relationship between general morality and fair play in sport is, thus, complex and nuanced. Although general moral rules still apply, they are limited and modified by the nature of the game that defines the ways in which one can do wrong and may even create new possibilities to act immorally. The nuanced nature of this relationship also provides further reasons for rejecting the view that fair play in sport can be understood simply as a subset of general moral values.

Fair Play As Play

In broad terms, much of the philosophical analysis of sport and its relationship to fair play has focused on the ideas that sport is play and sport is a contest. On the sport-is-play approach, the central feature of sport is its nature of being set apart. Sport is not a part of everyday life; it is freely chosen and entered into for its own sake. The appropriate attitude is, therefore, one of playfulness.[4] Keating (8) takes this to mean that the purpose of sport is the creation of enjoyment of the activity and that to do this, the appropriate attitudes are generosity and magnanimity. Keating claims that *sport* can be radically distinguished from *athletics*, the purpose of which is victory in a contest.

This distinction has been soundly criticized and rejected by Feezell (5) and others as unworkable, unhelpful, and false to the facts. On Feezell's Aristotelian account, sportspersonship is a mean, the balanced recognition and acceptance of the essential non-seriousness of sport combined with the utmost dedication and commitment in its pursuit.

While Feezell's objections to Keating's distinction are sound, it would be a mistake to reject out of hand Keating's emphasis on the freely-chosen nature of sport participation along with his distinction between sport and athletics. We will argue below that Keating has, in effect, missed a step in his argument. He moves directly from the set-apart, freely-chosen nature of sport to the conclusion that enjoyment is the goal. The step he misses is an understanding and explanation of just why it is that sport is both freely-chosen and enjoyable. That is, he argues as if the pleasure or enjoyment of sport was somehow separable from the practice of sport itself. On Keating's account, it is not clear why a person who sought enjoyment through the practice of some sport wouldn't just switch to stamp collecting—or indeed take a good drug—if they held out the prospect of greater enjoyment. We will argue that it is the activity of sport itself that brings its own rewards and pleasures. It is through commitment to a sport and the standards and skills it requires, that we gain enjoyment in its practice. We do not seek pleasure, then plug in means to that end. Rather, we commit to activities, then derive pleasure from them.[5]

Sport As Contest: Fair Play As Fair Contest

An alternative approach is to look at sport as a test or contest and try to derive fair play or sportspersonship from that. Within this general approach, the greatest debate has centered on the precise definition of the nature of the test or contest in which competitors are engaged. Most approaches start with the analysis that sports competitions are examples of games. Because they are games, they are created and defined by their rules, as are the permissible means of scoring goals or runs, and hence, winning. Athletes agree to test their skill against each other at a sport. The sport defines the nature and limitations of skill. If an athlete breaks the agreement to compete, he or she ceases to compete, and so, can no longer be in a position to win. That is, if one cheats one cannot win.[6] This is an essentially negative conception of fair play and sportspersonship, one which starts from a definition of cheating, then proposes that fair play and sportspersonship are the absence of cheating. This has two problems, the first definitional and the second evidential. The definitional problem concerns the nature of cheating. If we accept that cheating is the breaking of an agreement, we need to identify precisely the content of the agreement. Some authors (7, 18) argue that the agreement is defined by the rules of the sport. If one breaks a rule (especially if one intentionally breaks a rule), then one has broken the agreement to compete to test skill, so one has cheated, and hence, cannot win.

This position is viewed as too restrictive by both Leaman (11) and Lehman (12) who argue that the nature of the agreement must make some reference to the way the game is, as a matter of fact, played. If the game is generally taken to include the possibility of a "professional foul," then a player will not have cheated, or ceased to compete, if he or she commits a professional foul (11, 12).

The moral status of cheating flows from its definition. If cheating is all rule-breaking or even all intentional rule-breaking, then not all cheating is morally wrong.[7] However, if cheating is breaking one's agreement, then all cheating is morally wrong, but not all rule-breaking is cheating.

The evidential problem is that we tend not to view fair play or sportspersonship as the mere absence of cheating. While we may reject the overblown excesses of the early part of this century, fair play certainly has positive rather than merely negative connotations. To say that someone exhibits fair play seems to say more than: He or she clearly follows the rules or keeps to his or her agreements.

Just as Keating's analysis, while inadequate, stressed the important points that sports are participated in for their own sakes and bring enjoyment, the analysis of sport as contest, while also inadequate as an account of fair play, stresses the essential point that agreement must lie at the heart of contest.

In what follows, we will look in a little more detail at two common conceptions of fair play that develop the idea of sport as an agreement based on rules. We will argue that neither approach captures our positive sense of what constitutes fair play or sportspersonship. We will then move to our own positive conception of fair play as "respect for the game."

Fair Play As Respect for Rules

The International Council for Sport and Physical Education (ICSPE) defines *fair play*, first and foremost, as respect for the rules of the game. Fair play "requires, as a minimum, that [the competitor] shows strict, unfailing observance of the written rule" (1: p. 23). This is glossed by the suggestion that respect is due the spirit, rather than the letter of the rules, but the intent is the same. This understanding of fair play is important in that it draws attention to the rule-governed and -defined nature of sport. Games exist and are defined by their rules. This position is also important, because it acts as the foundation of the logical incompatibility thesis, the thesis which demonstrates that one cannot win if one cheats (21).

Fair play as respect for rules is, however, an inadequate formulation for capturing some of our intuitions about the idea. For example, we sometimes want fair play to apply to situations within sport but outside of the rules of the sport. For instance, Lumpkin et al. (13) pose the case of Josie, the squash player. Josie is your opponent in an important match and has arrived (not to her fault) without a racquet. She will forfeit the game. You use the same kind of racquet and grip as she, and you have a back-up racquet. She is the only competitor at this event who could seriously challenge you and without her, you would almost certainly win the championship. The game against her will be tough, and you are far from certain you can win. What should you do?

The fair play answer seems clear. Indeed one of the earliest fair play awards (to bobsledder Carlo Monti in 1952) was presented in a similar case. Monti loaned another team his brake when theirs was inoperable. The other team went on to beat Monti. You should lend Josie your racquet. But why?

Respect for rules does not help. You break no rule in declining to lend Josie your racquet. Lumpkin et al. (13) use the case as an illustration of the principle of beneficence. This is a standard moral notion, the idea that one ought, generally, to do nice things for people. As a general moral principle it certainly applies here. Anyone who could, should lend Josie a racquet. But you are in a special position—you are her opponent—and as such, have better reasons than generalized beneficence for lending her your racquet. (Although, at first glance, it appears that it is in your self-interest not to lend her your racquet.) As we will argue below, a formulation of fair play as respect for the game will show just why it is you would want to give Josie your racquet.

As an aside, the general applicability of beneficence to sport is unclear. While fair play dictates that you must let your opponents play and that you will only use legal means to stop them, there is no compulsion to be nice to them, for instance, by allowing them to make their best shots or play to their strengths.

Fair play as respect for rules cannot account for actions we take to be required by fair play but which are not directly covered by any rule.

The rule-based conception can also err in the opposite direction. As Lehman (12) has argued, before one can make judgments of cheating or unfairness, one must consider more than just the rule book and should look at the context in which the game is played.[8] If the contestants agree that, for instance, undetected spitballs are an accepted part of modern professional baseball, then "Spitball Perry" did not cheat.[9] Similarly so for the so-called "professional foul" when a player performs an illegal act and willingly accepts a penalty, because it would seem to create a competitive advantage to do so. While we can argue with Lehman about the best approach to take to the rules of a game—should one play to their spirit, to their letter, or to what one can get away with undetected or insufficiently punished—he makes an important point, similar to D'Agostino's (3): Games are played in a context, a context that uses more than just the rule book to define cheating. Fair play as "respect for rules"—which is primarily derived from what D'Agostino has referred to as a "formalist account of games"—does not take into account the variety of sport as played and practiced.

Fair Play As Contract or Agreement

It could be argued that fair play can be seen and explained on the model of a contract or agreement. While this is an interesting and important component of fair play, it is insufficient to characterize the concept fully. Fair play as contract starts from the position, mentioned above, that games are created by their rules. A sporting competition is, thus, a test of skill within the parameters prescribed by the rules. When athletes enter a contest, they agree, and form a tacit contract, to test their skills in the ways permitted by the game concerned. On this account, unfairness or cheating is wrong, because it breaks the agreement. Fair play as contract is open on the content of the agreement. On some versions of this view, the content of the contract is created solely by the rules. In other versions, it is the rules as practiced and understood by the athletes.

This approach is important, because it shows the athlete's own role in accepting the rules of his or her own sport. By making an agreement to compete, the athlete binds him- or herself with self-imposed conditions. This approach does not permit the athlete to view the rules (and the officials who enforce them) as somehow "out there" imposing rules against the athlete's will and interest. The contest is defined by the rules, and in entering the contest, the athlete agrees to measure skill, defined by the rules, against competitors doing the same.

Because this account leaves open the exact content of the agreement, it is flexible enough to account for the variability in the way in which the same sport is played in different places and at different competitive levels. Here the agreement to compete would be framed by the rules but with the added clause "as defined or interpreted" at the relevant level (3). On this account if, for instance, the game is played to the referee—that is, one is expected to break certain rules if the referee is not looking—then the two opponents could agree to a match played in this way, and it would be fair.

This method of viewing things accounts for a number of problems. Athletes often dismiss calls for fair play with the derisive response that "the game is not played that way." Their claim is that their agreement defines what is fair, not simply the rules. Some competitive discrepancies can also be accounted for by the tacit nature of the agreement. If one team is playing the game one way, for instance to the referee, and the other practices a different ethos, for instance, playing to the spirit of the rules, then they may well not have agreed to compete in the same way. This inevitably leads to bitterness and charges of unfairness. This problem could be solved by making as public as possible the nature of the tacit agreement to compete. Note, however, that the central idea is still one of agreement. This rules out the possibility of one team, or player, playing fairly, but operating by a different set of rules from their opponents.

The alternative view would rule out consideration of the ethos of the game by insisting that the content of the agreement be taken as the rules of the game and nothing more. This renders the fair-play-as-agreement position very similar to fair play as respect for rules, with the added benefit of emphasizing the athlete's role in accepting and living up to his or her part of the agreement.

Fair play as agreement is an important further step, but it does not go far enough. The idea of governing sport by contract reduces fair play to an essentially negative concept. Fairness is the absence of unfairness, and unfairness is defined by the breaking of one's word or contract. So fair play is merely doing no less than you said you would do. Without wishing to get overly romantic about the concept, fair play is generally taken (and sportspersonship is always taken) to be something positive, something that cannot be fully explained by mere adherence to one's word, although that is certainly required. When we talk of fair play, the standard we tend to adopt is one that refers to the spirit of the game, rather than the letter of its rules.

For example, some sports still carry rules against "unsportsmanlike conduct" or "bringing the game into disrepute." These rules go undefined, and of course, they can readily be abused to punish people unfairly. However, despite their lack of clarity, we will argue that these sorts of rules can not only be rendered coherent and justified, but that they carry an important concept, a concept we should do our best not to lose.

The Josie-the-squash-player example from the last section is again useful here. Your contractual agreement with Josie is to play fairly, to keep to the rules of the game. You break no rule, and hence, break no promise, by declining to lend her your racquet. Yet we want to say that fair play dictates that you lend her your racquet. So, fair play cannot be reduced entirely to keeping an agreement. It may be a necessary condition but not a sufficient condition.

In the next part of this paper, we will examine fair play as respect for the game and argue that this idea builds on the nature of the sporting agreement and provides the positive structure of our concept of fair play—a structure that will give a logical account for the intuitions in Josie's case.

Fair Play As Respect for the Game

We wish to defend the position that fair play in sport can be understood as respect for the game. As we unpack this idea, we will see the behavioral implications that flow from this central attitude. We will argue that the standard intuitive ideas of fair play are linked, and conceptually grounded, in the idea of "fair play as respect for the game."

There are two commonly used and rather similar senses of respect. In the first, weaker sense, one can respect merely by observing or following. In this sense, we respect the rules of the road by adhering to the speed limit, stopping at stop signs, and so on. The second sense of respect is stronger and carries connotations of honoring, holding in regard, esteeming, or valuing.

It is this second sense of respect that is operative in moral discussions of respect for autonomy, or equal respect for persons. Here, the idea is that one should, from a moral point of view, value the interests, rights, preferences, and so on, of others as one values one's own.

In the context of sport, it is easy to run the two senses together. Because sports are games made up by their rules, there is the requirement that we respect the rules of the game. This could mean that we treat the rules of the game in the same way we treat the rules of the road. We observe or follow them, perhaps for the sake of expediency or as a courtesy. However, it is not obvious how one could honor or esteem traffic regulations. But it is precisely in this latter sense that we wish to defend the idea that fair play can be understood in terms of respect for a game. We will argue that if one honors or esteems one's sport, not only will one wish to exhibit fair play, but one will also have a coherent conceptual framework for arbitrating between competing claims regarding the fairness, or otherwise, of actions.

We will argue below that sports are practices and that practices are the sorts of things that can have interests. Respect for the game will thus entail respect for the interests of the game (or sport) as a practice.

Sports Are Games

As we accepted earlier, sports are games. This means they are artificially constructed from their rules. Participation in a game takes one outside of everyday life. A game creates its own world with its own standards of excellence and its own ways of failing. What counts as skill and what counts as winning and losing are defined through its rules within the game.

Respect for the game, therefore, entails respect for the rules of the game. The rules of a sport make the activity itself possible. Because participation in a game is chosen, because the activities of sports are inherently worthwhile,[10] the rules that make those activities possible are due honor and respect.[11] But respect is a critical and reflective notion. One can criticize while still respecting. In fact, if one respects, one has a duty to criticize. But the criticism must be open and public and should be constructive rather than destructive.

Sports Are Contests

As noted above, although fair play cannot be straightforwardly derived from sport-as-contest, the test and contest nature of sport are important components of our approach. As Kretchmar points out, a contest is always against another and consists in the competitors trying to do the same thing better than each other (9). That the competitors are engaged in the same activity is crucial. If two people are engaged in different activities, there is no one activity they can be competing in. This begs questions about the identification, and identity, of actions or activities. In the sports context, we support the view that contests are defined by a combination of rules and ethos. The rules, constitutive and regulative, form the basis of an agreement that can then be modified by practice and further agreement—the ethos of the game. The fluid nature of the ethos of a particular game played at a particular level reinforces the necessity of agreement between the competitors. Because there are choices to be made about the way the game is to be conducted, we need to agree on what will count as fair in the contest and what will not. Otherwise we run the risk of engaging in different enterprises and thus failing to contest at all. If players wish to contest, they must agree on the precise nature of the contest.

Sports Are Practices

MacIntyre in *After Virtue* defines a *practice* as:

> any coherent and complex form of socially established co-operative human activity through which goods internal to that form of activity are realized in the course of trying to achieve those standards of excellence which are appropriate to, and partially definitive of, that form of activity, with the result that human powers to achieve excellence, and the human conceptions of the ends and goods involved, are systematically extended. (14: p. 187)

He then goes on to cite chess and football as examples of practices in the sense he intends. What practices do is create opportunities to pursue goods and to extend, expand, and realize our conceptions of what is worthwhile in life. MacIntyre makes the (by now) commonplace distinction between internal and external goods. Internal goods are those benefits or goods only available through the practice concerned. External goods, such as money or fame, can be pursued through a variety of means.

Being engaged in a practice means standing in a particular relationship to the practice itself and to other practitioners:

> A practice involves standards of excellence and obedience to rules as well as the achievement of goods. To enter into a practice is to accept the authority of those standards and the inadequacy of my own performance as judged by them. It is to subject my own attitudes, choices, preferences and tastes to the standards which currently partially define the practice. (14: p. 190)

This should not be taken to mean that a practice requires slavish and unquestioning obedience. MacIntyre stresses that practices have histories and traditions and form living, vibrant, and changing entities. Practices change—they must—but the change comes from within and operates inside the context formed by tradition.

It is the latter part of that last quotation—the idea that, as a practitioner of a practice, one's preferences, tastes, attitudes, and choices are partially shaped by the practice—that is most significant for our present purposes. We will argue that "respecting one's game" requires that one takes on or assumes the interests of that game.[12]

Respect for the Game As an Assumption and Transformation of Interests

If you are engaged in a practice, if you respect a practice, you acquire and assume a new set of interests—those of the practice itself. It may seem a little odd to speak of the interests of a practice, but we think the idea can be made clear enough. Let us take the practice of philosophy as an example. It is in the interests of philosophy for there to be innovative scholarship, lively and vigorous debate on contested issues, the study and analysis of historical work, a vibrant community of scholars (highly paid tenured faculty?), broad teaching of the concepts and techniques of philosophy, and so on. Philosophy should make a difference in people's lives. It is not in the interests of philosophy for its research to become sterile, its teaching stale, or its issues irrelevant. And, of course, philosophy being what it is, there should continue a lively debate about just what should constitute the interests of philosophy.

As philosophers we take on those interests as our own. If we care about philosophy, we care about our own roles and performance within the practice. We take on the interest in creating innovative scholarship, engaging in debate, teaching, and so on. We wish to add our own little brick to the philosophical edifice. Excellence in philosophy is in our interests, just as it is in the interests of philosophy itself.

This acquisition of interests has important consequences. To continue the philosophical example, as philosophers, we are committed to the quest for truth—wherever that might lead. That means that we are committed to following the argument, even if the argument runs against our most cherished positions. It is in the interests of a philosopher, as a philosopher, to see his or her own positions demolished in the name of truth.

The same principle holds good for other practices. To return to sport, the athlete takes on the interests of his or her sport. Those interests become the interests of the athlete. If you respect the game, you honor and take seriously the standards of excellence created and defined by that game. For example, an athlete who respected the game of soccer would take seriously its requirements and standards. Such an athlete would care about soccer skills and tactics. He or she would accept the fitness requirements of the game of soccer and would strive to meet them. Because such an athlete accepts the standards of soccer excellence, he or she would work to acquire and exhibit soccer skills. This general point is true whatever one's level of ability or commitment to training. Even if we can commit only small periods of time to our game, or even if we recognize that we will never have the skill to be truly great, the person who respects a game will still accept the standards imposed by the sport. (Naturally, one can also respect a game one does not play, for instance, as a spectator or official—but in all cases the same point applies: One accepts the standards of the game concerned and acts accordingly.)

The idea of the interests of the game provides a means of judging one's own actions in relation to the sport. We approach any activity with mixed motivations and interests. Taking the interests of the game seriously means that we ask ourselves whether or not some action we are contemplating would be good for the game concerned, if everyone did it.[13]

The transformation of interests that occurs when we take on the interests of a game has a second important consequence. Because the interests of the game are now our own interests, we have a motivation for striving for the good of the game. As we will see, this means we have a motivation both to play fairly and strive for excellence.

Respect for the Game and Intrinsic Motivation

The connections between fair play, respect for the game, intrinsic motivation, and the internal goods of a practice—really require a paper of their own. The association of respect for the game and intrinsic motivation offers rich practical and conceptual implications that warrant detailed analysis. However, for our present purposes, it is sufficient to introduce the ideas and draw the conceptual connections. It is a commonplace observation that people participate in sport for an enormous range of reasons. A very few participate because they are paid. Many participate for fitness and companionship or to achieve the respect and admiration of others. But for the great mass of people, the reasons for participating in sport lie within sport itself: People play games because they are fun. For many, perhaps most, participants in sport, its activities are intrinsically rewarding. They bring a feeling of pleasure and provide experiences that are enjoyable and worthwhile.

In the literature of the psychology of sport, the phenomenon of performing an action or activity for its own sake has been studied as an issue of *intrinsic motivation*. What follows is a brief synthesis and review of that literature, which is necessary to defend the premises of our argument on fair play as respect for the game.

The standard contrast in discussions of motivation is between intrinsic and extrinsic motivation. Extrinsic motivation is available for a variety of activities. For instance, one can acquire money or fame in a variety of ways. One might become a lawyer or a pop star, so, insofar as one wants fame or money, one is motivated to be a lawyer or a pop star. If one is motivated by the desire for fame or money, the question one faces is merely of the most efficient means of achieving those ends. For those who are physically gifted, professional sports may well provide the means to both money and fame. But extrinsic motivation is more pervasive than that. The admiration that comes from one's peers for outstanding athletic performance or for the beauty of one's body are extrinsic motivations for pursuing sporting achievement. This is similarly true for "most valuable player" awards, trophies, and the like. Engaging in sport to prove one's own self-worth is also a form of extrinsic motivation (23).

In contrast, an action or activity is intrinsically motivated if it is engaged in for its own sake. This idea has been operationally defined in the psychological literature in two quite different ways: (a) actions or activities engaged in, in the absence of external rewards, or (b) activity in which participants express an interest or enjoyment (4). The difference between the two definitions is important. In the first, one cannot be intrinsically motivated if one receives any extrinsic reward for the activity in question. This begs the question of the relationship between intrinsic and extrinsic rewards. At this stage, we would like to leave open the interchange and relationship between intrinsic and extrinsic motivation.[14]

So far we have merely contrasted intrinsic and extrinsic motivation and suggested that intrinsic motivation is connected to performing an activity for its own sake. But what is it about an activity that makes performing it for its own sake worthwhile? There seem to be four key components for an activity to be experienced as sufficiently worthwhile to be intrinsically motivating.

1. The activity must be interesting. There must be room for the individual participant to express creativity, to experiment (perhaps within limits) with new ways of performing the task.
2. It must be challenging. That is, the task the person is presented with must extend, but not over- or under-extend the person's competence to perform the required action. If the task is too simple, it will be boring, and if it is too difficult it will be stressful. This notion of challenge embraces the possibility of mastery. If the activity is appropriately challenging, the person will feel that he or she has the prospect of meeting and mastering that challenge.
3. The activity must provide feedback. The person needs to be able to assess how well or badly he or she is performing the task at hand.
4. The activity must be freely chosen. Participation should be uncoerced or voluntary (4, 23, 24).

The perfect example of the effects of deep intrinsic motivation can be found in the experience first described by Czikszentmihalyi (2, 6) over 20 years ago as "flow." When one is in flow, all of one's energies and attention is focused on the task at hand. Time seems to stop moving as one is absorbed in the activity. Czikszentmihalyi has researched this phenomenon in a number of sport and nonsport settings. For the flow experience, one should be engaged in a task that is interesting and challenging but within one's capabilities.

As it stands, this is dry and uncompelling. Flow, in fact, is the pinnacle of sporting experience. Flow is the joy of sport distilled. It is the experience felt when one's self and one's environment are one, when the plays are flowing as they should, when one's teammates are moving with almost mystical grace and ease, when one's whole being is focused on the moment, the movement, when the ball or the puck moves as if on wires, when everything in the game is right. The flow experience is highly variable and highly prized. It can also be had at any level of sport. Because an activity that permits the flow experience must be challenging, the level of the game required to create the flow experience will improve as the player becomes more and more skilled.

Flow is the experience one has as one is achieving the internal goods of a sport. As can probably be detected from the above, discussions of flow are notoriously difficult. While the features of flow—focus, attention, absorption, and so on—are common to all flow experiences, the feelings will be different for the flow experience of the basketball player, the chess player, and the surgeon.

Interaction Between Intrinsic and Extrinsic Motivation

The obvious assumption, when one considers motivation, is that motivations would be additive. If you have one reason for doing something, then two reasons would motivate you even more. The relationship is not this straightforward. Several studies show that the presence of extrinsic motivations, such as money, food, and good player awards, all tend to decrease intrinsic motivation (4, 23).[15] It would be premature, however, to assume that extrinsic rewards automatically decrease intrinsic motivation. In another study on scholarship athletes, it was found that those in high profile sports, like basketball and football, showed decreased intrinsic motivation in the presence of extrinsic rewards, whereas those in low profile sports, such as wrestling, and women with scholarships did not (4).

The theoretical explanation for these differences, and the complexity of the interaction between intrinsic and extrinsic motivation, lies in the way the extrinsic rewards are perceived. If the extrinsic rewards are seen as controlling or coercive, they will tend to diminish intrinsic motivation. Typically, extrinsic rewards are used to pressure or coerce people into doing things they do not otherwise wish to do. By association, therefore, extrinsic rewards can be seen as coercive and controlling. But this result is not logically necessary. It is suggested that women athletes, and those in low profile sports, do not tend to view scholarships as controlling but rather see them as informational feedback and a recognition of competence and skill.

An essential component of intrinsically motivated activity appears to be that it is freely chosen. Conversely, if people perceive their actions to be controlled, they are less likely to be intrinsically motivated to perform the actions concerned (even when the same, inherently interesting tasks are examined [23]).

Although there is relatively little research on the direct effects of intrinsic motivation on sport performance and perseverance, the general position on intrinsic motivation is that people who are intrinsically motivated to perform an action, or engage in an activity, get more enjoyment from the activity and persevere longer than those who have been extrinsically motivated (23). People who are intrinsically motivated also tend to be more creative in their approach to the tasks at hand, whereas those who are extrinsically motivated tend to do the minimum required in order to receive the reward.

The connection between intrinsic motivation and internal goods of a practice should be obvious. In effect, internal goods and intrinsic motivation are the philosopher's and the psychologist's view of the same phenomenon. The substance of intrinsic motivation is the internal goods of a practice.

The psychological literature of intrinsic motivation and how it is enhanced and nurtured and how it is affected by different treatments of opponents, competition, and so on, offers a rich source for practical approaches to teaching fair play. For our purposes right now, intrinsic motivation emphasizes the achievement of internal goods that, in turn, reinforce a commitment to the process of playing a game. A commitment to the process of playing the game is a commitment to, and respect for, the game itself, with all that that implies. Because respect for the game requires respect for its rules and traditions, intrinsic motivation is its natural practical ally and support.

Practical Implications

We can think about the implications of viewing fair play as respect for the game at two levels. At the personal level of the individual athlete, fair play as respect for the game will provide guidelines as he or she considers what ought to be done. At this personal level, respect for the game will influence actions on the field of play, attitudes toward one's opponents, and even one's own level of commitment to the game. Fair play as respect for the game also has implications for actions and decisions at the level of policy. Most sports have, in MacIntyre's sense, institutions. These institutions are comprised of sports governing bodies, rule committees, administrative superstructures, and so on. At this level, too, fair play and respect mandate particular decisions—decisions that refer to the best interests of the game concerned.

For any game or sporting contest, it is possible to describe an ideal against which other contests might be measured.[16] While the particular description will naturally vary from sport to sport, we can identify some necessary conditions. Each item on the list can be justified and explicated in terms of promoting the interests of the game.

1. The contestants should be evenly matched. The ideal contest requires that the contestants be at comparable levels of skill and fitness;
2. The contestants should play at or near their best;
3. The outcome of the contest should be in doubt until the end. (This should be guaranteed by having evenly matched contestants playing at their best.)
4. The outcome of the contest should be determined by sporting skill or ability, not extraneous factors such as egregious luck or errors in officiating. Conditions of play, such as weather, may create additional obstacles but must not be so severe as to undermine the exhibition of skill;
5. The match must be fairly contested, that is, played within the rules of the game;
6. For an ideal match, the contestants must have a high degree of skill. Good contests can, however, take place between evenly matched opponents at any level of skill.[17]

The structure of sports and games is such that skills cannot be tested or demonstrated in isolation. The interests of both athletes and the game itself lie in excellent competitions. Athletes who respect and honor their sport have an interest in participating in good sporting contests. One shows and measures one's sporting skills in competition against others seeking to do the same. For the athlete, a competition is a chance to show and test his or her skills, to play the best game that he or she is capable of. In this case, the interests of the athlete are in producing the best possible game. But the best possible game, from a sporting point of view, is not a lop-sided contest where one player or team demonstrates its skill while the other helplessly looks on. In the best possible competition, excellent, evenly matched competitors push each other to the limits of their ability.

The competitive interest of an athlete who honors his or her sport is to play the best possible game against evenly matched opponents playing their best possible game. This interest dictates an important attitude toward one's opponent. The best possible game requires not only that you play to your best, but also that your opponent does. It is not, therefore, in your interest to have your opponent play below his or her best, except where your methods of bringing that about are part of the game itself. For instance, it is part of basketball to pressure a player as he or she attempts to shoot—defensive skill is all about creating such pressure, and shooting skill is about dealing with it—but it is not permissible to cough while your opponent serves in tennis.

Respect for the game, thus, creates important behavioral consequences in competition. The athlete who respects the game wishes to play as well as possible against a worthy opponent playing as well as possible. The only legitimate reason for wanting your opponent not to show his or her skill to its best advantage is where the limitation is imposed by your sporting skill. This means that you allow your opponent every opportunity—as defined by the game—to play his or her best.

If you ask athletes what their goal is in playing sport, they may say "winning." This appears to describe the athlete's interest in sport as winning and makes no reference to the manner in which the victory is achieved. Without question, any athlete who respects his or her sport will try his or her best to win whenever he or she plays. However, respect for the game requires that the athlete view winning only as a good if it comes as a result of a particular process: the well-played, well-matched game.

The athlete who honors the game has taken on the interests of the game as his or her own. It is not in the interests of sport to have undeserving competitors win. If it is not in the interests of sport, it is not in the interests of athletes who respect sport.

Winning is important only if it comes to the player or team that has played best on a given day. (And even then, it may be tainted if the teams or competitors are unevenly matched or if one team plays well below its capabilities.) If winning comes as a result of a well-played, evenly-matched game, both the victor and the vanquished can view the win as providing important performance feedback, an essential part of intrinsic motivation.

Because respect for the game entails an understanding of the relationship between a game and its rules, the athlete who respects the game realizes the truth of the logical incompatibility thesis. If one cheats one ceases to play, and if one does not play one cannot win. Because such an athlete values the process of playing, he or she has no motivation to cheat and would not value a victory awarded as a result of any unfairness.

A victory won through cheating is worthless. While a certain amount of luck is part of any sporting contest, there are some situations where the luck all seems to run one way. In such a case the winners would feel that the outcome was not a true representation of the display of skill in the contest. The further a contest is from the model of the ideal described above, the less satisfaction is available for the victor.

The attitude of respect for the game can be seen to lead readily to an attitude toward one's opponents. If one values and seeks the well-played game, one cannot view one's opponents as an obstacle to be overcome in one's drive for victory. Rather, one's opponents are an essential part of one's quest for the well-played game. Not only can an athlete not get what he or she wants without opponents, what is desired cannot be achieved without those opponents playing as well as they are able. Opponents must therefore be seen as co-questors for excellent sport (in Fraleigh's term, *facilitators*). One's competitors share the same goals and hold the same game in the same respect. They must therefore be seen as colleagues and compatriots, not enemies.

Violence outside of the rules is a form of cheating and so would be avoided by any athlete who honors or respects his or her game. Violence within the rules is more difficult. Many games make a virtue of physical strength and power. In these contact sports, an important part of the game may be to inhibit your opponent's actions and movements by means of your physical strength. The critical issue has to concern injury and potential injury. It cannot enhance the game to take an opponent out of the game by injuring him or her (which is, as a matter of fact, precisely the goal of boxing). Intending to injure would thus be unfair and should be avoided. Causing pain is a different matter. It is perfectly legitimate, for instance, to try to disrupt a quarterback's play by tackling him hard but fairly. If his fear of a legitimate but painful tackle causes him to rush his game, your team has fairly gained a tactical edge. Football (and rugby and hockey and wrestling and boxing and many other sports) test physical courage and strength as part of their tests of skill. Fairness as respect for the game does not rule out as unfair games that permit the infliction of pain.

While it could be argued that such sports are barbarous and should be banned or seriously modified, that moral claim operates from outside of the sport rather than from within. As such it is not really an issue of "fair play" at all. The claim would thus need to be made on moral or social policy grounds rather than fair play. This indicates the limitations of the view that fair play is respect for the game. The concept of fair play should not be expected to provide an answer to any and every moral problem that arises in or around the practice of sport. What our approach can do is provide a framework for settling fair play issues that is grounded in the nature of sport itself.

Intimidation needs sport-by-sport analysis. It may be argued that verbal intimidation may have a place in physical sports such as those listed above. Where the intimidation takes the form of boasting about one's physical prowess and the vigorous things you intend to do, and where it takes place within or around the game, it may be unpleasant but not morally reprehensible. Where it takes place outside of the game, or in the context of noncontact sports, it seems far less appropriate. Lumpkin et al. (13) recount the case of a football coach who used to send dead flowers and obituary notices to his team's opponents and another case of tennis players coughing during the opponent's serve or deliberately failing to let their opponents warm up properly. Both examples seem somewhat pathetic, as well as inappropriate. The respect for the game model of fairness can be used to support this feeling. Do these practices enhance the playing of the game? Do they make for better sport? Do they test game-related skills? Quite obviously not, so on the grounds of fair play, they should be avoided.

It is possible to take two quite different views of rule infractions and their penalties. One view says that a rule against, for instance, handling the ball in soccer, means that handling the ball is prohibited, then dictates a penalty (a direct free-kick) if the rule is broken. On this view, a player should not handle the ball. Another view says that handling the ball is generally imprudent (in sporting terms) because the cost—a direct free-kick—normally outweighs any possible benefits. But this is a defeasible condition. In some circumstances, for instance to stop a certain goal near the end of a vital game, the cost, the free-kick, may be worth paying. Such offences, as we discussed earlier, are usually referred to as "professional fouls," and the view that gives rise to them is one that values the outcome over the process of playing.

In effect these two views describe different games. In one game (soccer 1) the players do not consider handling the ball. In the other (soccer 2) handling is always an option to be assessed in light of its consequences. The two games would measure and test different skills, one of which (soccer 2) would be the tactical skill of assessing consequences of rule infractions. (For if this attitude is taken to the rule against handling the ball, it could, presumably, be taken for any rule.) Is the latter game, soccer 2, better, more skillful, more interesting to play and watch than soccer 1? Respect for the game will not dictate an answer, only a process for reasoning. Rules and our attitude toward them are constructed and can be changed. What is required is a debate and a decision that refers to the interests of the game of soccer.

While we cannot lay out this debate in its entirety, we can point to the sorts of arguments that might be raised. Soccer is a game where, relatively speaking, the play is continuous. Allowing players to constantly consider the relative cost of breaking the rule is likely to result in more rule infractions and hence more stoppages. This would change the nature of the game for the worse. Soccer skills include dribbling the ball with the feet and beating opponents. If handling the ball is a constant option (especially outside of the penalty area), traditional soccer skills will become of less value. This will make for less skillful soccer and would be a bad thing. Of course, proponents of soccer 2 may wish to argue that the new attitude will permit the development of new skills—strategic penalty evaluation, for instance, and they will further have to argue that these developments make soccer better. As the debate gets deeper, we will come closer to the heart of what makes soccer the game that it is. We cannot specify the outcome of this debate in advance, but the ground rules for discussion are the nature and interests of soccer itself. The outcome of the debate will be a decision.

Once that decision is made, we have the content of the agreement we enter into when we play. If the soccer community decides soccer 1 is better and promulgates that view, introduces harsher penalties for relevant infractions, and so on, it will not then be open to a player or team to play soccer 2, for that would constitute a breach of the agreement.

Respect for the Game and Racquetless Josie

In our analysis of the inadequacy of the rule- and agreement-based conceptions of fair play, we made use of the example of poor racquetless Josie. By now, it should be obvious that the notion of respect for the game provides ample reasons for lending Josie the racquet. At the personal level, if you respect the game, you enjoy the process of playing, competing, and testing your skills. You are intrinsically motivated to compete at your sport. You would forego a valuable experience and personal test if you decline to play Josie. At a more general level, the sport of squash is enhanced by people playing and competing at their best whenever possible. Squash at the institutional level would not be served by neglecting to play a possible and scheduled match. You should want to lend Josie your racquet.

Unfortunately, we do not have the time in this paper to explore in any depth the connections between our view of fair play and sportspersonship. (While we feel the connections are interesting, we do not feel that our account of fair play stands or falls on its relation to the concept of sportsperson.) In the context of sporting activity itself, we feel that fair play as respect for the game captures the attitude of the sportsperson. Such a person will be committed to the highest possible standards of play—for both himself or herself and his or her opponents. The attitude of the sportsperson is one that subsumes personal interest under the interests of fair and excellent play. This attitude is clearly grounded in our notion of fair play as respect for the game.

But there is more to the concept of the sportsperson than mere fair play and conduct within games. A person may be called a good sport for importing the general claims of morality into a sporting situation and for exporting a game playing attitude outside of sport.

In the latter case, we might call someone a sportsperson if he or she demonstrated the characteristic sporting attitude in situations outside of sport. In this type of case, the person may subsume personal interests under a broader commitment to the task at hand. For instance, to return to the academic example we used above, it would be sporting for someone to pass on information about a job or position to a potential rival. The concern that any qualified person be considered and the hope that the best person get the job is an obvious extension of the principles of fair play as respect for a practice applied outside of sport.

But there is an additional use of the concept sportsperson that does not obviously fit with our model. In cases of this type, the term is applied to someone who imports the general requirements of morality into a sporting situation. For example, in the 1988 Olympics in Seoul a Canadian yachtsman abandoned his race (when apparently, he had an excellent chance of winning a medal) to save another yachtsman in distress. If it was indeed the case that the other man would have died without the intervention, then the action is hardly one of moral heroism. We would all agree that it is right to save a life over completing a race. However, the more likely scenario is that many of us would judge that someone else could have completed the rescue, while we go on. Our hero's actions are good sporting behavior precisely because he was not willing, even in a situation as dramatic as an Olympic final, to allow the increased risk of waiting for someone else to make the rescue. What such a person appears to have is a fine sense of the relative importance of sport. Sport can be all-absorbing, and great sport is always pursued with the utmost dedication and commitment. But in the end, it is not worth a life. It is not clear to us how this sense of sportsperson fits within our model. We do not, however, take this use of sportsperson as a counterexample to our position that fair play can best be understood as respect for the game.

Conclusion

We set out to argue that standard views and treatments of fair play were incoherent and indefensible. Rather than presenting a unified conception of fair play, they either present a shopping cart of miscellaneous values or fail to capture our intuitions.

Respect for the game is a rich and powerful conception of fair play. It captures our intuitive understanding of the concept while providing a fully-worked out philosophical foundation for those intuitions. Respect for the game, rather than presenting ready made solutions to the issues of fair play, provides a process—a process that is grounded in sport—for working out what we should do.

Because of the connection between respect for the game and intrinsic motivation, the concept has its own, sport-based motivations for fairness. Teaching fair play as respect for the game increases intrinsic motivation, and teaching intrinsic motivation enhances fair play. The result is a philosophically credible and practically effective approach to fair play. Fair play as respect for the game is applicable at all levels of sport and readily lends itself to adaptation and implementation in education programs.

One could object that fair play as respect for the game preaches only to the converted. That is, it is applicable only to those who antecedently participate in sport for its own sake. It is true that fair play as respect for the game will resonate most clearly with those who already see sport in this way. We believe, however, that the approach is important even for those who do not currently have this view of sport. Our argument is both moral and psychological. On the moral side we are happy to argue that sport should be participated in for its own sake. Sport is only coherent if it is taken seriously on its own terms. The claims of fair play, however construed, will always be unheeded by those who insist on viewing sport instrumentally. (If one is not interested in sport itself, only the rewards that come from being hailed as the winner, there is no possible reason not to cheat if one thinks one can get away with it.)

From a psychological perspective and as a matter of fact, not only do people typically come to sport for intrinsic reasons, people who continue to play for intrinsic reasons have more fun. Those of us who care about sport and who care about fairness have an obligation to promote a view of sport that sees it practiced for its own sake.

Fair play as respect for the game is philosophy in action. It is an attempt to ground the treatment of actual sporting concerns and issues on philosophically sound foundations. As such it lays itself open to criticism from the members of two practices: sport and philosophy. As practitioners of both disciplines and, as we hope, good sports, we invite your criticism and collaboration as we attempt to make the world a slightly better place—through sport and through philosophy.

Notes

1. Although we do not support this method of understanding fair play, one could certainly do worse than apply the four cardinal virtues: wisdom, courage, justice, and self-control (temperance) to sporting situations.

2. We have made a similar point elsewhere. In *The Ethical Rationale for Drug-Free Sport* (19), we distinguish between arguments for banning doping that work from the "outside-in" and those that work from the "inside-out." The former rely on general moral principles and apply them to the specific issue of doping, while the latter work from principles found in sport itself. There, as here, we prefer the latter.

3. It could also be argued that games not only modify the scope of moral rules by limiting their applicability, but they also create new ways in which one can do moral wrong. On this view, intentionally handling the football during a game of soccer (assuming one is not the goalkeeper) and concealing that one did so, would constitute a moral wrong, one only possible given the rules of the game of soccer. We think that what would constitute the immorality of handling the soccer ball lies in the nature of the agreement of the players to compete. As such, the immorality would come from the general prohibition against breaking one's agreements rather than from soccer, which merely provides the context and content of the agreement.

4. Suits refers to this attitude as *autotelicity* (20).

5. This argument has a long history in ethical discussions of the self-defeating nature of simplistic views of hedonism. See *Reason at Work* (6).

6. Suits refers to this as the "logical incompatibility thesis" (21).

7. We can illustrate this with an example from golf. If, when playing alone, I throw my ball out of the rough, I break a rule of golf but do no moral wrong. (Although, we could say that I stop playing golf and start playing my own, modified version of golf.) If, however, I then tell others what my score was, or if I were playing against other people, without indicating my modification of the rules of golf, I would have committed the moral wrong, in the former case, of misrepresentation or, in the latter, of breaking my agreement to compete.

8. D'Agostino refers to this as the *ethos* of the game (3).

9. For a full account of this kind of discussion see Morgan (15).

10. It could be objected that sports are, in fact, paradigm examples of activities that are inherently worthless. In the grand scheme of things, it is irrelevant whether one can adequately perform a lay-up or put topspin on a backhand. This debate turns on what one takes to be worthwhile. We accept the position that activities that bring pleasure or meaning to lives (provided they are not ruled out on the basis that they cause harm to others) are candidates for being classified as worthwhile. Sports are often such activities.

11. This point applies particularly to the constitutive (and regulative) rules of a sport.

12. It could be objected that only individuals capable of having experiences or sensations are capable of interests at all. In what sense, then, could a practice have interests? At best, on this account, the interests of a practice would be the aggregate of the interests of its practitioners. Obviously we reject this view. The interests of a practice in one sense do derive from the interests of persons. Practices are human enterprises. There would be no such practice if human needs, desires, or preferences were not somehow behind the practice. But a practice takes on a life of its own and has the power to transform the lives and interests of those who participate. When this happens, the practitioner takes on the interests and values of the practice, to the extent sometimes

of neglecting or abandoning other aspects of regular human life. A devotee can even sacrifice himself or herself to the practice he or she loves. In this context it is natural and helpful to talk of the interests of a practice.

13. The requirement of universality is included for two reasons. First, if we are considering the good of the game we must assume that innovations be accessible to all practitioners. Second, the contested nature of sport requires that each competitor be permitted to use the same means to achieve the goal of the game.

14. We argue elsewhere (20) that the mere presence of payment does not necessarily obliterate intrinsic motivation.

15. Similar results are also found for college athletes with scholarships. Athletes who were on athletic scholarships listed more extrinsic reasons for playing and expressed less enjoyment of their sports than did college athletes without scholarships.

16. See, for example, Fraleigh's description of a good badminton match (7: pp. 30-33).

17. This list owes much to discussions by both Fraleigh and Kretchmar.

Bibliography

1. Bredemeier, B., and D. Shields. *Character Development and Physical Activity*. Champaign, IL: Human Kinetics, 1994.

2. Czikszentimihalyi, M. *Beyond Boredom and Anxiety*. San Francisco: Jossey-Bass, 1975.

3. D'Agostino, F. "The Ethos of Games." In: *Philosophic Inquiry in Sport*, W. Morgan and K. Meier (Eds.). Champaign, IL: Human Kinetics, 1988, pp. 63-72.

4. Deci, E., and R. Ryan. *Intrinsic Motivation and Self-Determination in Human Behavior*. New York: Plenum, 1985.

5. Feezell, R. "Sportsmanship." In: *Philosophic Inquiry in Sport*, W. Morgan and K. Meier (Eds.). Champaign, IL: Human Kinetics, 1988, pp. 251-262.

6. Feinberg, J. "Psychological Egoism." In: *Reason at Work*, S.M. Cahn, P. Kitcher, and G. Sher (Eds.). San Diego, CA: Harcourt Brace Jovanovich, 1984, pp. 25-35.

7. Fraleigh, W. *Right Actions in Sport: Ethics for Contestants*. Champaign, IL: Human Kinetics, 1984.

8. Keating, J. "Sportsmanship as a Moral Category." In: *Philosophic Inquiry in Sport*, W. Morgan and K. Meier (Eds.). Champaign, IL: Human Kinetics, 1988, pp. 241-250.

9. Kretchmar, S. "From Test to Contest: An Analysis of Two Kinds of Counterpoint in Sport." In: *Philosophic Inquiry in Sport*, W. Morgan and K. Meier (Eds.). Champaign, IL: Human Kinetics, 1988, pp. 223-230.

10. Kretchmar, S. *Practical Philosophy of Sport*. Champaign, IL: Human Kinetics, 1994.

11. Leaman, O. "Cheating and Fair Play in Sport." In: *Philosophic Inquiry in Sport*, W. Morgan and K. Meier (Eds.). Champaign, IL: Human Kinetics, 1988, pp. 277-282.

12. Lehman, C. "Can Cheaters Play the Game?" In: *Philosophic Inquiry in Sport*, W. Morgan and K. Meier (Eds.). Champaign, IL: Human Kinetics, 1988, pp. 283-288.

13. Lumpkin, A., S. Stoll, and J. Beller. *Sport Ethics: Applications for Fair Play*. St. Louis, MO: Mosby, 1994.

14. MacIntyre, A. *After Virtue* (2nd ed.). Nortre Dame, IN: University of Notre Dame Press, 1984.

15. McIntosh, P. *Fair Play: Ethics in Sport and Education*. London: Heinemann, 1979.

16. Morgan, W. "The Logical Incompatibility Thesis and Rules: A Reconsideration of Formalism as an Account of Games." *Journal of the Philosophy of Sport*. 24:1-20, 1997.

17. Morgan, W., and K. Meier. *Philosophic Inquiry in Sport*. Champaign, IL: Human Kinetics, 1988.

18. Pearson, K. "Deception, Sportsmanship, and Ethics." In: *Philosophic Inquiry in Sport*, W. Morgan and K. Meier (Eds.). Champaign, IL: Human Kinetics, 1988, pp. 263-266.

19. Schneider, A., and R. Butcher. *The Ethical Rationale for Drug-Free Sport*. Ottawa, Canada: Canadian Centre for Drug-Free Sport, 1993.

20. Schneider, A., and R. Butcher. "For the Love of the Game: A Philosophical Defense of Amateurism." *Quest*. 45:460-469, 1993.

21. Suits, B. "Words on Play." *Journal of the Philosophy of Sport*. 4:117-131, 1977.

22. Suits, B. *The Grasshopper: Games, Life and Utopia*. Toronto: University of Toronto Press, 1978.

23. Vallerand, R., E. Deci, and R. Ryan. "Intrinsic Motivation in Sport." In: *Exercise and Sport Sciences Reviews* (Vol. 15), K. Pandolf (Ed.). New York: Macmillan, 1987, pp. 398-425.

24. Weiss, M., B. Bredemeier, and R. Shewchuk. "An Intrinsic/Extrinsic Motivation Scale for Youth Sport Settings: A Confirmatory Factor Analysis." *Journal of Sport Psychology*. 7:75-81, 1985.

3

CHAPTER

On Winning and Athletic Superiority

Nicholas Dixon

How do we decide which team or player is better in a competitive sporting contest?[1] The obvious answer is that the winner is the superior team or athlete. A central purpose of competitive sport is precisely to provide a comparison—in Kretchmar's terms (7), a contest—that *determines* which team or player is superior. However, we can easily find undeserved victories in which this purpose is not achieved—in other words, contests in which the player or team that wins is not, according to both our intuitions and plausible accounts of the goal of competitive sport from the philosophy of sport literature, better than the losing player or team.[2] This paper is an examination of several such situations in which competitive sport fails to provide an accurate measure of athletic superiority. For brevity's sake, I will at times refer to such events as "failed athletic contests," meaning contests that have failed in their central comparative purpose, even though they may have succeeded in other goals like entertaining spectators.

An early draft of this paper was presented at the Philosophic Society for the Study of Sport conference in Clarkston, WA on Oct. 3, 1996. This final draft has greatly benefited from suggestions by the editor of the *Journal of the Philosophy of Sport* and three anonymous referees, to all of whom I am most grateful.

Reprinted, by permission, from N. Dixon, 1999, "On winning and athletic superiority," *Journal of the Philosophy of Sport, XXVI:* 10-26.

My purpose is threefold. First, studying various ways in which athletic contests fail to achieve their central comparative purpose is intrinsically interesting. While the philosophy of sport literature is replete with discussions of the purpose of competitive sport, it does not, to my knowledge, address the question of how well athletic contests fulfill that purpose. An instrumental benefit of this discussion is that a clear delineation of the wide variety of sources of unjust outcomes in sporting contests, showing that winning is not the be-all and end-all of athletic superiority, may help to weaken the motivation to resort to morally objectionable means to secure victory. Second, in the process of examining unjust victories, we will deepen our understanding of the concept of athletic superiority. More specifically, we will be forced to confront the issue of how much weight we should give to such psychological traits as guile and poise in our determinations of athletic superiority. Third, consideration of how much weight we should give to one particular psychological trait—the ability to perform well under pressure—in our judgments about athletic superiority will lead to the conclusion that the "playoff" system by which championships are determined in American team sports is a relatively inefficient method of determining which team is best.

For the first four sections, I will use "the better team" as interchangeable with "the team that deserves to win." Both expressions refer to the team that performs better (however we choose to define superior performance) in a particular athletic contest. In section 5, the two concepts diverge, as I discuss the possibility that the team that performs better and deserves to win may still not be the better team.

Refereeing Errors

Suppose that a soccer referee is either incompetent or openly biased in favor of the home team. He or she disallows as offside three perfectly good goals for the away team, even though replays clearly indicate that all the attacking players were onside. The home team wins by a single goal after the referee awards a "phantom" penalty, even though replays conclusively show that no contact was made with the attacker who slumped to the ground in the penalty area. Furthermore, the away team was constantly on the attack, pinning the far less skillful home team in its own half throughout the entire match. In this case, I suggest, the home team did not deserve to win. The better team did not win.[3] Several different views on the goal of competitive sport support this claim, assuming that the team or player that best meets this goal is the better one and deserves to win. For instance, Robert Simon's view that competitive sport is "the attempt to secure victory within the framework set by the constitutive rules" (11: p. 15) indicates that the away team is superior, since, had the referee applied the rules of the game correctly, it would have won. The injustice of the home team's victory follows from another of Simon's views, namely "the idea of the sports contest as a test of skill, a mutual quest for excellence by the participants" (11: p. 50), since the away team displays more skill and excellence. For the same reason, the away team's superiority also follows from Kathleen M. Pearson's view that the purpose of competitive sport is

> to test the skill of one individual, or group of individuals, against the skill of another individual, or group of individuals, in order to determine who is more skillful in a particular, well-defined activity. (10: p. 183)

But let us pause to consider some objections that would deny that refereeing errors lead to undeserved victories and, hence, to failed athletic contests.

First, we might insist that the referee's word is final and that, as long as no cheating occurs, any results based upon the referee's decisions are just. As a long-serving baseball commentator in Detroit was apt to point out, when people challenged an umpire's calls, tomorrow morning's box scores will always prove that the umpire was right after all. The problem with this argument is that it clumsily conflates power with infallibility. The jury in the first trial of the LAPD officers who assaulted Rodney King certainly had the power to acquit them. Those of us who disagreed with the verdict believed that, even though the correct *procedures* for a jury trial may have been followed, the *outcome* was unjust. Similarly, even though the procedural rules of soccer do indeed give the referee the final word, this in no way guarantees that the referee's calls will be correct. And referees' errors can lead to unjust results.

Second, and rather more plausibly, some people argue that a great team should be able to overcome bad calls by the referee and win anyway. There may be some truth to this claim, but it does not undermine my thesis, which is that the *better* team can be prevented by refereeing errors from winning, not that great teams can be. The away team in my example may not be good enough to overcome the referee's poor calls, but it is certainly the better team, and deserved to win, according to the rules of the game.

A third objection takes a very different tack. Rather than denying that the winning team (in my example, the home team) is superior, this final objection consists in arguing that the home team does not win at all. For instance, Suits (12: p. 9) argues that "a player who does not confine himself to lusory means may not be said to win, even if he achieves the pre-lusory goal." Thus the home team's alleged victory, which has been achieved by methods that violate the permitted lusory means, even though the referee negligently failed to punish these violations, is not a victory after all. This approach has an interesting parallel in natural law theory's treatment of unjust laws. In justifying his violation of segregation laws, Martin Luther King cited St. Augustine's view that "an unjust law is no law at all" (6: p. 89). Just as an unjust law, according to natural law theory, is superseded by the moral law that it violates, so an apparent victory by illicit means is nullified by the very rules that have been violated.

A problem with this approach is that, in preserving the justice of the outcome of sporting contests by legislating out of existence victories by inferior teams due to refereeing errors, it creates the suspicion of an ad hoc maneuver designed to respond to a troubling objection by stipulation rather than by argument. More important, in considering the analogy with natural law theory, we need to examine a rival theory, that of legal positivism. According to legal positivism, whether a statute is indeed a valid law, we need only consider its "pedigree" (that is, whether it was enacted in accordance with the constitution or whatever other "rule of recognition" is operative) without deciding on its moral justifiability. So a bad law is still a law. The problem with natural law theory, according to legal positivists, is that it conflates the concepts of "law" and "good law," and fails to allow for the very possibility of a bad law. We would do better, they suggest, to focus our attention on moral evaluation and criticism of immoral laws than to dispute their status as law.[4] The implication of legal positivism for our debate over refereeing errors is that, rather than disputing the fact that the home team won the game, we should instead concentrate on describing the injustice of this victory. Ordinary usage has a meaning for the expressions "hollow victory" and "undeserved victory," and we should be suspicious of an approach that would render these concepts meaningless by fiat.

Showing that refereeing errors can lead to undeserved victories by inferior teams has not required us to make any controversial assumptions about our criteria for athletic superiority. The fact that the visiting team was far superior in terms of physical skills and performance seems sufficient, in our example, to identify it as the better team. In the next section, however, we will have to broaden our concept of athletic superiority beyond mere physical prowess.

Cheating

My purpose in this section is not to offer a comprehensive account of cheating, a complex topic that deserves a much more detailed discussion than is possible in the confines of this paper. I offer instead what I hope will be an uncontroversial sufficient condition for cheating—namely, an attempt to break the rules of a game while escaping detection and punishment. Whatever else may count as cheating, we can be sure that anything meeting this description does. My goal is to explore the implications of this minimal definition for my topic of the relationship between victory and athletic superiority.

A victory that depends in large part upon cheating seems neither deserved nor a sign of athletic superiority. This is, presumably, why Ben Johnson was stripped of his gold medal in the 1988 Olympic Games after he tested positive for illegal steroids. Granted, Johnson did outperform his rivals. But he would also outperform them if he spiked their food or drink with a performance-impairing drug. In neither case does Johnson's victory prove him to be a superior athlete, because his violation of the rules gives him an unfair advantage over his opponents, thus subverting the race as a legitimate test of athletic excellence. Cheating can also occur *during* a game: A golfer may move the ball from a bad lie when her opponent is not looking, a pitcher may doctor the baseball, or a player in a tennis match without an umpire may wrongly call a ball out. An especially infamous act of cheating was committed by Diego Maradona, one of the most gifted soccer players of all time, who illegally punched the ball into the net to score a goal for Argentina against England in a 1986 World Cup quarterfinal. The referee did not spot the infraction that replays revealed, and Maradona afterwards boasted that the "hand of God" had scored his goal. In general, the reason why cheats do not deserve to win is that their victories are due not to their athletic superiority, but to their violation of rules which their opponents, in contrast, obey. This claim is based on the assumption that the athlete who deserves to win is the one who performs better *within the game's rules* and *under conditions of equality*.

However, we need to consider an audacious defense of cheating as playing a legitimate role in competitive sport. Oliver Leaman (8) describes cheating as the use of "wits" in addition to skill and strategy and suggests that it adds a new dimension that makes sport more interesting. As long as cheating occurs in the context of *overall* obedience to the rules by the cheater and other competitors, it will not result in anarchy, and the overall character of games will be preserved. Moreover, if we were to recognize cheating as a *legitimate* tactic for athletes to use, then the cheater would no longer have an unfair advantage, since *all* athletes would feel free to cheat. Indeed, the ability to cheat without being detected might even become a prized aspect of athletic skill. So, if Leaman is correct, even the orthodox view that the best athlete, the one who deserves to win, is the one who displays most skill does not necessarily preclude cheating. Perhaps Maradona's ability to deceive the referee into believing that he had used his head and not his hand to score the infamous goal against England is itself evidence of his genius. Machiavellian conflict between ruthless competitors would be the best test of this new, broader concept of athletic prowess.

Regardless of the merits of Leaman's defense of cheating, he has said enough to indicate that we need to broaden our concept of athletic superiority to include more than mere physical prowess. An excellent athlete must not only have superior physical skills but also the acumen to use them wisely, employing shrewd tactics and strategy that are designed to maximize the benefits of his or her skills while simultaneously neutralizing those of opponents. A soccer team that has exquisite ball control skills, but unwisely commits all 11 players to a constant onslaught on the opposing team's goal will often leave itself vulnerable to fast breaks from the opposition. Should the opponents win the game by virtue of a goal scored during just such a fast break, the technically superior losers cannot justly claim to be the superior team, since they have failed to exhibit an integral part of athletic excellence. If, as Leaman argues, the ability to cheat is itself a legitimate component of the "strategy and tactics" dimension of athletic excellence, then perhaps the cheating winners listed at the beginning of this section did after all deserve their victories.

Of course, moral condemnations of cheating in sport are easy to formulate.[5] However, Leaman's point is precisely that athletes are protected by a kind of moral immunity to the criticisms that would rightly be directed at them were they to cheat outside the context of sport.[6] We might compare this immunity to that enjoyed by defense attorneys in the U.S. Even when an attorney is convinced that her client committed a despicable crime, she is professionally obligated to mount a zealous defense, trying to get key evidence excluded on constitutional grounds, challenging truthful prosecution witnesses, and trying to persuade the jury of alternative possibilities that she herself believes did not happen. The end product of the attorney's actions may be the acquittal of a dangerous, factually guilty defendant.

Now the attorney's moral immunity is an essential part of the legal adversary system, which is itself justified by the belief that even the most despicable defendant deserves a loyal ally to protect his or her rights. Whether or not Leaman's argument for the moral immunity of athletes succeeds depends on the existence of a similar rationale for allowing cheating in sport. Is cheating essential to sport in the way that an attorney's loyalty to clients is essential to the legal adversary system? The answer seems to be no. Granted, widespread cheating would add an extra layer of intrigue and excitement to sport, but it hardly seems to further any of sport's central values. On the contrary, it sabotages one of competitive sport's least controversial goals: to determine which team has most athletic skill, including, as we have just seen, mental abilities like shrewd tactics as well as physical prowess, *as permitted by the rules of the game*. Certainly, successful cheating requires some skill and cunning and even, in some cases, considerable physical ability, but this is very different from the kind of legitimate use of tactical and physical prowess that competitive sport aims to test.[7]

My goal in this subsection is not morally to condemn cheating, even though good reasons exist for doing so. It is, instead, to evaluate the relationship between cheating and athletic superiority. However, for the same reason that teams cannot claim moral immunity for their acts of cheating—that is, they subvert the test of athletic skill that is a central goal of competitive sport—the claim that the team that uses cheating to win is *ipso facto* the best team and deserves to win is unconvincing. This judgment is reflected in the heavy penalties that sporting federations have imposed on athletes whom they catch cheating. More than the long term suspension that was imposed on Ben Johnson for his illegal drug use, the fact that his Olympic gold medal was taken away from him indicates the belief that he did not deserve to win. In terms of the abilities that competitive sport is designed to test, Johnson was *not* the best athlete. So, at least in some cases, cheating can prevent competitive sport from providing an accurate measure of athletic superiority.

Gamesmanship

Gamesmanship is a slippery concept that is hard to define. Unlike cheating, it does not involve violating the rules of the game in the hope of avoiding detection. Examples include using legal but morally dubious designed tactics to unsettle opponents: trash talking, taking an inordinate amount of time between points in a tennis match, and so on. A different kind of gamesmanship is the so-called "professional foul," which is committed in order to prevent an opposing player from scoring an easy goal or lay-up. Unlike outright cheating, such fouls are committed openly, in the expectation that a penalty will be imposed. Perhaps what all gamesmanship has in common is an apparent violation of the *spirit* of a game.[8] My purpose here is not morally to assess gamesmanship. It is, rather, to argue that an athlete or team that successfully uses gamesmanship as a major weapon in securing victory may not deserve to win in the sense of being the best athlete or team. Gamesmanship, then, provides another category of situations in which athletic contests can fail in their aim of accurately determining athletic superiority. We should note that at this stage we may only call gamesmanship an *apparent* violation of the spirit of a game. Should we conclude that successful use of gamesmanship is one sign of a good athlete, then we must withdraw the judgment that it violates the spirit of competitive sport.

I begin by considering the professional or "strategic" foul. Some philosophers of sport outright condemn such fouls,[9] while Robert Simon has given a nuanced, qualified defense of professional fouls in some circumstances (11: pp. 46-49). He points out that in basketball, for instance, the intentional foul is widely regarded as a legitimate strategy. The only issue, on Simon's view, seems to be the prudential one of whether preventing an easy lay-up is worth the penalty incurred for intentional fouls. For the sake of argument, I will grant Simon's point that a professional foul is sometimes a legitimate strategy. My goal in this section is to show that sometimes it is *illegitimate* and subverts the goal of measuring the relative athletic ability of the contestants.

For such an example, let us consider a soccer game that has been dominated by the home team but that remains scoreless going into the final few minutes. The home team finally mounts a decisive attack, and one of its players is about to tap the ball into an empty net when he is brutally rugby-tackled by an opponent, preventing him from scoring. The goalkeeper then saves the resultant penalty. In the final seconds of the game, the away team mounts a similar attack. The home team, in contrast, refrains from resorting to a professional foul to prevent the attacker from scoring, and the away team scores the winning goal with the last kick of the game. In such a case, I suggest, the away team did not deserve to win, because it did not demonstrate superior athletic skill. Its victory is due, instead, to its cynical willingness to exploit the rules of the game that "permit" the professional foul to teams willing to incur the resultant free kick or penalty. The recent (but unevenly enforced) decision by FIFA (the Federation of International Football Associations) to automatically penalize the professional foul by ejection from the game (without substitution) indicates that soccer's highest governing body regards it as a violation of the game's spirit.

How we view a professional foul may depend on the type of foul involved: we naturally view hard fouls more harshly that risk injuring opponents. Especially in basketball, we are more apt to condemn such fouls when they occur late in the game, since they are more likely to determine its outcome than those that occur earlier. The difference in attitude to the professional foul in basketball and soccer is arguably attributable to the vastly different impact that it can have in each sport. Basketball is a high-scoring sport, in which preventing a lay-up and requiring the offensive player to earn points from the free throw line normally has a minimal impact on a game's outcome. Soccer, in contrast, is a low-scoring sport, in which a single professional foul can prevent what would have been the decisive winning or equalizing goal. In such sports, a team that wins as a result of a professional foul is not necessarily the best team, in terms of the criteria we have so far allowed as relevant for athletic excellence: physical skill and tactical acumen, both exercised within the rules of the game.

The use of psychological tricks—for example, trash talking or delaying the game—to try to unsettle opponents is a very different kind of gamesmanship that forces us to confront another dimension of our concept of athletic excellence. We have already widened the concept to include mental as well as physical attributes. We now need to consider whether the mental element of athletic superiority should include such emotional characteristics as coolness under pressure, in addition to the cognitive abilities (for instance, strategy) that we have already added. In favor of such a widening of our understanding of athletic excellence is the view that players who allow themselves to be distracted by such tactics do not deserve to win. Truly great players, one might argue, will use their vastly superior skill to compensate for whatever loss of composure they suffer as a result of opponents' psychological tricks. However, we need to remember that the question here is not whether *great* players always win but, rather, whether the *better* player wins when gamesmanship is a decisive factor. And we can easily imagine examples in which a clearly superior, but not great, player is so rattled by her opponent's gamesmanship that she loses her cool and the game. According to the uncontroversial view that the primary purpose of competitive sport is to determine which team or player has superior athletic skill (understood as including both physical ability and astute strategy as permitted by the game's rules), players who use this kind of gamesmanship to win do not appear to deserve their victory.

In response, apologists for gamesmanship will respond that it *is* a legitimate strategy in competitive sport. If the ability to use gamesmanship (and to remain impervious to opponents' use of it) is part of athletic excellence, then the technically superior player who allows herself to be unsettled by her opponent's psychological tricks is deficient in one of the mental elements of athletic excellence and is not, after all, the better athlete. The issue, which we may safely leave unresolved at this stage, hinges on whether we include "psychological coolness" or temperament as part of the mental element of our definition of athletic excellence. In section 5, I will discuss in more depth the relationship between temperament and athletic excellence. I will conclude there that, while repeated defeats due to extreme nervousness may disqualify a team's claim to be the best, we must also allow for the possibility that a team that loses a big game due to nervousness may nonetheless be the better team. What has already emerged from this section is that at least one kind of gamesmanship—the professional foul in low scoring games like soccer—can result in undeserved victories in which the better team does not win, and the athletic contest has failed.

Bad Luck

The next set of putative failures of athletic contests to accurately measure athletic superiority involves neither mistakes by referees nor misconduct by players. It arises, rather, in games in which one team dominates the other but still manages to lose the game, because of a succession of strokes of bad luck.[10] The distinction between high- and low-scoring games is relevant here. In a high-scoring game like basketball, a few unlucky breaks are unlikely to sway the outcome. In contrast, in a low-scoring game like soccer, a small number of unlucky breaks can be decisive. Nor do we have to resort to thought experiments: most soccer fans have seen games dominated by one team that hits the woodwork several times and still ends up losing to a single goal scored on one of its opponents' few serious attacks. Suppose further that the dominant team has several goal-bound shots deflected by erratic gusts of wind, others stopped by thick mud on the goal line, and others still inadvertently stopped by a poorly-positioned referee. When, moreover, the winning goal is caused by a freakish deflection by a defender, the dominant team may justly claim that it was the better team and deserved to win. Unlucky losers appear, therefore, to provide another category of failed athletic contests. Let us pause to consider some objections.

First, mirroring an argument we have already considered, one might insist that a great team makes its own luck, and teams that fail to do so do not deserve to win. But this argument is vulnerable to a response already given: While a truly great team may indeed be able to salvage victory despite horrendously bad luck, a less talented team may be unable to do so, while still being clearly the better team and deserving to win. Granted, if a team with a long-term poor record claims that its losses were all due to bad luck, we would suspect self-deception and suggest that its players take a little more responsibility for their performances. Luck does tend to even out in the long run. However, in the short run—for instance, an individual game—we may plausibly say that a team was unlucky and did not deserve to lose.

A second objection reminds us that the purpose of any competitive game is to score more points than opponents. When a team dominates the action, keeping the opponent pinned in its own half, yet still manages to lose, it may be the lack of two legitimate considerations in determining athletic superiority, a killer instinct and good strategy, not bad luck, that accounts for its losses. Such charges were made, for instance, against the French soccer team in the 1982 World Cup, when it played beautiful, crowd-pleasing soccer but was eliminated in the quarter-finals. However, even granting for the sake of argument that some dominant teams do not deserve to win, we can still produce cases in which a team loses undeservedly due to bad luck. In the hypothetical case at the beginning of this section, the dominant team did not play pretty but innocuous soccer. It employed shrewd strategy and displayed a killer instinct, translating its dominance into several accurate shots on goal that were stopped only by the woodwork and by aberrational interventions by the wind, the mud, and the referee. Had these interventions not taken place, had any one of these shots gone just a few inches inside, and had the freakish deflection not occurred, the team would have won. Under these admittedly far-fetched circumstances, the better team did not win. However, more mundane examples of unlucky losses do occur in the real soccer world. Even the best players cannot direct their shots to the nearest inch, and the precise placement of any shot is partly a matter of luck. When a team repeatedly hits the goalpost without scoring, it is usually unlucky.

A final objection draws a line in the sand and insists that, no matter how close a team may have been to scoring several goals, it does not deserve to win if it does not score. According to this defense, the team that wins by a freakish goal on an isolated attack, despite several lucky escapes, including having its own goal's woodwork rattled repeatedly throughout the game by opponents' shots, deserves to win. The problem with this impregnable-sounding argument is precisely that it is *too* impregnable. Instead of honestly confronting the role of luck in sport, it tries to legislate it out of the picture by simply *defining* the best team as the one that scores most points. Arguments, not question-begging stipulative definitions, are needed to decide the question. And the arguments that I have presented in this and previous sections indicate that refereeing errors, cheating, unacceptable gamesmanship,[11] and bad luck can all result in undeserved victories by inferior teams.

Before moving on to a different aspect of the relationship between winning and athletic superiority, I pause to consider an argument that stipulative definitions of the kind I have just criticized are not necessarily question-begging. According to this argument, winning is an *operational definition* of the concept *the better team* in the same way that a score on an IQ test is an operational definition of the everyday concept of intelligence, and a legal verdict of guilty is an operational definition of the intuitive concept "that guy did it!" Operational definitions generally provide clear, objectively-ascertainable criteria for concepts whose everyday usage is more ambiguous and complex. (Legal guilt is an exception, in that rules of evidence and burden of proof requirements may make determinations of guilt appear more complex than the intuitive sense of "he did it!" Nonetheless, like all operational definitions, it provides an objective decision procedure—in this case, has the prosecution proven beyond a reasonable doubt that the defendant performed the *actus reus* with the requisite *mens rea?*—for determining a question that might otherwise be subject to arbitrary personal preference.) Since operational definitions do not claim to capture all the connotations of the everyday concepts that they replace, we should not be surprised by divergences between the two. People whom we judge very intelligent may perform poorly on IQ tests, and people who we know committed the act of which they are accused may be *correctly* found legally innocent. These divergences need reflect no fault in the operational definitions but, rather, the mere fact that they are operational definitions.

In support of viewing winning as an operational definition of athletic superiority, one goal of athletic contests is precisely to *determine* which team is better, and they have been designed to provide an accurate measure of excellence. Moreover, we sometimes modify rules in order to make contests a more accurate test of athletic superiority, for instance the offside rule in soccer, which prevents the tactic of booting the ball upfield to strikers who are permanently camped in front of the opposing goal, and encourages teams to play a more skillful passing game. To the extent that winning the contest is an operational definition of athletic superiority that has evolved over the years in the sporting world, it appears to be immune from the critiques that I have made, since my critiques are made from the point of view of the intuitive, everyday concept of athletic excellence. As we have seen, operational definitions do not claim to coincide with the everyday concepts that they are designed to replace.

In response, I do not deny that regarding winning as the criterion for athletic superiority is, *qua* operational definition, irreproachable. However, critiques of operational definitions from the point of view of intuitive concepts still perform two useful functions. First, too great a divergence between an everyday concept and its operational definition casts doubts on the adequacy of that definition. This is precisely what has happened with the concept of IQ, which has been criticized because of major discrepancies between it and intuitive judgments about intelligence. Victories by inferior teams or athletes, on the other hand, are sufficiently rare to indicate that this particular criticism is not applicable to regarding the winner as the better athlete, which remains a workable operational definition. Second, and most important, "external" critiques from the point of view of everyday concepts serve to remind us that such concepts as legal guilt *are* only operational definitions. They remind us that a defendant may really have "done it," even though he was correctly found legally innocent. And, in the case of the intuitive concept of athletic superiority,[12] they remind us that, while regarding the winner as the better athlete is generally a harmless convention, on some occasions it leads to inaccurate judgments of athletic superiority. I intend this paper, in part, as just such a reminder.

Inferior Performances by Superior Athletes

Steffi Graf dominated women's tennis for several years from the late 1980s until the mid-1990s. Suppose that in the middle of her period of dominance, she plays devastating tennis to reach the final at Wimbledon without losing a set. Her opponent is an unseeded player who has battled her way to the final by means of a series of gutsy three-set victories over technically superior players. And suppose, finally, that the unseeded player continues her string of upsets with a famous victory over Graf in a long, desperately close game. Her victory is fair and square. It involves no refereeing errors, no cheating, no gamesmanship, and no notably good luck. She deserves her victory because, on that day, she is the better player. However, in another sense, she is not the better player. Steffi Graf, who would almost certainly beat the player nine times out of ten, is the better player. She just had an off day.

So we appear to have found another sense in which an athletic contest can result in an inaccurate measure of athletic excellence: The winning player can deserve to win and yet still be an inferior athlete. Superior athletes do sometimes have bad days and lose. Few people would deny this claim in the case of my Steffi Graf example, but when it comes to other sports, some sectors of the sporting community are surprisingly reluctant to concede the possibility of this source of failed athletic contests. Concurrent with discussing their obvious relevance for my central topic of the relationship between winning and athletic superiority, I will point out the implications of such inaccurate measures of athletic superiority for the playoff system used in the U.S. to determine the winners of team sports championships.

According to a popular approach in the U.S. sporting community, a football team with the best record during the National Football League's regular season and playoffs, winning all its games easily but losing the Super Bowl, is not after all the best team in the NFL. The surest sign of the best team, the view continues, is the ability to save its best performances for the biggest occasions, and this is precisely what the winning team does, despite its indifferent play during the regular season and the playoffs. Evidence of the prevalence of this view is provided by the astonishing scorn directed at the Buffalo Bills football team in the U.S. for a series of Super Bowl losses in recent years. Even though it had the best record in American football for several years and was agonizingly close to winning one of its Super Bowl games, the mere fact that it lost several of these finals not only prevented it from being considered the best team but also made it a despised laughing-stock among many sport journalists.

Michael Jordan's status as an all-time great was secured in the opinion of many American basketball fans the first year he led the Chicago Bulls to a National Basketball Association championship, even though his play, both quantitatively and qualitatively, may have been just as outstanding in previous seasons. Once again, the underlying belief is that the best players, especially great ones, are those who come through to achieve victory when it matters most: post-season playoff games.

More generally, the playoff system in the best-known professional team sports in the U.S.—baseball, basketball, football, and hockey—clearly presupposes that victory in the biggest games is the best measure of athletic superiority. The championship is awarded not to the team with the best regular-season record but rather to the team that excels in a relatively brief playoff tournament involving some of the teams with the best regular-season records. Athletic excellence is understood as the ability to perform well under pressure, when the stakes are highest, rather than as the ability to perform well over the course of an entire season.

As a matter of contingent fact, the two rival criteria for athletic excel-lence—performance over an extended period (a season) versus performance in a brief, high-pressure playoff tournament—usually point to the same player or team. With rare exceptions, playoff winners tend to have very strong regular-season records, if not the best. Strong teams win most of their games, including high-pressure playoff games. The most interesting cases from the point of view of our discussion of athletic superiority, though, are those where a team with a mediocre regular-season record wins the playoffs, for example a wild-card team winning the Super Bowl. What reasons exist for the belief that this Super Bowl winner is, *ipso facto*, that season's best NFL team? Think back to the example about Steffi Graf, where a single defeat in a major tournament to an unranked player would not have dislodged our belief that she was the best women's tennis player in the world during her years of dominance. By analogy, why don't we also believe that the team with a perfect regular season record, which has dominated its opponents throughout the regular season and playoffs, is still the best team in the NFL, despite its subpar performance in its Super Bowl loss to a wild-card team? Certainly, a difference of degree exists between the two situa-tions. Whereas a single loss in a major tournament is relatively insignificant in the context of Steffi Graf's dozens of victories in many other tournaments, the Super Bowl is clearly the most important game in a very brief NFL season, consisting of a *single* tournament with a maximum of only 20 or so games. However, this difference in degree seems insufficient to support the view that the team that wins the playoffs for the championship is necessarily the best team. My scenario in which the season's dominant football team has an off day and loses the Super Bowl makes a strong enough *prima facie* case that it is still the best team in the NFL to require in response an *argument* for, and not just an assertion of, the accuracy of the playoff system in measuring athletic excellence.

And perhaps such an argument is not too hard to find. The ability to perform well under pressure, so the argument goes, is a sign of *psychological toughness*, which is an essential ingredient of excellence in competitive sport. We have already encountered in section 3 one element of psychological toughness, namely the ability to remain impervious to opponents' gamesmanship. Now little doubt exists that psychological toughness is an important quality for winning athletic contests. The key question is how much weight we assign to it in assessing athletic excellence.

I agree that a claim to athletic excellence would be hollow in the case of an athlete who *always* choked in any competitive game, not just big games in big tournaments. We would suspect that a general lack of athletic ability, and not just a suspect temperament, is responsible for the repeated losses. Furthermore, we could even require a baseline of psychological toughness as a prerequisite for athletic excellence, and concede that, however gifted an athlete may be, repeated losses in major tournaments due to nerves, undue sensitivity to opponents' gamesmanship, or a failure to be "up" for the occasion preclude us from considering her as the best athlete in her field. However, we also need to avoid the danger of setting our standard for psychological toughness so high that only actually *winning* the tournament or playoff series or Superbowl qualifies us as mentally strong enough to be the best athlete or team. In other words, we should leave conceptual space for regarding the team that has shown supreme skill, strategy, *and* psychological toughness throughout the entire regular season and playoffs, before losing the final game in the playoffs in a subpar performance, as nonetheless the best team. If we fail to allow for this possibility, the belief that the best team always comes through on the big occasions has become an article of faith rather than a hypothesis that is open to confirmation or falsification by open-minded examination of our concept of athletic excellence.

To further challenge the centrality of psychological toughness to athletic excellence, consider, by analogy, the importance that we place on the ability to perform well under pressure in other activities. For instance, is excellence in teaching best judged by a job candidate's classroom performance during a one-day campus visit, or by observing her classes for an entire semester? While we admire the candidate who rises to the occasion to deliver a dynamic guest lecture, most search committees recognize that nerves caused by the momentousness of the occasion can obscure the ability of even excellent teachers. A far better, but logistically impractical, way to evaluate a candidate's teaching ability would be to observe her over a longer period of time in a more relaxed setting. Why should we regard performance under pressure as so much more important in judging athletic excellence when in other fields we regard pressure as a factor that can *obscure* excellence? Of course, important disanalogies exist between teaching and sport, which is by its very nature competitive and tense. However, this does not explain why people regard performance under the greatest pressure as *the best* indicator of athletic excellence.

One reason for this may be that we in the U.S. are accustomed to the playoff system, which puts a premium on performing well in a small number of high-pressure games. And the very fact that we do have such a system may cause teams to approach the season in such a way that does indeed make the playoff system a reasonably accurate measure of excellence. In other words, professional teams in the U.S. recognize that reaching and sustaining a peak level of performance during the playoffs is far more important for winning the championship than compiling the best regular-season record. They may, therefore, regard the regular season primarily as a training period of little intrinsic importance, the main purpose of which is to allow them to fine-tune their skills and strategy for the playoffs for which they reserve their maximum effort. Given that we have such a system, the best teams will successfully channel their talents into developing the ability to produce excellent performances under extreme pressure in the brief playoff period.

However, we should not let this blind us to the more fundamental question of whether the playoff system is the best way of measuring talent in the first place. The force of my arguments in this section is that it is not. We seem to have fetishized the ability to perform well under pressure and given it far more importance as a criterion of athletic excellence than it deserves. It is instructive to compare the playoff system with the organization of professional sports in other countries. For example, in professional soccer leagues in Europe and South America the most prestigious trophy goes to the team with the best record at the end of the season. No post-season or playoffs exist. Single-elimination cup tournaments also exist, but they run concurrently with and independently of the so-called league championship. The underlying belief is that the most accurate measure of athletic excellence is performance against all rival teams over an entire season. Why does the introduction of the high pressure that accompanies playoff series provide a better measure? A further advantage of the "over the entire season" method of evaluation is that it minimizes the impact of refereeing errors, cheating, gamesmanship, and luck, much of which will tend to even out over the length of a season, whereas any one of them may be decisive in a playoff tournament.

In the case of international tournaments such as the soccer World Cup or the Olympic Games, simple logistics require a brief, high-pressure "knock-out" or single elimination tournament. A season-long series of games or track meets would not be feasible for such international competitions. And doubtless powerful financial considerations underlie the American playoff system, in that it sustains fans' interest and attendance at games far deeper into the season than does the league table approach, which can effectively eliminate most teams from contention well before the season ends. None of my arguments in this section are intended to diminish the value of success in such tournaments or in post-season playoff series in American professional sports. The ability to rise to the occasion and succeed in competition against the best athletes in the nation or the world is indeed a sign of athletic excellence. In the absence of crucial refereeing errors, cheating, unacceptable gamesmanship, and exceptional luck, winners of these tournaments are fully deserving of our admiration. They are indeed the best athletes and teams, in the sense that they performed best on the days of the tournament and deserved their victories. In most cases, they are also the best athletes and teams, judged on their form throughout the current or past season.

My objections have been directed solely at the view that insists that the winning team or athlete in a playoff or a similar tournament is *by definition* the best one, not just on the day but for the entire season or year. My point has been that a subpar performance resulting in a loss, whether due to nerves, insufficient motivation, or some other psychological factor, does not necessarily negate an athlete's or a team's claim to be the best. Psychological toughness is a legitimate component of the mental element in athletic excellence, and a serious deficiency in it greatly weakens an athlete's claim to athletic superiority. But we should beware giving psychological toughness so much importance in our understanding of athletic excellence that it eclipses all other elements.

The most important consequence of my reasoning in this section is that we should reexamine our attitude toward the playoff system in American professional sport. The best way to measure relative ability in domestic professional sport is the system used in European countries for such sports as soccer: a league championship, which is awarded to the team with the best record after an entire season of play. This system minimizes the impact of unjust results in individual games due to such factors as poor refereeing, cheating, gamesmanship, and bad luck. And while end-of-season games will sometimes involve enormous pressure, and while the ability to perform well under this pressure is a legitimate aspect of athletic excellence, the over-a-season method of evaluation is superior to the playoff system in not placing an inordinate weight on this ability in determining which team wins the championship. Unlike international tournaments like the Olympics and the World Cup, logistics do *not* demand that we base championships in American professional sport on brief tournaments. If we persist in using the playoff system, we need to acknowledge that this is a choice, not a necessity. And this choice involves sacrificing a more accurate measure of athletic excellence—the season-long championship—in order to enjoy the financial benefits of the playoff system. By choosing this system, we decrease the probability that the best team wins the championship.

Justice and Results in Sport

Despite the relatively uncontroversial nature of the list of situations I have described in which a sporting contest fails to provide an accurate measure of athletic superiority (sections 1-4), we are reluctant to concede that sometimes sporting contests may have unjust results. We like to think of sport as a supremely democratic arena where ability and dedication are the only determinants of success, at least in those sports that do not require expensive equipment and country club memberships. And there is some truth in this belief: A child from the shanty-towns around Rio may face insurmountable socio-economic obstacles that prevent him from any realistic chance of becoming a lawyer, but exquisite soccer skills may by themselves be sufficient to raise him to fame and fortune with the Brazilian national team. My conclusion that even sport is not a pure meritocracy may, therefore, appear to tarnish its image. However, the fact that a conclusion may disappoint us is not a good reason for rejecting it.

A helpful parallel to my thesis about sporting results exists in ethics. A venerable tradition associated with Kant holds that I am morally responsible only for what is within my control. I am not responsible for any consequences of my actions that I did not intend and had no reason to foresee. Strictly speaking, the only human actions that are subject to moral evaluation are our *intentions*, which, unlike the consequences of our actions, seem to be fully within our control. However, in the last 25 years or so, philosophers have realized that *moral luck* may play a significant role in determining our moral "record."[13] Factors beyond our control, including genetics, upbringing, and even where and when we happen to be born, influence what kind of people we become and even what kind of intentions we form. Nor does recognizing the role of moral luck require that one make controversial metaphysical assumptions about the absence of free will. Even if we grant that people have free will, we must concede that two people with exactly similar moral character may be faced with vastly different challenges and obstacles during their lives, resulting in one's leading an unobjectionable life, while the other becomes a moral monster. But for the historical accident of living in Germany during Hitler's rise, a Nazi war criminal might well have led a morally innocuous life, while his morally innocuous counterpart who spent his entire life as a farmer in South America might have played a gruesome role in the Holocaust had he lived instead in Nazi Germany.[14] Yet if we were to try to strip away the unfair influence of these external factors and confine our moral evaluation to the part of ourselves over which we have complete control, we would be left with no subject for our ethical judgments.[15] If we are to have moral assessment at all, we have to concede the role played by moral luck.

Similarly, my arguments show that displaying superior athletic skill, strategy, and mental toughness to those of our opponents—in other words, doing everything that is within our control while obeying the rules and spirit of the game—does not guarantee victory. Poor refereeing decisions, cheating, gamesmanship, and bad luck can all deny us the victory that we deserve. Perhaps the realization that morality itself is sometimes unfair, in the sense that we are not in complete control over our moral record, will soften the blow of the unfairness that sometimes arises in sporting results.

In contrast, my discussion of inferior performances by superior athletes (section 5) does not indicate any unfairness in the results of sporting contests. After all, the team that plays better on the day against superior opponents *deserves* to win. What my arguments in that section do show is that even a just result is sometimes not an accurate indicator of the relative athletic excellence of the teams. The only sense in which such a result is unjust is reflected in the statement that the losing team did not do justice to itself.

So we have seen many factors that can prevent the better team from winning. Bad refereeing decisions, cheating, gamesmanship, and bad luck can result in a loss for the team that performed better and deserved to win. And a subpar performance can result in a deserved loss by a team that is better than its opponents. The concept of athletic superiority that has emerged from our examination of these situations includes not only physical prowess but also mental attributes. And relevant mental attributes include not only cognitive skills like astute strategy but also affective qualities like poise and toughness. However, we should beware of placing undue stress on these affective qualities in our determinations of athletic superiority. A welcome consequence of our realization that a wide range of situations exists in which the better team or player does not win may be to weaken the obsession with winning that exists among some athletes, especially in the U.S. Putting winning and losing in a saner perspective may reduce the motivation to resort to cheating, distasteful forms of gamesmanship, and trash talking and other forms of taunting. And, while the desire to win is a necessary ingredient of competitive sport, realizing that winning is not the be-all and end-all of athletic excellence may help to foster the cooperation that is part of healthy competition and prevent it from degenerating into alienation.[16]

Notes

1. For the sake of convenience, I will refer throughout most of this paper to the "better" team or player. While the comparative "better" applies most naturally to contests between pairs of players or teams, I also intend my discussion to include competitions involving several players or teams. Understanding "better" in such contexts to mean "better than the rival(s)" will enable me to avoid the cumbersome construction "better or best."

2. For the sake of brevity, I will henceforth usually refer only to the better team, except when explicitly discussing individual sports, in which case I will refer to the better player. The reader should understand, however, that my entire paper pertains to both team and individual sports.

3. An actual example of a victory resulting from a refereeing error was the University of Colorado football team's infamous "5th down" win over the University of Missouri in 1990.

4. For an excellent summary of this central tenet of legal positivism, see Hart (4: sec. 1).

5. See, for example, Edwin J. Delattre's critique (2).

6. "Cheating in sport need not be compared morally to cheating in our everyday affairs since sport is 'just a game' and not simply a reflection of our everyday behavior. It may be morally acceptable to do certain things in sport which are not acceptable in everyday life" (8: p. 196).

7. See Simon (11: pp. 37-51) for a very perceptive analysis of the incompatibility between cheating and sport as a test of athletic skill.

8. Fine questions arise concerning whether a professional foul can be such a violation of D'Agostino's concept of the ethos of a game (1) that it constitutes an outright act of cheating rather than gamesmanship. Such questions, while of great intrinsic interest, are beyond the scope of this section. My concern is with whether such acts, *however* we characterize them, can result in an undeserved victory by an inferior team, and with what implications this has for our concept of athletic superiority.

9. See Warren Fraleigh (3) for a persuasive example of such critiques.

10. By luck I mean factors that are beyond the control of either team and that

have, hence, no bearing on the teams' athletic ability, whether understood in purely physical or psychological terms. Uncontroversial examples of bad luck are being on the wrong end of a net cord in tennis or losing a golf game when one's opponent's tee shot on the final hole rebounds freakishly from a tree into the hole.

11. I add the qualifier "*unacceptable* gamesmanship" to allow for my concession to Simon, for the sake of argument, in the previous section—namely, that some gamesmanship may be permissible. By implication, a team that succumbs to opponents who use *legitimate* gamesmanship may have lost the right to call itself the better team.

12. I remind the reader that what I refer to as the "intuitive" concept of athletic superiority is not a blind appeal to intuition. The account developed in this paper is based on uncontroversial views on the purpose of competitive sport by such philosophers of sport as Kretchmar, Simon, and Pearson, and modified in the light of Leaman's radical critique.

13. Two ground-breaking articles are Thomas Nagel (9) and Bernard Williams (13).

14. This is a variation on an example that Nagel gives (9: p. 26).

15. Nagel: "The area of genuine agency, and therefore of legitimate moral judgment, seems to shrink under this scrutiny to an extensionless point" (9: p. 35).

16. For an excellent account of healthy, non-alienated competition in sport, see Drew A. Hyland (5).

Bibliography

1. D'Agostino, F. "The Ethos of Games." *Journal of the Philosophy of Sport.* 8:7-18, 1981.

2. Delattre, E.J. "Some Reflections on Success and Failure in Competitive Athletics." *Journal of the Philosophy of Sport.* 2:133-139, 1975.

3. Fraleigh, W. "Why the Good Foul Is Not Good." *Journal of Physical Education, Recreation and Dance.* 53(1):41-42, 1982.

4. Hart, H.L.A. "Positivism and the Separation of Law and Morals." *Harvard Law Review.* 71:593, 1958.

5. Hyland, D.A. "Opponents, Contestants, and Competitors: The Dialectic of Sport." *Journal of the Philosophy of Sport.* 11:63-70, 1984.

6. King, M.L. "Letter from a Birmingham Jail." In: *I Have a Dream: Writings and Speeches That Changed the World.* San Francisco: Harper Collins, 1992.

7. Kretchmar, R.S. "From Test to Contest: An Analysis of Two Kinds of Counterpoint in Sport." *Journal of the Philosophy of Sport.* 2:23-30, 1975.

8. Leaman, O. "Cheating and Fair Play in Sport." In: *Philosophic Inquiry in Sport* (2nd ed.), W.J. Morgan and K.V. Meier (Eds.). Champaign, IL: Human Kinetics, 1995.

9. Nagel, T. "Moral Luck." In: *Mortal Questions.* Cambridge, UK: Cambridge University Press, 1979.

10. Pearson, K.M. "Deception, Sportsmanship, and Ethics." In: *Philosophic Inquiry in Sport* (2nd ed.), W.J. Morgan and K.V. Meier (Eds.). Champaign, IL: Human Kinetics, 1995.
11. Simon, R.L. *Fair Play: Sports, Values, and Society*. Boulder, CO: Westview Press, 1991.
12. Suits, B. "The Elements of Sport." In: *Philosophic Inquiry in Sport* (2nd ed.), W.J. Morgan and K.V. Meier (Eds.). Champaign, IL: Human Kinetics, 1995.
13. Williams, B. "Moral Luck." In: *Moral Luck: Philosophical Papers 1973-1980*. Cambridge, UK: Cambridge University Press, 1981.

4

CHAPTER

Some Reflections on Success and Failure in Competitive Athletics

Edwin J. Delattre

The initial objects of my reflections are the great and transporting moments of participation in competitive athletics. Reflection on these moments draws our attention to the conditions under which they are possible and to the kinds of people who are capable of achieving them. Reflection on these, in turn, enables us to see at once the touchstone relationship of competitors, and the moral and logical incompatibility of competing and cheating. Most of all we are reminded throughout these reflections that success in competitive athletics is not reducible to winning, nor failure to losing.

Richard Harding Davis was sensitive to the great and transporting moments of participation in competitive athletics. In the late fall of 1895, he wrote a gripping account of the recently contested Yale-Princeton football game. He captured both the involvement of the spectators and the struggle of the participants in revealing ways.

With the score at 16-10 in favor of Yale, but amidst a Princeton comeback, the description proceeds:

Reprinted, by permission, from Edwin Delattre, 1976, "Some reflections on success and failure in competitive athletics, *Journal of the Philosophy of Sport, II:* 133-139.

It was obviously easy after that to argue that if the Tigers had scored twice in ten minutes they could score at least once more . . . or even snatch a victory out of defeat. And at the thought of this the yells redoubled, and the air shook, and every play, good, bad, or indifferent, was greeted with shouts of encouragement that fell like blows of a whip on one side and that tasted like wine to the other. People forgot for a few precious minutes to think about themselves, they enjoyed the rare sensation of being carried completely away by something outside of themselves, and the love of a fight, or a struggle, or combat, or whatever else you choose to call it, rose in everyone's breast and choked him until he had either to yell and get rid of it or suffocate. (2: p. 9)

Forgetting "for a few precious moments to think about" oneself, being "carried completely away," can be among the high points of human existence. Yet being so transported in the wrong way, or in the wrong context, becomes fanaticism, irresponsible loss of self-control, even madness. Here we will not concern ourselves with the problematic dimensions of being "carried completely away," since they are not relevant to our reflections.

As the objects of eros are many, we can become passionately involved in diverse pursuits and activities, concerns, persons, even places. Inquiry can be transporting, the quest to discover—was anyone ever more obviously carried completely away than the Leakeys at Olduvai Gorge? The love of another, a symphony, dance; the range of our passionate concerns is virtually endless. In this list, of course, is the game: competitive athletics. Because of its special place on this list, which will emerge in our discussion, competitive athletics merit our attention and reflection.

Let us return then to Davis' description for it becomes even more revealing about the transporting moments in competitive athletics:

The clamor ceased once absolutely, and the silence was even more impressive than the tumult that had preceded it. It came toward the end of the second half, when the light had begun to fail and the mist was rising from the ground. The Yale men had forced the ball to within two yards of Princeton's goal, and they had still one more chance left them to rush it across the line. While they were lining up for that effort the cheering died away, yells, both measured and inarticulate, stopped, and the place was so still that for the first time during the day you could hear the telegraph instruments chirping like crickets from the side line. (2: p. 9)

What is crucial in this passage is not the silence of the crowd, but the occasion for it. The silence is occasioned by the resolution of the game into this moment, this spellbinding moment when the competition is most intense. Think of the moment not as a spectator, but as a competitor. Think of the overwhelming silence of the moments when the game is most of all a test, the moments of significance in the game, the turning points, which all the practice and diligence and preparation point to and anticipate.

Such moments are what make the game worth the candle. Whether amidst the soft lights and the sparkling balls against the baize of a billiard table, on the rolling terrain of a lush fairway or in the violent and crashing pit where linemen struggle, it is the moments when no let-up is possible, when there is virtually no tolerance for error, which make the game. The best and most satisfying contests maximize these moments and minimize respite from pressure. When competition achieves this intensity it frequently renders the outcome of the contest anti-climactic, and it inevitably reduces victory celebrations to pallor by contrast.

We see here the basic condition of success in competitive athletics. We must be able mutually to discover worthy opponents, opponents who are capable of generating with us the intensity of competition. Exclusive emphasis on winning has particularly tended to obscure the importance of the quality of the opposition and of the thrill of the competition itself. It is of the utmost importance for competitors to discover opponents whose preparation and skill are comparable to their own and who respect the game utterly.

We are recalled to this insight by the applicability to competitive athletics of the phrase "testing one's mettle." The etymological roots of "mettle" are the same as those of metal; indeed these were originally variant spellings of the same word. Just as the quality of a metal ore was determined long ago by the intensity of the color streak produced by rubbing it against a mica-like material called a touchstone, so in competition, one's opponent is his touchstone. In rubbing against a worthy opponent, against his skill, dedication and preparation, the quality of a competitor's mettle is tested.

As all philosophers know, Socrates employed the metaphor of the touchstone in the dialogues. Fellow participants in dialogue are the touchstones by which one tests the epistemic quality of his beliefs. That I have used the same metaphor must not be allowed to obscure the point that inquiry, dialogue, is, without qualification, not competitive. To view inquiry as competition, argument as something won or lost, is to misunderstand both. Dialectical inquiry is the shared and cooperative pursuit of the best approximation of the truth. In successful dialogues, false and confused beliefs are exposed as such, and those who held them benefit by the disclosure of their inadequacy. The testing of one's mettle in competitive athletics is quite another thing. The distinction is vital because when inquiry is treated as competition it is destroyed as inquiry.

Competition, contesting, if you will, thus requires commensurate opponents. The testing of one's mettle in competitive athletics is a form of self-discovery, just as the preparation to compete is a form of self-creation. The claim of competitive athletics to importance rests squarely on their providing for us opportunities for self-discovery which might otherwise have been missed. They are not unique in this by any means—the entire fabric of moral life is woven of such opportunities—but there is no need for them to claim uniqueness. They provide opportunities for self-discovery, for concentration and intensity of involvement, for being carried away by the demands of the contest and thereby in part for being able to meet them, with a frequency seldom matched elsewhere. It is in the face of these demands and with respect to them that an athlete succeeds or fails. This is why it is a far greater success in competitive athletics to have played well under the pressure of a truly worthy opponent and lost than to have defeated a less worthy or unworthy one where no demands were made.

We may appreciate this last point through a final look at Davis' chronicle:

> And then, just as the Yale men were growing fearful that the game would end in a tie, and while the Princeton men were shrieking their lungs out that it might, Captain Thorne made his run, and settled the question forever.
>
> It is not possible to describe that run. It would be as easy to explain how a snake disappears through the grass, or an eel slips from your fingers, or to say how a flash of linked lightning wriggles across the sky. (2: p. 9)

We cannot separate the significance of the Yale victory and the Princeton defeat from the fact that there was involved a player capable of such a run. For Princeton to have played well against a team with such a back, to have held a back of such quality to a single long run, to have required magnificence of Thorne for him to score, is a great success in itself.

How different this is from the occasion for Jack London's concluding lament in his coverage of the Jack Johnson–Jim Jeffries fight:

> Johnson is a wonder. No one understands him, this man who smiles. Well, the story of the fight is the story of a smile. If ever man won by nothing more fatiguing than a smile, Johnson won today.
>
> And where now is the champion who will make Johnson extend himself . . . (4: p. 513)

Jeffries was game in that fight, and he took a terrible beating. But the fight was no real competition because the opponents were not commensurate. Worse, Jeffries was ill-prepared, he was not the opponent he might have been. Accordingly, the extent of success possible for Johnson was extremely limited by the time the fight began.

As we noted previously, more is required for successful competition than commensurate opponents. Opponents, to be worthy, must utterly respect the game. Let us return now to explore that claim, for it involves not only important moral considerations but also rather more subtle logical or conceptual ones. An example will help us to expose and deal with both.

It is well known that during his career as a golfer, Bobby Jones several times called penalty strokes on himself. By 1926, he had won the American and British Opens and the American amateur title. In that year he granted an interview on golf style to O. B. Keeler, who asked Jones about those self-imposed penalties:

> "One thing more, Bobby. There is a lot of interest in those penalty strokes you have called on yourself. At St. Louis and Brookline and at Worcester—they say that one cost you the championship—and the one at Scioto, in that awful round of 79 when the ball moved on the green—" Bobby held up a warning hand. "That is absolutely nothing to talk about," he said, "and you are not to write about it. There is only one way to play this game." (3: p. 222)

From the point of view of morality, competitors must consider it unworthy of themselves to break deliberately the rules of the game. When a person violates the rules which govern competition, he treats his opponents as means merely to his end of victory. The symbols of victory have status or meaningfulness only because they stand for triumph in competition; without the opposition, they are worthless. Attainment of these symbols by cheating is therefore the exploitation of those who competed in good faith. Competitors are equally reduced to means merely in cases where the end of the cheater is prize money or gambling profit. Without the competition there can be neither prize nor wager, and the cheater simply uses the bona fide competitors solely for his own gain. Cheating is thus a paradigm case of failure to act with respect for the moral status of persons as ends.

From the point of view of logic, the need for the players' utter respect for the game is equally crucial. Competing, winning and losing in athletics are intelligible only within the framework of rules which define a specific competitive sport. A person may cheat at a game or compete at it, but it is logically impossible for him to do both. To cheat is to cease to compete. It is for this reason that cheaters are the greatest failures of all in competitive athletics, not because of any considerations of winning or failing to do so, but because they fail even to compete.

In the case of golf, as in the Bob Jones example, failure to impose a penalty on oneself where it is required by the rules is to cease to compete at golf. For one can compete with others only in accordance with the rules which govern and define the competition.

Or consider the case of pocket billiards. In all pocket billiard games it is a rule violation to touch any object ball or the cue ball with one's hands or clothing, etc. during play. It is also a violation for the cue to touch any object ball in the execution of a shot; any player who violates these rules has committed a foul. The penalty for a foul in all cases is termination of one's inning or turn. Now suppose that during a game of straight pool in the execution of a shot where the cue ball must be struck at a steep angle because of an object ball immediately behind it, a player knowingly touches that object ball with his finger, undetected by his opponent or a referee. If he continues to shoot, if he does not terminate his inning voluntarily, he has ceased to compete at straight pool. And because he is no longer competing, he cannot win at straight pool. He may appear to do so, he may pocket the prize money or collect on the wager or carry off the trophy, but since he is not competing any longer, he cannot win. The cheater is logically prohibited from competing and therefore from winning. He can lose by disqualification.[1]

We may wish here to recall Bernard Suits' discussion of rules in "The Elements of Sport." Suits distinguishes the constitutive rules of a game, those which proscribe certain means of achieving the end of the game, from rules of skill which apply to how to play the game well or effectively. He points out that to ". . . break a constitutive rule is to fail to play the game at all." (5: p. 52) He mentions also a third kind of rule, namely the kind of rule which if violated requires the imposition of a specific penalty, the sort of rule we have been discussing. He urges rightly that violating such a rule is neither to fail to play the game nor to fail to play it well, since the penalized action may be nonetheless advantageous to the competitor. But he also notes that such rules are extensions of the constitutive rules. This is the emphasis of my argument. In particular, to commit an act which merits a penalty, to do so knowingly and not to incur the penalty is to cease to play the game. To ground a club in golf or to commit a foul in pool is not to cease to play the game. But to ignore the penalty imposed by the rules surely is, and it is in this sense that we understand rules with penalties as extensions of constitutive rules.

Both morally and logically, then, there is indeed only one way to play a game. Grantland Rice makes clear his appreciation of this insight in his autobiography, *The Tumult and the Shouting*. For emphasis, he employs the example of a rookie professional offensive lineman. The athlete responds to Rice's praise for his play during his rookie year by observing that he will be better when he becomes more adept at holding illegally without being caught. Of course, to Rice this confused vision of successful competition is heartbreaking.

We have seen now that success in competitive athletics requires being and discovering worthy opponents, and that worthy opponents must be relative equals with utter respect for the game and their fellow competitors. We have related success to competing well, performing well, under pressure. No one can be a success in competitive athletics if he fails to compete, either by avoiding worthy opposition or by cheating.[2]

Of course, our treatment of competitive athletics is rather narrow; it does not deal with the variety of reasons and purposes people have for engaging in competitive athletics. Our reflections do not really pertain to people who play at competitive games merely for fun or relaxation or exercise, who use, as it were, the format of competitive games for purposes largely indifferent to competing and to winning. We are talking only about people who seek to compete with those whose investment in a game, whose seriousness of purpose and talent, are comparable to their own and who therefore play to win.

Now people vary greatly in talent and available time for preparation, opportunity, training and so on. This means that success in competitive athletics cannot be tied unconditionally to absolute quality of performance. Whether a competitive athlete is a success hinges on numerous relevant factual considerations. We acknowledge this point as part of our sense of fairness through handicapping, establishment of weight divisions in boxing and wrestling, age divisions in junior and senior competition, and division of amateur and professional, to mention only a few.

What then of the athlete as competitor, the athlete who competes with equals, who, in the very act of competing, sets victory among his goals? Is winning everything in such competition, the only thing, the sole criterion of success?

We have been told so often enough, and we have seen the young encouraged to believe that winning and success are inseparable, that those who win are "winners" and those who lose, "losers." This view, however, must be tempered by our previous insights; we must not become preoccupied with individual victories to the exclusion of recognition of the importance of patterns of outstanding performance. As Thackeray saw, "The prize be sometimes to the fool. The race not always to the swift." (6: p. 57)

Sometimes performance in victory is mediocre, in defeat awesome. Many Super Bowls are testimonial to the former. There are countless other examples of mediocrity in victory, from Little League games to professional contests. So too of excellence in defeat. To cite only one:

Anyone who saw Wohlhuter's heroic performance in Munich won't soon forget it. In the first qualifying heat, he tripped, and his pipestem body scraped along the track. Scrambling to his feet, he chased after the field—but was shut out by a stride.

"I was startled," he recalls. "To this day, I don't even know why or how I went down. When there're 80,000 people watching you, you want to have a good day. I had a choice—walk off the track or give it a try. I chose to be competitive." (1: p. 48)

To stress victory to the point of overlooking quality of performance is to impoverish our sense of success in competitive athletics.

It matters whether we win or lose. It also matters whether we play the game well or badly, given our own potential and preparation. It matters whom we play against and whether they are worthy of us, whether they can press us to call up our final resources. Satisfaction in victory is warranted only when we have played well against a worthy opponent. Otherwise victory is no achievement, and pride in it is false.

Notes

1. We might ask whether other members of a team are competing if one member is cheating. We would ask immediately whether they knew of it, and deny that they were competing if they knew and did nothing. We would be more perplexed if they did not know. But we would still deny, I think, that the team as a unit was competing. Notice that a team can be disqualified for the violations of one member. The same considerations apply to cheating in the form, say, of recruiting violations.
2. Obviously there is no failure involved in the decision not to participate in athletic or nonathletic competition. Some people are constitutionally unsuited for athletics, some for competition, while others find the demands of games artificial or fabricated and therefore unsatisfying. That there is failure in cheating or in constantly playing unworthy opponents neither suggests nor entails that there is anything wrong with unwillingness to enter at all into competition.

Bibliography

1. Bonventre, Peter. "The Streaker," *Newsweek* (February 17, 1975).
2. Davis, Richard Harding. "Thorne's Famous Run," *The Omnibus of Sport.* Grantland Rice and Harford Powel (eds.). New York: Harper and Brothers,

1932. Reprinted from: "How the Great Game Was Played," *The Journal* (November 24, 1895).

3. Keeler, O.B. "Bobby Jones on Golf Style," *The Omnibus of Sport*. Grantland Rice and Harford Powel (eds.). New York: Harper and Brothers, 1932.

4. London, Jack. "The Story of a Smile," *The Omnibus of Sport*. Grantland Rice and Harford Powel (eds.). New York: Harper and Brothers, 1932.

5. Suits, Bernard. "The Elements of Sport," *The Philosophy of Sport: A Collection of Original Essays*. Robert G. Osterhoudt (ed.). Springfield, Illinois: Charles C Thomas Publisher, 1973.

6. Thackeray, William M. "Sportsmanship," *The Omnibus of Sport*. Grantland Rice and Harford Powel (eds.). New York: Harper and Brothers, 1932.

5

CHAPTER

Opponents, Contestants, and Competitors: The Dialectic of Sport

Drew A. Hyland

"For that man be delivered from revenge, that is for me the bridge to the highest hope, and a rainbow after long storms" (5: p. 211). As is so often the case, these words of Nietzsche, though certainly not intended specifically for athletes, would seem to have particular meaning for those of us devoted to sports. All too often athletes, in the intensity and passion of a game, fail to be delivered from the spirit of aggression and revenge, or to use another of Nietzsche's apt terms, from *ressentiment.* I should say that I take the notion of "aggression" to be significantly different from "aggressiveness." Aggressiveness, in the sense of enthusiastic hustle, is a *desideratum* in sport and need not be accompanied by alienation. I find in the term "aggression," on the contrary, the strong sense that it is indeed accompanied by alienation, by *ressentiment*; that is why it is a problem for us, and that is why Nietzsche's observation is germane.

I will begin with what I take to be an empirical fact. The incidence of excessive aggression and violence in sport is great enough that many regard it as a significant problem. One hardly need rehearse the number of sports

Reprinted, by permission, from Drew Hyland, 1985, "Opponents, contestants, and competitors: The dialectic of sport," *Journal of the Philosophy of Sport, XI:* 63-70.

in which this problem has become serious enough to become an issue of public concern. The fighting in hockey, the "cheap shots" in football, soccer, and basketball, throwing "bean-balls" and spiking opponents in baseball—these are just the most sensational manifestations of a problem that many believe now affects sports the world over. Nor is the phenomenon limited to professional or elite levels; from high school and club sports to weekend "pick-up" games, we have had to recognize that the possibility of encountering excessive aggression and violence is a risk that one incurs in playing sports. It seems that the intense involvement and passion that is part of the attraction of most sports carries with it the concurrent risk that such intensity will devolve into alienation and violence.

So pervasive is this phenomenon that it has led many to the point of accepting it as a "fact" of sporting life. That is, many have concluded, however reluctantly, that violence and aggression are an inevitable part of sports competition, that if you put aggressive, competitive people in the intense emotional situation of sporting competition, it is simply too much to ask them not to become alienated and even violent. Keating (4) has intimated as much in his assertion of the difference between sport and athletics, and it has become a regular part of the "defense" of the inevitability of violence by some spokesmen for hockey and football, to name two of the most problematic cases.

The catch is, such alienation and violence is demonstrably not inevitable. I submit that everyone who has witnessed or participated in sporting events which have become alienated or violent (that is, I presume, nearly everyone) has also witnessed or participated in sporting events, equally intense, that occur in the mode of friendship. The Olympic Games offer us perhaps the most gratifying examples of this. I think especially of the well-known spirit of camaraderie and good will that exists among the world-class shot-putters throughout the world, or the manifest mutual respect held by professional basketball players Earvin Johnson and Larry Bird, notwithstanding the fact that they will give their all to beat each other. But at every level, from elite sports to sandlot competition, we know that athletic competition can be an occasion of friendship. However often aggression and violence occur, then, it is clearly not inevitable. Why then does it occur from time to time, and what is its meaning and significance?

In several earlier articles (2; 3), I have considered these questions from a fundamentally Platonic perspective. Several of the central theses of these studies bear reiteration here, without, of course, the supporting documentation. First, I paid heed to the etymology of the word "competition": *competitio,* to strive or question together. Now, etymologies of words are never perhaps conclusive arguments, but neither are they meaningless, unless one considers origins to be meaningless. In this case, the etymology of "competition" points first to the element of cooperation involved, that something is being done together, and second, to the element of a striving or questioning toward something that presumably one does not already have. The original significance of competition, then, seems to entail a shared striving or questioning toward something one lacks and which one could not achieve, or at least could not achieve as well, without the cooperation. Second, I suggested that this understanding of competition was commensurate with and indeed grounded in the stance of play as "responsive openness," in brief, a heightened openness toward possibilities and at once a heightened responsiveness toward them.

Two aspects of this stance are particularly germane to our present discussion. On the one hand, play as the stance of responsive openness preserves a precarious balance between the two alternative and somewhat polar stances of mastery or dominance and submission. Insofar as the player fails to preserve that balance, that is, insofar as he or she moves more exclusively toward the two polar stances, alienation is likely to occur. The player begins to construe the game in terms of an either/or: either master or be dominated—perhaps an inherently alienating situation. This explains in part the recurrent risk of alienation in play. On the other hand, responsive openness can equally well be seen as arising out of a certain duality in human being, that we are at once incomplete, striving for wholeness, yet overfull and desirous of pouring ourselves out toward the world, of expressing ourselves. In turn, this understanding of human being, it was suggested, is an elaboration of, and so is ultimately grounded in, the nature of human being as erotic. Human being is eros. The critical upshot of this somewhat elaborate ontological grounding of play was the thesis that the *telos* of competition, competition insofar as it attains to its highest possibility, is a mode of friendship, and that conversely, alienated play must be understood in every case as a defective mode of competition, as a failure to attain the highest potential game.

That truth may bear repeating, but that is not the reason why I present this brief outline of my earlier position. That position is one perspective, and I am inclined still to hold to it, without insisting that it is a comprehensive or total one. Herein, I wish to look at the same phenomenon from a different but, I believe, finally compatible perspective, in the hope that more light will be shed on alienation and violence in sport by looking at it from this other perspective. I shall loosely call it an Hegelian perspective.

Let me begin with a brief outline of Hegel's notion of dialectic. Spiritual activity, which for Hegel meant activity that is a manifestation of spirit *(Geist),* is dialectical through and through. Dialectic might thus be construed as the logic of spiritual activity, and it has a triadic structure which is captured by the virtually untranslatable German word *Aufhebung.* Its first "moment" is negation. Any spirit in acting "negates" as adequate whatever the situation was in the light of which it was moved to act. When I chose, say, to write this paper, I "negated" my previous papers on the subject as completely adequate or comprehensive statements of the truth; similarly, with the Declaration of Independence the United States "negated" its status as a colony of England. But a dialectical act is never merely a negation of some previous situation. Its second moment is a lifting up of the truth of the negated situation, and its third a preserving of that lifted-up truth in the ongoing dialectical movement.

To appeal again to the above examples, although my writing this paper indeed negates the adequacy of my previous efforts, it does not merely destroy them or leave them behind; rather, the present paper lifts up and preserves what I take to be the truth of the previous articles in the ongoing movement of this paper. Similarly, although the Declaration of Independence negated the states' status as a colony of England, it lifted up and preserved much of the spirit, the culture, the principles, of the English tradition. Any dialectical movement, then, any *Aufhebung,* embodies this triadic structure of negation, lifting up, and preserving. Of this structure a number of observations are germane to our present concerns.

First, the critical importance and the subtle complexity of the initial moment of negation must be emphasized. As my previous examples suggest, it is one thing to negate my former papers as adequate; it is quite another to declare independence from a country and thereby precipitate a bloody war. Hegel (1: pp. 27, 43, 94) himself vacillates in his metaphors for this moment of negation between the metaphor of a fruit "negating" the blossom from which it emerges and, on the other hand, his characterization of the dialectical movement of history as a "slaughterbench" on which "many an innocent flower is crushed." This testifies to Hegel's recognition that the negativity inherent in all dialectical activity can be benign or can be violent. Perhaps more fully, there is no doubt an enormous range of manifestations which this moment of negation can take. But there will always be negation. Negativity is an irreducible element of spiritual life. It can be as violent as a murder or bloody war, as benign as the sign for logical negation or the correction of a philosophical error.

Second, however, it must be emphasized that the moment of negation is the initial, not the final, moment in any dialectical action. Negation, that is, occurs to be transcended into something higher. Mere negation, which only negates and leads to no more positive *Aufhebung,* is thus radically incomplete, undialectical, and so, unspiritual.

Third, I emphasize again that all genuinely spiritual activity for Hegel is inherently dialectical; this means that if he is right, then sporting activity, as an activity of finite spirits, should be dialectical through and through. I believe Hegel is right.

It is not difficult to see the appropriateness of a dialectical interpretation of competitive sport. I suggest first that the "oppositional" character of competitive sport represents the moment of negativity; one individual or team must win, one must lose. In order for me to accomplish the goal of winning the game, I must negate the efforts of the other player or team to win. But as the competitive sport situation makes clear (and as Hegel perhaps fails sufficiently to emphasize), the other player or team will not accept passively my efforts at dialectical negation; they will resist, counter my efforts with their own attempt to negate me. But being negated is not always pleasant or welcome; sometimes the situation can become alienated, and the efforts at negation violent. Violence and alienation in competitive sport, then, are located in a radicalization of this negative dialectical element inherent in the effort to "beat" the other team, to win the game.

Thus the possibility, but not the necessity, of violence and alienation in sport can be accounted as consistent with Hegel's own suggestion that the negative moment can be violent or a less violent, more benign form of negation. The latter, I suggest, is the ontological location of the possibility of friendship in competition. To be sure, my efforts to win the game, and so to negate the other team's concurrent efforts to win, can become alienated and violent; indeed, all too often they do. But we also know that they are not always so; negation is not necessarily alienated and violent. Competitors can and do from time to time engage in a more "benign" mode of mutual negation which can even be an occasion for friendship, for striving or questioning together. The situation, then, is that alienation and violence in competitive sport arise as one possibility inherent in the negative moment of all spiritual activity. Both its possibility but also its contingency, that it does not have to occur, is thereby explained. Both aggression and friendship are revealed as ontological possibilities of the dialectical moment of negation.

So far, however, the co-presence of the possibility both of violent and of benign negation would seem to be simply a dialectical fact; nothing in the nature of dialectical movement *per se* would seem to argue for the superiority of benign to violent negation. There seems—to the dismay of many students of Hegel—to be something amoral about dialectic, or at least about its negative moment. If so, a consistently Hegelian interpretation of competitive sport would seem to demand the conclusion that some instances of sport competition will be violent, some more nonviolent, and no judgment can legitimately be made as to the superiority of friendly to alienated competition. Yet as I earlier reiterated, the *telos* of athletic competition is friendship, and every instance of alienated competition must be understood as a defective mode. Can such a thesis be maintained within an Hegelian context? I believe so.

If negation were the whole of dialectical movement, we would be forced to the conclusion that no claim could be made for the superiority of friendly to alienated competition. However, negation is not the *telos* of dialectic but its first moment. The negative moment in dialectic, and so the oppositional character of sport competition, exists to be overcome. The question then is, what is the athletic counterpart to the *Aufhebung,* the lifting up and preserving, which is the transcendence of the negativity of the oppositional element that each team in a game will strive to beat the other? Presumably, it will have something to do with each of the contestants being raised to new heights in and through the competition which they could not otherwise have achieved.

At least this much is now clear; it cannot be the case, from an Hegelian perspective, that "winning isn't everything, it's the only thing." For if winning, beating the opposition, were the sole *telos* of the contest, then the situation would not be dialectical but the simple negation of one by the other opponent. Athletic competition would thus be a radically incomplete, inadequate, unspiritual activity—nothing, finally, but an occasion for negation. But if this were so, if winning were the sole goal of sport, then, as we say, "anything goes"; we should do absolutely anything necessary to win, including all manner of cheating. That this is not so attests that winning, though certainly a goal of the competition, is not the only one. What, we must now ask, are the other, higher *teloi* of athletic competition which constitute the *Aufhebung* of the oppositional component?

Their number no doubt is legion. I shall not even attempt exhaustively to catalogue the possible goals of athletic competition. Instead, I shall focus on only a few of those *teloi,* with the particular intention of showing that these higher goals can better be accomplished in situations in which the oppositional component is not alienated or violent, and so that the comprehensive dialectical structure of athletic competition is such that friendship is indeed its superior mode and alienated or violent competition is defective.

I begin with the theme that Paul Weiss emphasized so well in his *Sport: A Philosophical Inquiry* (6: chapter one): namely, the quest for excellence. Weiss is surely right that one of the strongest attractions of sport, both for participants and spectators, is the concern for excellence. Think of a sport in which you have no desire to improve, to achieve a level of excellence; I submit that it is almost certainly a sport that either you never have played or that you almost never play. Virtually any sport to which we become committed, about which we are at all likely to say that we enjoy it, is a sport in which we are concerned to achieve excellence. Why, for example, are we frustrated when we do not play well on a given day, if not that one of our strong concerns is precisely to play well, to be excellent at our chosen sport? Weiss also noted appropriately that this is one of the strongest attractions of sport for young people; long before they are capable of achieving excellence in other domains—business, politics, ethics, science—they are capable of achieving it in athletics. In a very real sense, athletics offers to many of us our first taste of excellence; it is fair to say that most of us like that taste.

Thus the quest for excellence is one of the important *teloi* of sport. But does it function as part of the *Aufhebung* of the merely negative, oppositional moment in sport? A number of examples suggest that it does. The first involves a pair of common experiences: on the one hand, there have been occasions when we have won the game (and therefore, on the "winning is everything" thesis we should be delighted) but nevertheless have not felt good about it. The victory, as we sometimes say, "leaves a bad taste in the mouth." Why? Almost always, I submit, because we did not play well, we did not achieve that excellence for which we strive as much as we strive to win. On the other hand, we have also had occasions when we lose the game, perhaps to a superior team, but nevertheless experience a feeling of satisfaction because we played our very best, perhaps the best we ever played.

In both cases, the negative moment inherent in the sport situation—that one team wins and the other loses, gives way to or is transcended by the overriding factor of the desire for excellence. But what if the particular game happens to be one in which alienation and violence is rampant? What is the likelihood of this transcendence of negativity occurring? Is it not altogether more likely that when the negativity, the alienation and violence, becomes dominant, it precludes any more positive transcendence? The possibility of such transcendence, in this case the possibility of achieving that sense of excellence, is enhanced insofar as the competition is unalienated.

My second example follows upon the first. If our sole concern in playing games were winning, this would dictate a rather clear strategy in choosing opponents; always choose opponents over which you are vastly superior. This should guarantee that except for the most bizarre of circumstances we would always win, and usually by an overwhelming score. But few of us do this. We seek out opponents who will genuinely challenge us, opponents who are sufficiently good that the outcome of the game is really in question. In our sandlot games we choose sides in order to make the teams as close as possible in ability. Even at the elite level of professional sport, there is a well-known concern to achieve competitive balance among the teams. And it is a virtual coach's cliche that a team plays to the level of its opponent. If you want your team to play well, to achieve excellence, play good teams.

Again, what does all this suggest? Our concern to achieve competitive balance in sport, to find opponents who will really challenge us, who will "bring out the best in us," flies in the face of the claim that our sole concern is with winning. Winning, to be sure, is one goal—we might say the immediate goal—of many sports. Our Hegelian analysis suggests why. As the moment of negativity in sport, wherein the winning team negates the efforts of the losing team, it exists to be transcended to something higher. Again we can ask, when that initial negative moment is radicalized into alienation and violence, is this transcendence inhibited or enhanced? Experience confirms Hegelian analysis; when the negativity gets radicalized into violence, the most you can come away with is a victory. But that is to fail to achieve the transcendence that athletics holds for us.

Finally on the issue of excellence, this point has always been encapsulated for me in the symbolic significance of the handshake at the end of a hotly contested game. Some would hold that the handshake symbolizes that now that the aggression and violence are over we won't hold a grudge. It has long struck me that the handshake symbolizes rather, "Thanks, friend, I could never have achieved what I did without you."

The striving for excellence is one of, but not the only, *teloi* of athletic competition which brings about the transcendence of the initial moment of negation. Perhaps the most obvious goal of sport that accomplishes this is fun. I remember well my college basketball coach exhorting us from time to time that "If you don't want to win, don't walk out on the floor." But at other times, when we were on the verge of making the goal of winning too exclusive, he would exhort us instead, "If all this isn't fun, you shouldn't be doing it." It took us a while to realize that the two exhortations are altogether compatible.

Fun, I have discovered, is almost impossible to define in a nontrivial way. Yet it is something that we sense is at the very core of our participation in sport. Even professional athletes, ostensibly now playing a sport not for the fun but for a livelihood, often insist that when the game ceases to be fun they will retire. I do not hear other business people say that nearly so often. Earvin "Magic" Johnson of the Los Angeles Lakers basketball team has become a virtual cultural hero recently, in part because he so manifestly and ebulliently enjoys what he is doing. We like that; we sense that Magic is playing the game the way it is supposed to be played, that is, with enormous enjoyment. On a considerably less elite level, I continue to participate in our faculty lunchtime basketball games at Trinity College, certainly not because I keep a thorough record of the thousands of games I have played there over the years and have discovered that I win more than I lose, but because it is still fun.

Obviously, then, fun is a *telos* of athletic competition, one that contributes to the *Aufhebung* of the sole concern with winning. No less obviously, I take it, the possibility of fun is enhanced insofar as alienation and violence are avoided. In fact, the point is more subtle than it looks, because experience confirms that most athletic competition is more fun if everybody hustles, plays hard, even with passion. Here we can see why genuine involvement in athletic competition again and again risks alienation, because in order to derive the most fun from our play we must invest in it the kind of enthusiasm and passion which can, with an all-too-subtle change in circumstances, devolve into alienation. So to get the most fun in our athletic competition we must risk alienation. That does not deny but instead confirms the view that such fun will be best achieved if the alienation into which it might degenerate is avoided. If someone retorts, "But I always have the most fun when I am alienated and violent," we make our private assessment of such a person and seek our playmates elsewhere.

My third and final example of a *telos* of athletic competition which transcends the negativity of beating the opposition is the phenomenon commonly referred to as a "peak experience." Many of us are aware of and have even experienced in our athletic competition these very special moments when, as we sometimes say, "everything comes together," when the long hours and even years of practice and preparation culminate in an occasion when everything happens as it should, apparently effortlessly, without calculation, as if our ability now flowed instinctively from our bones and muscles. They are special moments, these peak experiences, and even if they happen relatively rarely, they constitute a possibility of athletic participation which, when it occurs, surely embodies a kind of transcendence. Is the possibility of such experiences enhanced or inhibited by alienation and violence? Again the answer seems obvious; when I am alienated, when I am in a mood for violence, that mood dominates my consciousness. There is not room for the kind of openness and responsiveness which invite anything like a peak experience. Put differently, an obsession with "getting the opposition," especially when it escalates to alienation and violence, closes off these other *teloi;* it arrests the dialectic at the moment of negativity.

Still, one might object that winning remains one goal of competition and possibly the most immediate one, and it is better accomplished if one is alienated and willing to do violence to achieve it. That has surely been asserted by many a coach. To this view I have two responses. First, even if it were true, my Hegelian analysis has suggested that there are other *teloi* of athletic competition, *teloi* which in fact even supersede the goal of winning. Since these higher *teloi* are better accomplished without the presence of alienation and violence, that in itself should lead us to avoid alienation whenever possible, even if this means we lose another game here and there.

But second, is it even true that winning is better accomplished in the mode of alienation? The most we could say, I suggest, is that some people seem psychologically incapable of doing their very best unless they are alienated, unless they "hate" the opposition. But this is part of the particular psychology of certain individuals, not an inherent aspect of athletic competition. There are many other people who, when they become alienated, "fall apart" and do not play well at all. Why, then, should we allow such idiosyncracies to justify alienating the game for others? We should not.

Hegel and Plato, of course, are very different philosophers. But they are both concerned to account for the nature of human experience, and since athletic competition is a meaningful and significant experience, it is instructive to apply their insights directly to the realm of sport. Notwithstanding their important differences, I have tried to suggest that their philosophies lead to very compatible conclusions regarding the issue of aggression and violence in sport.

My earlier thesis, defended from a Platonic perspective, that the ends of athletic competition are best accomplished when the competition is in the mode of friendship, and that alienation is therefore a defective mode of competition, is supported from the very different Hegelian perspective. From the latter standpoint, alienation is an instance of arrested dialectic. It represents the failure to see the real directions, the higher *teloi,* of athletic competition. It generates masters and slaves, not athletes. Genuine athletes, who recognize the full dialectical possibilities inherent in sport and strive to achieve them, would therefore do well to recall the spirit of Nietzsche's words evoked at the beginning of this paper: *Keine Rache!* No revenge!

Bibliography

1. Hegel, G.W.F. (1983). *Lectures on the Philosophy of History.* Translated by R.S. Hartman as *Reason in History.* New York: Bobbs-Merrill Inc.
2. Hyland, Drew. (1978). "Competition and Friendship." *Journal of Philosophy of Sport,* pp. 27-38.
3. Hyland, Drew. (1983). "Competition, Friendship, and Human Nature." In B.C. Postow, *Women, Philosophy, and Sport: A Collection of New Essays.* Metuchen, NJ: Scarecrow Press.
4. Keating, James W. (1979). "Sportsmanship as a Moral Category." In E.W. Gerber & W.J. Morgan (Eds.), *Sport and the Body: A Philosophical Symposium.* Philadelphia: Lea & Febiger.

5. Nietzsche, Friedrich. (1983). *Thus Spoke Zarathustra, Part II.* Translated by W. Kaufmann in *The Portable Nietzsche.* New York: Viking Press.
6. Weiss, Paul. (1969). *Sport: A Philosophical Inquiry.* Carbondale: Southern Illinois University Press.

6

CHAPTER

Cheating and Fair Play in Sport

Oliver Leaman

It is not as easy as it might initially be thought to define cheating in sport, and it is just as difficult to specify precisely what is wrong morally with such behaviour, and why fair play should be prized. In this article I intend to try to throw some light on the notions of both cheating and fair play, and to suggest that stronger arguments than those so far produced in the literature are required to condemn the former and approve the latter.

Let us try to deal first with the definitional problem of what sorts of behaviour constitute cheating, and come to the ethical issue later. Gunther Luschen boldly starts his essay on cheating in sport with this definition:

> Cheating in sport is the act through which the manifestly or latently agreed upon conditions for winning such a contest are changed in favor of one side. As a result, the principle of equality of chance beyond differences of skill and strategy is violated. (1976, p. 67)

A problem with this definition is that it omits any consideration of intention. After all, if a player unwittingly breaks the rules and thereby gains an unfair advantage he will not necessarily have cheated. For example, if a boxer has a forbidden substance applied to bodily damage without his knowledge, then he has not cheated even though the rules have been broken to his advantage.

Reprinted from *Sport and the Humanities: A Collection of Original Essays* (pp. 25-30), (1981), edited by William J. Morgan, Bureau of Educational Research and Service, University of Tennessee. Reprinted by permission.

Were he to be penalized or disqualified, it would not be because of his cheating but due to the rules having been broken by those who attend to him in the intervals.

A superior account of cheating is then provided by Peter McIntosh, who claims that:

> Cheating . . . need be no more than breaking the rules with the intention of not being found out . . . Cheating, however, implies an intention to beat the system even although the penalty, if the offender is found out, may still be acceptable. (1979, pp. 100-101)

But McIntosh next claims that:

> This definition, however, is too simple. It is not always the written or even the unwritten rule that is broken; tacit assumptions which one contestant knows that the other contestant acts upon may be rejected in order to gain an advantage . . . A more satisfactory definition is that of Luschen. (1979, pp. 182-3)

McIntosh's adaptation of Luschen's account makes possible the useful distinction between intending to deceive, which he calls cheating, and breaking the rules without having that intention. He concludes that: "Cheating is an offence against the principles of justice as well as against a particular rule or norm of behaviour" (1979, p. 185). This is presumably because the attempted deception is an attempt at unfairly putting the cheater in a superior position vis-à-vis the person cheated. This distinction is made clearer if we compare cheating with lying. We may tell someone an untruth without at the same time lying, because we may not intend to present the audience with a proposition which we know not to be true. This comparison suggests that McIntosh's dichotomy is not sufficient since it does not cover those cases where the rules are deliberately broken without any intention to deceive. A player may commit a professional or tactical foul in front of the referee or umpire because he considers that it is better to break the rules and suffer the penalty rather than not to commit the foul at all. Of course, such a player would *prefer* the offense to be unobserved, but cannot reasonably expect it in those circumstances to be overlooked. It is not obvious whether this sort of case is an example of cheating or not. If the intention to deceive is a necessary condition of cheating, then obviously such a case is not one of cheating, for not only did the player not intend to deceive, but he could not even reasonably have expected such an intention to be realized. Yet the rules of the game have been broken, and it might well be argued that it is the intention to break the rules rather than the intention to deceive which will do as a necessary condition of cheating. We can see why this should be so if we return to the analogy of telling an untruth. There is nothing wrong with telling an untruth as such; the fault lies in intending to tell an untruth. If I intend to tell an untruth then my action may or may not deceive you. The falsehood may be so blatant that it is obviously not intended to deceive, but perhaps merely to confuse or gain time. Such a falsehood may nonetheless be called a lie since it seeks to place its author in a position of undeserved superiority vis-à-vis the audience, and this runs against a principle of justice, other things being equal, namely, that the truth ought to be told. If I tell you that p is the case, and I know that p is false, *and* I intend to deceive you with respect to the truth of p, then this is no doubt a more serious lie than if I just intentionally tell an untruth without attempting to deceive. Other things being equal, we have a right to be told the truth, and if we are lied to then we are not dealt with justly. The injustice is magnified if we are at the same time deceived, or if there is an intention that we be deceived, but the injustice is there whether we are deceived or not, and whether there is any intention to deceive or not.

We may now be a bit clearer about the nature of cheating, but there are nonetheless problems in specifying precisely when a player cheats. Luschen's definition refers to a principle of equality over and above differences in skill and strategy. Using such a definition makes it difficult to give determinate answers to a variety of cases. For example, it might be that player A knows that player B is put off his play by such actions as A's coughing, or doing up his shoe-laces, or altering the pace of the game by doing things which are not directly part of the game, and so on. There are, of course, all sorts of actions which can put players off which are not in themselves illegal. A player may have considerable skill at a game and yet be quite easily beaten by an opponent who understands what sorts of (legal) behaviour the superior player dislikes. If such behaviour is indeed legal, must we say that A is cheating because he is breaking one of the "latently agreed upon conditions for winning such a contest"? It might well be argued that A is cheating since the sorts of skill and strategy which are acceptable in a game involve being better at the motions of the game than one's opponent and successfully exploiting his weaknesses and one's own strengths. Such weaknesses and strengths should be limited to the moves of the game and not to the defects in psychological make-up which are not directly related to the moves of the game. On this view, if B is put off his tennis by A's continual practice of doing up his shoe-laces, and A acts thus because he knows that it puts B off, then A is cheating by acting in this way even though he is not doing anything illegal. (There is naturally a continuum of cases here, where the yelling of hostile imprecations of a sexual nature by A at B would no doubt be adjudged illegal.)

It might be thought that calling A's actions in this sort of case an example of cheating is to go rather too far. After all, perhaps it should be up to a sportsperson to conquer his feelings about slowing a game down by tactics such as A's when such actions are within the rules of the game. B may be a "better" player in terms of skill and strategy than A, yet also more temperamental than A, and A might play on this defect to win more often than B in their contests. This sort of case emphasizes yet again the unsatisfactory nature of the definitions of cheating which Luschen and McIntosh offer. The latter's description involves trying to beat the system and deception, which A's behaviour does not necessarily do. A may take no pains to hide the fact that he is trying to put B off, and he is not trying to beat the system in so far as he is keeping to the explicit rules of the game. So on the McIntosh model A is not cheating at all. On Luschen's account A might be cheating, since he is violating "the principle of chance beyond differences in skill and strategy." However, as we have just suggested, it might be argued that being a good player involves being able to control one's emotional states and overcome annoyances of the time-wasting variety.

What we can conclude is that both accounts fail to tell us how to classify this very common form of behaviour in sport. McIntosh is clear in having to think that A is not cheating, yet this is only because of a simplistic view of the limited possibilities of cheating which is based upon deception and which has already been criticized. Luschen can provide no answer at all. The question of cheating can either be answered in terms of B's obligation as a skillful player to control his temperament (in which case A is not cheating) or in terms of A's behaviour violating a "latently agreed upon" condition for winning a contest (in which case A is cheating). The latter disjunct may seem temptingly acceptable, yet it should be pointed out that there are serious problems with talking about "latent agreements," especially when in practice quite a few players do not act in accordance with such agreements. Noncompliance by some players makes the problem of identifying precisely what the latent agreement is allegedly about insoluble. In fact, we frequently resort to talking about latent agreements when some people do not want to comply with a behavioural norm and we are trying to prove that they ought to by appealing to some non-explicit rule which they are obliged to follow. Yet this sort of argument is always open to attack by saying that no person is obliged to abide by an agreement, explicit or latent, to which he is not a party.

The tentative conclusion, then, is that there are a good number of difficulties in defining cheating in sport. Now it remains for me to argue that there are similarly many difficulties in specifying precisely what is *wrong* with cheating. It is a commonplace of the literature that cheating in sport is rather like lying in our everyday affairs, and falls under the same moral reproach. That is, if I am not morally entitled to hit someone over the head when competing for a business contract, then I am just as ethically constrained from injuring a competitor in a sporting contest. After all, the practice of sport comes under the same moral rules as the carrying out of any other inter-personal activity (see the work of Aspin, Keenan, Osterhoudt and Zeigler on this topic). Indeed, this rather unexciting comparison has been used to suggest that physical education has a large part to play in moral education. Huizinga has expressed the generally accepted view of what is wrong with cheating in sport by arguing that: "To our way of thinking, cheating as a means of winning a game robs the action of its play-character and spoils it altogether, because for us the essence of play is that the rules be kept—that it be fair play." Aspin makes an interesting observation on this passage. He claims that it ". . . underlines the point about the central virtue of athletic competitions . . . that their whole framework rests upon our desire to see excellence achieved according to rules which attempt to ensure equality, fairness, and impartiality for all" (1975, p. 55). Now, as we have just seen, it is not at all clear what "equality, fairness and impartiality for all" means in a sporting context, nor when they are being denied to a player or players in a contest. It is not a simple matter to determine when the rules of the game are being kept—it depends upon whether a narrower or broader interpretation of the notion of the rules of the game is accepted. So Huizinga's justification of fair play in sport does not as it stands explain why players are morally obliged to reject cheating.

Let us consider a more radical argument concerning fair play. Why should keeping the rules, on whatever interpretation of that expression, be "the essence of play"? In a very basic sense it is obvious that if all or some of the players in a game disobey the rules as a matter of course in their entirety, then they are not playing the game in an ethically dubious manner—they are not playing it at all. Yet this general breakdown of the rules, and consequently of the game, is not what is meant by cheating. The cheater's behaviour is on the whole conforming, since otherwise he would not be allowed to break the rules of the game. Someone who does not in any way conform to the rules of the game will presumably be forbidden, at some stage or other, to continue in it. The cheater seeks to gain an advantage over the opposition in a game and through the game, and so he wants to stay in the game and not destroy it. In addition, those occasions in which he intends to deceive would be robbed of their possible success if it is obvious that he is not adhering to the rules of the game.

If it is acceptable to assert that the presence of cheating in a game does not necessarily invalidate the game, then does it really follow that either the players or the audience should be in favour of fair play in a contest? It might be suggested that many competitions, especially those with some sort of authority present to regulate cheating, would be more interesting if cheating takes place within it, or if several players try to stretch the rules. Such deviant behaviour adds a new dimension to the game which can also add to its interest. Now, I do not want to suggest that cheating cannot disturb the game's rhythm and so make it less interesting to both players and spectators. Perhaps this is what happens in the majority of cases where cheating is prevalent in sport. Yet it need not be the case in all sporting contests. In so far as the contest is one of wits as well as one of skill and strategy, it can be exciting to compete with and against someone who uses his wits to try to cheat and it can be exciting for an audience to observe such intelligent behaviour.

It might be argued that if both players and spectators have such a laissez-faire attitude to cheating, then they will suffer, or be likely to suffer, harmful influences upon their moral character. We have already referred to the link which is sometimes taken to hold between physical and moral education, to the idea that someone who is taught to break the rules of hockey (or to enjoy watching those rules broken) when it suits his side is more likely to break social rules when it is in his personal interest to do so. Whether any such link exists is an unproved empirical proposition, and there is surely no a priori way of establishing its truth or otherwise. On the other hand, it is surely true that it is possible to inculcate virtues into players and spectators by giving them the opportunity to interact with other people on the sports-field in a morally acceptable manner and thereby to practice such mutually beneficial roles which they might then apply later in a purely general public context. Yet my argument seems to be that it does not matter how players behave provided that it does not interfere with the interest of the game. Any such claim that sport is amoral in nature would collapse, however, since the actions of players fall under the same very general moral rules as any other sort of behaviour which affects the welfare of others. What I am suggesting is that the fact that people may cheat is part of the structure of sport and is taken into consideration in the rules of the sport, so that cheating in a sport can be built into audience and player perceptions of the game. If it is true that cheating is recognized as an option which both sides may morally take up, then in general the principles of equality and justice are not affected. It may be that player A is a better cheater than player B, yet if cheating is recognized as part of the skill and strategy of the game, then A's advantage is merely an aspect of his being a better player than B. If we dislike the idea of cheating being part of the structure of the game, then perhaps we might consider this passage from Huizinga:

. . . the game depends upon the temporary acceptance by the players of a set of rules which 'cut off' the activity within the games from events in the 'real' world . . . Play as type of leisure activity . . . entails the temporary creation of a sphere of irreality. . . .

Huizinga's remarks support the idea that cheating in sport need not be compared morally to cheating in our everyday affairs since sport is "just a game" and not simply a reflection of our everyday behaviour. It may be morally acceptable to do certain things in sport which are not acceptable in ordinary life. In his description of violence in hockey, Vaz comments that the:

. . . implicit objective is to put the opposing star player out of action without doing him serious harm. Illegal tactics and 'tricks' of the game are both encouraged and taught; rough play and physically aggressive performance are strongly encouraged and sometimes players are taught the techniques of fighting. Minimal consideration is given to the formal normative rules of the game, and the conceptions of sportsmanship and fair play are forgotten. . . . Gradually the team is molded into a tough fighting unit prepared for violence whose primary objective is to win hockey games. (1972, p. 230)

If this is an accurate description of the general preparation for the playing of professional hockey then both the players and (Vaz suggests) the spectators will expect a skillful player to be good at cheating, where this involves breaking the rules when it is most advantageous to his side. Where such a policy is generally pursued there is no general deception practiced, and players are on equal terms in so far as the conditions for winning the contest are concerned. It is difficult then to see what is morally wrong with such behaviour. After all, it is presumed that the players and spectators are free agents in their participation and attendance. The players know how they are going to behave and the spectators know what they are going to see, namely, cheating carried out when it is considered to be in the best interests of the cheater and his side. If our objection to this practice is to be more than empty romanticism then some stronger arguments in favour of the moral obligatoriness of fair play in sport must be produced.

Perhaps, though, we have unduly stressed what actually happens in some sports at the expense of what ought to happen. That is, if people undertake to play a game, then they may be taken to have understood and agreed to the rules of the game and the principles upon which any fair victory in that game must rest. As Keenan puts it: ". . . if cheating in any form occurs among those parties to the game, they simply fail to adopt the principle of fair play and the morality of justice" (1975, p. 117). As Robert Nozick has expressed this argument: ". . . the principle of fairness . . . holds that when a number of persons engage in a just, mutually advantageous, cooperative venture according to rules and thus restrain their liberty in ways necessary to yield advantages for all, those who have submitted to these restrictions have a right to similar acquiescence on the part of those who have benefited from their submission" (1974, p. 90). Yet what are "the rules of the game" to which players supposedly commit themselves when they enter a game? If we look at the ways in which some sports are played it becomes evident that the rules of the game involve following the formal rules in so far as it is to the advantage of one's own side and breaking them when that is perceived, perhaps wrongly, to be to the side's advantage, where the possibility of suffering a penalty is taken into account. The existence of an authority in games enshrines cheating in the structure of the game; the authority is there to ensure that cheating does not interfere with the principle of fairness in a game. He is there to regulate cheating so that it does not benefit one side more than the other except where one side is more skillful at cheating than the other, and to see that the amount of cheating which takes place is not so great as to change the general form of a particular game. That is, the formal rules of the game must in general be adhered to by all players since otherwise in a clear non-moral sense the game is not being played. But if we are profitably to discuss the notion of the rules of the game, and of cheating and fair play, we must address ourselves to the ways in which players and spectators perceive those rules rather than to an abstract idea of the rules themselves. The next step is to determine what notion of fair play is applicable within the context of the ways in which players actually participate in sporting activities. An injection of realism into philosophical discussions of cheating and fair play in sport is long overdue.

Bibliography

1. Aspin, D. "Ethical Aspects of Sport and Games and Physical Education." *Philosophy of Education Society of Great Britain,* 1975, 49-71.
2. Huizinga, J. *Homo Ludens: A Study of the Play Element in Culture.* Boston: Beacon Press, 1950.
3. Keenan, F. "Justice and Sport." *Journal of the Philosophy of Sport,* 1975, 2, 111-123.
4. Luschen, G. "Cheating in Sport." In D. Landers (Ed.) *Social Problems in Athletics.* Urbana: University of Illinois Press, 1977.
5. McIntosh, P. *Fair Play: Ethics in Sport and Education.* Heinemann, London, 1979.

6. Nozick, R. *Anarchy, State and Utopia.* Oxford: Blackwell, 1974.
7. Osterhoudt, R. "The Kantian Ethic as a Principle of Moral Conduct in Sport and Athletics." In R. Osterhoudt (Ed.) *The Philosophy of Sport. Springfield, Illinois:* Charles C Thomas, 1973.
8. Vaz, E. "The Culture of Young Hockey Players: Some Initial Observations." In A. Taylor (Ed.) *Training: Scientific Basis and Application.* Quebec: Laval University, 1972.
9. Zeigler, F. "The Pragmatic (Experimentalistic) Ethic as It Relates to Sport and Physical Education." In R. Osterhoudt (Ed.) *The Philosophy of Sport* (op. cit.).

II
PART

THE LIMITS OF BEING HUMAN: THE CASE OF PERFORMANCE-ENHANCING DRUGS

A great deal of time, energy, and money are spent on enforcing bans on doping in sport. There is, however, growing agreement amongst researchers and those charged with implementing the regulations that enforcement of bans is not only doomed to failure but also somehow misses the point. Many people argue that we need educational programs that show athletes how doping is antithetical to sport. In this way doping would be prevented rather than its offenders being punished.

The success of this educational task requires demonstrable and sound reasons for banning doping and enforcement of those bans. But such reasoning is hard to find in the actions and practices of those who set the rules and enforce the bans. For example, the International Olympic Committee's (IOC) Medical Commission sets the standards that all Olympic competitors must comply with. The IOC maintains a list of substances and practices that are banned from the Olympic Games. What the IOC lacks, however, is an ethical framework that could justify the banning of the items on the list by showing them to be relevantly different from other substances and practices that are currently permitted.

Though the IOC does not present a justification for its banned list, it does refer to some general reasons:

A. Considering that the use of doping agents in sport is both unhealthy and contrary to the ethics of sport, and that it is necessary to protect the physical and spiritual health of athletes, the values of fair play and of competition, the integrity and unity of sport, and the rights of those who take part in it at whatever level . . . (IOC, 1990a:p.1)

After further preamble the Olympic Charter goes on to list prohibited doping classes and methods.

Thus, protection from harm (both physical and through the violation of rights), fair play, and the integrity of sport are the three underlying justifications in this passage. In addition, later in the preamble of the Olympic Charter, the IOC refers to its role in the society's larger "war on drugs" (it sees doping in sport as a symptom of the larger problem of social drug use) and to supporting athletes' calls for more stringent controls and sanctions. As they stand, these points do not constitute reasons or justifications for banning doping. The purpose of this part is to put flesh on these bones and to critically evaluate the justifications that are presented for banning doping in sport.

Each of the reasons listed in the IOC preamble can be found in more fully developed forms in the literature of the philosophy of sport. The reasons can also be expanded in arguments to justify bans in more than one way. Those arguments can then be categorized on the basis of the type of appeal they make: cheating and unfair advantage, harm, the idea that doping perverts the nature of sport, and the contention that doping is dehumanizing. Generally speaking, these are the four clusters of arguments proposed to justify banning drugs in sport. All of them have some merit from an ethical standpoint. As they stand alone, however, some philosophers would argue that none of them provide a sufficient justification for banning doping.

Cheating and Unfairness

It is sometimes argued that doping is banned because it is a method of cheating or gaining an unfair advantage. The problem with this position is that an activity becomes cheating only once there is a rule prohibiting it. So although the fact that doping is cheating may well provide a reason for enforcing the rules against doping, and may well give other athletes a reason for having an extremely negative attitude toward those who dope, it does not provide a reason for creating the rule banning doping in the first place.

A similar argument can be made from the unfairness standpoint. The simplest idea of fairness concerns adherence to the rules; an action is unfair if it violates the rules. This position suffers the same fate as the preceding one. An alternative notion of fairness that is independent of the rules of sport could be postulated. This idea would entail that "fairness" is somehow prior to, and independent of, the particular rules of any sport. That is, that some practices are prohibited in sport—because they are unfair. But this notion would have to show how doping was somehow inherently unfair, even if the contestants agreed to do it and even if the rules of the game permitted it. Due to its circular nature, it is not clear how an argument like this could succeed.

Harm

The argument from the standpoint of harm comes in a variety of forms: harm to athletes who dope, harm to other (clean) athletes, harm to society, and harm caused by bans.

Harm to Athletes Who Dope

Here the suggestion is that doping should be banned to protect the athletes who dope. As it stands this argument is paternalistic, inconsistent, and incomplete. It is paternalistic because we do not generally permit intrusion into the lives of competent adults to protect those people from harm they may inflict on themselves. It is inconsistent because sport, especially elite-level sport, is necessarily an extremely hazardous enterprise. It is not clear why athletes should be protected from the harm that might result from doping when we do not see fit to protect them from the harms inherent in the sports they practice and the overtraining they endure. The argument is incomplete because the evidence of harm for the practices currently considered doping is mixed at best. Although steroids in high doses may cause adverse side effects, in relatively low doses they seem not to. Autologous blood doping has not been shown to have adverse side effects at all.

Harm to Other (Clean) Athletes

The argument here is that drug use is coercive. Because doping may improve results, coercive pressure is placed on those who wish to compete without drugs. If drug users are competing, then non-drug users are forced to dope to keep up. This argument has some merits but is still incomplete. It is incomplete because elite-level sport is already highly coercive. If full-time training, altitude training, or diet control is shown to produce better results, then everyone is forced to adopt those measures to keep up. It is unclear why doping is any more coercive, and sufficiently so to warrant being banned, than, say, full-time training. On the other hand, the coercion argument has merit if it can be shown how doping is irrelevant to a particular view of what is important to sport. If sport is about testing skills, then it can be argued that the improved performance that comes with doping is irrelevant to that test of skill (especially when one bears in mind that if some athletes dope, others will be forced to dope to keep up, thus obviating the original advantage that came with doping). If doping is irrelevant to sport we can shun it as being unnecessarily coercive as compared to, for example, extended training, which may improve one's skill at the contest at hand.

Harm to Society

This position says that doping harms others in society, especially children, who see athletes as role models. This argument works in two ways. The first is that for children to see athletes having no respect for the rules of the games they play tends to undermine their respect for rules, and law, in general. This argument works only if doping is already against the rules. The argument cannot therefore function as a justification for rules that ban doping in the first place. The second version sees athletic drug use as part of a wider social problem of drug use. If children see athletes using drugs to attain sporting success, then they may see other drugs as a viable means to other ends. The limitation of this argument is that many things exist that we consider appropriate for adults but not for children. Alcohol, cigarettes, and sex are obvious examples; we don't ban these substances or activities for adults just because they are inappropriate for children.

Harm Caused by Bans

So far we have looked at reasons for bans based on the harm the banned substances cause. Unfortunately, because we need to enforce the bans we create, the bans themselves also cause harm. Enforcement of bans on substances or practices designed to help one train rather than improve one's performance on the day of competition requires year-round random, unannounced, out-of-competition testing. This testing requirement is an extreme intrusion into athletes' private lives. Thus athletes are harmed by being required to consent to such testing procedures to be eligible for competition.

Perversion of Sport

According to this view doping should be banned because it is somehow antithetical to the true nature of sport. This view requires an account of sport that shows why doping is incompatible with it. As yet, no plausible account of sport is available to demonstrate its incompatibility with doping. (Part of the problem is that sport is socially constructed, and there is no obvious reason that it could not be constructed to include doping.)

Unnaturalness and Dehumanization

Here the argument is that doping should be banned because it is either unnatural or dehumanizing. The unnaturalness argument does not get very far, for two reasons. The first is that we do not have a good account of what is deemed "unnatural." The second is that we are inconsistent. Some "unnatural" things are permitted in sport (e.g., spiked shoes) whereas other, "natural" ones (e.g., testosterone) are on the banned list.

The dehumanization argument is interesting but incomplete, because everyone does not agree on what it means to be human. Without this consensus it is difficult to see why some practices should be considered dehumanizing. The argument is also inconsistent. Some practices, such as psychodoping, the mental manipulation of athletes using the techniques of operant conditioning, are not banned, whereas the reinjection of one's own blood is. For this argument to work, we need some sort of framework that gives us an idea of human excellence that will permit us to see how the pursuit of athletic excellence can, and should, be limited in ways that exclude doping from the pursuit of sport.

7

CHAPTER

Listening to Steroids

John Hoberman

For a decade after his reign as the premier American marathoner of the early 1980s, Alberto Salazar failed to win a major race, and no one could figure out why. His years-long quest for medical advice that might salvage a distinguished career became well known among those who follow the running scene. Finally, the long-awaited breakthrough came with a victory in the 56-mile Comrades Marathon in South Africa in June 1994. But this personal triumph was accompanied by an odd and, for some observers, unsettling piece of news. After consulting with a sports physician and an endocrinologist, Salazar had concluded that years of intensive training had "suppressed [his] body's endocrine system." The treatment that he and his advisers chose was a drug that had no previous association with athletic performance and did not violate international rules: the now-legendary antidepressant Prozac.

No one familiar with the history of drug use in sports will be surprised by an athlete's innovative use of a medication, especially one that is prescribed to create courage and self-confidence in timid, lethargic, or demoralized people. Over the past century there have always been athletes willing to

Reprinted, by permission, from John Hoberman, 1995, "Listening to Steroids," *Wilson Quarterly, Winter 1995:* 35-44.

ingest substances, including potential poisons such as heroin and strychnine, to boost their performance. That many of them have been assisted by physicians and pharmaceutical companies reminds us that sports medicine has always been part of what one German sports scientist has called "a gigantic experiment on the human organism." At the same time, we must not overlook the quasi-scientific or pseudoscientific character of most experimentation. Consider, for example, the fuzzy medical logic employed by Alberto Salazar and his counselors. While Dr. Peter D. Kramer's phenomenal best seller *Listening to Prozac* (1993) makes many claims for the drug, the treatment of endocrinological disorders is not one of them. Equally revealing is the vagueness of the self-diagnosis that pointed Salazar toward the world's most popular antidepressant: "It wasn't that I was depressed or sad," he told an interviewer. "I just never had any energy or zest. I knew there was something wrong with my whole system."

Alberto Salazar's encounter with Prozac forged a high-profile link between doping in sport and the wider world of pharmacology that affects us all. The existence of powerful drugs forces us to think about human nature itself and how it can or should be transformed. As modern science increases our power to transform minds and bodies, we will have to make momentous decisions about how the human beings of the future will look and function, how fast they will run, and (perhaps) how fast they will think. To what extent do we want to preserve—and to what extent do we want to alter—human traits? It is already clear that in an age of genetic engineering advocates of the medical transformation of human beings sound reasonable, while the proponents of preserving human traits (and, therefore, human limitations) are likely to sound naive and opposed to progress in principle. The unequal contest between those who favor experimentation upon human beings and those who oppose it will be the most profound drama of 21st-century postindustrial society. Yet few people are aware that its essential acts have already been rehearsed during the past century of scientific sport.

Drugs have been used to enhance sexual, military, intellectual, and work performances as well as sportive ones. Yet sport is somehow different. Its exceptional status as a realm of inviolable performances becomes clear if we compare it with some other vocations. Consider, for example, another group of performers for whom mental and physical stress is a way of life. Their life expectancy is 22 percent below the national average. They suffer from tendinitis, muscle cramps, pinched nerves, a high incidence of mental health problems and heart attacks, and anxiety levels that threaten to cripple their performance as professionals. These people are not fire fighters or police officers or athletes; they are orchestral musicians, and many use "beta-blocker" drugs to control their stage fright and thereby improve their performances. The use of these same anti-anxiety drugs has been banned by the Medical Commission of the International Olympic Committee as a form of doping.

What accounts for this discrepancy? What makes sport the one type of performance that can be "corrupted" by pharmacological intervention? One might argue that an orchestral performance, unlike a sporting event, is not a contest. Since the performers are not competing against one another, deceit is not an issue. Yet even if we leave aside the prominent international music competitions, this argument overlooks the fact that an entire field of equally doped runners who knew exactly which drugs their competitors had taken would still violate the ethics of sport, which require both fair competition and the integrity of the performance itself—an untainted, and therefore accurate, measure of human potential. But why is the same requirement not imposed on the orchestral musician? Indeed, one would expect "high" cultural performances to carry greater ethical and anthropological significance than sportive ones. Sport's role as a special index of human capacity makes drug use by athletes uniquely problematic.

The "doping" issue within pharmacology thus originates in a tension between the licit and the illicit, a conflict that is inevitable in a society that both legitimizes and distrusts pharmacological solutions to human problems. The enormous market for substances that are supposed to boost the human organism in various ways benefits from the universal presumption that almost any attempt to expand human capacities is worth trying. Technological civilization always tends to turn productive activities into measurable performances, catalyzing an endless search for performance-enhancing technologies, from psychotherapy to caffeine tablets.

The modern obsession with performance enhancement is reflected in the wide range of substances and techniques enlisted on behalf of improving the human organism and its capacities. Commercial "brain gyms" employ stress-reduction devices such as flotation tanks, biofeedback machines, and somatrons (which bombard the body with musical vibrations) in an attempt to affect the brain waves and thereby increase intelligence, boost memory, strengthen the immune system, and combat phobias. So-called "smart drugs," none of which have been proven effective in scientifically valid trials, are sold to promote "cognitive enhancement."

The never-ending contest between the performance principle and the cultural restraints that work against it blurs the line separating the licit and the illicit. Consider, for example, the response in 1993 to charges of steroid doping among Chinese swimmers. A Chinese newspaper responded that the swimmers' world-class performances had been made possible by a "multi-functional muscle-building machine" that sends electronically controlled bursts of electricity through the muscles. That is to say, an accusation of illicit performance boosting of one kind was met with earnest assurances that Chinese athletes had succeeded by employing an equally artificial (but still legal) procedure. Few anecdotes could better illustrate the prevailing opportunism in the field.

Doping in sport has been banned for the past 25 years, yet less than a century ago European scientists were discussing pharmacological aids to athletic performance without any qualms. The physiologists of that time understood that the pharmacologically active substances they worked with displayed a range of effects: they could be medicines, stimulants, depressants, intoxicants, antiseptics, narcotics, poisons, or antagonists of other drugs. But during this phase, physicians and others had little interest in using drugs to improve athletic performance. Sports simply did not have the social and political importance they have today. At the same time, the athletic world did not yet recognize drugs as a threat to the integrity of sport. The distinction between performance-enhancing and therapeutic medications—a prerequisite of the doping concept—was not yet established.

The absence of such a norm explains why the French scientists who gave experimental doses of drugs such as alcohol and kola nuts to cyclists in the 1890s were untroubled by ethical doubts. The pioneering sports physician Philippe Tissié, for example, could both carry out experiments on human subjects and warn against the medical dangers of stimulants. Tissié saw athletic physiology as one approach to the study of the human organism. His attempt to prolong a cyclist's endurance by feeding him rum and champagne during a 24-hour distance trial may have been the first scientifically controlled experiment of its kind. Yet he was consistently cautious on medical grounds about the use of stimulants.

Tissié's attitude toward athletic stimulants appears strangely conflicted to those of us accustomed to the antidrug propaganda of the sports world today. How could the same physician who had urged his cyclist around the track for the purpose of identifying effective stimulants also condemn them as dangerous? To dissolve this apparent contradiction, we must abandon our conditioned reactions to the idea of doping and project ourselves back into Tissié's world. If he had no qualms about energizing his cyclist, it was because his experiment occurred before stimulants had come to be regarded as a threat to equitable competition. In any event, Tissié was not interested in producing record-breaking cyclists. It was medical prudence, not morality, that prompted his frequent cautionary remarks about stimulants. Indeed, his condemnation of alcohol is immediately followed by a recommendation that "the better beverage" for boosting performance is sugar water.

A similar ethical nonchalance is evident in a 1913 article, "Sport and Stimulants," by the early German sports physician Ferdinand Hueppe. Modern life is impossible without stimulants, he wrote, and the task of the physician is to replace harmful substances with more benign alternatives. Hueppe's disapproving references to "doping"—an internationally understood term even at this early date—concerned the uselessness or potential dangers of drugs, not their possible use as illicit performance-enhancers.

Condemnation of doping on ethical grounds appeared during the 1920s as sport became a genuine mass-cultural phenomenon. The growth of international sporting events after the first modern Olympics, held in Athens in 1896, created a new arena for nationalistic competition that served the interests of various governments. Larger financial investments and the prominence of sport in the emerging mass media gave elite athletes a new social and political significance, which helped foster new suspicions about the competitive practices of others. Having left its age of innocence behind, sports medicine was now embarked upon a new experimental phase involving the collaboration of athletes, trainers, physicians, and the pharmaceutical industry. At the same time, a new international sports establishment arose championing an ideal of sportsmanship that was threatened by the use of drugs.

The debate over doping in Germany during the 1920s and '30s anticipated today's doping controversy in almost every respect. Drug use among German athletes was widespread and openly discussed. The German sports literature of this period offered antidoping sermons, justifications for the use of various substances, and rationales for drawing lines between what should and should not be forbidden. Some German physicians dearly believed that certain substances did improve athletic performance, and they were not reluctant to prescribe them. The prominent sports physician Herbert Herxheimer, for example, claimed in 1922 that the commercial product "Recresal" (primary sodium phosphate) produced a detectable increase in physical fitness. More interesting than his endorsement, however, were the verbal gymnastics that followed. With the approach of the spring sports season, he said, the aspiring athlete would need his full dose of phosphates. Without mentioning the word "doping," he went on to assure his readers that this ergogenic "aid" was not comparable to the many "stimulants" in use, since it merely "supported" basic physiological processes. Echoes of Herxheimer's argument have been heard in recent years from former East German sports scientists who still seek to portray steroid use as a form of beneficial "hormonal regulation" for athletes under stress.

By 1930 a less restrained attitude toward the use of Recresal was evident. W. Poppelreuter, a professor of medicine in Bonn, claimed that wartime tests on German troops and later experiments on mountain climbers had confirmed positive laboratory results. Feeding this substance to horses, cows, and pigs had caused them to grow larger, look better, sweat less, work harder, give more milk, and produce better litters. Poppelreuter's own experiments indicated that Recresal also improved arithmetic performance: the speed of mental calculations rose while the number of errors went down—an important finding, he said, because the mental dimension of athletic performance had become increasingly clear. He was adamant about the propriety of Recresal therapy, which he called "a normal hygienic procedure" that merely supported basic physiological processes.

The most controversial technique in Germany at this time was the use of ultraviolet radiation (UV) to invigorate all or part of the athlete's body. From one standpoint, UV was about as invasive and "artificial" a procedure as standing in sunlight. But from another perspective, UV light was the product of "technical and machine-like devices" that threatened to destroy the "honorable competition" sport was meant to be. The debate over UV became a textbook confrontation between the antidoping purists and their more up-to-date opponents for whom performance was the first priority.

Such problematic distinctions between "nutrients" and "stimulants," between supplemental nutrition and more ambitious regimens, constitute the core of the "doping" issue. The sports medical literature of the interwar period is filled with arguments over variations on this fundamental dichotomy: the "natural" versus the "artificial," rehabilitation versus performance enhancement, restoring the organism versus boosting it, and so on. Then as now, debates over specific drugs or techniques were less important than the larger question of whether society should impose limits on athletic ambition and certain methods that serve it, whether athletes should attempt to improve performances by resorting to what one German physician of this period called "deviations from a natural way of life."

Medical objections to doping in Germany did not command universal support among physicians for two reasons. Some of these medical men, like their modern counterparts, were simply spellbound by the prospect of boosting athletic performance in ingenious new ways. But the more fundamental problem, then as now, was that there were simply too many ways to rationalize the use of what were believed to be performance-enhancing drugs within the standard guidelines for medical practice. The line between healing the organism and "improving" it could not be drawn in a clear and definitive way.

Lacking a systematic definition of doping, biomedical conservatives adopted a position based on a kind of moral intuition. Dr. Otto Riesser, director of the Pharmacological Institute at the University of Breslau, was one of the few who understood the biochemical complexities of doping and its uncertain effects. In an address to the German Swimming Federation in 1933, he deplored widespread doping in German sport and blamed physicians for their collusion in these unethical practices. Riesser's response to the problem of defining doping was to say that in difficult cases "common sense and conscience must be the final judges." Such homespun wisdom, though it could not always prevail over the temptation to cheat, was an important statement of principle. Similarly, when Riesser wrote about digitalis in 1930, he speculated that it might help the long-distance skier. "I don't know whether that sort of thing has been tried," he commented. "But all of us feel a healthy inner resistance to such experiments in artificially boosting athletic performance, and, perhaps, a not unjustified fear that any pharmacological intervention, no matter how small, may cause a disturbance in the healthy organism."

The history of doping tells us that our "healthy inner resistance" to such temptations is constantly being subverted by the problem of distinguishing between licit and illicit techniques. The idea of doping—and its notoriety—are, after all, cultural constructs. The rise of an antidoping ethos during the 1920s shows that the culturally conservative response to drug use in sport required about a generation to formulate itself. The culturally conservative response to performance-enhancing drugs, in society at large as well as in sport, is today under siege as it has never been before. In *Listening to Prozac,* Peter Kramer makes a point of undermining what he calls "pharmacological Calvinism," defined as "a general distrust of drugs used for nontherapeutic purposes." Pharmacological Calvinism, he suggests, "may be flimsy protection against the allure of medication. Do we feel secure in counting on our irrationality—our antiscientific prejudice—to save us from the ubiquitous cultural pressures for enhancement?" As Kramer (and his critics) well know, we do not. Indeed, the transformation of Otto Riesser's "healthy inner resistance" into "antiscientific prejudice" is one more sign that Kramer's enormously popular brief on behalf of "cosmetic psychopharmacology" has benefited from (and strengthened) an increasingly activist view of therapeutic intervention.

The rise of the therapeutic ideal has made the stigma attached to performance-enhancing drugs seem increasingly implausible. In the therapeutic model, the distinction between enhancement and the treatment of specific disorders is blurred. Therapy aims at human improvement, not necessarily the curing of a specific malady. Precisely because we now treat the legitimacy of "therapy" as self-evident, we overlook its expanded role in modern life. Drugs in particular have a vast range of applications that extend far beyond the treatment of organic diseases. Drugs now in wide use help

people cope with such "normal" challenges of daily life as work performance and mood control. The elastic concept of therapy easily accommodates the physiological conditions and psychological stresses experienced
by high-performance athletes, and the fusion of everyday stress and extreme
athletic exertion makes it difficult to condemn doping in sport on a priori
grounds. We simply do not employ a typology of stressful experiences that
distinguishes on a deep enough level between the pressures of everyday life
and sportive stress. The modern English (and now internationalized) word
"stress" homogenizes an entire spectrum of experiences and simultaneously
implies the need for "therapies" to restore the organism to its original healthy
state.

The power of this therapeutic ideal is already transforming the status of the
male hormone testosterone and its anabolic-androgenic steroid derivatives.
These hormonal substances have been leading a double life as (legitimate)
medications and (illegitimate) doping agents for almost half a century. Over
the past three decades, steroid use by male and, more recently, female elite
athletes has become epidemic, covertly supported by a prosteroid lobby
among sports physicians that has received almost no media coverage outside
Germany.

The legitimate medical career of synthetic testosterone compounds began
within a few years of the first laboratory synthesis in 1935. By the early
1940s, methyl testosterone and testosterone propionate were being promoted by pharmaceutical companies and administered to patients as an
experimental therapy for a variety of disorders both real and imagined: to
treat the "male climacteric" (fatigue, melancholia, and impotence) in older
men, to deal with impotence in younger men, to treat hypogonadism
(testicular deficiency), to restore libido in women, and to reverse homosexu-
ality—a particularly problematic use of testosterone, as was recognized at
the time. Early practitioners groped toward safe and effective treatments,
sometimes administering megadoses (for breast cancer) that dwarfed the
lifetime consumption of the most heavily doped East German athletes of the
1970s and '80s. These clinicians divided into more and less cautious
factions, but no one questioned the legitimacy of hormonal therapy as a
medical technique.

Even at this early date, ambitions for testosterone transcended strictly
clinical uses. The idea that synthetic testosterone might become a restorative
therapy for millions of people dates from the early period of its commercial
development. In 1938 a Yale scientist told a meeting of the American
Chemical Society that testosterone propionate "rejuvenated" old men by
relieving depression. While the idea of using testosterone to boost athletic
performance does not appear in the medical literature, it was becoming

apparent to this generation of scientists that testosterone played a role in physical fitness. In 1942, for example, three American researchers correctly guessed that the combination of megadoses and exercise would alter "responses to fatiguing exercise"—an early harbinger of steroid use in elite sport.

Paul de Kruif's popular book *The Male Hormone* (1945) promoted the idea that testosterone would soon become a mass therapy for the fatigue and waning sexual potency of aging males, and pharmaceutical companies advertised testosterone preparations in professional journals during the decade. Yet testosterone never caught on as a mass-market drug.

A half-century later, new developments are again encouraging the widespread use of testosterone. For one thing, hormone therapy is now a conventional procedure, even if certain applications remain controversial. Pediatric endocrinologists, for example, treat thousands of children of subnormal stature with synthetic human growth hormone (HGH). At the same time, they face increasing demands from parents to prescribe the same therapy for children who are only somewhat short. Such pressures are likely to legitimate the wider use of HGH. Inevitably, some parents will want HGH to boost the athletic potential of their children. Others have already requested steroids for the same purpose. A National Institutes of Health (NIH) plan to recruit healthy children to test the efficacy of biosynthetic HGH is yet another sign that social barriers to hormonal treatments are falling. According to the NIH panel that approved this clinical trial several years ago, "There is substantial evidence that extreme short stature carries distinct disadvantages, including functional impairment and psychological stigmatization." The commercial interests of drug companies also play a role in promoting hormone therapies. In October 1994, less than a week before the federal government was to outline complaints at a congressional hearing against the two major manufacturers of synthetic HGH, Genentech and Caremark, Inc., both companies agreed to curtail aggressive marketing campaigns.

Testosterone therapy is now a standard treatment for hypogonadal males. The resulting demand has stimulated a growing market for testosterone patches that athletes (among others) can use for nonclinical purposes. But again the significance of hormonal therapy extends far beyond the clinic and into the public sphere, where medical "disorders" and "crises" are defined in accordance with social and commercial demands. Thus in 1992 the National Institutes of Health requested research proposals to test whether testosterone therapy can prevent physical ailments and depression in older males. We may now ask whether the aging process itself is about to be officially recognized as a treatable deficiency disease. "I don't believe in the male midlife crisis," commented Dr. John B. McKinlay, an epidemiologist at the New England Research Institute who is a specialist on aging. "But even though in my perspective there is no epidemiological, physiological or clinical evidence for such a syndrome, I think by the year 2000 the syndrome will exist. There's a very strong interest in treating aging men for a profit, just as there is for menopausal women." The emergence of such a syndrome would bring with it new definitions of physiological normality and male identity, and it would help to legitimize other grand ambitions to "boost" the human organism.

The advent of mass testosterone therapy would represent a dramatic cultural change. The use of sex hormones as a "popular nutritional supplement" (as one German expert has put it) to strengthen aging muscles would be a major step toward equating therapy with performance enhancement. And if testosterone products proved to have a restorative effect on sexual functioning in the elderly, this would surely foster a new ideal of "normal" sexual capacity that many people would regard as a "health" entitlement. The certification of low doses as medically safe would transform the image of these drugs, "gentrifying" testosterone products and paving the way for wider use by athletes and body builders.

The meteoric career of Prozac is culturally significant because Prozac is regarded not strictly as a treatment for a specific disorder but as a performance-enhancing drug for a competitive society. The history of Prozac is a case study in how the legitimization of a performance-enhancing drug proceeds. *Listening to Prozac* is a fascinating book because it presents in autobiographical form the entire cycle of initial discovery, ethical doubt, therapeutic concern, and transformative ambition that constitutes the history of doping in the 20th century. (Whether Prozac has actually transformed the lives of a large number of patients remains a matter of dispute.) The author's periodic references to his own doubts about the ethics of prescribing Prozac function as evidence of his bona fides: "I became aware of my own irrational discomfort, my sense that for a drug to have such a pronounced effect is inherently unnatural, unsafe, uncanny." The resolution of this ethical discomfort is an important aspect of Kramer's narrative, and it is achieved by witnessing the relief afforded his patients by Prozac therapy. The transformative phase is where real ethical peril lies, and once again Kramer sees himself swimming with the historical tide. "If I am right, we are entering an era in which medication can be used to enhance the functioning of the normal mind." It will take bravery for human beings to decide to change themselves, he suggests, but history is on the side of Prozac and psychobiological transformation.

By now the voice of a famous cultural diagnostician from the last century has become faintly audible. We return to the text for further clues and read that Prozac "seemed to provide access to a vital capacity that had heretofore been stunted or absent." The trail grows warmer. We read on and find that Prozac "lends people courage and allows them to choose life's ordinarily risky undertakings." Now the voice is more distinct. Finally, on the last page of the book, the missing theme falls into place. The most profound moral consequence of Prozac, we learn, will be "in changing our sense of constraints on human behavior, in changing the observing self." The idea of human self-transcendence has been the key all along. Now we understand that Kramer is the prophet of a Nietzschean pharmacology that exalts a more dynamic, biochemically enhanced human type.

Doping is Nietzschean pharmacology because it defies biomedical conservatism in the name of a biochemically engineered superperson. But the legitimization of doping takes place not under the charismatic banner of the Nietzschean superman but under the humane rubric of therapy. The use of doping substances is driven by the ambiguous status of drugs that have (or may have) legitimate medical applications as well as performance-boosting value for elite athletes. The "dual-uses" of such drugs make it difficult to argue that they should be banned from sport as medically hazardous. Medical researchers have already confirmed the benefits of human growth hormone for AIDS patients. The amino acid L-carnitine, which appears on a list of legal "steroid alternatives" compiled by the U.S. Food and Drug Administration, is another "dual-use" drug that is targeted at both the physically powerful and the physically enfeebled. Sold to athletes in Europe as "supplementary nutrition," it has also been promoted by researchers who claim that it may play a role in preserving mental and physical capacities in the elderly. Making L-carnitine a standard part of geriatric medicine would certainly promote its legitimacy as a performance-enhancing drug for both athletes and the general public.

The gradual "gentrification" of such drugs will have diverse effects. Testosterone products will be more available to the elderly and thus more acceptable to everyone, creating a market much larger than the estimated one million American males who now buy these drugs on the black market. Gentrification will also undermine the campaign against doping in sport. At the same time, destigmatizing these drugs will enable physicians to treat large groups of patients in new ways. Ironically, the criminalization of steroids has been an obstacle to their use for legitimate purposes. At the Ninth International Conference on AIDS, held in Berlin in 1993, physicians urged that anabolic steroids become a standard treatment for AIDS patients and people who are HIV-positive. The potential market represented by these patients already numbers in the tens of millions around the world.

The official pharmacological Calvinism of organized sport is thus under siege from within and without. While drug use has been epidemic among elite athletes since the late 1960s, the new respectability of testosterone products will put international sports officials in an unprecedented bind. How will the Medical Commission of the International Olympic Committee maintain the official notoriety of steroids once these drugs have become a standard medical therapy for millions of ordinary people? In a word, the hard line against doping is not likely to survive the gentrification process. This outcome of the contest between our "healthy inner resistance" to doping and ambitions to "improve" the human organism will have fateful consequences. New roles for drugs will promote the medicalization of everyday life at the expense of our sense of human independence from scientific domination. It will certainly affect our thinking about licit and illicit applications of genetic engineering.

While it is easy to endorse the medical wisdom of warnings against the widespread use of steroids and other potentially dangerous drugs, the history of athletic doping in this century shows that it has been very difficult to enforce such pharmacological Calvinism in the face of growing demands for the "therapeutic" benefits of enhanced performance. The elastic concept of therapy will help to legitimize hormonal manipulation as a mass therapy of the future. It is interesting to speculate about how the advertising experts will promote these products. It is hard to imagine that they will not turn to elite athletes, portraying them as pharmacologically improved examples of supercharged health. One can see the athletes now, lined up at the start of an Olympic final early in the next century, their drug-company logos gleaming in the sun.

CHAPTER

Good Competition and Drug-Enhanced Performance

Robert L. Simon

Competition in sport frequently has been defended in terms of the search for excellence in performance.[1] Top athletes, whether their motivation arises from adherence to the internal values of competition or desire for external reward, are willing to pay a heavy price in time and effort in order to achieve competitive success. When this price consists of time spent in hard practice, we are prepared to praise the athlete as a worker and true competitor. But when athletes attempt to achieve excellence through the use of performance-enhancing drugs, there is widespread condemnation. Is such condemnation justified? What is wrong with the use of drugs to achieve excellence in sport? Is prohibiting the use of performance-enhancing drugs in athletic competition justified?

The relatively widespread use of such drugs as anabolic steroids to enhance performance dates back at least to the Olympics of the 1960s, although broad public awareness of such drug use seems relatively recent. Anabolic steroids are drugs, synthetic derivatives of the male hormone testosterone, which are claimed to stimulate muscle growth and tissue repair. While claims about possible bad consequences of steroid use are controversial, the American College of Sports Medicine warns against serious side effects. These are believed to include liver damage, atherosclerosis,

Reprinted, by permission, from R.L. Simon, 1984, "Good competition and drug-enhanced performance," *Journal of the Philosophy of Sport:* 6-13.

hypertension, personality changes, a lowered sperm count in males, and masculinization in females. Particularly frightening is that world-class athletes are reportedly taking steroids at many times the recommended medical dosage—at levels so high that, as Thomas Murray (4: p. 26) has pointed out, under "current federal regulations governing human subjects . . . no institutional review board would approve a research design that entailed giving subjects anywhere near the levels . . . used by the athletes."

The use of such high levels of a drug raises complex empirical as well as ethical issues. For example, even if steroid use at a low level does not actually enhance athletic performance, as some authorities claim, it is far from clear whether heavy use produces any positive effects on performance. At the very least, athletes who believe in the positive effects of heavy doses of steroids are not likely to be convinced by data based on more moderate intake.

As interesting as these issues are, it will be assumed in what follows that the use of certain drugs does enhance athletic performance and does carry with it some significant risk to the athlete. Although each of these assumptions may be controversial, by granting them, the discussion can concentrate on the ethical issues raised by use of performance-enhancing drugs.

I. What Is a Performance-Enhancing Drug?

If we are to discuss the ethics of using drugs to enhance athletic performance, we should begin with a clear account of what counts as such a drug. Unfortunately, a formal definition is exceedingly hard to come by, precisely because it is unclear to what substances such a definition ought to apply.

If it is held to be impermissible to take steroids or amphetamines to enhance performance, what about special diets, the use of coffee to promote alertness, or the bizarre practice of "blood doping," by which runners store their own blood in a frozen state and then return it to their body before a major meet in order to increase the oxygen sent to the muscles?

It is clear that the concept of an "unnatural" or "artificial" substance will not take us very far here, since testosterone hardly is unnatural. Similarly, it is difficult to see how one's own blood can be considered artificial. In addition, we should not include on any list of forbidden substances the use of medication for legitimate reasons of health.

Moreover, what counts as a performance-enhancing drug will vary from sport to sport. For example, drinking alcohol normally will hurt performance. However, in some sports, such as riflery, it can help. This is because as a depressant, alcohol will slow down one's heart rate and allow for a steadier stance and aim.

Rather than spend considerable time and effort in what is likely to be a fruitless search for necessary conditions, we would do better to ignore borderline cases and focus on such clear drugs of concern as amphetamines and steroids. If we can understand the ethical issues that apply to use of such drugs, we might then be in a better position to handle borderline cases as well. However, it does seem that paradigm cases of the drugs that are of concern satisfy at least some of the following criteria.

1. If the user did not believe that use of the substance in the amount ingested would increase the chances of enhanced athletic performance, that substance would not bc taken.
2. The substance, in the amount ingested, is believed to carry significant risk to the user.
3. The substance, in the amount ingested, is not prescribed medication taken to relieve an illness or injury.

These criteria raise no concern about the normal ingestion of such drugs as caffeine in coffee or tea, or about medication since drugs used for medicinal purposes would not fall under them (1). The use of amphetamines and steroids, on the other hand, do fall under the criteria. Blood doping seems to be a borderline case and perhaps this is as it should be. It is employed only to enhance performance, is not medication, is not part of any normal training routine, yet seems to pose no significant risk to the user.[2]

However, the important issue for our purposes is not the adequacy of the three criteria as a definition for, as I have suggested, any search for a definition in the absence of the correct normative perspective will likely turn out to be a fruitless hunt for the nonexistent snark. Rather, the major concern is not with defining performance-enhancing drugs but with evaluating their use. In particular, it is one thing to claim that the three criteria (or any other proposed set) are satisfied to a particular degree. It is quite another to make the normative claim that use of the substance in question is morally questionable or impermissible.

Why should the use of possibly harmful drugs solely for the purpose of enhancing athletic performance be regarded as impermissible? In particular, why shouldn't individual athletes be left at liberty to pursue excellence by any means they freely choose?

II. Performance-Enhancing Drugs, Coercion, and the Harm Principle

One argument frequently advanced against the use of such performance-enhancing drugs as steroids is based on our second criterion of harm to the user. Since use of such drugs is harmful to the user, it ought to be prohibited.

However, if we accept the "harm principle," which is defended by such writers as J.S. Mill, paternalistic interference with the freedom of others is ruled out. According to the harm principle, we are entitled to interfere with the behavior of competent, consenting adults only to prevent harm to others. After all, if athletes prefer the gains that the use of drugs provide along with possible side effects to the alternative of less risk but worse performance, external interference with their freedom of choice seems unwarranted.

However, at least two possible justifications of paternalistic interference are compatible with the harm principle. First, we can argue that athletes do not give informed consent to the use of performance-enhancing drugs. Second, we can argue that the use of drugs by some athletes does harm other competitors. Let us consider each response in turn.

Informed Consent

Do athletes freely choose to use such performance-enhancing drugs as anabolic steroids? Consider, for example, professional athletes whose livelihood may depend on the quality of their performance. Athletes whose performance does not remain at peak levels may not be employed for very long. As Carolyn Thomas (6: p. 198) maintains, "the onus is on the athlete to . . . consent to things that he or she would not otherwise consent to. . . . Coercion, however, makes the athlete vulnerable. It also takes away the athlete's ability to act and choose freely with regard to informed consent." Since pressures on top amateur athletes in national and world-class competition may be at least as great as pressures on professionals, a comparable argument can be extended to cover them as well.

However, while this point is not without some force, we need to be careful about applying the notion of coercion too loosely. After all, no one is forced to try to become a top athlete. The reason for saying top athletes are "coerced" is that if they don't use performance-enhancing drugs, they may not get what they want. But they still have the choice of settling for less. Indeed, to take another position is to virtually deny the competence of top athletes to give consent in a variety of sports related areas including adoption of training regimens and scheduling. Are we to say, for example, that coaches coerce athletes into training and professors coerce students into doing work for their courses? Just as students can choose not to take a college degree, so too can athletes revise their goals. It is also to suggest that *any* individual who strives for great reward is not competent to give consent, since the fear of losing such a reward amounts to a coercive pressure.

While the issue of coercion and the distinction between threats and offers is highly complex, I would suggest that talk of coercion is problematic as long as the athlete has an acceptable alternative to continued participation in highly competitive sport. While coercion may indeed be a real problem in special cases, the burden of proof would seem to be on those who deny that top athletes *generally* are in a position to consent to practices affecting performance.

Harm to Others

This rejoinder might be satisfactory, critics will object, if athletes made their choices in total isolation. The competitive realities are different, however. If some athletes use drugs, others—who on their own might refrain from becoming users—are "forced" to indulge just to remain competitive. As Manhattan track coach Fred Dwyer (3: p. 25) points out, "The result is that athletes—none of whom understandingly, are willing to settle for second place—feel that 'if my opponent is going to get for himself that little extra, then I'm a fool not to.'" Athletes may feel trapped into using drugs in order to stay competitive. According to this argument, then, the user of performance-enhancing drugs is harming others by coercing them into becoming users as well.

While the competitive pressures to use performance-enhancing drugs undoubtedly are real, it is far from clear that they are unfair or improperly imposed. Suppose, for example, that some athletes embark on an especially heavy program of weight training. Are they coercing other athletes into training just as hard in order to compete? If not, why are those athletes who use steroids "coercing" others into going along?[3] Thus, if performance-enhancing drugs were available to all, no one would cheat by using them; for all would have the same opportunity and, so it would be argued, no one would be forced into drug use any more than top athletes are forced to embark on rigorous training programs.

Perhaps what bothers us about the use of drugs is that the user may be endangering his or her health. But why isn't the choice about whether the risk is worth the gain left to the individual athlete to make? After all, we don't always prohibit new training techniques just because they carry along with them some risk to health. Perhaps the stress generated by a particularly arduous training routine is more dangerous to some athletes than the possible side effects of drugs are to others?

Arguably, the charge that drug users create unfair pressures on other competitors begs the very question at issue. That is, it presupposes that such pressures are morally suspect in ways that other competitive pressures are not, when the very point at issue is whether that is the case. What is needed is some principled basis for asserting that certain competitive pressures—

those generated by the use of performance enhancing drugs—are illegitimately imposed while other competitive pressures—such as those generated by hard training—are legitimate and proper. It will not do to point out that the former pressures are generated by drug use. What is needed is an explanation of why the use of performance-enhancing drugs should be prohibited in the first place.

While such arguments, which describe a position we might call a libertarianism of sports, raise important issues, they may seem to be open to clear counter-example when applied in nonathletic contexts. Suppose for example that your co-workers choose to put in many extra hours on the job. That may put pressure on you to work overtime as well, if only to show your employer that you are just as dedicated as your colleagues. But now, suppose your fellow workers start taking dangerous stimulants to enable them to put even more hours into their jobs. Your employer then asks why you are working less than they are. You reply that you can keep up the pace only by taking dangerous drugs. Is the employer's reply, "Well, no one is forcing you to stay on the job, but if you do you had better put in as many hours as the others" really acceptable?

However, even here, intuitions are not a particularly reliable guide to principle. Suppose you have other less stressful alternatives for employment and that the extra hours the others originally work without aid of drugs generate far more harmful stress than the risk generated by the use of the stimulant? Perhaps in that case your employer is not speaking impermissibly in telling you to work harder. If not, just why does the situation change when the harmful effects are generated by drugs rather than stress? Alternatively, if we think there should be limits both on the stress generated by pressures from overtime *and* the risks created by drug use, why not treat similar risks alike, regardless of source? Similarly, in the context of sport, if our goal is to lower risk, it is far from clear that the risks imposed by performance-enhancing drugs are so great as to warrant total prohibition, while the sometimes equal risks imposed by severe training regimens are left untouched.

Harm and the Protection of the Young

Even if athletes at top levels of competition can give informed consent to the use of performance-enhancing drugs, and even if users do not place unfair or coercive competitive pressures on others, the harm principle may still support prohibition.

Consider, for example, the influence of the behavior of star athletes on youngsters. Might not impressionable boys and girls below the age of consent be driven to use performance-enhancing drugs in an effort to emulate top stars? Might not high school athletes turn to performance-enhancing drugs to please coaches, parents, and fans?

Unfortunately, consideration of such remote effects of drug use is far from conclusive. After all, other training techniques such as strict weight programs also may be dangerous if adopted by young athletes who are too physically immature to take the stress such programs generate. Again, what is needed is not simply a statement that a practice imposes some risk on others. Also needed is a justification for saying the risk is improperly imposed. Why restrict the freedom of top athletes rather than increase the responsibility for supervision of youngsters assigned to coaches, teachers, and parents? After all, we don't restrict the freedom of adults in numerous other areas where they may set bad examples for the young.

III. Drugs and the Ideal of Competitive Sport

Our discussion so far suggests that although the charges that use of performance-enhancing drugs by some athletes harms others do warrant further examination, they amount to less than a determinative case against such drug use. However, they may have additional force when supported by an account of competitive sport which implies a distinction between appropriate and inappropriate competitive pressures. What we need, then, is an account of when risk is improperly imposed on others in sport. While I am unable to provide a full theory here, I do want to suggest a principled basis, grounded on an ethic of athletic competition, for prohibition of paradigm performance-enhancing drugs.

My suggestion, which I can only outline here, is that competition in athletics is best thought of as a mutual quest for excellence through challenge (2: pp. 133-139). Competitors are obliged to do their best so as to bring out the best in their opponents. Competitors are to present challenges to one another within the constitutive rules of the sport being played. Such an account may avoid the charges, often directed against competitive sports, that they are zero-sum games which encourage the selfish and egotistical desire to promote oneself by imposing losses on others.

In addition, the ideal of sport as a *mutual* quest for excellence brings out the crucial point that a sports contest is a competition between *persons*. Within the competitive framework, each participant must respond to the choices, acts, and abilities of others—which in turn manifest past decisions about what one's priorities should be and how one's skills are to be developed. The good competitor, then, does not see opponents as things to be overcome and beaten down but rather sees them as persons whose acts call for appropriate, mutually acceptable responses. On this view, athletic competition, rather than being incompatible with respect for our opponents as persons, actually presupposes it.

However, when use of drugs leads to improved play, it is natural to say that it is not athletic ability that determines outcome but rather the efficiency with which the athlete's body reacts to the performance enhancer. But the whole point of athletic competition is to test the athletic ability of persons, not the way bodies react to drugs. In the latter case, it is not the athlete who is responsible for the gain. Enhanced performance does not result from the qualities of the athlete *qua* person, such as dedication, motivation, or courage. It does not result from innate or developed ability, of which it is the point of competition to test. Rather, it results from an external factor, the ability of one's body to efficiently utilize a drug, a factor which has only a contingent and fortuitous relationship to athletic ability.[4]

Critics may react to this approach in at least two different ways. First, they may deny that drug use radically changes the point of athletic competition, which presumably is to test the physical and mental qualities of athletes in their sport. Second, they may assert that by allowing the use of performance-enhancing drugs, we expand the point of athletic competition in desirable ways. That is, they may question whether the paradigm of athletic competition to which I have appealed has any privileged moral standing. It may well be an accepted paradigm, but what makes it acceptable?

Drugs and Tests of Ability

Clearly, drugs such as steroids are not magic pills that guarantee success regardless of the qualities of the users. Athletes using steroids must practice just as hard as others to attain what may be only marginal benefits from use. If performance enhancers were available to all competitors, it would still be the qualities of athletes that determined the results.

While this point is not without force, neither is it decisive. Even if all athletes used drugs, they might not react to them equally. The difference in reaction might determine the difference between competitive success and failure. Hence, outcomes would be determined not by the relevant qualities of the athletes themselves but rather by the natural capacity of their bodies to react to the drug of choice.

Is this any different, the critic may reply, from other innate differences in athletes which might enable them to benefit more than others from weight training or to run faster or swing harder than others? Isn't it inconsistent to allow some kinds of innate differences to affect outcomes but not the others?

Such an objection, however, seems to ignore the point of athletic competition. The point of such competition is to select those who do run the fastest,
swing the hardest, or jump the farthest. The idea is not for all to come out
equally, but for differences in outcome to correlate with differences in ability
and motivation. Likewise, while some athletes may be predisposed to
benefit more from a given amount of weight training than others, this trait
seems relevant to selection of the best athlete. Capacity to benefit from
training techniques seems part of what makes one a superior athlete in a way
that capacity to benefit from a drug does not.

Competition and Respect for Persons

At this point, a proponent of the use of performance-enhancing drugs might
acknowledge that use of such drugs falls outside the prevailing paradigm of
athletic competition. However, such a proponent might ask, "What is the
moral force of such a conclusion?" Unless we assume that the accepted
paradigm not only is acceptable, but in addition that deviance from it should
be prohibited, nothing follows about the ethics of the use of performance-
enhancing drugs.

Indeed, some writers seem to suggest that we consider new paradigms
compatible with greater freedom for athletes, including freedom to experiment with performance-enhancing drugs. W.M. Brown seems to advocate
such a view when he writes,

> Won't it [drug use] change the nature of our sports and ourselves? Yes.
> . . . But then people can choose, as they always have, to compete with
> those similar to themselves or those different. . . . I can still make my
> actions an "adventure in freedom" and "explore the limits of my
> strength" however I choose to develop it. (1: p. 22)

I believe Brown has raised a point of fundamental significance here. I wish
I had a fully satisfactory response to it. Since I don't, perhaps the best I can
do is indicate the lines of a reply I think are worth considering, in the hope
that it will stimulate further discussion and evaluation.

Where athletic competition is concerned, if all we are interested in is better
and better performance, we could design robots to "run" the hundred yards
in 3 seconds or hit a golf ball 500 yards when necessary. But it isn't just
enhanced performance that we are after. In addition, we want athletic
competition to be a test of *persons*. It is not only raw ability we are testing
for; it is what people do with their ability that counts at least as much. In
competition itself, each competitor is reacting to the choices, strategies, and
valued abilities of the other, which in turn are affected by past decisions and

commitments. Arguably, athletic competition is a paradigm example of an area in which each individual competitor respects the other competitors as persons. That is, each reacts to the intelligent choices and valued character-istics of the other. These characteristics include motivation, courage, intel-ligence, and what might be called the metachoice of which talents and capacities are to assume priority over others for a given stage of the individual's life.

However, if outcomes are significantly affected not by such features but instead by the capacity of the body to benefit physiologically from drugs, athletes are no longer reacting to each other as persons but rather become more like competing bodies. It becomes more and more appropriate to see the opposition as things to be overcome—as mere means to be overcome in the name of victory—rather than as persons posing valuable challenges. So, insofar as the requirement that we respect each other as persons is ethically fundamental, the prevailing paradigm does enjoy a privileged perspective from the moral point of view.

It is of course true that the choice to develop one's capacity through drugs is a choice a person might make. Doesn't respect for persons require that we respect the choice to use performance enhancers as much as any other? The difficulty, I suggest, is the effect that such a choice has on the process of athletic competition itself. The use of performance-enhancing drugs in sports restricts the area in which we can be respected as persons. Although individual athletes certainly can make such a choice, there is a justification inherent in the nature of good competition for prohibiting participation by those who make such a decision. Accordingly, the use of performance-enhancing drugs should be prohibited in the name of the value of respect for persons itself.

Notes

1. This paper was presented at the Olympic Scientific Congress in Eugene, Oregon (July, 1984) as part of a symposium, sponsored by the Philosophic Society for the Study of Sport, on the use of performance-enhancing drugs in sport. Some of the material in this paper is included in Robert L. Simon, *Sports and Social Values* (Englewood Cliffs, NJ: Prentice-Hall, 1985), and published by permission of Prentice-Hall.
2. The ethical issues raised by blood doping are discussed by Perry (5).
3. The charge of coercion does seem more plausible if the athlete has no acceptable alternative but to participate. Thus, professional athletes with no other career prospects may fit the model of coercion better than, say, a young amateur weight lifter who has been accepted at law school.

4. Does this approach have the unintuitive consequence that the dietary practice of carbohydrate loading, utilized by runners, also is ethically dubious? Perhaps so, but perhaps a distinction can be made between steroid use, which changes an athlete's capabilities for athletically irrelevant reasons, and dietary practices, which enable athletes to get the most out of the ability they have.

Bibliography

1. Brown, W.M. (1980). "Ethics, Drugs and Sport." *Journal of the Philosophy of Sport,* VII, 15-23.
2. Delattre, Edward. (1975). "Some Reflections on Success and Failure in Competitive Athletics." *Journal of the Philosophy of Sport,* I, 133-139.
3. Dwyer, Fred. (1982). "The Real Problem: Using Drugs to Win." *The New York Times,* July 4, 2S.
4. Murray, Thomas H. (1983). "The Coercive Power of Drugs in Sports." *The Hastings Center Report,* 13, 24-30.
5. Perry, Clifton. (1983). "Blood Doping and Athletic Competition." *International Journal of Applied Philosophy,* 1, 39-45.
6. Thomas, Carolyn E. (1983). *Sport in a Philosophic Context.* Philadelphia: Lea & Febiger.

CHAPTER

Paternalism, Drugs, and the Nature of Sports

W.M. Brown

During the marathon run at the 1972 Munich Olympics, Frank Shorter is said to have sipped decarbonated Coca-Cola provided along the route by his assistants as he headed for a gold medal. Clearly, for Shorter, caffeine was the drug of choice for that most demanding of running events. Since that time, caffeine has become one of an increasingly long list of banned drugs no longer permitted by the International Olympic Committee for competing athletes.[1] The list includes both a variety of chemically synthesized drugs as well as naturally occurring substances that are artificially prepared for human use.[2] The central issue of the use of such substances is not their so-called recreational use, the most prominent example of which is probably the widely publicized use of cocaine by some professional athletes. (Alcohol is apparently not currently a prohibited drug for Olympic athletes.) Rather, the issue is the use of drugs to enhance the benefits of training and to improve peak performance in competition.

Controversy on this issue centers on several factors which have both an empirical aspect and a moral one. The empirical questions concern both the effectiveness of drug use for training and competition and the possible harm such use can have for users.[3] The moral questions concern the appropriate-

Reprinted, by permission, from W.M. Brown, 1984, "Paternalism, drugs, and the nature of sports," *Journal of the Philosophy of Sport, XI:* 14-22.

ness of the use of drugs in sports, especially when their use is seen as a kind of cheating, a breach of principles of fair play. It is sometimes claimed, too, that the use of drugs in sports is somehow unnatural or incompatible with the very nature of sports. I intend to discuss these matters, but from the perspective of the moral principle of paternalism that I believe motivates many people who are concerned with this issue. First I want to look closely at the issue of drug use in sports by children and young people—cases which may appear to justify paternalistic choices—and then turn to the harder case of the paternalistic control of drug use by adults in sports.

Even John Stuart Mill (7), in his sustained attack on paternalistic restrictions on individual liberty, limited the application of his principles to mature individuals, adults in the full possession of their cognitive and emotional capacities. In the case of children, and perhaps others whose mature development of these capacities and a wider experience of life's possibilities has yet to be achieved, restrictions on individual liberty may be justified as preventing significant harm that might not otherwise be recognized and avoided. In such cases it seems clear that paternalistic interference is not only permissible but may indeed be obligatory to prevent harm and allow for a full flourishing of the child's potential development. Of course, judgment must be balanced: An important part of growing up is making mistakes and learning from them. All parents know the anguish of allowing failure to help guide the maturation of their children. Following Joel Feinberg and Gerald Dworkin, we can distinguish between "soft" and "hard" paternalism (2;3;4).[4]

Soft paternalism is defined by Dworkin (3: p. 107) as "the view that (1) paternalism is sometimes justified, and (2) it is a necessary condition for such justification that the person for whom we are acting paternalistically is in some way not competent." The key element here is clearly the determination that the person for whom we are acting is in fact not acting voluntarily, perhaps due to various circumstances including immaturity, ignorance, incapacity, or coercion. It may be that the nonvoluntary character of the behavior is evident or justifiably assumed on other grounds. This is typically the case with young children; but it is sometimes also true of adults whose situation makes clear that their actions are not fully voluntary. The more problematic cases are those of adult behavior that is not obviously nonvoluntary, but whose consequences are potentially dangerous or serious enough to call for careful deliberation. In these cases, as Feinberg (4: p. 8) suggests, we may be justified in intervening at least temporarily to determine whether the conduct is voluntary or not.

If soft paternalism is most clearly relevant to intervention in the lives of children and incompetent persons, hard paternalism must deal with cases of fully voluntary action and show nevertheless that paternalism is justified.

Here we may have every reason to suppose that the action in question is voluntarily undertaken by someone who has carefully appraised the consequences, weighed all available information, is emotionally responsive to the circumstances, but still opts to act in ways that involve the probability of serious harm, degradation, or impairment of opportunity or liberty. The most frequently cited cases are of those who seek to sell themselves into slavery, or persist in ignoring basic safety precautions such as wearing helmets while riding motorcycles. I shall return to the hard paternalistic thesis and its application to the case of adult sports after considering first the view of the soft paternalist and its application to the case of children and young people and their participation in sports. I shall not be directly concerned with the soft paternalist attitude toward adult sports except as an extension of its application to the case of children.

The soft paternalist argues that limitation of one's liberty is justified when one's behavior or actions are not fully voluntary because they are not fully informed, or because one is not fully competent or is in some relevant way coerced. All of these factors may plausibly be seen as present in the case of children's sports. By virtue of their youth, limited education, and inexperience, young people may frequently act in imprudent and potentially harmful ways, ways that may have unforeseen but long-term or irreversible consequences. Before considering the case of drugs, let me review several other cases in which the soft paternalist has what seems to be a strong argument for intervention or control of the young athlete's participation in sports.

The first kind of situation can best be called "safety cases."[5] These involve efforts by coaches, trainers, parents, and others to ensure that young players are provided with proper safety equipment and that they use it while engaged in playing the sport. Especially in contact sports such as football or hockey, such equipment as helmets and padded uniforms may be essential to protect the players against serious injury. Other sports may require other kinds of precautions. For example, swimmers may be prohibited from training alone in a pool, runners may be required to wear proper shoes, contact lenses may be forbidden, and so on. Some of these precautions may simply be prescribed by thoughtful parents or coaches, but others may be written into the rules of the sports by athletic associations, schools, or boards of education, thereby restricting participation to those who are properly equipped, or prohibiting certain kinds of play as too dangerous.

Indeed, most of the rules governing contact between players are formulated with the intention of ensuring the safety of enthusiastic and energetic players. The reasons for these requirements and rules are evident. Young athletes are frequently marvelously competent and talented in performing the intricate or arduous or swift feats called for in their sports. But they are typically equally unaware of their own limitations, their susceptibility to injury, and the long-term consequences of injuries to their development or effective participation. What justifies intervention in these cases, of restrictions on what young athletes may do, is precisely the belief that they are thus being prevented from harming themselves and that on mature reflection they themselves will come to see the reasonableness of the restrictions now placed on them. As their own experience broadens, and as their knowledge of themselves and their actions deepens and their values mature, they are, we anticipate, likely to join in accepting the restrictions they may have seen before as irksome and unnecessary.

A second set of cases I propose to refer to as "health cases." Insofar as injuries are closely connected with our views of health, there is clearly a considerable overlap between these two types of cases. Nevertheless, I believe there are some significant differences that warrant a separate category. Even in the absence of injuries and of circumstances likely to promote them, other matters of health rightly should concern the parent or coach of young athletes. I have in mind here matters that concern training, medical examinations and corresponding medical treatment or therapy, and nutrition and rest. They may involve the need for periodic medical examinations, the proper treatment of injuries, insistence on adequate nutrition and rest, and thoughtful organizing of training schedules that carefully consider the age, preparation, and health of the athlete.

In these cases, the young person typically lacks information to make adequate judgments—information that may be the purview of specially trained persons with long experience working with athletes and others. Furthermore, the young person is not generally expected even to be aware of his or her own ignorance or of the importance of acquiring medical or other information at an age when health may be taken for granted. Moreover, even when information is available, its significance may not be readily appreciated, habits of restraint and caution may be ill-formed, and self-discipline in maintaining therapeutic or training regimens may be minimal. The opposite may also occur. Youthful determination may manifest itself in excessive restraint, debilitating training, or stubborn persistence. Here ancient wisdom of balance, moderation, measure or variation may be the needed antidote, provided by more experienced people who insist on more wholesome approaches to sports preparation.

Of course, other factors than ignorance and inexperience may need to be overcome in paternalistic control of youthful sports. Peer and perhaps especially adult pressures are often a critical factor that adult advisors must deal with firmly and sensitively. One other important distinction should be mentioned here. So far, I have ignored the difference between health as the absence of disease or injury and health as a positive feature of growth and development. If it is clear that adults are justified in controlling the sports activities of young people in the interest of preventing injuries or speeding recuperation, and in maintaining the health of their children and students in the sense of keeping them injury-free and minimally healthy, it is also plausible that they are justified in seeking a greater degree of health or fitness for them. This seems to involve more centrally an educational function, though this feature is clearly present in the other two kinds of cases I have discussed, and I now turn to consider what might be called "educational cases."

Sports in our schools and universities, even when they involve intercollegiate competition, are almost invariably associated with departments of physical education. I mention this because it seems that a neglected but focal role for parents and coaches is educational, and the educational function goes far beyond the training of skills to include the inculcation of attitudes and values, the dissemination of information, and the formation of habits of mind as well as of body. It is difficult to illustrate cases in which paternalistic issues arise here, because the guidance of parents and coaches is often so subtle and pervasive as to be unnoticed by those it influences. Its character as interfering with or controlling the behavior of unwilling charges is more difficult to discern. Nevertheless, I think there are some fairly clear cases.

One type of case brings us back to efforts to prevent injury and to foster wholesome development by prescribing training schedules and nutritional standards designed to maximize training effectiveness. The effort here should never be merely to prescribe, but also to educate by explaining the rationale for the requirements, presenting the evidence available to substantiate the judgments, and requiring that the student understand as much as possible how the decisions were made. What can be expected here will vary with the age and educational level of the student; but resistance can often be expected, not only to following the requirements but to making efforts to understand them. I offer no formula for success in these efforts. As in all educational contexts many options are available to gifted teachers: cajolery, punishment, rewards, example, the inducements of affection, friendship, and respect, and lessons of failure and success. But I do wish to stress that these efforts are made because we believe the lessons should be learned, willingly or not, in the gym and playing field as well as the classroom. In doing so we counter the thoughtless or irrational or emotionally immature behavior of our students with paternalistic measures we believe are acceptable to fully rational and emotionally mature individuals.

A second type of educational case involves values. I have in mind instances of cheating or foul play in which adults may intervene to correct unfair, dishonest, or unsportsmanlike actions. Here again the goal is not merely to remedy or referee but is fundamentally educational. We should seek to instill values of fairness and honesty, countering whatever tendencies to the contrary we observe on the grounds that such action is not in the best interest of the players, whatever they may think about it. The development of values like the acquisition of knowledge in general is but one aspect of the central aim of education, which is the discovery of self-knowledge. Since, especially in young people, this is inextricably bound up with what they will become as well as with what they now are, the paternalistic guidance by adults must both inform and shape in light of what the adults believe to be the characteristics of persons in the fullness of their cognitive and emotional powers.

We are now ready to discuss control of the use of drugs by children and young people as an aspect of their participation in sports. Although I think a good general case can be made for proscribing drug use by young people, and even that a recreational use of drugs has some negative relevance to participation in sports, I plan to limit my remarks to a consideration of the use of drugs to influence athletic training and performance. I have not hesitated to offer here what I consider to be defensible moral judgments on the topics and issues I have raised. My point is not to insist that these judgments are unavoidable, but to suggest that they correspond with widely held intuitions relating to the acceptability of paternalism in regard to children and their sports activities.

Two aspects of drug use can be distinguished in advance, one being the use of drugs as medication. When medical treatment does not prevent sports participation entirely, it may significantly curtail that involvement. And when injury or illness requires medication which nevertheless will allow some sports activity, the decisive criterion will be improvement of the participant's health, not athletic achievement. There may also be times when use of medication is unrelated to sports and seems in no way to affect participation, except perhaps to allow it where otherwise it might not be possible. (An example might be drugs used to control mild epilepsy.) Here, too, the primary concern is the health and safety of the child. Such use may enhance participation in the limiting sense of making it possible, but where the purpose and effect of such usage is limited to medically justifiable ones, we may reasonably disregard this trivial enhancement. In the event that a medication did significantly improve performance over what would otherwise be expected, we could consider it in the next category.

This category involves cases in which drugs are used by otherwise healthy people for the express purpose of enhancing training or competition. There are a number of reasons why such usage should be prohibited. Foremost, of course, are the clear threats to the health and safety of the persons taking them. Among the many drugs available to athletes are some that have a powerful effect on the balance of the hormonal system, such as testosterone and other steroids, or human growth hormone, or L-dopa and β-blockers which can stimulate such hormones. Psychomotor or central nervous system stimulants can have a variety of powerful effects on the human body. Young people are especially vulnerable not only to the primary effects of such drugs but also to many deleterious side effects and to possible long-range effects that in many cases are only now beginning to be determined.[6] Damaging effects on growth patterns, and on psychosocial development, are probable high risks of such drugs for children and young people—risks far outweighing any possible benefits of temporary superior athletic prowess.

I should mention that in this respect, drugs are not different in kind, though perhaps in degree, from other features of sports which conflict with our values of health for young people. Arduous and extreme training methods, excessively rough contact between players, and insufficient recuperation or recovery from illness or injury, for example, may all violate our reasonable standards of wholesome athletics. Indeed a paramount concern for any tendency to overemphasize achievements in young people's sports is that it encourages a disregard for the health and balanced development of the young players.

I suspect that these judgments are relatively uncontroversial. But I now want to renew our discussion of the relation of such possible drug use and the development of attitudes and values by young players which I have already defended as among the legitimate paternalistic concerns of guardians and athletic supervisors. Drug use of the kind we are discussing (and of course many other features of training and competition) is clearly associated with winning, indeed with winning at virtually all costs. The chief consideration will always be how use of drugs will enable a young athlete to develop more quickly and effectively the strength, speed, or endurance needed to win, and how subsequent use will provide an improved competitive performance. This attitude is one that we can fairly consider to be nearly a defining characteristic of professionalism as it has come to be understood.

This use of drugs therefore carries with it, or encourages the development of, attitudes and values that conflict with those we hope to instill in children and young people through their very early participation in athletics. Among these latter values are sportsmanship, honesty, fairness, self-reliance as well as cooperation, grace under pressure, and health. Others could also be mentioned. But a central value is that of experiencing achievement through personal effort, of responding willfully to challenge, and thereby of coming to realize, that is, both to create and to understand, one's self, the complex bundle of skills, dispositions, beliefs, values, and capacities which constitute a personality.

Merit in a young athlete should reflect factors that are fully within his or her control. Ability and achievement should be a reflection of the amount of effort and self-motivation that are consonant with a normal life not characterized by fanaticism (an unreasonable purposiveness). We seek to stress a history of training and competitive effort that may to some extent cancel the uncontrollable differences among people so that superior skill is the result of a growing strength or personal resolve. In our paternalistic limiting of the freedom of young athletes, we are not emphasizing freedom to do anything or to have anything done to one, but rather the freedom of self-determination which accords with ideals of a reasoned, autonomous, well-balanced life, led in relation to a sensible ranking of values. It is because success due to some special technique or technology is only marginally reflective of athletic skill or training or motivation that we discount it or forbid it in the repertoire of young athletes.[7]

I want to emphasize that sports are not the only context in which these values are developed; indeed, they may not even be the best one. But they are a place, and for many people a very important one, where this learning process does occur. The conflict raised by drug usage of the kind we are discussing is that, by emphasizing one value over all others, it skews the context of learning and growth so as to deny sufficient credibility to other values. Moreover, it may conflict directly with efforts to encourage the young athlete to grasp the relation between personal effort and achievement so closely tied to both the experience of joy, excitement, and satisfaction of the athletes themselves, and to a similar appreciation by spectators.

It should be clear that we can extend the claims of soft paternalism, which I have so far discussed in regard to children, to various cases of adult behavior which presume incapacity of some sort, for example, ignorance, lack of opportunity or resources, or immaturity. But these are the easy cases for the soft paternalist and I shall not dispute them here. The difficult cases are surely those that give us every reason to believe that the actors are rational, informed, emotionally mature adults. The soft paternalist in turn must dispute such presumptions. We could of course hold that adult athletes who take drugs to enhance training or performance are in some way irrational, that they do not fully appreciate the dangers of such actions or the seriousness of side effects, or cannot adequately weigh the evidence that drug usage is not beneficial to performance. Moreover, we could claim that such athletes, in addition to ignoring relevant information, are unable to resist the pressures of others to succeed at all costs, that their weakness of will warrants paternalistic interference.

But such a reply is unconvincing, at least in many readily imaginable cases. It cannot be the very use of drugs which is the sole evidence for irrationality or self-destructiveness or weakness of will, on pain of begging the central question. And the evidence, once in, is very unlikely to support the claim that all cases of drug use are nonvoluntary in the requisite way. Rather, the truth seems to be that in these cases other values come into play. Adult values and motivations are not always the same as those we may encourage for young people. Adult life is more complicated, and though we intend the training in values and skills of childhood and youth to carry over to maturity, we are well aware that they will inevitably compete with other values that are often at odds with those we can reasonably insist on earlier. Often for adults winning *is* more important, and the circumstances of life may encourage a new range of motives: fame, wealth, power, social mobility, patriotism, pride of class, or race or ideology.

We may not accept such values or wish to encourage such motivations, but in a free society they are permissible; we may not deny them, to those who choose them, on grounds of paternalism. Where such values predominate, the risks of drugs may be outweighed by the benefits they may bring. Perhaps we come here to one of the sources of the distinction between "amateur" and "professional." If so, the distinction does not match the one I am suggesting between the values of youth and adulthood. Some professional skills and the knowledge of professional experience are clearly applicable to youth sports, and, conversely, professional values need not conflict with other values. It is always a matter of emphasis, role, age, commitments, and goals that determine which values dominate.

Indeed, even in our approach to sports for children, and especially of youths, we will at some point begin to anticipate some of the competing values that will increasingly vie for their attention and commitment as they grow older. As always, there are important questions of timing, emphasis, role, and age. But teachers and parents must at some point help facilitate the transition to full autonomy at which earlier limits to freedom can no longer be tolerated.

The soft paternalist could of course insist that where drug use or sports activities carry with them high risk, even risk of death or permanent injury, we are justified in intervening to prevent serious costs to the rest of us even when the athletes are willing to take the risks.[8] But society does not typically support the costs of such injury, and we could in any case require proper insurance for the athletes. Moreover, the psychic cost to others is surely minimal and, even in cases such as boxing, it is normally outweighed by the psychic gains of the spectator: the vicarious thrill and excitement, the shared pride, the satisfactions of knowledgeable viewing. In any case the balance of risks and benefits concerning drug usage is not likely to be clear. Efforts are no doubt being made to control for undesirable side effects, and the benefits may often need to be measured only in fractions of seconds. And why should we single out one class of risks when others, perhaps equally great, are already tolerated for the sake of excellence? Finally though it involves interference in the lives of others, such a response does not seem paternalistically motivated.

At this point, we may resort to something like a principle of "hard" paternalism if we are to persist in our efforts to control the choices and options of athletes. We are in effect seeking to impose on those who resist it an alternative set of values. But what would justify such an imposition? There seems no reason to suppose that taking risk in sports, even great risk, is inevitably irrational, self-destructive, or immature, as we have seen. Nor is it plausible to suggest that we forbid all of the sports which involve such risk, such as mountain climbing, sky-diving, or even boxing. As Mill argued, such intervention in people's lives would itself be a greater wrong than the possible injury of activities voluntarily chosen.

It may nevertheless be argued that the use of drugs is somehow inconsistent with the nature of sports, and that sports in turn are linked with a broader set of values—a conception of the good life—which is betrayed by the use of drugs, so that interference in the choices of athletes in this respect is done to preserve a greater good, one they may have lost sight of in their preoccupation with the more narrow concerns of training and competition. Such an argument a priori, as I have argued elsewhere, is not cogent (1). There is, I believe, no single conception of sports on which we need agree. In competitive sports we stress fairness and balanced competition; but in more solitary pursuits these values seem irrelevant. In the case of drugs, fairness may dictate equal access and widely available information. But even this is not clear: athletes and coaches seem justified in keeping secret their training regimens, and even, when permitted by the rules, equipment modifications.

Often, too, we stress human factors such as determination, fortitude, and cooperativeness over risk taking and technology. But in other cases—luge, skiing, mountain climbing, hang-gliding—risk and technology dominate. We believe in the capacity of sports to promote health and fitness, but many originated in the practice of war and routinely involve stress and injury, sometimes death. We fashion rules and continually modify them to reduce hazards and minimize serious injury, but few would seek to do so entirely. Perhaps we are tempted to require in athletes only what is natural. But our sports have evolved with our technology and our best athletes are often unnaturally, statistically, endowed with abilities and other characteristics far beyond the norm. It seems artificial indeed to draw the line at drugs when so much of today's training techniques, equipment, food, medical care, even the origin of the sports themselves, are the product of our technological culture.

Nevertheless, something more may be said for the claim that sports reflect a broader set of values. In discussing the justification of paternalism in coaching the young, I have stressed the formation of the values of honesty, fairness, and autonomy, values central to my conception of personhood. But they are not the only ones that might be stressed. Obedience, regimentation, service to others, or sacrifice might have been proposed. These, too, in the proper context, might also be developed together with the skills of athletics. The values, perhaps even a conception of what is good for human life, are associated with sports, not because of their nature, but due to the way we choose to play them. We can indeed forbid the use of drugs in athletics in general, just as we do in the case of children. But ironically, in adopting such a paternalistic stance of insisting that we know better than the athletes themselves how to achieve some more general good which they myopically ignore, we must deny in them the very attributes we claim to value: self-reliance, personal achievement, and autonomy.

Notes

1. The current ban on caffeine is defined in terms of a maximum level in urine of 15 μg/mL. For athletes this certainly means no direct ingestion of caffeine tablets, but also a need to avoid combinations of coffee, soft drinks, and over-the-counter medications like Anacin or Empirin which could lead to excessive accumulations of the drug.

2. A good example of such substances is the hormone testosterone. Since it occurs naturally in the body, it has been difficult to detect exogenous testosterone. A new test, however, now measures the ratio of testosterone to a metabolite, epitestosterone, which normally occur in a one-to-one ratio. Since exogenous testosterone isn't converted as readily to epitestosterone, it changes the ratio. The IOC requires the ratio of testosterone to its epimer in urine to be less than six to one. See Zurer (10).

3. Much of the evidence available to athletes in this regard is anecdotal, based on the personal experience of coaches, trainers, a few sports physicians, and the athletes themselves. The research literature is skimpy and the results conflicting. See Zurer (10) for a brief discussion of the conflicting views on the evidence. See also Williams (9).

4. These articles are conveniently reprinted in (8). Dworkin makes the distinction between "soft" and "hard" paternalism in (3). A slightly broader definition of paternalism is defended by Gert and Culver (5). (A version of this article appears in [6: Ch. 7].)

5. Dworkin (3: p. 108) uses this rubric, but for a different type of case.
6. Among the side effects of anabolic steroids are acne and liver tumors. For children and adolescents who are still growing, premature bone fusing and precocious puberty are likely results. See Zurer (10: pp. 73-75).
7. I'm grateful to Bill Puka for discussing this point with me, though in a somewhat different context.
8. Dworkin (3: p. 109) briefly discusses this argument for a different kind of case.

Bibliography

1. Brown, W.M. (1980). "Drugs, Ethics, and Sport." *The Journal of the Philosophy of Sport,* VII, 15-23.
2. Dworkin, Gerald. (1972). "Paternalism." *The Monist,* 56, 64-84.
3. Dworkin, Gerald. (1983). "Paternalism: Some Second Thoughts." *Paternalism.* Edited by Rolf Sartorius. Minneapolis: University of Minnesota Press.
4. Feinberg, Joel. (1971). "Legal Paternalism." *Canadian Journal of Philosophy,* 1, 106-124.
5. Gert, Bernard, and Culver, Charles. (1976). "Paternalistic Behavior." *Philosophy and Public Affairs,* 6, 45-57.
6. Gert, Bernard, and Culver, Charles. (1982). *Philosophy in Medicine: Conceptual and Ethical Issues in Medicine and Psychiatry.* New York: Oxford University Press.
7. Mill, J.S. (1978). *On Liberty.* Indianapolis: Hackett Publ.
8. Sartorius, Rolf. (1983). *Paternalism.* Minneapolis: University of Minnesota Press.
9. Williams, Melvin H. (1974). *Drugs and Athletic Performance.* Springfield, IL: Thomas.
10. Zurer, Pamela S. (1984). "Drugs in Sports." *Chemical and Engineering News,* April 30, pp. 69-79.

10

CHAPTER

As American As Gatorade and Apple Pie: Performance Drugs and Sports

W.M. Brown

As long as people have played at sports they have tried to develop their skills and capacities with all the means at their disposal.[1] In recent years, public discussion of such efforts has focused on the use of performance-enhancing drugs, in part because we are caught up in a quagmire of issues relating to illegal drug use, and in part because we are perplexed by ethical and practical issues relating to developments in biotechnology. Our sports have changed and our attitudes toward them and the athletes who perform in them are undergoing similar changes. By and large, the controversies over professionalism and race in sport are over, those over sex and gender are passing, but the controversy over performance drugs is unresolved.

This paper is a critique of a number of arguments that are frequently made to resolve that controversy by showing why performance drugs should be forbidden to all athletes participating in organized sports such as amateur and professional leagues and international competitions like the Olympic Games. The arguments have moral as well as practical aspects, focusing as they do on athletes' rights and principles of liberty or of avoiding harm.

Reprinted, by permission, from W.M. Brown, "As American as Gatorade and apple pie: Performance drugs and sports," *Ethics for Today and Tomorrow (edited by Jorm Graf Haber): 324-341.*

Surprisingly, perhaps, one of the most curious aspects of the controversy is what people mean when they argue about drugs in sports.

One reason for this is that much of the notoriety of drug use in sports is related to athletes' use of recreational drugs: cocaine, alcohol, and tobacco, for example. Few of these drugs are thought by anyone to enhance athletic performance. Indeed, aside from the illegality of some of them, they are deplored because they diminish one's skills and produce aberrant behavior on and off the playing fields. Another reason is that many of the substances used to enhance athletic performance are not usually thought of as drugs at all, for example an athlete's own blood, or hormones, or widely used food products like caffeine or sugar. And finally, there is puzzlement over the availability of synthetically produced substances that naturally occur in the human body such as testosterone, human growth hormone, and erythro-poietin which have widespread therapeutic uses and even uses for otherwise healthy individuals coping with the processes of aging.[2]

But having mentioned a few, I will not catalogue the list of substances that are used to enhance athletic performance or seek to define them.[3] The issues I will discuss cut across such lists and concern more general views about fairness, health, consensus, autonomy, and the nature of sports as they are brought to bear on the practice of enhancing athletic performance. Nor will the arguments I will consider hinge on the effectiveness of such substances. No one really knows whether many of these products are effective at all or in what ways or with what risks. Virtually no serious major studies of their use by athletes have been made, and most of our evidence is speculative and anecdotal, extrapolated from very different contexts or reported by journalists. So I will assume that some performance drugs are effective and some are not, that some are risky and some are safe, and proceed to explore what conclusions we can reach about their use by athletes.

1. Fairness

Perhaps the most frequently cited issue concerning drugs and sports is that of fairness. The claim is that taking "performance drugs" is a form of cheating, that it is therefore fundamentally unfair. After all, if some athletes are using something that gives them a decisive advantage, it is argued, it is unfair to the basic premise of competition in sports (whether competition against present opponents or competition for records). Competition in sports (as opposed to competition in love and war) assumes some basic similarities among all participants so that contests are close and, therefore, both bring out the best in the competitors and are exciting to watch. Such a situation also, it is claimed (rightly, it seems to me), makes it more likely that the contest will be won in the margin where various factors come into play that are dear to our traditions: effort, will, determination, fortitude, and courage, among others.

And it is true: when an athlete breaks the rules, such as those banning the use of performance drugs, that is clearly a form of cheating, and its practice introduces an aspect of unfairness into the sport. But in an important way this argument misses the point. The ethical issue we are addressing is precisely that of the value of such rules, of the wisdom or justification of prohibiting the use of performance drugs. It therefore begs the question to stress that such drugs are forbidden and so it is wrong to use them.

There is a version of this argument that seems to acknowledge this point, but goes on to claim that when some athletes use drugs and others do not (for whatever reason other than that they are banned), an inequality is introduced that renders competition unfair, not because of any cheating, but because of the discrepancy in performance that drug use may introduce. The short answer to this argument is that there are always likely to be differences among athletes (even if they are clones) and that these differences are (to mention a particular sport) what makes for horse racing. Without them, sports competition would surely hold little interest for us. Competition would resemble the predicament of Buridan's ass with unresolveable stalemates or contests won by random chance.

A more persuasive version of this argument is to note that in highly competitive sports where there are many pressures from family, coaches, teammates, managers, and owners, there can be no free choice to use performance drugs. At best it is a subtle form of coercion, a "forced choice," that produces for some athletes an unhappy dilemma: don't compete or take drugs.[4] We can acknowledge the crucial premise that individual autonomy is a central value. (Indeed, it is one I will employ frequently.) The additional factual premise that no one can be expected to withstand such pressures is more problematic. For one thing, it is clear that although many athletes now use performance drugs, many do not, and the latter are among the finest and most successful athletes now performing. But for another, every innovation or change in training, techniques, and equipment places similar pressure on athletes to adopt the changes or lose a competitive edge (assuming also that the changes are really effective in enhancing performance). The charge of coercion hinges on the prior assumption that the choice to use performance drugs is deeply objectionable and therefore many people would not want to use them. Of course, if their use is illegal or harmful, many athletes will be reluctant to use them. So athletes who choose not to use drugs are at an unfair advantage only if there is a good reason not to use them. And that, of course, is just the issue at stake. But these reasons need to be assessed. Someone might complain that he can be a boxer only if competitors are allowed to punch the head, and since that is very dangerous, he is unfairly forced to choose between boxing and getting his head punched (and punching others in the head) or not competing at all. The wise choice may be to switch to swimming, but the choice is not in any interesting sense coerced.

The argument can be changed, however, to make a different point, and this refinement involves noting that sports are often segregated into classes by such things as age, sex, and weight. In this form, the argument deserves a separate consideration, and I return to it in section 6.

In the discussion to follow, various additional arguments concerning the use of performance drugs are examined to assess their cogency and persuasiveness.

2. Health

Performance drugs are dangerous, so this argument goes, and banning their use is a way of protecting athletes from their own ill-conceived acts. The danger lies in the injuries that the use of performance drugs may cause. Recently, this case has been made most vociferously in regard to anabolic steroids, the drug of choice for athletes seeking to increase muscle mass useful for various sports ranging from football to track to gymnastics. But many other drugs are also available, including beta-blockers, growth hormones, and food ingredients such as caffeine; presumably the argument can be made in regard to them as well.

There are, however, two issues that need to be separated in this regard. One is an empirical issue concerning the actual harms likely to be caused by performance drug use. The other is the ethical issue of paternalism, the justification of restricting the actions of others ostensibly for their own good. A byproduct of this argument is what appears to be a remarkable case of hypocrisy.

As for the first issue, there is some evidence that the use of some performance drugs carries risks of injury to the users. But the evidence is remarkably sparse and, of course, differs for different drugs. Much of it is anecdotal—the lore of boxing and weight-lifting aficionados, the stuff of locker room banter. Such research-based evidence as is available is often inconclusive. Some studies suggest that steroids are effective in enhancing performance; others claim that there is no significant enhancing effect.[5] Athletes tend to discount the extreme claims of risk of injury because their own experience has not confirmed them; and much of the research evidence has been based not on studies of efforts to enhance athletic performance but rather on cases of medical therapy and extrapolation to nonmedical circumstances. What this suggests is that the factual claims concerning performance drugs remain significantly unsubstantiated both in regard to drug risks and in regard to performance enhancement.[6] The sensible thing to do would surely be to find out who is right by encouraging careful and competent research into both kinds of claims.[7]

But this would not be the end of it. It seems likely that some substances or procedures would be relatively dangerous and others relatively risk-free; some would be relatively effective, others ineffective. In this case, it could be argued that dangerous ones especially should be carefully used, if effective, to eliminate or minimize their side effects, but that all performance drugs should be studied and the results be widely and publicly available to athletes and their coaches and physicians.[8] The goal should be to eliminate or reduce the likelihood of harm to athletes, as it is for other risks in sport.

A brief comment is in order about relative risk. In many sports, the activities of the sports themselves are far more dangerous than the use of any of the performance drugs that have even a bare chance of being effective. Deaths and injuries due to the use of performance drugs are rare.[9] Scarcely more than a dozen deaths are noted by some authorities, and most of these can be attributed not to performance drugs, but to recreational drugs like cocaine and alcohol used off the playing fields and unconnected to competitive efforts.[10] But deaths and serious injuries due to the sports themselves number in the hundreds in sports like football, boxing, mountain climbing, hockey, cycling, and skiing.[11] Where the sports themselves are far more dangerous than anything risked by using performance drugs, one can only wonder at the hypocrisy that prompts the extraordinary tirades directed at the latter but seldom at the former. The most vociferous criticism of performance drugs seems far more closely linked to our national hysteria about illicit drugs in general than to the health of our athletes.[12]

Still, if we assume that there are dangers in using performance drugs, and clearly there are some even if their use is monitored by knowledgeable physicians, should we prohibit them on the grounds that athletes cannot be expected to make rational choices about their use and hence are at risk of excessive injury to their health? I have argued elsewhere that child athletes should be prohibited on paternalistic grounds from using such drugs.[13] But the issue is not so clear with adult athletes. Unlike airline pilots or subway train drivers, for example, athletes who use performance drugs pose no obvious dangers to others. Nor are the drugs in question related to diminished performance, but rather to enhanced and improved performance. So concerns about athletes' health are paternalistic in the strong sense of being directed not toward preventing harm to others, but to the drug users themselves. There often seems to be a discrepancy between concerns about athletes' health and safety in general and concerns about risks of using performance drugs. In any case, one could equally well argue that making their use safer while preserving the autonomy and freedom of choice of the athletes is a far preferable approach. If there are effective performance enhancing drugs (and there seem to be some), and if they are or could be relatively safe to use (and some are), then the health argument, as I have called it, seems ineffective as a general argument against their use.

One final note. Hormonal supplements for healthy adults are not a new item in the pharmacopoeia. More recently men and women are being given sex hormones and growth hormone supplements to offset the effects of aging, apparently with favorable results.[14] Women have taken estrogen for years to offset the effects of menopause. The World Health Organization is currently administering steroids as a male contraceptive in doses greater than those said to have been used by Ben Johnson when he was disqualified after his victory at the Seoul Olympics.[15] It is hard to argue in light of such practices that the use of performance drugs, even the most risky kinds, including steroids, should have no place in the training or performance of athletes.

3. Naturalness and Normality

The argument shifts at this point, therefore, to the claim that performance drugs are unnatural additives to the athlete's training or performance regimen. Even if their careful use is relatively harmless, the argument goes, they are objectionable because they are artificial and unnatural additives to sporting activities. There are two versions of this argument. One is that it is the drugs that are unnatural; the other is that it is the athletes who use them who are unnatural or abnormal.

The first version is the less plausible. The reason is that many of the drugs used to enhance performance are as natural as testosterone, caffeine, or an athlete's own blood.[16] True, some drugs are the product of manufacturing processes or are administered using medical technologies. But, of course, so are many of our foods, vitamins, and medicines, all routine parts of the athlete's regimen. If by *natural* one means not artificially synthesized or processed, or known to occur in nature independent of human intervention, few of the nutritional and medical resources available to athletes today would be allowed. Performance drugs, therefore, cannot be identified or forbidden under this rubric without taking many things we find indispensable down the drain with them.

The claim for abnormality may be a bit stronger. After all, to the extent that performance drugs work effectively at all, they are designed to render their users superior in ability and rates of success beyond what we would expect otherwise. And this, the argument concludes, renders them abnormal. Of course, this is in one sense true. If normality is defined in terms of statistical frequencies, then highly effective athletes are abnormal by definition. Such people are already abnormal if compared with the rest of us; their reflexes, coordination, neuromuscular development, and fitness levels already place them far to the right on the bell-shaped curves showing the range of human capacities and performance. Performance drugs are scarcely needed to place them among the abnormal, that is, the statistically rare individuals who can run a mile under 3:50, accomplish a gymnastic routine, slam dunk a basketball, or climb Mt. Everest without canisters of extra oxygen. Looked at another way, however, athletes are probably the most natural components of their sports; their efforts reveal to all of us various ranges of human abilities as currently manifested under the very artificial and unnatural constraints of our present-day sports and their assortment of bats, balls, rules, shoes, training techniques, and ideologies.

Surely, however, those who make this argument know this. Perhaps they are using the word *abnormal* in its other sense of connoting what is bad or undesirable, and since they can't quite articulate what is so bad about performance drugs, they rely on the claim of abnormality or unnaturalness to carry the weight of their condemnation. Here again, then, we need to move on to other arguments that may make the case more substantively and effectively, or at least make clearer what it is about the use of performance drugs that seems to some critics so deplorable.

4. Role Models

Athletes, especially professional athletes, are among the most widely publicized figures in Western societies and often in other countries as well. The reasons for this are many, but some are fairly obvious. Athletes are young, extraordinarily gifted in their physical abilities, and display the grace and power, and sometimes wealth, that many others may wish to share. For this reason they are often featured in commercial and nationalistic promotions as well. Given this prominence, sports figures easily become "role models" for others who seek to emulate their careers and behavior. This argument capitalizes on the social prominence of some athletes to claim that the use of performance drugs by them will be copied by others, especially young people, to their great detriment.[17]

I have some sympathy for this claim. There is some evidence for harmful
use by adolescent male body builders of steroids especially. And it may be
that publicized cases of professional athletes and others using such drugs
effectively has encouraged this behavior. But there has also recently been a
strong critical reaction to the status of athletes as role models. By far the most
notorious cases of athlete drug use have been concerned with recreational
drugs: alcohol, cocaine, and marijuana, not performance drugs. Further
criticism has come from those who note that the vast majority of professional
athletes do not live lives of grandeur and opulence, but rather ones characterized by brief and somewhat tawdry careers plagued by injury and the
bleak prospects in our society of the uneducated and untrained. The
attractiveness of athletes as role models is accordingly due more to media
and commercial exploitation than to the inherent qualities of the athletes
themselves. In reality they show roughly the same limitations in their
conduct as do the rest of us and the promotion of them as living exemplary
lives is, as Jonathan Schonsheck notes, a central hypocrisy of our times.[18]
Moreover, in other areas where people serve as role models, we do not seek
to institute policies that collectively control their conduct. And in the case of
athletes themselves, we do not attempt to forbid other forms of conduct that
might be objectionable to some: other forms of drug use (alcohol, caffeine,
nicotine), divorce, gambling, self-promotion, and greed (though all of these
at one time or the other have been the object of censure or prohibition).
Consistency at least requires that we question the singling out of one form
of behavior from others without good reason.

The issues here are so intermixed, juxtaposing as they do attitudes toward
drugs in general with our ambivalent views of sports as a focus of national
self-esteem, that it may be impossible to sort them out. Still, it seems
reasonable to argue that the promotion of other people than sports figures as
role models for the young, and a more sensible attitude toward the understanding and use of performance drugs, would accomplish much of what
those who deplore their use seek in this regard. Perhaps, too, we need a
reevaluation of our national policies toward recreational drugs and the
associated costs in enforcement, punishment, crime, and disease.[19]

5. The Nature of Sport

Some claim that there are central characteristics of sports that mitigate
against the use of performance drugs. I want to consider one such claim,
formulated by Alasdair MacIntyre, and developed by others.[20] The claim is
that sports are practices, coherent forms of organized social activity that

create certain goods and values intrinsic to them and which are attained by performing in accordance with the standards of excellence integral to the practices.[21] This characterization of practices gives rise to a distinction between those goods that are internal to the practices and those that are external to it. Internal goods arise out of the exercise of skills developed to fulfill the defining goals of the activities; external goods are rewards typically offered by institutions that support the practices but also tend to exploit them for reasons of their own that are unconnected with the practices' own immediate activities. Thus a well-thrown pitch, a stolen base, and a perfect bunt are exercises of skill within the practice of baseball and offer their own rewards. The fame, salaries, and trophies that are also rewarded are external to the game and provided by institutions not directly involved in the practice itself.

There is much to be said for this conception of sports. It highlights some of the features of a favorite view of them: the virtuous and innocent player motivated by the love of the game; the power and skill of the practitioner, a thing of beauty and grace; the corrupt and venal exploiters of youth and innocence for worldly gain. But it divides motives and satisfactions too neatly, borrowing the metaphor of inside and outside to suggest that practices are like the bodies of the players themselves, inwardly pure and driven by their own dynamics, confronted by external forces of corruption and greed. The idea is that performance drugs, like an invading microorganism, infiltrate from the outside to foul the internal workings of sports, the athletes themselves, distorting their skills, depriving them of the internal goods of the sports, and motivating them toward the external rewards of larger social institutions. The argument then goes something like this. Performance drugs are not relevant to the internal goods of sports which derive from "achieving those standards of excellence" characteristic of the practice. Their use tends rather to be driven by external goals of winning and victory and the fame or riches attendant on them.

But this argument is unpersuasive for several reasons. The first is that the basic distinction between internal and external goods, though serviceable for some purposes, blurs at crucial places. For example, there are clearly satisfactions to be gained from the exercise of the skills one develops in sport. Such skills are largely specific to given sports: taking a turn on a 400-m track and other tactical skills in a foot race, for example, are not easily carried over to golf or basketball. This is due by and large to the arbitrary character of sports, their curious separateness from the skills of the workplace and home. Nevertheless, such skills are sometimes carried over to other sports. And in sports where many diverse skills are called for—in the biathlon, triathlon, and decathlon, for example—skills developed in one sport are transferable to others. No matter that the combination often limits performance to less than that of the specialist; the satisfaction of each skill's development, not just in their combination, is still present. But now such skills and their attendant satisfactions must be both internal and external to specific sports, and if transferable to practices other than the sports themselves—as are the skills, many argue, of teamwork, cooperativeness, and planning—are doubly external.[22]

Or take the good of winning. Winning, it is said, is an external good of sports and as such would seem to cut across various sports.[23] But winning in one sport is surely not the same as winning in another, and winning at one level of competition is surely different from winning at another. Indeed winning surely emerges as the final, overall configuration of the game itself, internal to the dynamics of the play, its culmination, not an externally imposed determination by those external to the activity. Even in those rare cases where controversial results lead to reviews by others, they are decided by the internal constraints of the sport, not by external institutional needs. And the rewards of winning may be internal or external. True, fortune is usually introduced from outside sports these days, but fame and admiration run deep within the sports themselves and are not just the province of institutional or social renown.

Health and fitness would seem to be external goods imposed on sports, as we have seen in our earlier discussion of the effects of performance drugs. But both are elusive. Fitness is to sports as intelligence is to tests: both seem specific to the ways in which they are measured, by essentially arbitrary cultural norms. Just as there seems no clear way to measure a general intelligence or IQ, so there seems no way to measure general fitness beyond capabilities developed in specific sports or other activities. (Questions like, "Are musicians smarter than lawyers?" give place to "Are basketball players more fit than swimmers?") Health is a notoriously slippery concept. Indeed, it is an uneasy companion of sports like boxing, mountain climbing, football, and many others, which carry with them inherent risks of injury that may be reduced but not eliminated: those risks are integral to the sports themselves and help define the excitement and challenge that are among their internal goods.

So little is to be gained for our purposes from the distinction between internal and external goods. And this is brought out by the second reason, that performance drugs are intended to enhance performance, as measured by the sports' own activities and standards, their own internal goods. Schneider and Butcher have argued that such enhancement is tantamount to changing the skills required by a sport and thus "changes the sport."[24] But this claim is implausible. Training at high altitude greatly enhances the oxygen transport capacity of long-distance runners, but few would argue that it changes the skills required to run a marathon or changes the sport itself. The jump shot, a basketball skill first performed in the late 1940s, changed the sport only in the sense that it added excitement and challenge to the game. Indeed, Schneider and Butcher emphasize this point themselves.[25] And to the extent that performance drugs could enhance performance, they would contribute to the exercise of skills at a higher level where the challenges and satisfactions might be all the greater.

Surely this is the reason why athletes have always tried to better their opponents, to find ways to excel, in spite of the fact that no one doubts that their secrets to success will soon be out. No one would seek to ignore a new training technique, equipment modification, or diet on the grounds that since one's opponents will soon catch on, the discovery will just escalate the competition, soon making it harder than ever to win. To this extent, sports recapitulate life and reflect a constant striving to win and enjoy, to compete and share in the competition of the game. In this sense, performance drugs may be as relevant to sports and their internal goods as any other way of enhancing one's performance.

6. Difference

I combine here a number of points that challenge the general trend of my comments to other objections. They involve differences among athletes that may suggest grounds for acknowledging the differences performance drugs may make. One way to isolate the objections to performance drugs is to note that they apply to the participants in sports rather than to the constitutive rules of the sports themselves. Like proscriptions of earlier generations against some people participating in sports because of their race, sex, social status, or religion, forbidding the participation of those who use drugs may seem like a similar kind of discrimination since in using drugs, one is not breaking the rules of the sports themselves but rather challenging limits on who may play in them. The Negro baseball leagues followed the same rules as the white leagues, their players just weren't allowed to play on the same teams, or in the same competitions. How is the case different for drugs?[26]

There are a number of cases, however, where competition is decided on the basis of the players rather than on the rules of the game. Participation is often based, for example, on sex. Women were officially allowed to run in the Boston Marathon only in 1972, after several women, beginning in 1966, unofficially broke the sex barrier. Even so, when women began running the marathon in the Olympic Games in 1984 it was in a separate women's race. And similar divisions into men's and women's events are familiar in other sports. In other cases, such as boxing, wrestling, and crew, participation is also based on weight. (Body-building competitions are now organized into new "natural" or drugfree and traditional, "open" events, the latter widely assumed to feature contestants who use steroids.) In amateur sports such as running, tennis, swimming, and golf, participants are often classified by age as well as sex.

What are we to make of these differences among people as a basis for classifying sports? To some extent they no doubt reflect long social traditions and prejudices. Barriers to involvement in sports by girls and women, whether as overt prohibitions, as social practices based on rigid sex roles, or as subtle social pressures, have long been part of our society and others. But such practices also reflect inherently different developmental patterns of males and females, and these, when combined with the characteristics of sports developed largely for men, produce on the average striking differences in the athletic capabilities of men and women. Still, since the overlap of such traits is large, it would be easy to match some groups of women with similarly skilled groups of men to have sports with combined and roughly equally matched male and female participants. In fact, this often happens in informal sports in schools and elsewhere when (mostly) male exclusiveness is overcome and efforts are not directed primarily at competitive excellence. Why isn't this done more often?

One reason is that sports are one of the most effective ways our society has of reinforcing and maintaining gender identities just as they were once used to reinforce racial and socioeconomic or class identities. After all, biologically it is not always easy to distinguish male and female: these are not two platonic categories unblurred in their essential difference.[27] Genetic testing notwithstanding, who is to count as a male or female is finally a determination of social as well as biological intent. (Even age, with its inexorable chronological exactitude, must be reinforced by social constraints to become an effective determinant of participation in sports.) So the differences we are concerned with, though largely "natural," biologically or statistically, are also partly social constructs.

Adopting William James's remark that a difference to be a difference must make a difference, we can nevertheless look to some pragmatic indications of where our line-drawing can reasonably be made. As it turned out, race and social class make very little difference to the outcome of participation in sports, although the residue of the old arguments still simmers in fatuous claims about the inherent abilities of black athletes who now predominate in some sports, and social class and wealth remain entrance qualifications in yachting and polo. Age more clearly takes its toll on the skills and achievements of all athletes. Cutting across as it does all other categories, it can be left to exact its own inevitable classifications. But within limits, it doesn't matter. Most sports make no concessions to age save to even the competitive zest for those who find themselves past their prime. If older athletes do better than their younger competitors, they get their double victory.

Perhaps, however, sex does make a difference, in general. This is not a comment on gender equity issues in our schools and universities, but one on how, minus as best we can tell our social reinforcement of differences, things fall out for men and women in sports. At the levels of high-performance athletics, for intercollegiate and professional sports, men and women will perform on average so differently that it is often reasonable to organize sports by sex. The case is not nearly so clear for sports in elementary schools and for amateur adult sports. The dividing line at puberty makes high school athletics the place where separating participation by sex begins to make sense. If so, then for sports as they are now configured, the differences between men and women will produce corresponding differences in athletic performances and offer a rationale for preserving the competitive balance achieved when participants are organized by sex. Surely this is the rationale of weight classes in boxing, wrestling, and crew, although the absence of such classes in other sports where size and strength make a substantial contribution shows the degree of arbitrariness in such decisions.

But a similar case cannot be made, I think, for performance drugs. By and large, where such drugs work at all, and the evidence here is inconclusive, the results are usually relatively minor. Depending as they do on the initial characteristics of the athletes and their training, performance drugs may sometimes marginally enhance the performance of the athletes.[28] But to the same extent so, too, may a new training technique, different food, or better equipment. A striking exception may be the androgenic effect of anabolic steroids on female athletes. If we ignore for the moment the dangers of such drugs for women (and men), and if we assume that they do promote significant changes in muscle development and corresponding weight and strength, then my argument in the preceding paragraph is undercut and organizing sports by sex would lose some of its rationale (though perhaps for other reasons not all). If women were to close the gap between male and female developmental norms, there would be less justification for separating men and women in sports.[29]

My response here depends on an empirical claim, namely that the likely effects of performance drugs are slight. But suppose that the appropriate use of such drugs could result in substantial improvements in competitive performance. If this were the case, then wouldn't there be a reasonable basis for organizing sports for those who do and those who do not use performance drugs, the same basis adduced to justify classifying athletes by weight, for example? My inclination here is still to argue against such a division. The separation of sports based on drug use is poorly supported by an analogy to the cases of sex and weight classes where the performance ranges are inherently greater. A stronger analogy, that I will discuss further in section 7, is to new developments in training or equipment, or improvement in talent through selection from larger pools of potential athletes. Because of these changes, performances over the years have changed remarkably in virtually all sports, but this has not prompted new classification of athletes. It is worth noting, too, that the issue in this case would be not the banning of performance drugs altogether, but the relegating of those who do use them to separate categories.

But I must return specifically to the case of androgenic anabolic steroids for female athletes. I have argued that most performance drugs have marginal benefits for athletic performance, but this may not be the case for female athletes who use steroids. More importantly, however, are the effects of these drugs on the secondary sexual characteristics of those who use them. (This is true for men as well, but to a much lesser extent.) For women these effects are masculinizing, and hence directly affect their sexual or gender identities. I have already noted that sports tend to reinforce society's stereotypical gender classifications, and the use of steroids by female athletes may make these classifications increasingly problematic. (Indeed, early objections to the participation of women in sports were often based on gender stereotyping, including claims that sports would endanger women's reproductive organs, were unsuited to their inherent feminine natures, or would result in unseemly masculine women. Today, few people give credence to these claims.) There is the further concern that the use of steroids may have long-lasting or permanent androgenic effects, especially on women who use them in high doses and over long periods of time. Of course, athletes who perform at high levels of achievement for long periods of time face many long-term, even permanent, changes in their bodies whether from injury, stress, or training. Sports are even touted by some as being valuable for producing such changes: boys can become men, ninety pound weaklings may be transformed into strong, assertive, and confident citizens capable of leading and enjoying the goods of life. If there is truth to these claims, then sports already touch deeply on central features of personal identity.

Still, sexual or gender characteristics strike us as so central to human identity as to require separate consideration. If the use of steroids threatens such a core identity—physically, psychologically, and culturally—then their use may finally be too detrimental to sanction. But once again, the problem may not be as intractable as it appears at first. There is already a wide range of characteristics among females (as there is among males). Some are small and frail, others large and muscular; some have few masculine traits, some have many. The same is of course true of men. It is in the average that men and women diverge in significant ways, but the overlap is large and significant. And, as I have already mentioned, dividing us into male and female classes is not as easy as it might seem. Genetics, for example, is an important but not always decisive measure. Steroids, like the sports themselves, will therefore affect different women (and men) in different ways, depending on use and on the initial characteristics of the users. Sexual and gender identity concerns will also figure in different ways for different people, never arising for some and requiring careful choices for others.

Because, in our society and others, sports reflect the general cultural interests and values of men, female athletes are more likely to seek to emulate the performance capabilities of men than men are to seek those of women. (There are exceptions. The rare male transsexual, such as Renee Richards, or the female impersonator, such as Herman Ratjen in the 1936 Olympics, may seek to enter women's sports. Ironically, in these cases success has not been notable. Ratjen was beaten in his event, the high jump, by three female competitors.)[30] But this is already the case in sports today. Steroids may therefore have no more of an effect on women's sports than they do on men's. The growing athletic achievements of women, performance drugs aside, have already begun to put pressure on sports and the sex barrier to participation, just as women have increasingly put pressure on other male institutions, such as military academies and traditionally male professions, to allow women full participation. Resistance is strong, and we do not yet know whether the fuller participation of women will change women or change men and their institutions. The same questions with few answers also confront our sports.[31]

So, perhaps the efforts to ban performance drugs, especially steroids, in sports derive in part from a desire to preserve the predominant character of our sports as reflecting social norms of sexual and gender stereotyping. These norms are not likely to change soon or easily. But two directions of change might be possible. One would be to let classifications be blurred, opening participation to everyone based on qualifications to play safely and successfully. Perhaps women would dominate in long-distance swimming and running and in gymnastics and rhythmics, while men would continue to dominate in other sports. But a secondary effect might be to change the sports themselves, reducing the violence and brutality of some and introduc-

ing new sports requiring mixed skills that rarely develop together in men or
women. The other change would be to allow classifications throughout
sports to proliferate, recognizing a wider variety of human types, emphasizing relatively stable characteristics like height, age, and sex, where shifting
among the categories would be minimal, but perhaps also allowing for other
classes, like weight, gender identity, or handicaps which may shift and
change for individuals.

7. Slippery Slopes

I want to continue the arguments of the last section by pushing them a bit
harder. Another way, I think, of expressing worries that some have about
performance drugs is by seeing their claims as slippery slope arguments.[32]
I have considerable sympathy for such arguments because they force us to
consider longer-range consequences of proposals and to factor in both the
past history of human folly and the broad outlines of human behavior as
telling evidence for prospects of the future. I have touched on this kind of
argument by noting that we might imagine that performance drugs were
highly significant factors in athletic achievements rather than marginal or
sometimes even negative ones as they now in fact seem to be. In such
imaginary circumstances, it is probable that our sports would change.
Certainly high-performance sports or professional sports might well come
to seem far different for us as spectators from the everyday variety of sports
that most of us participate in as amateurs. But in many ways, this is already
true. Few of us play basketball or tennis or swim in ways that even our
fantasies can liken to professional or even collegiate athletics. So such
changes are not necessarily ones we need deplore. The range of abilities and
achievements in sports is already enormous and provides niches for us all to
enjoy our various skills and interests.

Furthermore, performances in sports have changed in astonishing ways
over the last century independently of what we now think of as performance
drugs. Training methods, diet, equipment, and above all the selection of the
most gifted potential athletes from larger pools have all contributed to these
changes that are, I suspect, far greater than any we might expect by the use
of performance drugs even in the distant future. In 1900, for example, the
record in the marathon was scarcely under three hours; in 1995 the record
time was 2:06.50. In the mile run, the record at the turn of the century was
4:12.75; today it is 3:44.39.[33] And no one can watch old films of football or
basketball games and suppose that today's players are of the same caliber.
Contrast these changes with Ben Johnson's margin of victory in the 1988

Olympics, one of the best known cases of documented drug use. Johnson ran in 9.79, winning by .13 second to Carl Lewis's second place 9.92, a wide margin for the 100-meter dash, bettering Johnson's world record of 9.83 the summer before. Both records have been denied by world track authorities. In 1995, the world record was considered to be Leroy Burrell's 9.85 (of 1994), only .06 second off Johnson's best time. Assuming no one else used performance drugs in this event, a dubious assumption, Johnson's best is likely to be beaten without drug use in the near future.

But if performance drugs are allowed, what's next? Aren't there further ways in which athletic performance could be enhanced? And are we to tolerate these, too, in the name of personal choice and autonomy on the part of athletes? For example, some years ago someone invented a mechanical device for moving one's legs fast enough to enable one to run at record-breaking speed.[34] We need only recall the fictional "bionic man" of television to imagine more sophisticated aids to physical activity. Such cases seem to challenge our very conception of athletic endeavor. As Robert Simon noted, "If all we are interested in is better and better performance, we could design robots to do it for us."[35] But, of course, what we are interested in is human performance, our own and that of those we watch as spectators, though we can easily imagine interest in android or robot performance, too, just as we acknowledge our interest in competition among other animals in dog and horse racing, for example. But the issue here is the limits of human performance, even the limits of what is to count as human for purposes of sport. So let's consider whether there are some reasonable stopping places on the slippery slope.

One place is the body's own basic boundary, the skin (though it is a porous and partial boundary at best). The differences between sports that are most evident are the differences in equipment and technical aids: the balls, bats, padding, skates, skis, cars, spikes, and other paraphernalia that define different sports, even the other animals who are used sometimes to augment human efforts. Changing the type of equipment in effect changes the identity of the sport. Changing the quality of the equipment also changes the sport, but not its identity, though it complicates efforts to compare performances across such equipment changes and sometimes requires minor changes in the rules. So where the slippery slope involves modifications of equipment, we can easily accept the new technologies as changing the sport.

The problem with performance drugs is that they are integrated into the body's own biosynthetic and metabolic pathways and so are intended to change the performance quality of the athlete, not the circumstances of the sport as defined by its goals, equipment, and rules. Here the slippery slope may yield the more difficult case where the last two possibilities come together, integration into the body of nonbiological technologies. If we condone the use of performance drugs, why not also the use of bionic implants, of artificial bones or organs? Most of the surgery available today for athletes is restorative, repairing the ravages of sports injuries. But not all. Some surgery may enhance performance, allowing greater muscle development or range of movement. And if this were possible on a wider scale, would we consider it, like performance drugs, to be liable to control? Should tissue implants to increase metabolic activity be forbidden? Should surgically improved visual acuity be outlawed? These are the stuff of science fiction for the most part, but we can begin to see the possibility of such procedures.

To some extent, we are at a loss to answer these questions, and not just for sports.[36] Our fears about such changes run deep. Would such procedures be fraught with severe side effects that would make their transient benefits pale by adverse comparison? Do they finally threaten our sense of human identity to a degree that we would find intolerable? Do they hold out the prospects of further divisions among us, not only by wealth, race, and belief, but also by health, talent, and access to biotechnology? I do not have adequate answers to these questions. Even after we satisfy ourselves of the reasonable safety of performance drugs or other performance enhancers (assuming that we could do that), many of these other questions would remain. But they are not limited to the case of sports. These fundamental issues are the spawn of biological technology in general and its possible future impact on our society. It is probably impossible to decide them in advance of the actual development of our knowledge and technology.

8. Personhood

I want now to look at an argument that is reminiscent of one I discussed earlier: the possibility that performance drugs may so affect athletes that their personal identities are threatened. There I looked at the risk that steroids in particular may change one's sexual identity. Here I want to look at a more general argument, that performance drugs, by stressing the physical competence of athletes, detract from their qualities as persons and hence corrupt the ideal of sport as competition among persons.[37] The gist of the argument seems to be that performance drugs somehow provide a physical boost to athletic ability that is totally separate from the personal qualities we often cherish in athletes, such as perseverance, good judgment, sportsmanship, grace under pressure, and a striving for excellence. Sometimes, the argument goes further in stressing that when some athletes use performance drugs, they force others to use them, contrary to their desires and hence can corrupt their autonomy and freedom as persons.

These are serious claims, but are they cogent? Two considerations suggest that they are not. One is that the use of performance drugs is no different in these effects than are other ways that athletes develop their skills and capacities or enhance their competitive performance. The other is that none of these approaches to developing their excellence need undermine the athletes' qualities as persons. Consider the first of these two points. Athletes use a variety of means to improve their skills and extend their capacities to perform in their chosen sports. Training methods and diets are obvious ones, but many other techniques are common including psychological counseling and, above all, practice and competition which can develop mental toughness and tactical acuity. Performance drugs can also be used to promote training and the development of athletic skills. They are never a substitute for the hard work of general athletic preparation, and, if they are useful at all, are helpful in enhancing the effects of that work, not in substituting for it. Living at high altitude promotes the body's production of red blood cells, but it is worth little if training is absent. The same is true in actual performance. Performance drugs do not provide skill, stamina, and knowledge; at most, they give a boost to those already developed.

So far, then, performance drugs seem no more a threat to an athlete's "personhood" than any other technique of training or performance. Little is to be gained by stressing that performance drugs have effects on one's body: that's the point of them, as it is of most athletic training and practice. But it is worth noting that there are few other experiences in life outside of sports where we feel so unified in mind and body, where the distinction between being persons and having bodies seems so fatuous. And nothing, so far as I can see, in the use of performance drugs need threaten the development of those personal qualities that we often value in athletes. If it is true that some performance drugs can alter mood and outlook, then careful study is needed to determine how these can affect one's personality.[38] But pep talks, rivalries, and counseling can also affect mood and attitude, as can the sports themselves, and are indeed relied on to do so as teams and individuals gear up for tough competition. If we are worried about performance drugs affecting moods, then we must also consider other tried and true methods for doing the same thing. Presumably it is only some moods, perhaps aggressive ones, that are said to be objectionable. If so, then much in the way certain sports are played and their players are developed must be changed as well. Performance drugs, like other athletic techniques, work primarily to enhance what is already there.

Again, it is said that athletes are coerced into choosing to use performance drugs, a curious contradictory claim in itself, by the fact that if some competitors use them, others must use them as well in order to compete successfully. But this is surely true of all changes in technique or training or tactics that athletes develop, as I have already noted. No one can introduce a successful change without others adopting it if they wish to compete successfully. We do not usually suggest that this denies athletes their autonomy. If you can't develop a good jump shot, or move to Colorado to train in the mountains, or develop a new tactical ploy, it is not your autonomy or free choice that is threatened. There may be an element of unfairness when the adoption of new techniques depends on wealth or special knowledge. But this may be the case for many features of dynamic and changing sports, not just for the use of performance drugs. The remedy would seem to be openness and research, not banning and secrecy.

9. Consensus

Finally, it is sometimes urged that we should dismiss the contentions involved in many of the arguments discussed here, just agree on what we want to do about performance drugs, and then do it.[39] Whether there is such an agreement or consensus about drugs is of course an empirical matter, but, it is claimed, surely there is a widely accepted, though perhaps inchoate, sense of the ideals of sports, and these can be teased out, much the way linguists have teased out the unconscious rules governing our linguistic competence. This view would be a kind of democratic position, allowing a vote perhaps on whether or not performance drugs should be banned.

The strength of this position lies in its acknowledgment of the degree to which sports are arbitrary—the rules that constrain possible moves, time limits, equipment, scoring, numbers of players, courses, and contact being to a considerable degree artifacts of historical accident and whim. And it seeks to restore a sense of popular control over how our sports are played. But whatever the value of these points of view, the position also has important limits. For one, it isn't at all clear that its empirical premise is even plausible, no matter how difficult it might be to test. There is little reason to suppose that there is a consensus even about broad aspects of sports practices which would constitute an ideal of sport, let alone about specific issues such as using performance drugs. Further, where such a consensus has been present to some degree in the past, its effect has often been to exclude some from participation on grounds such as race or sex that few of us would tolerate, as I have noted.

In any case, surely once we grant the curious arbitrariness of some sports, or at least some aspects of them, it does not follow that all other aspects or changes in the sports are similarly arbitrary. (Many of our sports seem to have originated in their simulation of other human activities having little to do with play, for example, the techniques of war.) Most of the changes that come to be accepted are adopted to make sports more exciting to watch, to increase competitive challenge, or to ensure the relative safety of those participating in them. Sometimes, too, changes are designed to help preserve the identity of a sport across time, though changes in technologies often make this difficult. So far from being capricious or arbitrary, such changes often have a deeper rationale. Indeed, it has been the goal of this paper to examine some of the rationales given for prohibiting performance drugs. And at least some of these rationales seem to touch on more basic ethical principles of personal liberty and of not causing harm. So even if a consensus could be reached, there is no guarantee that it would represent a reasoned or moral ideal.

A more sophisticated variant on this position uses an argument based on the prisoner's dilemma.[40] Here the "prisoners" are athletes who must decide whether or not to use performance drugs (rather than whether or not to confess to a crime and receive a lesser penalty than their fellow prisoners). If one athlete does and the other does not (assuming that the drugs are actually effective), the one wins and the other loses. If both use performance drugs, neither has an advantage; if neither uses them, neither has an advantage. But the argument here assumes that it is better if both do not use performance drugs than if both do, though in either case the competition is balanced. But being unwilling to lose and not wanting to risk competing with someone who uses performance drugs, both competitors end up using them and therefore end up in the (assumed) worst situation rather than the (assumed) best one where no one uses the drugs. Like prisoners who are allowed to communicate and thus coordinate their silence or confession, athletes could, it is argued, find ways to arrive at a consensus about performance drugs (it is assumed it would be negative) and then ask that the consensus be enforced by sports organizations to avoid the consequences of the prisoner's dilemma.

However, independent arguments must be adduced to defend the main assumption of the dilemma matrix, namely that if everyone uses performance drugs, everyone is worse off than if no one uses them. These arguments tend to be the ones we have already considered and found to be lacking in cogency. So the argument from consensus depends on the other arguments to establish that the agreement or consensus should be against using performance drugs. Without these arguments, the prisoner's dilemma matrix only establishes that using performance drugs may be unfair if some athletes use them secretly or illicitly and that mutual use or nonuse would be equally balanced. And this, of course, brings us back to our starting point. We have come full circle.

Our sports have changed over the years. The days of the leisured amateur performing with elegant insouciance seem quaint and puzzling in an age of professionalism and "high-performance" skills driven by commerce and nationalism. There is much to deplore in these changes,[41] but much also to commend. We have seen the end to racism in American sport and positive efforts to resolve the problems of full participation in sports for women. Amateur and school sports flourish as never before. But because sports present so visibly to us a view of what it is to be human (though to be sure in only one of the many ways we understand ourselves), they are a focus of the concerns we have about the impact on human life of modern technologies, especially biomedical technologies. We should not, I believe, either reject or embrace these technologies uncritically, but study and reflect on the way they are changing our lives and our conceptions of who we are. They will continue to change us and our sports. I have argued not so much for the use of performance drugs as for the flourishing in sports of a critical exploration of their use and its impact on how we understand our skills and achievements.[42]

Notes

1. See John M. Hoberman, *Mortal Engines: The Science of Performance and the Dehumanization of Sport* (New York: The Free Press, 1992), and William Morgan's review essay of Hoberman in *Journal of the Philosophy of Sport* XIX (1992): 101–106.
2. See, for example, the study by Daniel Rudman and his colleagues, "Effects of Human Growth Hormone in Men over 60 Years Old." *The New England Journal of Medicine* 323 (July 5, 1990): 1–6.
3. Definitions are myriad, ranging from anything that changes any biological process to synthetic chemicals. The IOC sensibly just lists banned substances, though it fails to keep up with new products. For NCAA and USOC listings, see Allen & Hanburys *Athletic Drug Reference '94,* ed. Robert J. Fuentes, Jack M. Rosenberg, and Art Davis (Durham, N.C.: Clean Data, Inc., 1994).
4. See Thomas H. Murray, "Drugs, Sports, and Ethics." In Thomas H. Murray, Willard Gaylin, and Ruth Macklin, eds., *Feeling Good and Doing Better* (Clifton, N.J.: Humana Press, 1984), pp. 107–126. Ruth Macklin elaborates a bit on Murray's argument in her essay in the same volume, "Drugs, Models, and Moral Principles," pp. 197–200. Similar arguments are developed by Warren P. Fraleigh, "Performance-Enhancing Drugs in Sports: The Ethical

Issue." *Journal of the Philosophy of Sport* XI (1984): 23–29, and by Angela J. Schneider and Robert B. Butcher, "Why Athletes Should Avoid the Use and Seek the Elimination of Performance-Enhancing Substances and Practices from the Olympic Games." *Journal of the Philosophy of Sport* XX–XXI (1993–4): 64–81.

5. See Gary I. Wadler and Brian Hainline, *Drugs and the Athlete* (Philadelphia: F.A. Davis Company, 1989), pp. 61 ff. It may be that steroids are very effective for athletes in some sports and not for others. Football linemen swear by them. But aside from the paucity of hard evidence, the issue is complicated by other factors. Steroids may accelerate training effects, for example, but not facilitate anabolic effects beyond what is possible without them.

6. The impression one gets in reviewing the literature is that both sides are much exaggerated: performance drugs are neither as dangerous nor as effective as their advocates are wont to claim. See the excellent series of reports on "Steroids in Sports," *The New York Times,* November 17–21, 1988.

7. Wadler and Hainline endorse this view (p. 67), though they note the practical problems of carrying it out. Presumably, careful study would also allow for greatly reduced risks of drug use. Perhaps the reason so few athletes are known to have been injured by performance drugs is that they are so often able to solicit professional medical advice.

8. Old standbys like caffeine seem to be somewhat effective and generally harmless, and new techniques like "blood doping" seem relatively effective and, if properly done, also harmless. See Melvin H. Williams, ed., *Ergogenic Aids in Sports* (Champaign, IL: Human Kinetics Publishers, 1983), Chs. 5 and 8. Robert Voy and Kirk D. Deeter, *Drugs, Sport, and Politics* (Champaign, IL: Leisure Press, 1991), pp. 21–23, briefly discuss the difficulties of research in this area.

9. See Voy and Deeter, pp. 20ff.

10. See Wadler and Hainline, p. 4ff.

11. The NCAA collects injury rates for intercollegiate sports in its Injury Surveillance System, a compilation of data voluntarily submitted by member schools. More serious injuries and fatalities are compiled by Frederick O. Mueller and Robert C. Cantu of the National Center for Catastrophic Sports Injury Research, University of North Carolina, Chapel Hill. See their "Eleventh Annual Report: Fall 1982–Spring 1993."

12. See Jonathan Schonsheck, "On Various Hypocrisies of the 'Drugs' in Sports Scandal." *The Philosophical Forum* XX/4 (Summer 1989): 247–285.

13. W.M. Brown, "Paternalism, Drugs, and the Nature of Sports." *Journal of the Philosophy of Sport* XI (1984): 14–22.

14. The Rudman study (see note 2) also warns against assuming that such supplements hold out hope for a general amelioration of the effects of aging.

15. John M. Hoberman and Charles E. Yesalis, "The History of Synthetic Testosterone." *Scientific American* (February 1995), 76–81.

16. One may be surprised to read that blood is a drug, but see H.G. Klein, "Blood Transfusions and Athletics: Games People Play." *New England Journal of Medicine* 312, 854 (1985): "Like other drugs, blood should be given only for medical indications." Quoted by Wadler and Hainline, p. 176.

17. For a good introduction to this issue, see Drew A. Hyland, *Philosophy of Sport* (New York: Paragon House, 1990), Chapter 1.
18. Schonsheck, p. 250.
19. See Schonsheck for a brief discussion of this point, pp. 275–281.
20. Alasdair MacIntyre, *After Virtue,* 2nd ed. (Notre Dame, Ind.: University of Notre Dame Press, 1984), Chapter 14; and Schneider and Butcher, pp. 95–97.
21. MacIntyre, p. 187.
22. As an aside, it may be noted that the association of skill and satisfaction in sports is a fluid one. Many people who scarcely compare to high performance athletes nevertheless take great satisfaction in the exercise of their more limited skills. The satisfactions lie here in improving and comparing skills, not just in having the finest developed ones and outdoing all others.
23. MacIntyre, p. 274.
24. Schneider and Butcher, p. 77.
25. Schneider and Butcher, p. 66.
26. See Hyland's discussion of this issue, pp. 61–63.
27. One individual out of 500 has sex-related genetic anomalies. See Joseph Levine and David Suzuki, *The Secret of Life: Redesigning the Living World* (Boston: WGBH Educational Foundation, 1993), p. 70.
28. Anecdotal evidence suggests that steroids have a greater effect in some sports, for example American football. But it is hard to judge the relative effects of drugs, training, selection, and other factors.
29. There may be other reasons why men and women will continue to find separate sports appropriate and satisfying. If Carol Gilligan and her followers are right, there may be striking differences in the development of moral sensibilities in boys and girls. Perhaps these different approaches to morality carry over to different values in competition and achievement in sports as well. See Carol Gilligan, *In a Different Voice: Psychological Theory and Women's Development* (Cambridge: Harvard University Press, 1982).
30. Levine and Suzuki, Chapter 3, note 4.
31. For example, what would sports be like in a society traditionally dominated by women? Would they not emphasize strength, speed, and size? Would it be difficult for the average man to compete in them? Would men seek to emulate women's sports achievements? (No men seek to compete today on the balance beam, a sport in which women excel.) Perhaps it is with questions like these that the findings of Gilligan and others are most relevant. (See note 29.) On the other hand, it is not clear that in such a society women and men would develop the same characteristics that they tend to in societies like ours.
32. For an excellent discussion of slippery slope arguments, see David Lamb, *Down the Slippery Slope: Arguing in Applied Ethics* (New York: Croom Helm, 1988).
33. The history of the mile run is fascinating. The greatest miler in the nineteenth century, Walter George, ran at least once in 4:10.2 in 1885, shortly before his first professional race in the sport then called pedestrianism; his fastest racing time was 4:12.75 in 1886, a record that was not beaten until Paavo Nurmi ran 4:10.4 in 1923. It was only in the 1930s that Glenn Cunningham and others

began to break the new 4:10 barrier, and in 1954 that Roger Bannister ran the mile in 3:59.4. See Cordner Nelson and Roberto Quercetani, *The Milers* (Los Altos, Calif.: Tafnews Press, 1985).

34. The device was motor driven and used slats attached to the legs to move them at great speed.

35. Robert Simon, "Good Competition and Drug-Enhanced Performance." *Journal of the Philosophy of Sport* XI (1984): 12.

36. See W.M. Brown, "Ability-Enhancing Drugs." In Steven Luper-Foy and Curtis Brown, eds., *Drugs, Morality and the Law* (New York: Garland Publishing, 1994), pp. 113–132, and Robert Simon's reply in the same book, "Better Performance Through Chemistry: The Ethics of Enhancing Ability Through Drugs," pp. 133–150.

37. See Robert Simon, "Good Competition and Drug-Enhanced Performance," p. 12, and "Response to Brown and Fraleich," *Journal of the Philosophy of Sport* XI: 30–32.

38. Interestingly, Peter Kramer argues in *Listening to Prozac* (New York: Viking, 1993) that far from destroying one's personality, some new mood-alternating drugs allow it to be expressed more fully and authentically.

39. See Michael Lavin, "Sports and Drugs: Are the Current Bans Justified?" *Journal of the Philosophy of Sports* XIV (1987): 32–43, and Robert Simon, "Better Performance Through Chemistry . . . ," pp. 134–137.

40. See Schneider and Butcher, pp. 73–74; and Gunter Breivik, "Doping Games: A Game Theoretical Exploration of Doping," *International Review for Sociology of Sport* 27 (1992): 235–252.

41. See, for example, the fine book by William Morgan, *Leftist Theories of Sport: A Critique and Reconstruction* (Urbana and Chicago: University of Illinois Press, 1994).

42. My thanks to my colleagues, Drew Hyland and Maurice Wade, for their challenging criticisms of earlier drafts of this paper.

Bibliography

1. Breivik, G. "Doping Games: A Game Theoretical Exploration of Doping." *International Review for Sociology of Sport* 27 (1992): 235–252.

2. Brown, W.M. "Ability Enhancing Drugs." In Steven Luper-Foy and Curtis Brown, eds., *Drugs, Morality and the Law.* New York: Garland Publishing, 1994, pp. 113–132.

3. ———. "Ethics, Drugs, and Sports." *Journal of the Philosophy of Sport* VII (1980): 15–23.

4. ———. "Paternalism, Drugs, and the Nature of Sports." *Journal of the Philosophy of Sport* XI (1984): 14–22.

5. ———. "Comments on Simon and Fraleigh." *Journal of the Philosophy of Sport* XI (1984): 33–35.

6. ———. "Practices and Prudence." *Journal of the Philosophy of Sport* XVII (1990): 71–84.

7. Fraleigh, Warren P. "Performance-Enhancing Drugs in Sports: The Ethical Issue." *Journal of the Philosophy of Sport* XI (1984): 23–29.
8. Gilligan, Carol. *In a Different Voice: Psychological Theory and Women's Development.* Cambridge: Harvard University Press, 1982.
9. Hoberman, John M. *Mortal Engines: The Science of Performance and the Dehumanization of Sport.* New York: The Free Press, 1992.
10. Hoberman, John M., and Charles E. Yesalis. "The History of Synthetic Testosterone." *Scientific American* (February 1995): 76–81.
11. Hyland, Drew A. *Philosophy of Sport.* New York: Paragon House, 1990.
12. Kramer, Peter D. *Listening to Prozac.* New York: Viking, 1993.
13. Lamb, David. *Down the Slippery Slope: Arguing in Applied Ethics.* New York: Croom Helm, 1988.
14. Lavin, Michael. "Sports and Drugs: Are the Current Bans Justified?" *Journal of the Philosophy of Sport* XIV (1987): 34–43.
15. Levine, Joseph, and David Suzuki. *The Secret of Life: Redesigning the Living World.* Boston: WGBH Educational Foundation, 1993.
16. Luper-Foy, Steven, and Curtis Brown, eds. *Drugs, Morality and the Law.* New York: Garland Publishing, 1994.
17. MacIntyre, Alasdair. *After Virtue,* 2nd ed. Notre Dame, Ind.: University of Notre Dame Press, 1984.
18. Macklin, Ruth. "Drugs, Models, and Moral Principles." In Thomas H. Murray, Willard Gaylin and Ruth Macklin, eds., *Feeling Good and Doing Better: Ethics and Nontherapeutic Drug Use.* Clifton, N.J.: Humana Press, 1984, pp. 187–213.
19. Morgan, William J. *Leftist Theories of Sport: A Critique and Reconstruction.* Urbana and Chicago: University of Illinois Press, 1994.
20. Mueller, Frederick O., and Robert C. Cantu. *Eleventh Annual Report: Fall 1982–Spring 1993.* Chapel Hill, N.C.: National Center for Catastrophic Sports Injury Research, 1994.
21. Murray, Thomas H. "Drugs, Sports, and Ethics." In Thomas H. Murray, Willard Gaylin and Ruth Macklin, eds., *Feeling Good and Doing Better: Ethics and Nontherapeutic Drug Use.* Clifton, N.J.: Humana Press, 1984, pp. 107–126.
22. Murray, Thomas H., Willard Gaylin and Ruth Macklin, eds. *Feeling Good and Doing Better: Ethics and Nontherapeutic Drug Use.* Clifton, N.J.: Humana Press, 1984.
23. Nelson, Cordner and Roberto Quercetan. *The Milers.* Los Altos, Calif.: Tafnews Press, 1985.
24. Schneider, Angela J., and Robert B. Butcher. "Why Athletes Should Avoid the Use and Seek the Elimination of Performance-Enhancing Substances and Practices from the Olympic Games." *Journal of the Philosophy of Sport* XX–XXI (1993–4): 64–81.
25. Schonsheck, Jonathan. "On Various Hypocrisies of the 'Drugs' in Sports Scandal." *The Philosophical Forum* XX/4 (Summer 1989): 247–285.

26. Simon, Robert L. "Better Performance Through Chemistry: The Ethics of Enhancing Ability Through Drugs." In Steven Luper-Foy and Curtis Brown, eds., *Drugs, Morality, and the Law.* New York: Garland Publishing, 1994, pp. 133–150.

27. Simon, Robert L. "Good Competition and Drug-Enhanced Performance." *Journal of the Philosophy of Sport* XI (1984): 6–13.

28. Simon, Robert L. "Response to Brown and Fraleigh." *Journal of the Philosophy of Sport* XI (1984): 30–32.

29. "Steroids in Sports." *The New York Times* (November 17–21, 1988), pp. 1, et seq.

30. Voy, Robert, and Kirk D. Deeter. *Drugs, Sport, and Politics.* Champaign, Ill.: Leisure Press, 1991.

31. Wadler, Gary I., and Brian Hainline. *Drugs and the Athlete.* Philadelphia: F.A. Davis Company, 1989.

32. Williams, Melvin H., ed. *Ergogenic Aids in Sport.* Champaign, Ill.: Human Kinetics Publishers, 1983.

11

CHAPTER

Sports and Drugs: Are the Current Bans Justified?

Michael Lavin

This paper explores some rationales for regulating drug use by athletes in order to determine what lessons the current drug crisis may have for philosophers of sport. I will proceed as follows. First, I distinguish between three classes of drugs in order to argue that only drugs in two of these classes raise special issues for sports. Second, I argue against some widely accepted distinctions regarding drugs, but argue that even if those distinctions are rejected it is still reasonable to be concerned about substances that give a player an edge or those which Robert Simon has called "paradigm" drugs.[1] Third, I discuss how edge-giving substances do raise issues of concern for philosophers of sport. I relate these issues to some arguments in favor of regulating, and even prohibiting, the use of certain substances by athletes. Finally, I reject those arguments, but conclude by offering a different kind of argument for regulation. My positive position strives to show that the failure of standard arguments for substance regulation does not force one to adopt the substance libertarianism of W.M. Brown (1, 2), even if one also rejects Robert Simon's contention (6) that regulation of substances may be justified in terms of *the* ideal of competitive sport.

Reprinted, by permission, from Michael Lavin, 1987, "Sports and drugs: Are the current bans justified?," *Journal of the Philosophy of Sport, XIV:* 34-43.

To think clearly about drugs in sports, it is wise to distinguish three classes of drugs: (a) recreational drugs, (b) restorative drugs, and (c) additive drugs. Examples are perhaps the easiest way to grasp the differences between these three classes. Recreational drugs are drugs such as alcohol, cocaine, heroin, marijuana, and a host of other street drugs. Typically, recreational drugs are taken without medical supervision, and many are illegal. Restorative drugs, by contrast, are drugs such as aspirin and antihypertensive medications. These typically permit people suffering from a medical disorder to approximate their normal functioning. Additive drugs, such as anabolic steroids, are the third class of drugs. These drugs let users reach performance levels exceeding what they might otherwise reach when healthy.

Once one keeps these intuitive distinctions in mind, it should be relatively easy to see that recreational drugs pose no special problems for philosophers of sport, who presumably care about issues relating to sport itself or men and women qua athletes. But athletes abusing recreational drugs do not use these drugs to further their careers qua athletes any more than drug-abusing certified public accountants do. Recreational drug abuse may be a national tragedy; it is not peculiar to sports. So, it is of no special concern for the philosopher of sport.

If drugs raise special issues for the sports philosopher, then the issues relate to the use of restorative and additive drugs. It at least seems that real issues are lurking here. Athletes, far more than other people, have incentives to keep their bodies functioning at peak levels. For professional athletes, their very livelihood depends on being at their best. So, let me further investigate restorative and additive drugs.

Despite what conventional wisdom might think, in practice distinguishing restoratives from additives and drugs from nondrugs proves difficult. Consider these four items:

Item 1—The International Olympic Committee (IOC) stripped Rick Demont of his 1972 Gold Medal in the 1500-meter Freestyle for swimming while under the influence of Marax, an antiasthma medication containing ephedrine. Ephedrine is a stimulant proscribed on the IOC's "dope list."

Item 2—Bill Walton, formerly a star for the Portland Trailblazers, sued the team on the grounds that its doctor concealed the hazards of playing on a fractured foot. The doctor, evidentally complying with management's preference, prescribed analgesics. Walton's foot was further damaged.

Item 3—A scandal occurred at Vanderbilt University when informed sources alleged that some players on the football team were using anabolic steroids in conjunction with their strength training.

Item 4—Italian distance runners participated in the 1986 New York City Marathon though suspected of blood doping. This technique involves reinfusing athletes with their own red blood cells, previously removed and saved for this purpose. Although outlawed by the governing bodies of track, blood doping is presently undetectable.

These items should serve to induce at least a modest skepticism about the basis for distinguishing between (a) restorative and additive drugs and (b) drugs and nondrugs.

To begin with, consider what might be thought of as an obvious difference between restorative and additive drugs: Restorative drugs, unlike additives, do not take athletes beyond their natural potential. Hence, although Marax may seem to be a restorative, it is not, since the stimulant, ephedrine, would permit nonasthmatic athletes to exceed natural peaks. However, if a natural peak is to be the litmus test for distinguishing between restoratives and additives, it should be possible to determine what a natural peak is. The necessity of doing this is most obvious if one is trying to determine whether an unfamiliar drug is a restorative or an additive. For athletes that will be no easy task. Athletes already engage in a multitude of practices specifically designed to take them beyond natural peaks. Nautilus training, high distance mileage, interval training, special diets, vitamin supplements, special equipment, and so on all converge to bring athletes far beyond anything remotely resembling a natural peak. If anything, the purpose of training is to improve what nature has provided.

Worse still, what is an athlete's peak, natural or otherwise? Athletic prowess is susceptible to myriad influences. Weather, time of day, training stage, age, emotional state, and so on vary constantly, but indisputably alter performance. Would one conclude that whenever an addition to an athlete's training program is followed by a peak performance, the addition counts as an additive? In that case far too many devices and drugs would count as additives. Moreover, distinguishing between restorative and additive drugs on the basis of their potential to alter performance for the good seems to lead to other undesirable results. It is indisputable that many restoratives could be used by healthy athletes with advantage. In the final analysis, who knows who might benefit from using a particular drug? In item 2, Walton made use of an analgesic in order to play in a championship match. Without the drug he could not have played at all. Healthy athletes could also use some analgesics to better their performance. After all, a common limiting condition on peak performance is pain.

Of course other proposals might successfully distinguish between restoratives and additives. For example, many people might not object to additives per se but to additives whose collateral effects are dangerous—without there being compensatory health benefits for the user. Hence restoratives do improve the health of an unhealthy athlete but do not improve the health of a healthy athlete. Additives of special interest to sports regulators would be those that place users at uncompensated health risk. Unfortunately, the notion of a health risk, as opposed to a nonhealth risk, is far from clear. Walton's use of analgesics made him more susceptible to injury, not less. In fact, it is safer for a noninjured player to play on painkillers than for an injured player to do so. The healthy player has no injury to aggravate. So the present proposal would yield the result that analgesics are additives when they are clearly restoratives. In the end, as Norman Fost (5) has noted, it is probably difficult to sustain a sharp distinction between restoratives and additives for superathletes.

Item 4 raises issues of a slightly different sort. Can drugs be distinguished from nondrugs? If blood counts as a drug, what does not? Attempts to make out a principled distinction do not inspire confidence. The federal Food and Drug Administration (FDA), which presumably has a passionate interest in the subject, opines that drugs are "articles (other than food) intended to affect the structure or any function of the body." Foods, one learns, are "articles used for food."[2] I presume articles other than drugs.

The FDA proposal has one feature easily overlooked. Drugs are identified not in terms of chemistry but in terms of intended effects. Specifying the chemistry of a substance will not enable one to distinguish drugs from foods. In practice, the FDA often has to list drugs. The current boom in designer drugs illustrates the difficulty. Drug peddlers produce a substance not on the FDA's list of controlled substances. The FDA then has to rush to get the new substance placed on the list. All of this suggests, but does not establish, that "drug" is a normative term used to identify what people buy from their pushers rather than their pharmacists, a term most likely to be used colloquially when one disapproves of a substance's effect. Simon (6), who defends regulating some drugs, is alert to this difficulty. He proposes to minimize it by limiting his attention to what he calls paradigm case drugs.[3] Although I believe it would be beneficial to stop talking about the regulation of drugs in sport and to start talking about what ought and ought not be regulated substances in sport, I doubt whether it ultimately matters whether one sides with me or with Simon on the seriousness of the definitional difficulty. Regulators in either case would have to keep in mind that there is no universally agreed upon objective criteria for identifying drugs and only drugs.

For Simon or me, the right question to ask is whether the traditional prohibitions against the use of substances such as anabolic steroids, amphetamines, and so on, Simon's paradigm drugs, are defensible. I contend that the traditional prohibitions are defensible, but not for either the traditional reasons or quite for Simon's reason.

Conventional wisdom recognizes a set of fairly common rationales as underwriting regulation of certain edge-giving substances in sport. Although other rationales certainly exist, the following are archetypical.

1. The argument from fairness: the substance gives the user an unfair advantage.
2. The argument from danger: the substance endangers the user to an undue degree.
3. The argument from coercion: the substance, if its use were permitted, would force athletes to use a dangerous substance that they would otherwise not genuinely wish to use.

These rationales are the common ones and are often jointly employed. They capture, I think, first-try justificatory defenses of traditional substance regulations in sport. Once the distinctions between drug and nondrug and restorative and additive substances are blurred, however, these rationales are far from compelling.[4]

The argument from fairness objects to the use of certain substances on the grounds that users secure an unfair advantage, and fails because it explains nothing. When athletes avail themselves of means that rules prohibit, they do act unfairly. Nobody doubts that. But the present demand is for a compelling rationale for making the use of certain substances against the rules in the first place. It is beside the point to say that use is against this or that nonconstitutive rule, for it is just such rules for which justifications are being requested. When people claim that using a particular drug is unfair, if they do not mean that its use is against the rules, they probably mean that it is either unnatural or secures players an advantage at grave risk to themselves or, ultimately, coerces others into taking those same risks.

I have already indicated above the appropriate reply to the claim that advantages secured by use of traditionally banned substances is unnatural. Many "unnatural" practices mark the athlete's regimen. It boggles the mind to believe that the routines or diet of a runner for Athletics West or a tackle for the Los Angeles Raiders is natural. In any case, the response leaves it a mystery as to why only some unnatural substances are banned. But the remaining two objections, which focus on dangers to the players, amount to the arguments from danger and coercion. I will now argue that they do not provide compelling rationales for current bans either.

Athletes striving for excellence incur health risks. High mileage jeopardizes the distance runner's knees. Sumo wrestlers become obese. Modern training regimens often keep players on the edge of injury. The phenomenon is an accepted part of athletic life. Traditional bans on drugs are, to be sure, often offered out of paternalistic concern. Sports regulators wish to protect athletes from undue risks. But serious reflection on the risks that regulators permit a player to run strongly suggests that risk alone does not select the present prohibitions and only the present prohibitions. Consider football. Players vary considerably in size and weight. These disparities, as many quarterbacks discover, can cause serious injuries. In principle, risks could be considerably reduced by placing size and weight limitations on players. That is not done. Now it might reasonably be claimed that most sports do not specify any limitations on who may or may not play in their constitutive rules. Competition is open to all. Suppose one accepts that. The principles for regulating what substances a player may ingest or inject are still difficult to justify if the justification is player safety.

As previously mentioned, players routinely resort to analgesics and anti-inflammatories, even though using them to play puts players at far higher risk than nonuse would. After all, without medicine's helping hand, in many cases the player could not play at all, which would indeed be the safest policy. To this the response may be made that it is up to the player to decide whether to play injured. But if that is the response, it does not explain why players are allowed to determine what risks they wish to run in that case, but not, say, in the training case. A straightforward response would be that permitting players to make the latter judgment would force others, out of a desire to remain competitive, to resort to using whatever means, however dangerous, as are necessary to remain competitive. Although similar considerations might appear to apply to the use of painkillers during a match, the fact that matches are the goal of training justifies permitting players to run extraordinary risks. If that is so, then the present objection amounts to the third rationale for prohibition.

Ordinarily, philosophers who offer the arguments from danger and coercion do so on paternalistic grounds. W.M. Brown (2), for example, seems to think that substance control involves weak paternalism in Dworkin's sense (4), and hence requires that a judgment be defended that adult players are unfit to judge their own good. However, Brown overlooks that Dworkin himself recognizes that not all apparently paternalistic practices are paternalistic. Players themselves may have a collective interest in securing freedom from certain risks. To do this, players might have to relinquish the use of something they would gladly forego if they were confident that most everybody else would also relinquish its use. Hence football linemen might prefer to stop using anabolic steroids if they had assurance that their competitors would likewise abstain. But even if that is so, the resulting prohibitions would presumably not coincide with the traditional list of banned substances. When one remembers the amount of money involved in professional sports, it should be clear that the amount of risk that is rational for athletes to endure will depend, in large measure, on their pay.

Consequently, there would be considerable disagreement about which substances to ban as one moves from one sport to another. But that is not the case. Prohibited substances tend to be the same for all sports. I should add that many athletes might prefer not to stop using even highly dangerous substances for a simple reason: namely, their ability to participate in the sport at all depends on their use, say, of hormones and what not. And if some athletes win their advantage by running the risks of extra training, why may not others win them by ingesting or injecting what they want? It will not do to claim, yet again, that extra training is unnatural. An American athlete undoubtedly owes many of his advantages over thirdworld athletes to diet and even nutritional advice that may put him at risk. Body builders have long known this. Is there then no rationale for the current prohibitions? I believe there is. My solution builds on a suggestion of Robert Simon (6) but does not depend, as Simon's solution does, on spelling out the details of a particular ideal of competitive sport.

In one way or another, the previous rationales for banning certain substances in drugs focus on morally objectionable properties that those substances, unlike other substances, are alleged to have. The root idea seems to be that certain prohibitions on substance use are morally required. Not surprisingly, it has turned out to be very difficult indeed to justify prohibitions along these lines. Entirely too many substances, not to mention activities, have the relevantly objectionable properties. Simon (6) tries to avert this difficulty by proposing to segregate appropriately regulated substances in terms of the ideal of competitive sport. As Simon has it, sports involve a mutual quest for excellence on the part of the competitors. He sees this as an attempt to bring out the best in a *person*. Drugs circumvent this ideal by showing only whose body responded best to performance enhancers.[5]

W.M. Brown (3: pp. 33-34) has offered the obvious, and to my mind correct, objection to Simon's account. No account of the ideal of sport has good enough credentials to do the work Simon wants it to do. There is, though, an alternative route to prohibitions. It is mindful of Simon's suggestion to segregate objectionable substances in terms of the ideal of sports, but accepts Brown's charge that no current ideal has good enough credentials. The alternative begins by recognizing the permissibility of imposing certain prohibitions. Consider, to take one instance, the length of baseball bats. Nobody could credibly claim that it is impermissible to limit the kinds of bats players use. Granted, that is an example involving a nonconstitutive rule of a particular game.

All the same, there is no reason to suppose that governing bodies of sport might not concur in what substances athletes may use. It is even relatively easy to discern a principle at work as soon as one forgets the traditional rationales. Prohibitions on what substances players may use typically do concern substances whose use endangers players or puts them at what most perceive, rightly or wrongly, to be an unfair advantage. But one further feature is involved. Prohibited substances share the property of being commonly, or at least publicly, disapproved. Other substances may very well be just as dangerous as forbidden substances but fail to meet the test of pervasive disapproval. Nobody seriously maintains that playing on painkillers is a boon for players. It does endanger them. Still, there is very little agreement on the permissibility of regulating the use of analgesics. If there were agreement, then regulations could, I claim, be justified.

As I would want to put it, something approximating democracy operates to justify prohibitions. However, what might *explain* why certain substances become subject to democratic regulation and prohibition while others do not? It is implausible, for example, to suppose that prohibitions on the use of caffeine by track athletes reflect a puritan abhorrence for coffee, tea, or Coke.

I propose that some core set of ideals of sport covertly operates to favor the adoption of certain prohibitions rather than others. Current prohibitions, then, do not capture a timeless ideal of sport. Nevertheless, they are explained, at least in part, if viewed as the product of covert, but quite commonly held, ideals of sport. Since those ideals may change, so may what is regulated. One might say that regulation is a democratic attempt to enforce and perpetuate widely accepted ideals. Insofar as the fostering of widely accepted and morally permissible ideals is defensible, the regulation and even prohibition of certain substances is also defensible. Hence, there being no one ideal of sport does not lead to Brown's pharmacological libertarianism. I believe Simon was on the right track, but his approach is needlessly ambitious if the goal is justifying the current prohibitions.

Some philosophers will undoubtedly have a patrician disdain for my proposal. After all, democracy poisoned Socrates, segregated schools, and prefers Rock to Bach. And so it is that no sane person equates what ought to be with what most people want. Accordingly, I might be asked to make assurances that my reliance on consensus does not pander to irrational aversions against the use of drugs. For consensus to justify an interference in the means athletes use to achieve their ends, the objection continues, it must be supplemented with good argument. However, since the arguments typically advanced to support drug regulation in sport are embarrassingly inadequate, my opponents might wonder what moral force the existence of a consensus without good arguments as a bodyguard can have.[6]

There is a sense in which I cannot give a fully satisfying response to this plea for good reasons. Let me suppose, though, for the sake of argument, that there would be a consensus on the desirability of regulating some subset of currently regulated substances. If there is no consensus, then my suggestion cannot serve to justify regulation. But given a consensus, I claim that its best explanation would refer to an unconsciously grasped ideal of competitive sport. It would of course require empirical investigation to determine the core content of the currently prevailing ideal or ideals. An example or two may help to get across what I have in mind.

In their own native tongue, people seldom have difficulty distinguishing grammatically correct from incorrect sentences. But few can articulate the rules employed to distinguish the one from the other. All the same, linguists such as Chomsky have demonstrated the fruitfulness of explaining linguistic competence with internalized rules. Similar strategies may help to explain moral competence. Americans, for example, tend to exhibit considerable agreement on what is right and wrong. It may be useful to try to explain such agreement on the basis of their having internalized many of the same moral rules. Of course, as in the case of grammar, it will often be difficult for those who have internalized such rules to articulate them. Take an example: My students invariably think it wrong to sell huge whole-life policies to the retarded, but have trouble offering good arguments against the practice. Nevertheless they remain (to my mind, rightly) attached to their judgment even after I point out how bad their arguments for it are.

Now to return to the ideals of competitive sport, I conjecture that (a) there is a core of current ideals of competitive sport, (b) it will help explain the consensus on what substances to regulate, and (c) discovering it will reveal the ends in terms of which it is possible to develop good arguments justifying the regulatory consensus. That is my hypothesis.

To assess its plausibility, it is essential to keep one previously made claim in mind. Earlier I argued that the imposition of regulation on substance use may be no more than morally permissible rather than morally required. That that is so does complicate my argument. How? Suppose that research reveals a consensus on what substances are appropriate for regulation. Suppose further that investigation has identified a set of ideals of sport in terms of which substance regulations are justifiable. It is important to notice that my proposal does not require regulation of all similarly damaging substances. Rather, regulation *furthers* achieving the end of realizing the current ideals of competitive sport. And since it is unreasonable to expect that every morally permissible and effective means to an end must be adopted, the beginning of an explanation as to why similar substances do not have to receive the same regulatory treatment is at hand, namely, these regulations secure the end well enough. Only controversial principles that mandate adopting all the most efficacious, morally permissible means to an end would require regulation of all relevantly similar substances.

The situation might be compared to setting a college's curriculum. Although I am sure it would be mad to maintain that my university's general education requirements are the very best means for achieving the ideal of an educated citizen (students will not, alas, fail the republic if they no longer have to take Philosophy 1511 or college algebra), I maintain that universities may impose requirements that reasonably work to secure that ideal. If a current ideal of competitive sports exists, it could serve to justify regulation in much the same way that the ideal of an educated citizen serves to justify a university's general education requirements. The ideal rationalizes, without mandating, specific regulations or requirements.

At this point the importance of having a consensus on what substances to regulate in sports may be clearer. For without a consensus, individuals and groups subject to regulation will tend to view it as a capricious imposition of values alien to them. Unfortunately, I do not know how to specify what is required to establish that a consensus exists, but three features seem important.

First, consensus should involve widespread and shared opinions of diverse interest groups. It will not do to let owners, players, the IOC, fans, the NCAA, and so on singularly proclaim a consensus. A consensus should, then, invoke a pervasive opinion. Widespread disregard of a regulation, when combined with frequent criticism of it, is surely an excellent sign that a consensus is lacking. Second, as it becomes clearer what the current ideals of competitive sports are, the use of substances targeted for regulation should evoke a visceral dislike. An almost instinctive and pervasive dislike of a substance may be taken as a fallible indicator that its use does run contrary to the current ideal. Third, regulation should respect history. Generally there will be scant support for the regulation of longstanding practices. Democratic regulation requires that regulation be mindful of a sport's history. Regulations indifferent to history threaten to undermine regulatory authority. Regulators will be perceived as unmindful of what competition in that sport requires. Longstanding practices become, as it were, natural. These practices tend to become the context in which athletes pursue excellence in their chosen sports. But of course opinion can change with time on the desirability of continuing a practice. In the absence of these three features of consensus, disillusionment with regulations will probably arise. Such disillusionment, in turn, will tend to express itself in abuse.

My discussion of ideals of competitive sport has assumed that these ideals do not involve morally impermissible ends. It seems reasonably safe to say that the ends are at least morally innocuous, being ends that some agents might wish to adopt. Consequently the only obvious objection to these ends must, I think, consist in saying that it is objectionable to impose them on all athletes. The insistence on a deep consensus is meant to meet this objection. What is more, it should be remembered that participation in professional and amateur sports is *voluntary* participation in a group activity. Those who do not share the core ideals of the group need not participate.

Still, one might grant that athletes should respect the prevailing ideals, but that they should be free to select the means for attaining those ideals. That claim, though, requires justification. Groups routinely set limitations on what means participants may employ for attaining a group end. So long as this is done democratically, it needs to be shown that such limitations are morally impermissible. This is especially so when no regulation would make the end less well achieved. If a group's end is to limit pollution, it may be necessary to specify what forms of polluting are permissible; otherwise, a failure to coordinate may result in a failure to achieve the end at all. Regulating substance choice by athletes, when in the pursuit of the current ideal of competitive sport, may make coordination possible. If it does, then the objection against restricting means has misfired.

This paper set out to identify drug issues of special interest to sports philosophers. To a large extent, the results have been negative. Recreational drug use poses no special issues. The common distinction between restorative and additive drugs, and for that matter between drugs and nondrugs, does not aid sports philosophers if they wish to justify regulating substances. And so it goes. But despite these negative results, justification is possible. Consensus often can do the work of reason. Sports philosophers do have a special interest in understanding the regulatory practices of sports bodies. Consensus, I believe, permits understanding in areas where that possibility seemed bleak. And although some philosophers may suspect that my proposal will be stillborn, I hope I have given reasons for rejecting that diagnosis. So, perhaps, regulating substances can be justified.

Notes

I wish to thank K.V. Meier and three anonymous referees for many helpful suggestions.
1. Simon (6: p. 7) believes that these drugs (a) increase the probability of superior performance, (b) put users at significant risk, and/or (c) are not prescribed for an illness or injury.
2. Cited in Fost (5: p. 6).
3. See Note 1 for what Simon takes the characteristic features of these drugs to be.

4. In fact writers less skeptical of those distinctions than I have rejected these rationales. See, for example, W.M. Brown (1) and Robert Simon (6). They differ over the appropriate response to the failure of the common rationales. Brown draws the skeptical conclusion. Simon seems to want to use an ideal of competitive sport to select out a class of unfair, coercive, or dangerous substances as appropriately subject to regulation or prohibition.

5. It should, in view of the arguments offered in this paper, be clear that Simon will have to put heavy stress on the possibility of distinguishing restoratives from additive substances. But even if he intends, as he does, to limit his concern to relatively uncontroversial instances of "restoratives," his regulatory justification is still open to the objections discussed above.

6. I am indebted to an anonymous referee for pressing me to respond to some variant of this argument.

Bibliography

1. Brown, W.M. "Drugs, Ethics, and Sport." *Journal of the Philosophy of Sport,* VII (1980), 15-23.

2. Brown, W.M. "Paternalism, Drugs, and the Nature of Sports." *Journal of the Philosophy of Sport,* XI (1984), 14-22.

3. Brown, W.M. "Comments on Simon and Fraleigh." *Journal of the Philosophy of Sport,* XI (1984), 33-35.

4. Dworkin, G. "Paternalism." *The Monist,* 56 (1972), 64-84.

5. Fost, N. "Banning Drugs in Sports: A Skeptical View." *The Hastings Center Report,* 16 (1986), n.4, 5-10.

6. Simon, R.L. "Good Competition and Drug-Enhanced Performance." *Journal of the Philosophy of Sport,* XI (1984), 6-13.

12

CHAPTER

Drug Testing of College Athletes: The Issues

Richard R. Albrecht, William A. Anderson, and Douglas B. McKeag

In the early morning hours of June 19, 1986, arguably the best college basketball player in the United States—Len Bias—was found dead on the floor of his University of Maryland dormitory room. It was later determined that Bias' death resulted from cardiorespiratory arrest brought about by the use of "crack" cocaine (McCallum 1986). A genuine desire to prevent this type of tragedy and the economic need to preserve the appearance of fair and equitable competition provided the members of the National Collegiate Athletic Association (NCAA) with the impetus to "develop an ongoing programme of drug testing to identify those students involved in intercollegiate athletic competition who have used either controlled or allegedly performance enhancing drugs" (NCAA 1984). Subsequently, with the passage of Proposal 30 at its 1986 convention, the NCAA initiated a drug testing programme at championships and certified postseason football games.

Over the past 6 years, the NCAA has subjected thousands of its student-athletes to screening for performance enhancing and social drug use. The casual observer may, therefore, mistakenly conclude that controversial issues plaguing the early days of drug testing have been resolved. This

Reprinted, by permission, from R.R. Albrecht, W.A. Anderson, and D.B. McKeag, 1992, "Drug testing of college athletes: The issues," Sports Medicine 14 (6): 349-352.

commentary discusses critical issues which, in our view, remain unan-
swered in the drug testing of college athletes. Some issues, such as the legal
defensibility of various drug testing procedures (Beresford 1989; Curran
1987; Meloch 1987) and the laboratory methodologies available (Wadler &
Hainline 1989), have been adequately addressed elsewhere. Therefore, we
focus specifically on issues that have been less frequently, if ever, examined.
A single question serves as both the beginning and the end point of our
discussion: should institutions of higher education, individually or collectively, involve themselves in the drug testing of college athletes?

1. Is It Morally Wrong for Athletes to Use Ergogenic Drugs?

Many of us need a morning jolt of caffeine and/or nicotine to do our jobs
properly. Actors and public speakers routinely enhance performance by
using drugs to ward off the negative effects of stage fright. Despite a society-
wide reliance on drugs to improve performance, it is frequently suggested
that when athletes use performance enhancing drugs, it somehow "distorts
and corrupts" the competitive process (Murray 1986; Vernacchia 1990; Will
1985). This view conveniently overlooks the fact that "high-tech sport has
redefined the concept of fair play" (Vernacchia 1990). Today's "techno-
athlete" cannot compete unless supplied with a variety of performance
enhancers. Only if provided with, for example, state-of-the-art equipment,
facilities, coaches, trainers, physicians, surgeons, nutritionists, biomechanists,
physiologists, and psychologists can elite athletes perform their best.
Performances considered natural are often aided by sophisticated computer
analyses, vitamin and mineral supplements, and elaborate biofeedback
laboratories. To argue that only performance enhancing drugs corrupt and
distort competition is hypocritical. It is not the ergogenicity of a drug *per se*
that concerns us, but rather, that athletes may feel compelled to use drugs
which have been shown to compromise the user's physical and psychological well-being.

2. Can a Drug Testing Programme Ensure "Fair and Equitable" Athletic Competition?

Advocating drug testing to ensure "fair and equitable" competition is
grossly misleading. The fact is, we do not (and probably never will) have the

ability to detect the presence of many potential performance enhancing substances (Taylor 1988; Yesalis 1990). Even if a means of detection existed, it would be impossible to screen for every substance theoretically capable of improving athletic performance. Some drugs, such as anabolic steroids, are used to enhance training capacity and, therefore, need not be present at the time of performance. Competitors can reap the ergogenic benefits of the drug yet "cleanse" their urine well in advance of performance related testing. In addition, simply testing for ergogenic drugs is not sufficient. Many substances can be taken to mask the presence of performance enhancing drugs. Testing to ensure fair and equitable competition would require the development of accurate screening techniques for all possible performance enhancing drugs (and their respective masking agents) and mandatory, unannounced, random, year-round testing of athletes. Obviously, drug testing can hardly be viewed as a means of ensuring fair and equitable athletic competition.

3. What Is the Rationale for Testing Student-Athletes for Social Drug Use?

Even if we accept the proposition that the athletic community has a compelling interest in testing athletes for performance enhancing drugs, what is the basis for subjecting this specific segment of the college population to testing for "social" drug use? Epidemiological data fail to support the contention that college student-athletes are more "at risk" of using social drugs than their nonathlete peers (Toohey 1978; Toohey & Corder 1981). Recent studies (Anderson & McKeag 1985; Anderson et al. 1991; Nattiv & Puffer 1991) have found the opposite—student-athletes use social drugs less than their nonathlete peers. To argue such testing is designed to protect the health of the student-athlete is to imply that student-athletes deserve a higher standard of health care than their nonathlete peers. In addition, if our real concern was the health and welfare of the student-athlete, we would test for the most health-compromising drugs of all—tobacco and alcohol. Instead, many athletic events are directly and indirectly subsidised by the advertisement, sale, and consumption of alcohol. Finally, some may believe that athletes must be tested for social drug use because they serve as role models for our youth. Although there is little doubt college athletes are idolised by many, what justifies subjecting them to drug testing while drug use among their peers, for example, aspiring musicians, movie stars, politicians, police officers, scientists, physicians, lawyers, poets, professors, religious leaders, is ignored?

4. Are Student-Athletes Giving Their Free and Informed Consent to Be Tested?

By its very definition, consent must be given freely and on the basis of complete and accurate information. Despite this, the official NCAA position remains: "Failure to complete and sign the [drug testing consent] statement . . . shall result in the student-athlete's ineligibility for participation in all intercollegiate competition" (NCAA 1986). Simply stated, athletes refusing to consent to drug testing are automatically banned from athletic participation. More importantly, they are forced to surrender their athletic scholarships. This issue is critical considering the inordinate number of athletes from educationally and economically disadvantaged backgrounds. For many, access to higher education is contingent upon receipt of the athletic scholarship. In these cases, refusal to consent to drug testing is tantamount to depriving themselves of the only means of escaping a lifetime of poverty and hardship. The serious consequences associated with the refusal to "consent" indicate that, for many student-athletes, consent is obtained through coercion. A second consent-related issue involves whether or not the consent forms are signed with a full understanding of the testing protocol. Our research has shown that 37% of athletes attending institutions which have initiated a drug testing programme are unaware of the fact they can be subjected to drug testing and approximately 70% cannot identify the testing procedures to which they may be held accountable (Albrecht et al. 1992). Although college athletes are consenting to be tested, questions remain as to whether this consent is freely obtained and fully informed.

5. Is It Realistic to Believe Positive Test Results Can Be Kept Confidential?

When college athletes "consent" to drug testing, they do so with the stipulation that results of these tests are confidential and will be disclosed "only to authorized representatives of the institution, its athletic conference (if any) and the NCAA" (Buckley Amendment: National Collegiate Athletic Association Student-Athlete Statement). In practice, however, such assurances become little more than "legal fictions." Disqualifying a high profile athlete from a championship event makes confidentiality impossible. Wadler and Hainline (1989) have even compiled a list of athletes who have, among other things, failed drug tests. Problems in keeping the results of positive drug tests confidential may also be exacerbated when individuals in positions of responsibility such as Robert O. Voy, former Chief Medical Officer and Director of Sport Sciences for the United States Olympic Committee, publicly state: "We have to expose those who cheat. If an athlete has cheated the process, we need to make that public" (Cowart 1989). We need only consider the extensive media coverage of previous positive tests to realise that it is impossible to keep the results of athletes' drug tests confidential.

6. Do a Few Positive Test Results Justify the Expenses of Testing?

In its first year of drug testing, the NCAA spent approximately $1 million to test 3500 of its student-athletes. This considerable expenditure resulted in 2.5% of the athletes testing positive for a banned substance (Wadler & Hainline 1989). The following year, only 12 NCAA athletes tested positive for drug use (Cowart 1988). In 1990, the NCAA budgeted between $1.6 and $3.2 million to cover the cost of its drug testing programmes (Yesalis 1990). When the sizable legal fees the NCAA has paid to stave off a number of constitutional challenges to its drug testing programme (Cowart 1988) are added, the cost of drug testing college athletes is staggering. It may be argued, by some, that the fact so few athletes test positive is evidence that testing is serving its intended purpose as a deterrent to drug use. Although deterrence is one explanation for the small number of athletes testing positive, deception is another. Without significant technological advances and mandatory, unannounced, random, year-round testing, it is impossible to make this differentiation. The small number of athletes testing positive for drug use raises questions as to whether comprehensive drug testing constitutes the best way to allocate resources to reduce drug use among college athletes.

7. Conclusion

We have suggested that it is: hypocritical to imply that only drugs, among all categories of ergogenic aids, are a threat to "natural" competition; impossible for drug testing to ensure fair and equal athletic competition; illogical and inconsistent with empirical evidence to test college athletes for social drug use; unethical to coerce athletes to consent to drug testing; unrealistic to believe the results of positive drug tests will remain confidential; and inefficient to spend millions of dollars each year to detect a handful of positive results. This being the case, why do NCAA member institutions continue testing athletes for drug use? For one thing, drug testing provides the illusion of fair and equitable competition—an illusion that must be maintained if existing economic interests are to prosper. In addition, once we concede that drug testing is the solution, we have concluded that drug use is the problem rather than a symptom of larger, more systemic imbalance. As a result, drug testing keeps us from asking thorny questions about the overemphasis placed on winning and an excessive reward structure that fosters a "win at all costs" philosophy (Yesalis 1990)—even if those costs include an athlete's physical and psychological health.

References

1. Albrecht RR, Anderson WA, McGrew CA, McKeag DB, Hough DO. NCAA institutionally based drug testing: do our athletes know the rules of this game? *Medicine and Science in Sports and Exercise* 24: 242–246, 1992.
2. Anderson WA, Albrecht RR, McKeag DB, Hough DO, McGrew CA. A national survey of alcohol and drug use by college athletes. *Physician and Sportsmedicine* 19: 91–104, 1991.
3. Anderson WA, McKeag DB. The substance use and abuse habits of college student-athletes (Report No. 2). Mission KS: The National Collegiate Athletic Association, 1985.
4. Beresford HR. Legal considerations. In Wadler & Hainline (Eds.), *Drugs and the athlete*, pp. 234–247. F.A. Davis Company, Philadelphia, 1989.
5. Cowart VS. Drug testing programs face snags and legal challenges. *Physician and Sportsmedicine* 16: 165–173, 1988.
6. Cowart VS. Athlete drug testing receiving more attention than ever before in history of competition. *Journal of the American Medical Association* 261: 3510–3511, 3516, 1989.
7. Curran WJ. Compulsory drug testing: the legal barriers. *New England Journal of Medicine* 316: 318, 1987.
8. McCallum J. The cruelest thing ever. *Sports Illustrated* 64 (26): 20–27, 1986.
9. Meloch SL. An analysis of public college athlete drug testing programs through the Unconstitutional Condition Doctrine of the Fourth Amendment. *Southern California Law Review* 60: 815–850, 1987.
10. Murray TH. Drug testing and moral responsibility. *Physician and Sportsmedicine* 14: 47–48, 1986.
11. National Collegiate Athletic Association. *Proceedings of the 78th Annual Convention of the National Collegiate Athletic Association.* Mission KS: The National Collegiate Athletic Association, p. A–107, 1984.
12. National Collegiate Athletic Association. *Proceedings of the 80th Annual Convention of the National Collegiate Athletic Association.* Mission KS: The National Collegiate Athletic Association. p. A–22, 1986.

13. Nattiv A, Puffer JC. Lifestyles and health risks of college athletes. *Journal of Family Practice* 33: 585–590, 1991.
14. Taylor WN. Drug issues in sports medicine part II: growth hormone abuse and anti-hypertensive drug selection in athletic, active patients. *Journal of Neurological and Orthopaedic Medicine and Surgery* 9: 165–169, 1988.
15. Toohey JV. Non-medical drug use among intercollegiate athletes at five American universities. *Bulletin on Narcotics* 30: 61–64, 1978.
16. Toohey JV, Corder BW. Intercollegiate sports participation and non-medical drug use. *Bulletin on Narcotics* 33:23–27, 1981.
17. Vernacchia RA. Ethical issues of drug use in sport. In Tricker & Cook (Eds.), *Athletes at risk: drugs and sport*, pp. 29–52. Wm C. Brown, Dubuque, 1990.
18. Wadler GI, Hainline B. *Drugs and the athlete*. F.A. Davis Company, Philadelphia, 1989.
19. Will GF. Editorial: Exploring the racer's edge. *Newsweek*, February 4, p. 8, 1985.
20. Yesalis CE. Winning and performance-enhancing drugs—our dual addiction. *Physician and Sportsmedicine* 18: 161–163, 167, 1990.

13

Privacy and the Urinalysis Testing of Athletes

Paul B. Thompson

Under what conditions, if any, is it ethical to require athletes to submit to urinalysis examinations? An answer to this question involves careful consideration as to the purpose of the examination, as well as an understanding of the athlete's right to privacy. The issue of urinalysis provokes serious questions regarding the separation of athletic activity from the athlete's personal life. Does a coach or team official have a right or responsibility to insure that an athlete's private conduct does not compromise his or her ability to perform in sport? If so, are there limits to this authority which would indicate the permissibility of requiring urinalysis examinations?

Urinalysis is a laboratory procedure which identifies the chemical composition of a urine sample. The procedure has become controversial in athletics because urinalysis can reveal the presence of drugs in an athlete's urine. This controversial use of urinalysis should not be confused with the noncontroversial procedure of analyzing a urine sample as a part of a regular physical examination. Controversial use of urine sampling also breaks down into two discrete categories. Urinalysis has been required of competitors in track and field events in order to identify the presence of stimulants, pain killers, steroids, and other drugs which are assumed to alter the competitive equilib-

Reprinted, by permission, from P.B. Thompson, 1982, "Privacy and the urinalysis testing of athletes," *Journal of the Philosophy of Sport, IX*: 60-65.

rium of the sport. Rampant drug use among professional athletes has prompted the suggestion that urinalysis might be used to detect the use of illegal and dangerous substances among athletes. The ethical analysis of these two different uses of urine testing requires differentiation on several key points.

I shall assume without argument that privacy is not a form of property, and hence that privacy rights must not be confused with property rights. An argument for this position is made by Larry May (2). This assumption is important for the discussion of urinalysis testing since, if privacy were merely a form of property, one might argue that privacy rights are surrendered to an employer or official under the contract which a professional athlete signs, or under the implicit contract of amateurism. The point of the assumption is to demand that privacy rights be renounced specifically, and not as part and parcel of a standard employer/employee relationship. There must be some reason specific to the activity of sport which supports the abnegations of privacy. We would not tolerate urinalysis as a matter of course as a condition of employment in a bank, a factory, or a hamburger stand. The fact that it is contemplated as a requirement for participation in sport needs, therefore, to be justified by some condition or phenomenon which distinguishes sport from other forms of human activity.

The use of urine sampling in the enforcement of a drug ban is largely an issue for the philosophy of competition. Although there may be controversy over *whether* a drug should be banned in a given sport, once the ban has been imposed as a condition of competition there is little question about the ethicality of using urinalysis as a means of enforcement. When entering a competition, an athlete makes an implicit commitment to abide by the rules of the competition, and also to respect the measures required to secure fairness in the enforcement of rules. Clearly, the collection of urine samples provides an objective and impartial means for the enforcement of rules prohibiting the use of certain specific drugs.

It must, of course, be admitted that the decision as to whether a drug ought or ought not to be banned can be tortuous and riddled with philosophical difficulties. It will depend upon our knowledge about the effects of the drug in question, but also upon our conception of sport itself. When does an advance in sports medicine alter the conditions of competition so drastically that, effectively, a *new* sport is defined? How do we define the conditions of competition for a given sport? Do these conditions imply a "natural" or nonenhanced concept of physical fitness? These are questions which will probably be answered on a sport-by-sport and drug-by-drug basis (1). Such questions do not, however, play a role in determining the ethicality of urine sampling once it has been established that the use of a particular substance is inconsistent with the conditions of competition for a sport.

The use of urinalysis to detect banned substances falls within the scope of rule enforcement; hence one might object that urinalysis is inconsistent with philosophies of sport which stress amateurism and voluntary compliance with rules. This is tantamount to suggesting that enforcement of rules is secondary to certain esthetic considerations in the ideal of sportsmanship. It is difficult to imagine a sport so conceived (on an ideal of pure sportsmanship) in which the question of urinalysis could arise at all. Urine testing for banned substances, by its very nature, is a practice applicable only to sports where competition has been formulated in terms of rather precise rules and enforcement procedures.

The more difficult and topical issue involves the use of urinalysis to determine whether an athlete is using illegal or dangerous drugs recreationally. Revelations of drug use made by well-known athletes have brought this issue to prominence in the sports press (cf. 3: pp. 66-82). Urinalysis has been proposed as a means of identifying athletes who use drugs. This proposal has been met with protests citing an athlete's right to privacy as a protection against involuntary testing for drug use (4; 5).

In order to understand the ethical questions involved in such an application of urine testing, several points must be clarified. First, urinalysis for detecting illegal drug use differs from urinalysis for detecting banned drugs in important respects. When a drug is banned, the prohibition of that drug becomes a part of the definition of the sport in question. Banned drugs are drugs used to affect the competitive outcome of a sport. The illegal drugs in question are not ingested in order to affect the outcome of the sport; hence they have no place in defining the conditions of competition for a sport. Since the drugs are not banned on competitive grounds, officials have no referential authority over their use; hence officials have no justification for initiating a procedure designed to detect their use. Athletes are presumed to use these drugs "on their own time," so to speak, and an athlete violates no rules of traditional sports by doing so.

Second, the use of urinalysis specifically to detect illegal substances can be distinguished from urine tests conducted in the course of regular physical examinations. Since the doctors who conduct such examinations will have knowledge of an athlete's drug use, a confidentiality issue arises in regard to the conditions under which this knowledge can and should be disclosed. This is a difficult issue for medical ethics, but it can and should be differentiated from the ethical question of ordering an athlete to undergo urinalysis specifically for the purpose of identifying illicit drug use.

Third, there may be occasions in which coaches or other athletic officials have clear *in loco parentis* responsibility for their athletes. Under such a situation, coaches may be responsible for the moral as well as physical development of their charges. This conception of the coach-athlete relationship is doubtlessly grounded in the philosophical view that a primary goal of athletics is "character development." It is a philosophical view which is probably on the wane in many phases of contemporary sport, and it is clearly inoperative in the professional sports where urinalysis has been proposed. Professional coaches have no responsibility for the moral development of their players. This point is worth mentioning since a coach or team official who did have clear *in loco parentis* authority could quite plausibly construe this to include authority to see that an athlete was not violating any laws. Even in such a case it is difficult to imagine a situation in which the mutual respect between coach and athlete implied by the *in loco parentis* responsibility could have deteriorated badly enough to make urinalysis justifiable.

Given a situation in which coaches and team officials have no special mandate to watch over an athlete's moral development, are there any sport-related special circumstances which could justify forced urinalysis? There are two relevant possibilities. First, since team officials assume some responsibility for the physical development of athletes, testing for drug use might be interpreted as helping athletes stay in optimal physical condition. Second, a team official might cite a negative impact on team morale or cohesiveness as a justification for the investigation of drug abuse.

The first possibility suggests that, in the long run, urinalysis is in the interest of the athlete himself. It will be argued that a drug user can be given counseling and treatment which will help him or her avoid further abuse. The ethical force of this suggestion is to argue that what at first glance appears to be a clear breach of an athlete's privacy rights can be justified in light of the overriding goodness of its consequences—namely that it helps him or her overcome a drug problem. Cast in this light, the argument is an example of the classic utilitarian problem of forcing someone to do something for their own good; it is a practice which utilitarians have concluded does more harm than good. The weakness of the "helping" argument is shown by examining its probable consequences.

It is clear that a policy of conducting urine tests and referring drug abusers to treatment centers will be helpful indeed for athletes desirous of treatment, but there is no need for urinalysis to identify this group. The problem arises with regard to athletes identified as drug abusers who do not wish treatment. Presumably these athletes will be presented with the alternative of accepting forced treatment or of losing some privilege (probably all opportunities to compete). If there is no penalty for "failing" one's urine test, there is no reason to conduct a test. We may speculate with some degree of assurance that some athletes forced into treatment will later be very grateful and agree that the identification and treatment of their drug use have been helpful.

These people are helped at the expense of those who either refuse treatment and suffer for it, or accept the condition of treatment but continue to resent the intrusion into their privacy and claim that the treatment is of little value. Even those who are helped are robbed of their autonomy as moral agents. It is hard to imagine why a coach's responsibility to train and condition players justifies such an abrogation of basic moral respect. The idea of helping athletes by forcing them to undergo urinalysis is also founded on the dubious assumption that all instances of drug use are health problems. Illicit drugs have become an insidious social problem precisely because *some* people have the capacity to resist the debilitating effects of drug use, even over relatively long periods of use.

In the matter of professional team sports, the claim that urinalysis is in the health interests of the player can be taken rather differently. Since the professional team athlete is in the employ of the team owner, and since the team owner derives profits (indirectly) from the athletic performance of such employees, the owner may claim that the health of the athlete is a matter of his (the owner's) financial interest. Such a claim breaks down to two components. One is a general claim regarding employer/employee relations; but this is merely the illegitimate preference of the employer's financial interest over the employee's privacy rights (discussed previously). The more difficult question here is whether the nature of sport itself, the requirement of a physical performance from an employee, alters the basic employer/employee relationship in such a way that an owner can be said to have a legitimate claim.

The strongest argument in favor of such a view is by analogy to other well-established sports practices. Current and former training measures have been accepted as more or less legitimate infringements upon the athlete's privacy. At one time, restrictions against sexual intercourse before a game (in extreme cases, throughout an entire season) were widespread. Even more commonly, athletes are subjected to periodic weight checks. Athletes who fail to meet a specified weight can be subject to fines and even firings.

The analogy to restrictions on sexual intercourse is particularly *à propos,* since this training rule has largely fallen into disuse for reasons directly relevant to the issue at hand. While it is reasonable to suppose that some athletes suffer reduced performance after relatively recent sexual activity it is doubtful that all or even most do. Since the issue is athletic performance, and not the underlying moral attitudes toward sex and/or drug use, the athlete should be judged on the basis of performance. Athletes who perform well regardless of sexual activity or occasional drug use would be unjustly restricted by training practices which infringe upon their private life to no apparent purpose. Those who are negatively affected can and should be disciplined or criticized for their reduced performance, and *not* for the private indiscretions which contribute to reduced performance.

The analogy to weighings breaks down for similar reasons. The history of sport is littered with stories of paunchy quarterbacks and outfielders who nevertheless deliver stellar performances. No team owner would have fired Babe Ruth for failing to make a weight limit. The issue, again, is performance. It seems more plausible that an athlete and a trainer might agree on an ideal weight, and that the weight check will be made as a means of monitoring compliance with this explicit contract. By analogy, it seems reasonable to condone an explicit agreement between a trainer and an athlete with a history of drug problems which involves periodic urinalysis as a means of monitoring compliance. The ethics of such agreements are entirely different from those of general and mandatory testing for drug use, since by assenting to the contract, the athlete submits to the test voluntarily, and hence, it is no invasion of privacy. This exception naturally assumes that the athlete has not been coerced into accepting the contract.

The final argument for forced urinalysis appeals to a philosophical concept of team spirit or morale. This justification can itself be broken into two principles. One might claim that individual athletes represent the whole; that is, a team, an organization or institution, or the sport itself. As such, officials of the sport have a "right" to insure that its representatives are of appropriate moral fiber. This form of argument is so patently paternalistic that it deserves little serious analysis. Although it might justify sanctions against known offenders, it can hardly be used to justify the extreme measure of taking urine samples in order to identify individuals who might be potential embarrassments to the whole.

A more serious argument involves the idea that individuals using drugs have a negative effect on the camaraderie and spirit so often noted with respect to team sports. The critical question, which is unresolved, is whether there is any demonstrable link between drug use and team spirit. At the very least, it seems that this argument cannot justify urinalysis as a matter of course. Some confessed drug abusers have played on championship teams. One may also speculate that the ignominy of being subjected to urinalysis might have a worse effect on morale than minor cases of drug abuse, but philosophically, such considerations are beside the point.

The appeal to team spirit assumes a dubious premise with regard to an individual athlete's personal autonomy. It requires an athlete to regard at least some aspects of his or her personal life as subservient to the team concept; furthermore, it gives team officials license to regulate personal affairs in advance of a clear indication that impacts upon the team are involved. While some philosophical visions of the team concept would certainly give credence to the first part of this assumption, the second part is tantamount to a surrender of all privacy rights whatsoever. This totalitarian vision of sport is surely inconsistent with the traditional spirit of athletic competition.

In conclusion, urinalysis can be defended ethically when it has been clearly established as a procedure for enforcing the rule of a given sport. This can be so only when the use of a drug or substance has been determined to be inconsistent with the normal conditions of competition for that sport. There are no special sports-related circumstances which justify the use of urinalysis to identify users of illegal drugs. The normal privacy rights enjoyed by everyone protect athletes from this intrusion into their private lives.

The intentions of the authority conducting a urinalysis are, thus, the critical factor in determining the ethicality of the test. When the purpose of the test is to insure compliance with the regulations of a sport, it poses no threat to privacy. Privacy, in other words, cannot be cited in order to prevent referees from detecting cheating. An individual's decision to participate implies consent to referential authority. Privacy rights, however, can and are cited in restricting the access of officials into the lives of individuals for the purpose of identifying and proving criminal activity. This restriction should apply most strongly when the investigating parties are not duly appointed public authorities, but persons who derive authority through the regulatory offices of sport or as employers of athletes. As such, when the intention of an official conducting a urine test is to identify criminal activity, as opposed to rule violations, the official has usurped the athlete's right to a life beyond sport. The criterion of intention also shows why a medical utilization of urinalysis is acceptable, since the examining physician's intent is to certify the physical well-being of the athlete, and not to ascertain facts about his or her private activities.

The privacy rights of athletes and the possible abridgement of these rights through urinalysis raise philosophical questions about sport and competition which go beyond the scope of the present paper. Given the analysis in terms of intention, the governing bodies of a given sport could technically redefine a sport so as to make the criminal activity of an athlete off the field a violation of the rules of the sport. The purpose for this would not be to justify the expulsion of known criminals; there is strong precedent in sport to establish an official's right to do this already. Rather, the rule change would be to give officials a clear authority to pry into the private activities of athletes by making these activities part and parcel of the sport. Needless to say, such a tactic runs counter to the intuitive concept of sport which, presumably, guides our understanding of rules in sport.

The issue of urinalysis is thus a crucial one in that it could alter the very concept of sport which informs the organization of competitive activity in our society. It is at the cutting edge of issues which ask us to evaluate the distinction between sport and life. Given the current delineation of that distinction, the intention of the official conducting the test determines its moral validity. The ill-considered demand for urinalysis as a way to identify criminal activity is, at best, morally unjustifiable. At worst it may undermine the philosophical foundations of competitive sports.

Bibliography

1. Brown, W.M. "Ethics, Drugs and Sport." *Journal of the Philosophy of Sport*, 7 (1980), 15-23.
2. May, Larry. "Privacy and Property." *Philosophy in Context*, 10 (1980), 40-53.
3. Reese, Don, and John Underwood. "I'm Not Worth a Damn." *Sports Illustrated*, June 14, 1982, pp. 66-82.
4. "Schram Favors Exams for Drugs." *The Dallas Morning News*, July 20, 1982, p. B1, B3.
5. "Schram Backs Checks for Drugs." *Houston Chronicle*, July 21, 1983, Section 2, p. 4.

CHAPTER

The Ethics of Blood Testing As an Element of Doping Control in Sport

Alister Browne, Victor LaChance, and Andrew Pipe

Through a convergence of interest on the part of athletes, sport organizations, governments, and the general public, the world of amateur sport has collectively adopted the principle of drug-free sport. As a consequence, doping control policies and programs have been developed to detect and deter the use of performance-enhancing substances and practices (3,4). Such approaches necessarily involve the testing of athletes; drug testing is crucial to the promotion of drug-free sport. Given the enormous rewards that can be associated with being a top-flight athlete and the numerous performance-enhancing substances and techniques that may help an athlete to become one, an operating presumption of this paper must be that doping practices can only be held in check by the application of effective testing procedures.

Urine is the current matrix of choice. But urine testing will not detect all effective doping methods. Blood doping, for instance, cannot currently be detected through an analysis of urine samples (4). This practice can

Reprinted, by permission, from A. Browne, V. LaChance, and A. Pipe, 1999, "The ethics of blood testing as an element of doping control in sport," *Medicine & Science in Sports & Exercise,* 497-501.

artificially enhance an athlete's level of hemoglobin (Hb)—and aerobic performance—via the administration of blood products or hormones designed to accelerate blood production. Blood testing would conceivably facilitate the detection of this doping technique and might aid in the detection of others. In this respect the question emerges: should mandatory blood testing become a part of the doping control strategies of the international sport community? This is the fundamental question we address in our paper. The issue is the subject of considerable debate within the amateur sport community, and we find a full spectrum of responses to it.

This article deals exclusively with the issue of blood testing as it pertains to adult competent and consenting competitors. The taking of blood from minors raises a number of complex legal and ethical issues that merit in-depth discussion and are beyond the scope of this article. Even if blood testing were to be considered ethical for adult athletes, one cannot simply apply an adult situation to minors. We, however, will argue that routine mandatory blood testing protocols should not be introduced at this time.

Several national and international sport organizations have either adopted blood testing for doping control purposes or have called for the introduction of blood testing as a necessary addition to the existing urine testing programs. Blood samplings and subsequent analyses were conducted by the International Ski Federation, for example, at the 1989 Cross-Country Ski World Championships and the 1994 Lillehammer Olympics (it should be noted that such testing was not conducted by the International Olympic Committee), and by the International Amateur Athletic Federation at a number of Grand Prix meets in Europe in 1993 and 1994 (1). Other organizations in addition to the International Olympic Committee, and including the Canadian Centre for Ethics in Sport, have rejected blood testing as an element of standard doping control protocols. They are not prepared to adopt blood testing until the scientific, ethical, and legal issues are fully explored and resolved in favor of proceeding with the use of blood samples for doping control purposes. (Some sport organizations now conduct blood tests for the express purpose of identifying competitors whose levels of Hb or hematocrit (Hct) exceed certain arbitrarily defined levels. These individuals are withdrawn from competition on the basis of a concern for their health and safety. Such approaches are not the focus of this discussion.)

Advantages and Disadvantages of Blood Testing

It is natural to approach this question by listing and then weighing the advantages against the disadvantages. Both lists are impressive.

Advantages of Using Blood Matrix

1. The procedure for collecting a sample is relatively rapid.
2. It is a minimal requirement for the detection of homologous (nonautologous) blood doping.
3. It provides the best matrix to detect autologous blood doping.
4. Blood may be useful to confirm the presence of exogenous testosterone detected in an athlete's urine sample (although urine provides much greater concentrations by which to detect testosterone doping).
5. Blood plasma provides advantages in identifying the presence of certain peptide hormones.
6. There are population-based reference ranges for clinical hematological tests.
7. It reduces the possibility of the manipulation of samples.

Disadvantages of Using Blood Matrix

1. It is an invasive sampling procedure requiring a specially trained person (phlebotomist).
2. Blood analyses require the handling of blood samples by collection officers and laboratory personnel. Such manipulations expose individuals to the risk of infection by bloodborne viruses and thus are more hazardous than analyses involving urine.
3. It requires preparation and the refrigerated transportation of the sample.
4. Reference ranges for peptide hormones and their secondary factors may be unknown.
5. The concentrations of certain compounds, in particular anabolic steroids, are much greater in urine than in blood.
6. Autologous blood doping or the administration of erythropoietin (EPO) cannot be reliably detected.
7. Hematological parameters may be altered by altitude and/or by hard training.
8. Concentration of drugs or medications with low molecular weights are lower than in urine by a factor of 100-1000.
9. There are compelling ethical and legal questions: Blood testing is invasive, and there is a significant potential for the invasion of privacy (e.g., other health problems will be detected, and unauthorized testing may be done for other conditions such as HIV).
10. Additional complications arising out of blood testing of minors, who make up a sizable portion of competitors.

It must be noted that significant reservations exist in the scientific community about the validity, accuracy, and reproducibility of doping-control analyses conducted using blood as a matrix (5). Those legitimate concerns are rightfully the focus of other discussions. There is, however, evidence of agreement on these advantages and disadvantages. There is further agreement that there should be blood testing if, and only if, the advantages outweigh the disadvantages. The problem is: How can this weighing be done? How can these incommensurable factors be balanced against one another so that we can say which side is weightier? In what follows we will first propose a list of factors relevant to deciding the issue and then make a recommendation about blood testing by applying those factors to the facts as we know them.

Weighing the Advantages and Disadvantages of Blood Testing: The Fair Competitor and Costs

Whether the advantages of blood testing outweigh the disadvantages or, what is the same thing, whether blood testing should take place, depends on two factors. The first is what the Fair Competitor wants; the second is the cost of what the Fair Competitor wants. We will take these in order. By the Fair Competitor, we mean one who wants to win but who does not want to use prohibited substances or techniques to do so and would rather compete using fair and ethical means. The Fair Competitor is thus to be contrasted to the Unfair Competitor, who wants to win and is prepared to use prohibited performance-enhancing methods. The Fair Competitor plays the same role in our account as "the reasonable person" plays in the law, namely, to provide a standard by which operational significance is provided to an otherwise hard-to-apply concept. In law, what is reasonable is settled by asking what the reasonable person would decide in those circumstances. In our model, the preferences of a postulated Fair Competitor determine what testing programs are appropriate. If the Fair Competitor feels that blood testing must be conducted to detect the use of certain banned substances, then that is a powerful reason for having such testing. For then we have evidence that such testing would be to the disadvantage of the Unfair Competitor (assumed for this discussion to be one likely to use banned practices to accentuate performance) and thus will help level the playing field for the Fair Competitor.

What kind of testing would the Fair Competitor want? This will be a function of six considerations:

1. The advantage gained from using the prohibited substances or techniques. Is this advantage negligible? Or is the advantage so significant that it is extremely difficult for the Fair Competitor to compete with users?
2. The incidence of the use of the prohibited substances or techniques among athletes. Is the incidence 1 in 3 athletes, 1 in 100, 1 in 10,000 or less?
3. The number of "false negatives" the specific testing procedure produces. (A false negative occurs when a test fails to identify a banned substance when it is present.) False negatives may be a result of the intrinsic unreliability of the test procedure or may occur as a consequence of the manipulation or misidentification of samples. The Fair Competitor may be indifferent as to

why false negatives are produced but will be keenly interested in whether athletes can use performance-enhancing substances and still pass the test and, if so, how many can escape detection.

4. The number of "false positives" the specific testing procedure produces. (A false positive occurs when a test mistakenly identifies the presence of a banned substance when it is not present.) Like false negatives, false positives may be the result of the intrinsic unreliability of the tests or the manipulation or misidentification of samples. Again, the Fair Competitor may not care about the cause of false positives but will be acutely sensitive to the likelihood that athletes who do not cheat can fail the test and thus be falsely accused of cheating.

5. Whether Unfair Competitors can adopt other methods of doping that will be effective yet remain undetectable by current testing technologies.

6. The risk to the Fair Competitor that he or she will suffer unfair or unwanted consequences as a result of participating in the testing process (e.g., the risk of public or semipublic revelation that he or she is a carrier of Hepatitis B or C, HIV, or other communicable disease; the potential for the blood sample to be frozen, stored, and used for other purposes without the express permission of the athlete).

It is easy to assume what the Fair Competitor would want in some circumstances. If athletes derive a significant advantage from using prohibited substances or techniques, if the incidence of their use is high, if blood testing provides no or very few false negatives and (more importantly) no false positives, if there are no easily accessible alternative ways of doping that are undetectable by blood testing to gain that advantage, and if there are no or minimal "risks" to the Fair Competitor who participates in the blood testing procedure, then the Fair Competitor will want blood testing to be conducted. That would significantly level the playing field, and hence the Fair Competitor would predictably regard the invasiveness of the procedure and its potential to compromise privacy or cause personal harm as acceptable prices to be paid.

At the other extreme, if there is no significant advantage to be derived from the banned practice detectable by blood testing, if the incidence of the banned practices is rare, and if blood testing produces many false negatives or any false positives, or if participation in the testing process exposes the Fair Competitor to a high probability of personal risk or harm, then he or she will not want blood testing. No Fair Competitor would reasonably regard the possibility of an unjustified disqualification occurring as a consequence of a false positive test result, or a significant compromise of privacy, worth a minimal leveling of the playing field. Similarly, if blood testing effectively closes down one method of cheating, but dopers can with ease move to another effective but undetectable technique, the Fair Competitor could not be expected to be enthusiastic about the testing. Blood testing will then have all its attendant disutilities without possessing any significant advantages.

Even if the preferences of the Fair Competitor are easy to predict in some circumstances, there are others in which they are not. To take only perhaps the most challenging one: suppose that doping is so effective that it is difficult to compete without doping. Suppose also that doping is very common, can be effectively curtailed only by blood testing, but that blood testing yields a small but significant number of false positives. Would the Fair Competitor want blood testing under these conditions?

Some Fair Competitors may say that the stigma of disqualification is so great that there should not be any blood testing as long as there is any possibility of a false positive. Others may take the lead from criminal law and say that blood testing should proceed if it will detect doping beyond a reasonable doubt. Still others may adopt the civil law standard and say that blood testing should take place if it will detect doping on a balance of probabilities. Fortunately we do not have to settle this question to come to a decision in the blood testing issue before us. That issue (we will argue) can be resolved by a much more intuitively obvious balancing of the six factors. However, technology and attitudes relating to doping may change so that this question will have to be faced in the future, and we flag it for that reason.

The second factor on which the issue of blood testing turns is the cost of the tests. The fact that the Fair Competitor desires a particular testing procedure is a powerful, but not decisive, reason for its implementation. For the testing that will be maximally advantageous to the Fair Competitor and maximally disadvantageous to the Unfair Competitor may be prohibitively expensive. In this respect it may be seen to be disadvantageous to the sport system. Fairness is an important value, but it is not the only one that guides the conduct of sport in the same way that safety is not the only value that guides the activities of NASA or justice the only value that guides the conduct of society. How much fairness we can afford will be a function of what we have to give up if we apply a given testing procedure of known cost, and the extent to which the Fair Competitor is disadvantaged in competition if we do not. We are thus brought face to face with a standard problem in distributive justice. Unfortunately, there is no standard answer to this dilemma. But the absence of a well-tested, generally accepted theory of justice need not be crippling in practice. For once the cost-benefit ledger has been determined, the answer may become obvious on any account. This, as we will suggest in the next section, appears to be so in the case of blood testing.

Recommendations

We now turn to our three recommendations.

Recommendation 1: That Blood Testing Not Be Conducted As Part of the Protocols for Doping Control Procedures in Sport

There are four reasons for the development of this recommendation.

First, the only significant performance-enhancing doping method which is, in our view, uniquely detectable by blood testing is homologous blood infusion (the administration of another's blood or blood products). But to introduce blood testing to detect this practice would likely only have the effect of causing a shift to autologous blood infusion (the administration of an individual's own blood, or blood products, previously withdrawn and stored) or the administration of EPO, both of which are not reliably detectable. This will reduce the health risks associated with homologous blood doping to which dopers are exposed but do nothing to level the playing field. The Fair Competitor must therefore be indifferent to testing for this reason, and the advantage of encouraging dopers to adopt a safer method of cheating would not seem to be worth the cost.

The second reason relates to the other two putative advantages of blood testing to detect doping. (i) Blood testing will detect certain substances more easily and accurately than will urine testing, and (ii) the possibility of the manipulation of samples is reduced. The Fair Competitor must be attracted to blood testing for both these reasons. They mean that more dopers will be detected and hence there will be an increased deterrent effect.

We must not, however, overestimate the extent to which all this will level the playing field. It is not clear that even the most enthusiastic Fair Competitor will regard the leveling effect of (i) and (ii) significant enough to justify the inconvenience, physical invasiveness, and compromise of privacy that blood testing places on guilty and innocent alike. It may be that the Fair Competitor would prefer to let that amount of doping go undetected and unpunished rather than be subject to those burdens.

Even if on balance the Fair Competitor thinks blood testing is best, there is still the question of cost to consider. Blood testing may save some money, time, and effort because it may eliminate some frivolous and vexatious appeals. But this saving will hardly offset the significant amounts of money, time, and effort needed to develop and implement a program of blood testing, and it is highly problematic that (whatever the Fair Competitor may think) these costs will be worth the limited advantages of the program.

Third, blood testing as a component of research activities designed to assist in the development of better techniques for the detection of doping, e.g., to determine normal reference ranges, should be able to be equally well done by voluntary testing. Given that the Fair Competitor will want optimal detection methods, there should be no shortage of volunteers, and other things being equal, voluntary programs are always preferable to mandatory ones.

Recommendation 2: A Vigorous Educational Program to Articulate and Inculcate the Advantages of Drug-Free Sport Should Go Forward

This will both reduce the incidence of doping and secure support for testing programs.

Recommendation 3: Scientific Research Designed to Facilitate the Development of Valid, Reliable Methods of Detection of Prohibited Performance-Enhancing Substances and Techniques Should Continue and Be Appropriately Supported

Given the unfortunate realities of competition, as long as effective testing for certain substances is not in place, there can be no guarantee that competition will be fair; and in the absence of fair competition, the benefits of sport will not be completely realized. All in sport have an obligation to develop, to the extent possible, a sporting environment in which the pursuit of excellence by fair and ethical means is seen, particularly by athletes, as the only socially acceptable mode of competition. The application of reliable, state-of-the-art, and proven testing technologies coupled with expert interpretation of test results and open transparent processes of reporting such deliberations is a necessary component of such an approach.

This discussion has demonstrated, we hope, an approach to the consideration of an important issue in doping control. The concept of the Fair Competitor provides us with an instrument that can be applied in such discussions. Such an application has led us to the conclusion that the use of blood testing procedures to detect certain doping practices is not yet justifiable in sport.

References

1. Birkeland, K.L., M. Donike, A. Ljungqvist, et al. Blood sampling in doping control. *Int. J. Sports Med.* 18:8–12, 1997.
2. Donike, M., H. Geyer, A. Gotzmann, et al. Blood analysis in doping control: Advantages and disadvantages. In: *Blood Samples in Doping Control,* P. Hemmersbach and K.I. Birkeland (Eds.). Oslo, Norway: On Demand Publishing, 1994, pp. 75–92.

3. International Olympic Committee. *IOC Medical Code and Explanatory Document.* Lausanne, Switzerland: International Olympic Committee, 1995.
4. International Olympic Committee. *International Olympic Charter Against Doping in Sport.* Lausanne, Switzerland: International Olympic Committee, 1988.
5. Webb, B. The case against blood tests. *FISA INFO.* Lausanne, Switzerland: Fédération Internationale des Sociétés d'Aviron, 2:8–9, 1993.

III
PART

WOMEN IN SPORT: GENDER EQUITY AND GENDER IDENTITY

The idea that sport (or even physical activity), particularly high-level competitive sport, is somehow incompatible with what women are, or what they should be, must dominate any discussion of the unique ethical issues for women in sport. Ideas of ideal sport, and ideal women, lie behind discussions of permitting women to compete, of choosing the types of sport in which women can compete, in developing judging standards for adjudicated as opposed to refereed sports (contrast gymnastics and basketball), in attitudes to aggression and competition, and indeed to the very existence of women's sport as a separate entity at all.

Before examining some of these issues in detail, it is worth pointing out that many of the moral issues in sport arise equally for men and women. At the personal level, the decision whether or not to cheat or what attitude you take to your opponents or the unearned win are moral problems every athlete must face. At the institutional level, decisions about rules prohibiting drug use or equipment limitations designed to improve participant safety should apply equally to women and men. As such, those moral problems common to the realm of sport, important as they are, are more appropriately discussed elsewhere. This part is devoted to the moral issues that arise specifically for women athletes. Thus the articles in this section focus on gender, ethics, and sport and the interrelationships among them.

Ideal Woman

The traditional ideal of womanhood during the times of the ancient Olympic Games was intimately tied to a particular view of woman's body. This ideal included such characteristics as being soft, graceful, weak, and beautiful. The desirable qualities for a woman in the time of the ancient Olympics can generally be summarized as beauty, chastity, modesty, obedience, inconspicuous behavior, and being a good wife and mother. Of course, these characteristics are tied to the roles of wife, mother, and daughter. These characteristics differ from those of the traditional ideal of man as hard, powerful, strong, and rational, which correspond to the roles of leader, warrior, and father. But more importantly, if we examine the underlying characteristics of the traditional ideal athlete, we can plainly see that the characteristics of the ideal man are very similar to those of the ideal athlete, particularly in the role of warrior. For a current personal account of the relationship between masculinity and sport in North America, see Messner and Sabo (1994). Conversely, we can plainly see that during the times of the ancient Olympic Games (and during the rebirth of the modern Olympic Games), the traditional ideal woman and the traditional ideal athlete are almost opposites, so much so that women were hardly ever mentioned in conjunction with sport. There were, however, also some exceptional counterexamples from ancient Greece, even though it is not well known that girls did compete in athletic festivals. Plato, at the peak of his writings, argued that women should be accorded the right to soar to the highest ranks he could conceive of in human excellence—that of the philosopher ruler— and should be equally educated in the gymnasium by exercising naked with the men. Other exceptional counterexamples from ancient Greece that stress physicality and a warrior nature for women are the archetypes of Artemis, Atalanta, and the Amazons, who all rejected women's traditional role (Creedon 1994).

The fundamental ethical issue in this discussion is who gets to choose which images of woman are permitted, desired, or pursued in sport. The primary ethical question for women in sport is inextricably linked to the question of power and autonomy. At the institutional level, if men decide the sports that women are permitted to attempt, the standards of physical perfection that women must attain in adjudicated sports, or the levels of funding accorded women's sports, then women are not being treated with due respect and have a legitimate grievance. Just as each man is responsible for deciding the kind of life he wishes to pursue, whether moral or otherwise, so too each woman has the right to deal with the challenges that she must face as a female athlete.

Paternalism and Autonomy

The *Oxford Dictionary of Philosophy* defines paternalism as "government as by a benign parent." Paternalism is not necessarily sexist, although it often has been in sport and sport medicine, and it is often well meaning. It occurs when one person makes a decision on behalf of or speaks for another according to what he or she believes is the other person's best interest. In the case of children, this is, of course, a necessary part of the parenting process. Paternalism is also morally acceptable in cases where the person concerned is unable to speak or make decisions for himself or herself. It is morally troubling when it occurs on behalf of competent adults.

The concept of autonomy in ethical decision making is very important. Autonomy is often referred to as "the capacity for self-government," as noted in the *Oxford Dictionary of Philosophy*. Furthermore, the *Oxford Dictionary of Philosophy* also states, "agents are autonomous if their actions are truly their own." An essential part of being human is having the right and the capacity to make the choices and decisions that most affect oneself. Each competent human adult has the right to choose to pursue the projects and endeavors that he or she most cares about. That right is naturally limited by the rights of others to pursue their own desires and interests, but the concept of autonomy takes for granted that no one is entitled to speak on another's behalf without that person's permission.

Sport Paternalism and Women's Participation

Is there any reason that women should not participate in sports that men have traditionally participated in? If a particular sport practiced by men were physiologically impossible for women, that would count as a reason for women not to participate. But no such sport exists. To qualify, the sport would probably have to centrally involve male genitalia; there are no institutionally sanctioned sports of this type.

A second possibility would be if there were a sport men played that no women in the world actually wanted to play. It is logically possible to imagine such a sport might be invented, but then the reason for women's nonparticipation would be that they have chosen not to play, not that someone else has decided they should not.

Morally unacceptable reasons for prohibiting women from playing sport include that it would be bad for women to participate, or that there is not enough money to allow women to participate. Let us look at each of these answers in turn.

"It would be bad for women to participate" is the standard line that has been used throughout the history of sport. The exact nature of the harm that would befall women varies. Some critics believe that sport participation defeminizes women (meaning that it makes some women less attractive, either physically or mentally, in some men's eyes), or that women (or sometimes their not-yet-conceived children) might suffer some physiological damage. Two points are relevant here. The first is practical: the assertions that women are harmed and men are not harmed by strenuous physical exertion are simply not true. But the second point is more important—women have the right, just as men do, to decide what risks of harm they will accept. Subject to the normal limitations on every person's freedom, it is immorally paternalistic to decide on behalf of another competent adult what personal risks that adult is willing to take on.

The argument that there is not enough money for women's sport participation can be a more difficult one to answer. This reason often masks an inequitable distribution of the available resources. If money is available for anyone to participate in sport, then that money must be available equally to both women and men. Men's sport is not intrinsically more important or more worthwhile than women's sport and therefore has no automatic right to majority funding.

Dealing with instances of gender oppression or neglect in sport requires complex combinations of social, biological, political, ontological, and epistemological approaches. These complex approaches enable the development of an ethical framework that can provide the means for discerning and solving problems surrounding women and sport and requires the acknowledgment that no clear line exists between ethics and sociopolitical concerns. Some of the most important moral questions regarding gender oppression and neglect in sport concern specifically male domination and female subordination. A coherent understanding of the causes of women's subordination to men in sport, coupled with a refined program of action designed to eliminate the systems and attitudes that oppress or cause neglect of women in sport, must guide these complex approaches. A detailed analysis of the distribution of power in each case can identify a particular factor as the primary cause of women's subordinate status in sport, which, for the most part, has traditionally been based on biology. However, to deal adequately with these problems, researchers must also look at economics, law, education, national boundaries, language, and so on, because all of these factors have contributed, more or less strongly, to the current status of women's sport. Researchers can, and should, attempt to ascertain the actual status of both sexes in sport and determine how far that condition deviates from what justice prescribes.

Suggested Readings

1. Blackburn, S. 1994. *Oxford Dictionary of Philosophy.* Oxford: Oxford University Press.
2. Bordo, S. 1990. "Reading the Slender Body." In *Body/Politics: Women and the Discourses of Science,* ed. M. Jacobus, E. Fox Keller, and S. Shuttleworth. New York: Routledge.
3. Cohen, G. 1993. *Women in Sport: Issues and Controversies.* Newbury Park, Calif.: Sage Publications.
4. Creedon, P., ed. 1994. *Women, Media and Sport: Challenging Gender Values.* Newbury Park, Calif.: Sage Publications.
5. Hargreaves, J. 1995. "A Historical Look at the Changing Symbolic Meanings of the Female Body in Western Sport." In *Sport as Symbol, Symbols in Sport,* ed. F. van der Merwe. International Society for the History of Physical Education and Sport (ISHPES) Studies, vol. 4, 249-59. Sankt Augustin, Germany: Academia Verlag.
6. Messner, M., and D. Sabo, eds. 1990. *Sport, Men, and the Gender Order: Critical Feminist Perspectives.* Champaign, IL: Human Kinetics.
7. Messner, M., and D. Sabo. 1994. *Sex, Violence, and Power in Sports: Rethinking Masculinity.* Freedom, Calif.: Crossing Press.
8. Schiebinger, L. 1993. *Nature's Body: Gender in the Making of Modern Science.* Boston: Beacon Press.

15

CHAPTER

Sex Equality in Sports

Jane English

What constitutes equal opportunity for women in sports? Philosophers have developed three major positions concerning equal opportunity, but they have focused on fields in which the sexes are either known or assumed to have equal potentialities. In sports, some relevant differences between the sexes, though statistical, do appear to be permanent. All three of the most widely held views on equal opportunity are deficient when applied to this area. Since there may be other permanent differences between the sexes, in such areas as spatial perception or verbal ability, it is useful to examine the problems of equal opportunity in sports.

I

One account of equal opportunity identifies it with nondiscrimination. On this view, if we do not pay any attention to the race of applicants to law school, for example, then our admissions are "color blind" and give blacks equal opportunity. Admission should be based on characteristics relevant to law school, such as intelligence and grades, while irrelevant characteristics such as sex and race should be ignored entirely. Most philosophers have

Reprinted, by permission, from Jane English, 1978; "Sex equality in sports," *Philosophy and Public Affairs 7(3): 269-277.*

rejected this account as too weak. If women lack motivation because they never see female lawyers on television, "sex blindness" alone will not provide equal opportunity. Although "formal" equality is necessary for justice, it is not sufficient. These philosophers would permit temporary violations of this ideal, but only in the transition to a just society.

When applied to sports, however, their view proves inadequate. If our sports were made sex-blind, women would have even less opportunity to participate than at present. Given equal incentives and more role models, women would have more interest in athletics, but few would qualify for high school, college, professional and Olympic teams. Statistically speaking, there are physiological differences between the sexes that are relevant to sports performance. Remedial programs and just institutions cannot obliterate all differences in size and strength. So far from being necessary for equal opportunity, sex-blindness can actually decrease it.

A second account of equal opportunity identifies it with equal chances. Oscar and Elmer are said to have equal opportunity to become brain surgeons if it is equally probable that they will become brain surgeons. Most philosophers have rejected this conception of equal opportunity as too strong. If Oscar is a genius with great manual dexterity and Elmer is uncoordinated and slightly retarded, then they should not have an equal chance to become brain surgeons. Our society is not unjust if it encourages Oscar and discourages Elmer from this profession, because these skills are relevant to the job.

When we turn to women in sports, however, the model of equal probabilities seems to have some merit. Sports offer what I will call *basic benefits* to which it seems everyone has an equal right: health, the self-respect to be gained by doing one's best, the cooperation to be learned from working with teammates and the incentive gained from having opponents, the "character" of learning to be a good loser and a good winner, the chance to improve one's skills and learn to accept criticism—and just plain fun. If Matilda is less adept at, say, wrestling than Walter is, this is no reason to deny Matilda an equal chance to wrestle for health, self-respect, and fun. Thus, contrary to the conclusion on the example of the brain surgeon, a society that discourages Matilda from wrestling is unjust because it lacks equal opportunity to attain these basic benefits.

The third account of equal opportunity calls for equal chances in the sense of equal achievements for the "major social groups." Blacks have an equal opportunity to be lawyers, on this view, when the percentage of lawyers who are black roughly equals the percentage of blacks in the population. Like the "equal probabilities" view, this one calls for equal chances, but it interprets this by averaging attainments across the major social groups.

When this third account is applied to sports, it seems to have the undesirable consequence that a society is unjust if less than half its professional football players are women. If we had to provide sufficient incentives or reverse discrimination to achieve this result, it would create a situation unfair to 170-pound males. (They may even clamor to be recognized as a "major social group.") More important, it seems wrong to argue that a low level of health and recreation for, say, short women, is compensated for by additional health and recreation for tall women; one might as well argue that women are compensated by the greater benefits enjoyed by men. Rawls and Nozick have argued against utilitarianism by pointing out that society is not a "macro-individual" such that the benefits of some persons cancel out the sufferings of others. But the major social groups are not macro-individuals either. Proponents of the third account have not, to my knowledge, replied to this objection.

Beyond the basic benefits of sport, some athletes reap the further benefits of fame and fortune. I shall call these the *scarce benefits* of sport. The term is not meant to imply that they are kept artificially scarce, but that it is simply not possible for prizes and publicity to be attained equally by everyone at once. Although everyone has an equal right to the basic benefits, not everyone can claim an equal right to receive fan mail or appear on television. For this, having the skill involved in the sport is one relevant factor. In short, I shall maintain that the second account, equal probabilities, should be applied to the basic benefits; whereas the third model, proportional attainments for the major social groups, should be applied to the scarce benefits. And I shall construct an argument from self-respect for taking the "average" across the major social groups in the case of scarce benefits.

II

The traditional accounts of equal opportunity are inadequate because men and women are physiologically different in ways relevant to performance in sports. What is a fair way to treat physiologically disadvantaged groups? Two methods are in common use, and I shall suggest a third option.

One common method is to form competition classes based on a clear-cut physiological characteristic, such as weight or age, well known to be a hindrance in the sport in question. For example, middleweight boxers receive preferential treatment in the sense that they are permitted to move up and compete against the heavyweights if they desire, while the heavyweights are not permitted to move down into the middleweight class.

Sex is frequently used to form separate competition groups. If we apply the boxing model, several conclusions about this practice follow. Women should be allowed to "move up" and compete against the men if they wish. Since sex is not relevant to performance in all sports, the sport should be integrated when it is not. For example, it is probably irrelevant in dressage, riflery and car racing. In other sports, the differences between the sexes may be too small to justify separate classes—as in diving and freestyle skiing. In still others, the sexes have compensating differences. In channel swimming, for instance, men are advantaged in strength, but women profit from an insulating layer of fat. Additional sports could be integrated if the abilities characteristic of the two sexes were valued equally. In many areas, such as swimming, it is simply unknown whether the existing differences are due to permanent physiological characteristics or to cultural and social inequalities. Additional empirical research is needed before it will be known where integration is appropriate.

An objection to the use of groupings by sex is that it discriminates against those males whose level of performance is equal to that of the abler females. For example, if we have a girls' football team in our high school, is it unfair to prohibit a 120-pound boy who cannot make the boys' team from trying out for the girls' team? If we provide an additional team for boys under 140 pounds, does that discriminate against girls under 100 pounds? Against short boys over 140 pounds? It is impossible to provide a team for every characteristic that might be relevant to football performance. The objection has force because the differences between the sexes are only statistical. Our 120-pound boy is being penalized for the average characteristics of a major social group to which he belongs, rather than being treated on the basis of his individual characteristics.

The justification for maintaining separate teams for the sexes is the impact on women that integration would have. When there are virtually no female athletic stars, or when women receive much less prize money than men do, this is damaging to the self-respect of all women. Members of disadvantaged groups identify strongly with each other's successes and failures. If women do not attain roughly equal fame and fortune in sports, it leads both men and women to think of women as naturally inferior. Thus, it is not a right of women tennis stars to the scarce benefits, but rather a right of all women to self-respect that justifies their demand for equal press coverage and prize money.

This provides a justification for applying the third account of equal opportunity to the distribution of scarce benefits. It also explains why the "major social groups" have this feature, while arbitrary sets of individuals do not. A group singled out for distinctive treatment and recognized as a class tends to develop feelings of mutual identification which have an impact on the members' self-respect. It also affects the respect and treatment they get from others. In an androgynous society, we might be as unaware of a person's sex as we now are of left-handedness. Then roughly equal attainments would no longer be required, on my reasoning, for unequal attainments would not injure self-respect. Conversely, although there is some evidence of late that blacks have physiological traits such as a longer calf that give them an advantage in jumping and sprinting, I do not conclude that we should form separate track or basketball leagues for whites, since the self-respect of whites is not endangered by this modest advantage possessed by blacks.

III

A different method often used to give the disadvantaged equal access to the basic benefits of sport is to group individuals by ability alone. This occurs when we find second- and third-string games, B-leagues, intramural meets or special matches for novices or amateurs. Groupings by age, sex, or weight are often just attempts to approximate ability groupings in a convenient and quick way. When convenience is the intent, then, it must not be rigidly imposed to keep talented girls off the first string.

Groupings by ability are much easier to justify than groupings by the specific characteristics just discussed. There is no discrimination against less able members of the dominant group. Ability groupings take into account all the traits that may affect performance. Competition with those close to one's own ability usually provides the most incentive and satisfaction, except where style of play is very different. It is imperative to make recreational leagues on all levels of skill available to people of all ages, sexes, income levels, and abilities, because everyone has an equal right to sport's basic benefits.

Groupings by ability must not lead to disrespect for those playing in the lower ability groups, however. Sports is an area in which we have tended to confuse respect with what has been called "esteem." I may have a low (and accurate) estimate of myself as a tennis player without losing respect for myself as a person. Although competition does entail winners and losers, it does not entail disrespect for the losers. Much has been said recently about this among other evils of competition. But competition per se is not bad. It offers fun, excitement, entertainment, and the incentive to perform at one's best. The problems arise when losers are scorned or discouraged from playing, and when winning becomes the end rather than the means to basic benefits. It is ironic that sports, long recommended for building character and teaching how to be a good loser and winner, have often taught aggression and elitism. Experts have become idols and millionaires, while the rest of us watch rather than participate. With effort, the entry of women into sports could foster a reawakening to these values, which are widely shared but have been lost lately in the shuffle of big business sports. Some such reawakening is necessary if ability groupings are to be effective.

IV

So far I have assumed that women are a physiologically disadvantaged group in need of protection or special handicaps. In recent years, women have been making impressive progress in narrowing the gap between male and female performance. But there are apparently some permanent biological differences that affirmative action and consciousness raising will never change: women are smaller than men, they have a higher percentage of fat, they lack the hormones necessary for massive muscle development, they have a different hip structure and a slower oxygenation rate.

Before we conclude that women are permanently relegated to inferiority, however, let us note that what is a physiological disadvantage in one activity may be an advantage in others: weight is an asset to a Sumo wrestler and a drawback for marathon running; height is an aid in basketball but not on the balance beam. In some sports, women have natural advantages over men. The hip structure that slows running gives a lower center of gravity. Fat provides insulation and an energy source for running fifty-mile races. The hormones that hinder development of heavy muscles promote flexibility. Even small size can be an asset, as jockeys and spelunkers know.

An example of an athletic activity which emphasizes the female advantages is ballet. Some ballerinas can stand on one toe while extending the other leg up into a vertical position where it touches the ear! While admittedly few women can do this, even fewer men can. Men are simply physiologically disadvantaged in the body flexibility that ballet emphasizes. Perhaps the most extreme example of a sport favoring women's natural skills is the balance beam. Here, small size, flexibility and low center of gravity combine to give women the kind of natural hegemony that men enjoy in football.

This suggests a third approach to aiding physiologically different groups. We should develop a variety of sports, in which a variety of physical types can expect to excel. We tend to think of the possible sports as a somewhat fixed group of those currently available. Yet even basketball and football are of very recent invention. Since women have been virtually excluded from all sports until the last century, it is appropriate that some sports using women's specific traits are now developing, such as synchronized swimming.

This method is different from forming handicapped groups or second-string leagues, and it is superior in its impact on the self-respect of the affected groups. It contributes to a woman's self-respect to see or read about the best women golfers. But this pride is tempered by the knowledge that they are "only" the best *women*. The very need for a protected competition class suggests inferiority. The pride and self-respect gained from witnessing a woman athlete who is not only the best woman but the very best athlete is much greater. Perhaps most white male readers have not experienced this sort of identification characteristic of "minority" groups. But it is clearly displayed in the extraordinary interest in gymnastics among adolescent girls inspired by Olga Korbut, and the pride blacks derived from Jackie Robinson.

V

In calling for the development of new sports, I am suggesting that our concept of "sports" contains a male bias. Historically, this is understandable, because sports were an exclusively male domain, probably based on war and hunting, and actually used to assert male dominance. The few athletic activities permitted to women—mostly forms of dance—were not thought to fall under the *concept* of sport, and are still classified as arts or entertainment instead. Speed, size, and strength seem to be the essence of sports. Women *are* naturally inferior at "sports" so conceived.

But if women had been the historically dominant sex, our concept of sport would no doubt have evolved differently. Competitions emphasizing flexibility, balance, strength, timing, and small size might dominate Sunday afternoon television and offer salaries in six figures. Men could be clamoring for equal press coverage of their champions.

Here it might be argued that our concept of sport cannot be altered to make women equal, because speed, strength, and size are inevitable elements of *spectator* appeal. But it is participating rather than watching that is central to sport. Although speed is exciting, so is precision. Nor do audiences always choose to watch the experts. More important, spectator interest is a cultural product, tending to follow rather than lead media attention.

VI

The just society, in my view, would contain a greater variety of sports than we now have, providing advantages for a wider range of physical types. The primary emphasis would be on participation, with a wealth of local teams and activities available to all, based on groupings by ability. Only where style of play is very different would groupings by weight, age, or sex be recommended. The goal would be to make the basic benefits of health, teamwork, and fun equally available to everyone. Just distribution of the scarce benefits is somewhat more complex. Level of skill, audience appeal, and the self-respect of major social groups all have to be considered.

Current problems of the real world are far removed from such a utopia. Rights to the basic benefits dictate immediate changes in the distribution of our sports resources. Most obvious is the need for equal facilities—everything from socks to stadiums. If this means we must disturb a "Pareto optimal" situation—selling the football team's videotape machine if we are to provide a jogging path for the middle-aged—so be it. More subtle is the need for equal incentives. As well as equal scholarships and prizes, women need peer approval and changed sex-role stereotypes.

In short, I have suggested a division of the benefits of sport into the "basic" and the "scarce" ones. From the assumption that everyone has an equal right to the basic benefits of health and recreation, I have argued that the access to participator sports should not be based upon having the ability to play the sport well. And this ability is only one factor in the attainment of the scarce benefits. Since I believe that the right of women to roughly half of the scarce benefits, overall, stems from the right to self-respect, I have argued that a society which invents alternative sports using women's distinctive abilities and which rewards these equally is preferable to a society which only maintains protected classes for women in sports at which men are advantaged.

16

CHAPTER

Women, Sex, and Sports

Raymond A. Belliotti

Jane English (2) has presented several arguments related to sexual equality in athletics. Crucial to these arguments is the distinction between basic and scarce athletic benefits. Basic benefits are those to which everyone has an equal right; scarce benefits are those to which everyone does not have an equal right. Examples of basic benefits are health, the self-respect to be gained by doing one's best, learning cooperation and competition by working with teammates and battling against opponents, and the opportunity to improve one's skills. Examples of scarce benefits are fame and fortune. It is clear that basic benefits, at least in theory, can be available to all and are achievable by all; scarce benefits by their very nature cannot be attained by all (2: pp. 270-71).

I

English (2: p. 273) advances the following argument in defense of the claim that women have a justifiable demand for equal coverage and prize money:

The Argument From Self-Respect

1. Members of disadvantaged groups identify strongly with each other's successes and failures.

Reprinted, by permission, from R.A. Belliotti, 1979, "Women, sex, and sports," *Journal of the Philosophy of Sport, VI:* 67-72.

2. If women do not attain roughly equal fame and fortune in sports, it leads both men and women to think of women as naturally inferior.
3. When there is a wide disparity in these attainments between men and women, this is damaging to the self-respect of all women.
4. All women have a right to self-respect. This right to self-respect justifies the demand for equal press coverage and prize money for women.

Premises (1) and (4) can be quickly accepted. Self-respect is an indispensable factor for both enjoying our lives and living fruitfully with others. And, surely, it is true that individuals are often classified into groups, and that this group affiliation often leads them to be treated in particular ways and also leads them toward certain expectations and goals—hence the call for "role models" by many advocates for affirmative action.

Premises (2) and (3) are much less convincing. Even if the performances of the most capable women in sports in which objective performance measurement is possible (e.g., golf and bowling) are below the performances of the most capable men, we should not conclude that women are naturally inferior. Past cultural and social inequalities may well account for at least some of the disparity. And if women do not attain equal fame and fortune because of this performance disparity and because of market conditions, this need and should not lead anyone to conclude that women are *naturally* inferior as athletes; and it should certainly not lead anyone to conclude that women are inferior *people.*

Why should *all* women lose self-respect because of a dearth of female athletic stars or because professional women athletes receive less prize money than men receive? It is only when society teaches us that our self-respect is connected integrally with athletic attainments that this might occur. It is one thing to say that members of disadvantaged groups identify strongly with each other's successes and failures, and quite another to say that unequal financial attainments in athletics will result in a loss of self-respect for all members of the group.

The fact is that we should not respect ourselves because of our own or our group's attainments of fame and fortune in professional sports; we should respect ourselves and those we identify with on the basis of the kind of people we are, the kind of moral lives we lead, and the characters we possess. And the strange part of all this is that English (2: p. 274) seems to recognize this later in her article, for she states, "I may have a low (and accurate) estimate of myself as a tennis player without losing respect for myself as a person." Here she is certainly correct.

All women may have low estimates of themselves as athletes and athletic attainers without losing respect for themselves or their sisters as people. There simply is no necessary connection between a person's athletic

attainments and that person's degree of self-respect; and there should not
be any empirical connection. Again, there is an empirical connection only
if society as a whole or the major social group itself teaches and values
athletic performance measured by fame/fortune as an important aspect of
the group's or individual's self-respect. But society and the major social
groups need not and should not teach this and, hence, there need be and
should be no empirical connection between athletic attainments and self-
respect.

However, it should be rejoined that even if there is no *necessary* connection between athletic attainments and group self-respect, and even if there
should be no empirical connection, there still *is* an empirical connection, at
least in our society.

But I think that this is false, at least in the case of women. Do all women,
or even a majority of women, really lose self-respect because Chris Evert
Lloyd does not make as much money as Bjorn Borg; or because Nancy
Lopez is in a lower tax bracket than Jack Nicklaus; or, if we look to the past,
because Mickey Wright received far less press coverage and prize money
than did Arnold Palmer? I would conjecture that the vast majority of women
could care less about Chris Evert Lloyd and Nancy Lopez, and that very few
even know who Mickey Wright was. I believe that the majority of women do
not even take an active interest in female professional sports, much less lose
self-respect because of disparities in female and male sports attainments. So,
I do not think there is any empirical connection between female athletic
attainments and female self-respect.

II

English (2: p. 270) identifies properly the role of self-respect in athletics
when she states that "self-respect (is) to be gained by doing one's best." The
notion of individual self-respect being connected with effort expended in
fulfilling athletic potential is much sounder than the attainment principle (3).
Much athletic ability is natural, personally undeserved, and such that we
cannot take credit generally for our possession of it. It seems inappropriate
and mistaken to allow our self-respect to hinge upon so arbitrary a factor.
However, much of what we personally deserve is directly determined by the
effort and energy we expend in certain pursuits. That is why we often praise
a less gifted competitor who is making the most of her ability and denigrate
a more talented performer who seems to be an underachiever.

Athletics, if it is to be a factor in determining our self-respect, should be
valued for its basic, and not for its scarce, benefits.

The argument from the right to self-respect does not concentrate on equality of performance between men and women professional sports stars, but rather upon equality in press coverage and financial rewards. To those who believe that fame/fortune in professional sports should be proportionate to performance, it would not seem unjustified to compensate women less, or to allow them less media coverage, if the reason for doing so is not simply that they are women, but rather that they do not perform as well. At least in some sports objective performance is clearly measurable and comparable (e.g., golf, bowling, and skeet shooting); in other sports (e.g., basketball, tennis, and baseball) the top men professionals are held uncontroversially to be significantly superior to the top women. One could argue that the whole point of awarding prize money and lavishing fame is to single out the most proficient athletic performers. To reward equally the best men and women in a sport, when the former are objectively better performers than the latter, is to stray from the correlation of reward and performance.

I am assuming that in any occupation, professional athletics or otherwise, if females demonstrated that they could perform comparably to the top males, then unequal recognition and pay would clearly be justified, unless some special market conditions could be cited. Suppose that women could demonstrate this parity of performance, but were still denied equal recognition and pay. How would they respond? Rather than losing self-respect, I suspect, they would be outraged, angered, and indignant. Women under these circumstances would have no reason to lose self-respect, since they would have proven they were just as capable as comparable males. No one would conclude that women were naturally inferior in any respect. So I think that (2) is false. The connection between thinking women naturally inferior is connected, if it is connected at all, with inferior athletic *performance* and not inferior athletic *fame* and *fortune*. Further, as I have previously tried to indicate, even inferior performance in athletics need not lead everyone to conclude that women are *naturally* inferior athletes; and it should lead no one to conclude that they are inferior human beings.

Let us suppose that women could be shown to be inferior performers to comparable males in *all* occupations in which both groups labored. What would be the response of women in this case if they were recognized and rewarded less? The response might well be a loss of self-respect, since they might be led to conclude (rightly or wrongly) that women were naturally inferior to men in certain important skills. But note two things: (1) This loss of respect would be connected with inferior performance much more than with inferior fame/reward; (2) This loss of self-respect would not occur if women were judged inferior in only one, or a few, occupation(s), since they could point to other occupations in which they equalled or surpassed comparable male performers. So, again, I conclude that premises (2) and (3) are, at best, overstatements, and, at worst, simply false.

III

Recognition and monetary reward for athletics and all occupations are determined to a large extent by market conditions. Public demand for, and attendance at, sports contests determine in large part the money available to be awarded as prizes and the amount of media coverage for the event. But, of course, public interest can be altered by the media; increased media coverage of an event can have an important effect on increasing public demand for these types of events.

Do females have a justified demand for increased media coverage as a means of thwarting their loss of self-respect? Let us consider the case of high fashion models. There are several women who have recently become famous as models: Jean Shrimpton, Twiggy, Margeaux Hemingway, and Farrah Fawcett-Majors, among others. There are no relatively famous male fashion models. Female models at this level receive substantially more pay than male models. Yet this situation has not led all men to lose self-respect for several reasons: (1) Men are not taught that the rewards and recognition of this occupation are an integral part of their group's self-respect; (2) Even if it could be shown that male models perform less capably than their female counterparts—although I do not know how, if at all, the performances of models are measured—men can still point to other, more important, occupations in which they excel. Hence, they need not think themselves naturally inferior people; and (3) Men have been conditioned to regard all aspects of fashion less important to them than to women.

But suppose it were possible via an intensive program of public relations gimmickry to make fashion very important among men. Suppose by focusing a great deal of media coverage upon male fashion that the market could be manipulated and male demand for fashion increased greatly. Men would suddenly demand equal fame and recognition for male fashion models, since the self-respect of all men will be diminished if parity is not attained. However, the performance of male fashion models still lags behind the performance of comparable female models. So additional media and market manipulation is required in order to protect the self-respect of all men, and parity is achieved.

Would we really want all this to occur? I judge that if market and media manipulation in fashion is justified at all it should be concerned with deemphasizing the importance of fashion consciousness among both men and women. An individual's make-up, clothes, and sartorial style should play a very small role in determining one's self-respect. And so too with professional athletics. Instead of manipulating media and market influences to achieve a parity of fame and fortune for female stars whose objectively measured performances are inferior to comparable male stars, we might consider manipulating these influences (if at all) to achieve a deemphasis on professional sports themselves. Again, an individual's and a group's self-respect need not and should not be connected with the monetary attainments of professional athletic stars.

IV

Much of what English says is very perspicacious. The emphasis on athletics should be participation and not spectating; expenditures for big time male high school and college sports ought to be cut in deference to increasing the opportunities for participation for females, non-varsity males, and the community as a whole; equal opportunity for the *basic* benefits of athletics must be available to all; and sports other than those of traditional male domain should be considered valuable (2: p. 275).

However, she is wrong in arguing that the scarce benefits of athletics must be equalized for women in order to maintain the self-respect of all women. She is wrong because: (1) The attainments of top professional athletes need not and should not be a significant factor in determining the self-respect of all women; (2) As an empirical matter of fact, these attainments *are not* an important factor in the way the vast majority of women determine their respect for themselves; (3) Unequal objective performances, *ceteris paribus*, should not be rewarded and recognized equally; (4) Society should be more concerned with teaching us to identify our self-respect with our moral traits and characters, rather than vicarious identification with professional sports stars; and (5) Even if I am incorrect about the truth of (1)-(4), to say that X (women) have a right to Y (self-respect) and that Z (parity in attainments for female sports stars) is necessary for Y, it does not follow that X have a right to Z or a justified claim to Z.

To say that someone has a right to life and right to privacy, and to establish that certain things are necessary for that someone to continue living or continue to have privacy, does not establish that the person has a right or justified claim to these certain things.[1] Among other considerations, some of these necessary things may require that others perform supererogatory acts, and no one has a *right* that others perform supererogatory acts for her. Parity for female sports stars in terms of financial attainments may well require

supererogatory acts on the part of society, especially in view of the fact that
these stars have not demonstrated parity in terms of objectively measured
performance.

There may be other arguments that can be advanced in support of
equalizing the scarce benefits of professional sports (e.g., as *compensation*
for past cultural and social deprivations); I suspect that these would not be
successful. Finally, it seems clear that English's argument from the right to
self-respect fails, or so I am claiming.

Note

1. For clarification of this point and related notions see my "Negative Duties,
   Positive Duties, and Rights" (1).

Bibliography

1. Belliotti, Raymond A. "Negative Duties, Positive Duties, and Rights." *The
   Southern Journal of Philosophy,* XVI (1978), 581-588.
2. English, Jane. "Sex Equality in Sports." *Philosophy and Public Affairs,* VII
   (1978), 269-277.

17

CHAPTER

Gender Equity and Inequity in Athletics

Robert L. Simon

For a large portion of American history, highly competitive sport often was thought not to be appropriate for women. During a good part of the twentieth century, more formal athletic competition for women tended to take the form of noncompetitive "play days" or participation on teams that received little of the support accorded to men's sports. Although great female athletes such as Althea Gibson, Babe Zaharias, and Mickey Wright flourished during this period, athletic competition was available only in attenuated form for most females in most sports.

Thus, in 1971, slightly less than three hundred thousand girls participated in high school sports, while nearly four million boys participated (8: p. 3). James Michener, in his book *Sports in America,* in writing about the period shortly before passage of Title IX, reported that

> one day I saw the budget of . . . a state institution (a university) supported by tax funds, with a student body divided fifty-fifty between men and women. The athletic department had $3,900,000 to spend,

Reprinted, by permission, from R.L. Simon, 1995, "Gender equity and inequity in athletics," *Journal of the Philosophy of Sport, XX-XXI:* 6-22.

and of this, women received exactly $31,000, a little less than eight-tenths of one percent. On this face of it, this was outrageous. (6: p. 120)

This situation changed radically along with, and surely in great part because of, the passage of Title IX, the federal legislation that prohibited discrimination by gender in all federally funded programs, including athletics. Thus, by 1979, two million girls were participating in high school athletics. Similar growth took place at the intercollegiate level as well (8: p. 3).

Although the growth of participation in women's sports on the interscholastic and intercollegiate level has been enormous since the passage of Title IX, issues of gender equity in athletics are still very much with us. For example, in intercollegiate athletics in the United States, less total income is spent on female athletes than on male athletes, female athletes receive significantly less attention from the media than male athletes, and females continue to participate less than their male counterparts. Thus, issues of justice and fairness for each gender remain significant in organized athletics, including at the intercollegiate level.

Title IX lays down the legal criteria of nondiscrimination in athletics. Gender equity sometimes is taken as a broader notion having to do with morally fair and just treatment. But how are we to tell when men's and women's athletic programs within the same institution are treated equitably? What are the criteria of equity in this area?

In this essay, I will try to identify and explore some of the major issues that arise under the heading of gender equity in athletics. I will try to sketch out the landscape and indicate where controversies lie. My main focus will be on intercollegiate athletics in the United States, although the discussion certainly will have broader application, and on some of the important questions of gender equity that arise in such a context.

Gender Equity and Intercollegiate Sport

The general kind of consideration underlying the case for gender equity in sports is that no individual should be deprived of access to beneficial activities or opportunities merely on the basis of gender. Participation in athletics can provide important benefits ranging from what Jane English has called the basic benefits of sport, such as healthy exercise and the opportunity to learn to compete, as well as scarce benefits such as fame and fortune (3: pp. 329-330). In addition, there are what might be called constitutive benefits, that is, goods that are comprehensible only within the framework defined by the constitutive rules of the game and that have no value to those who do not appreciate the nuances of the game itself (5: pp. 175-178). Thus, the pleasure of pulling off a perfect double play in baseball, the faking out of a defender in basketball, or the execution of a difficult fade to a pin cut in the right corner of a well-protected green in golf are all examples of such constitutive goods, which may be virtually meaningless to nonplayers, but which may be remembered for a lifetime by participants and fans. Finally, as Jan Boxill emphasizes in her contribution in this issue, sports not only constitute a widely available means of unalienated self-expression but also open doors for other sorts of opportunities in our society. The case for gender equity presupposes that to restrict access to these sorts of goods by gender is unfair and unjust.

However, it doesn't follow from this that educational institutions, particularly colleges and universities, should support athletic teams and engage in the existing practice of intercollegiate sport. Whether colleges and universities ought to support intercollegiate athletics in the first place is a different issue from what counts as gender equity once such programs are already established. Indeed, many observers are skeptical of the value of intercollegiate sports. (Leslie Francis expresses such skepticism in her contribution to this issue.) In part, this may be because of highly publicized abuses in major college athletic programs. Even where such abuses are eliminated, however, skepticism might still arise from concerns about the time athletes are required to commit to their sport, the expenditures on athletics that critics feel might be applied to more central educational concerns, the exploitation of athletes, and the tremendous emphasis on athletic (as opposed to academic) success at some U.S. universities. In other words, intercollegiate athletics are seen to be in conflict with the central academic mission of the university.

While such skepticism cannot be fully assessed here, it is relevant to our concerns about gender equity, since most proponents of gender equity are concerned about equity within the present framework of intercollegiate sports. A more radical approach (which Francis goes some way towards endorsing) would encourage making fundamental changes in the framework itself, or perhaps even eliminating it.

In assessing skepticism about intercollegiate sports as presently constituted, two points do need to be kept in mind. First, it is important to distinguish the high pressure, "big-time" athletic programs of the major intercollegiate athletic powers from other sorts of intercollegiate athletic programs. Division III is the largest division of the National Collegiate Athletic Association (NCAA), and its schools, which do not award athletic scholarships, are explicitly committed to the ideal of the scholar-athlete and to the priority of academics over athletics. In addition, a number of conferences in Division I, such as the Ivy League and the Patriot League, embrace a similar philosophy. Moreover, many of the major athletic powers appear to run "clean" programs and recruit academically successful athletes. Differences among the different kinds of athletic programs clearly can be relevant to the moral evaluation of them.

Second, although a case can be made casting doubt on the educational value of participation in athletics, it is important to remember that much can be said on the other side. Thus, one can plausibly (although controversially) argue that intercollegiate athletics at their best do serve educational functions that are compatible and that may even reinforce the central academic tasks of the university. Effective performance in intercollegiate sports requires commitment, the ability to analyze one's weaknesses and the means to improve them, the capacity to perform under pressure, and the ability to work together with many different sorts of people towards a common goal. Similar values are necessary for academic success. The test of excellence, which constitutes the athletic contest, can be an important educational experience in which the participants learn about themselves and others. Moreover, effective performance by athletic teams can illustrate the values of dedication, coolness under pressure, courage, and intelligence in performance for the entire community within a common framework to which individuals from different genders, religions, ethnic backgrounds, cultures, and academic disciplines can all relate.

Whether such an argument is ultimately justifiable is controversial. However, it is relevant to the question of gender equity in intercollegiate athletics. If the practice does provide important educational benefits to participants, as well as opportunities for recognition and fun, a strong presumptive case exists against making distinctions by gender in cases of access to participation or treatment of participants. Moreover, even if (as Francis claims) intercollegiate athletics is a morally flawed practice that ought to be modified or even radically changed, presumably the benefits it does provide should be available to each gender.

In any case, the discussion that follows primarily concerns the framework of intercollegiate athletics. Because the gross abuses found in some major athletic programs need not be part of such a practice, and in fact violate existing rules of the NCAA and go beyond the scope of gender equity, they are not considered here. Instead, the issues concerning gender equity within intercollegiate athletics, as so constituted, are addressed.

Concepts, Conceptions, and Tests of Equity

It is puzzling when one finds all the parties to an ethical dispute appealing to the same value. Why then is there a dispute? Often, it is because the parties have different and conflicting conceptions of the value in question. For example, two individuals may both profess to believe in equal opportunity in hiring. However, one might understand equal opportunity as requiring simply the hiring of the best candidate as measured by standard meritocratic criteria, while the other may view virtually any set of meritocratic criteria as culturally biased. Such an individual may understand equal opportunity as requiring reasonable representation of disadvantaged groups in the work force. Clearly, although both individuals believe in "equal opportunity," what each considers equal opportunity is vastly different.

A similar point seems to apply to the value of gender equity in athletics. Although conceptual lines have not been drawn very clearly by participants in the public policy discussion, it is far from clear that all are working with the same conception of gender equity or that important conceptual distinctions have been made.

Thus, the Gender Equity Task Force of the NCAA declares that an athletics program is equitable to each gender "when the participants in both the men's and women's sports programs would accept as fair and equitable the overall program of the other gender" (4: p. 3). This account seems related to the idea of role reversal and impartiality in moral theory, but leaves open many of the questions raised by such approaches.

For example, does this mean that members of each gender should assess the program of the other gender using their own values and criteria? Or should they "bracket" those values and criteria and try to view things as if they had the values of the other gender? (Do values differ, even statistically, by gender?) Should they try to view things from some neutral perspective, perhaps behind a Rawlsian veil of ignorance, which would obscure from them the knowledge of just which gender they belong to?

Moreover, even if we could agree on the perspective from which we were to evaluate the program of the other gender, it is far from clear that all those who took that perspective would agree in their evaluation. For example, Jones might believe that coaches in high-visibility men's sports work under higher pressure than coaches of the same sports in women's programs and so should be paid more even if all other qualifications are equivalent. Smith, however, might disagree. Such persistent disputes need not be largely factual (Are coaches of men's sports necessarily under more pressure to win than coaches in parallel sports in the women's program?) but may be primarily normative. Jones may see nothing wrong with men's sports getting a disproportionate share of national publicity, since that is what the public wants, but Smith may see the media as having a moral duty to promote more equal coverage regardless of public demands.

Such concerns may not do justice to the intent of the Gender Equity Task Force, because their goal almost surely was not to present a philosophically adequate theory of gender equity. Their account in terms of taking the perspective of the other gender may be quite useful, not as a philosophical theory, but as a ground rule for discussion. Be that as it may, such a requirement is not sufficient to dictate agreement on what counts as gender equity, or whether it has been achieved in a specific context, both because of ambiguity in what counts as taking an alternate perspective and because disagreement may persist even among people evaluating from the same perspective. Thus, even individuals of the same gender often will disagree among themselves when evaluating the fairness of an athletics program.

While disagreement is possible even among people using the same conception of gender equity, disagreement is also possible over which conception should be employed. Even worse, parties to a dispute may not even notice they are using different conceptions of gender equity. Thus, if X identifies gender equity in college athletics with proportional representation of men and women in the athletic program, and Y identifies it with similar treatment of parallel teams, for example, similar budgets for men's and women's volleyball, then gender equity may exist according to Y's conception but not X's. A genuine issue they need to discuss is whose conception of gender equity is more defensible.

Moreover, we also need to distinguish tests or procedures for discovering what gender equity requires. For example, one might hold that gender equity substantively requires representation of each gender proportional to the gender's representation among the student body. One might justify this by appeal to the test of taking the perspective of the other gender. The latter functions as a kind of role-reversal test at the level of justification, while the former requirement is alleged to be what those who actually do reverse roles would come to agree upon.

Thus a full conception of gender equity in intercollegiate athletics has several levels, including a level of justification that involves procedures or methods of moral evaluation and a level of substantive criteria or requirements that specific programs should satisfy. Conceivably, different justificatory approaches could support the same substantive requirements. It is equally conceivable that those who use the same justificatory approach might disagree about what requirements are justified, perhaps because they apply the justificatory method differently or disagree on factual matters relevant to the argument.

Rather than attempt to distinguish all the possible conceptions of gender equity, it will be useful for our purposes to simplify so as to advance the discussion. Let us say that an athletics program is gender equitable if it makes no unjustified distinctions between the genders. This approach has two advantages. First, it avoids begging key questions by stipulation because it leaves open what a justifiable distinction is. That is to be settled on a case by case basis by discussion, although general principles of justifiability may emerge from the examination of cases. Second, this approach is related to the one used to interpret Title IX that has recently been developed by the Office of Civil Rights (OCR). Thus, relevant aspects of the legal discussion over Title IX can be incorporated into the moral discussion of gender equity.

The OCR's Three-Tiered Test

Sometimes individuals who are frustrated by what they perceive as the lack of equity for women in intercollegiate athletics will express disbelief that progress has been so slow two decades after the passage of Title IX. It is only recently, however, that relatively clear (although still contestable) guidelines for the legal interpretation of Title IX have been promulgated by the OCR. Indeed, prior to special legislation by Congress, the Supreme Court had ruled in *Grove City vs. Bell* (1984) that Title IX only applied to those programs within educational institutions that directly received federal funds. If Congress had not passed special legislation in 1988 overriding that decision, it is unclear that Title IX would have applied to intercollegiate athletics at all since few if any intercollegiate athletic programs receive funds directly from the U.S. government.

The guidelines promulgated by the OCR are of interest both because they specify allowable exceptions to a general presumption of equal treatment and because they raise some interesting problems in their own right. The OCR identifies three major areas of compliance with Title IX: athletic scholarships, accommodation of athletic interests and abilities, and other athletic benefits and awards. We will be concerned with the second area, accommodation of athletic abilities and interests, since it clearly is most fundamental.

The OCR proposes the following three-part test for gender equality in the accommodation of athletic abilities and interests. One must consider

- whether opportunities for participation in the intercollegiate athletics program for students of each sex are substantially proportionate to their respective enrollments;
- if not, whether the institution can show a history and continuing practice of expansion of the intercollegiate athletic program responsive to

developing interests and abilities of members of the underrepresented sex;

- if not, whether the interests and abilities of the underrepresented sex are "fully and effectively accommodated" by the existing program (1: p. 7).

Legal compliance is established by satisfying any one of the three tests. An intercollegiate athletic program that fails an earlier element might still be in compliance with Title IX by satisfying one of the later prongs. The first is a "safe harbor" in the sense that a finding of proportionality will at the very least establish a strong and indeed virtually overwhelming presumption of compliance. However, failure to show proportionality (it is doubtful if any institutions of higher education in the country now satisfy this requirement strictly construed) is not sufficient to establish noncompliance since the other criteria still might be met.

The three-part OCR test has some important resemblances to the presumptive approach to gender equity. It assumes both genders will be treated equally and specifies some allowable reasons for inequality. Representation of gender in proportion to its share of the overall student body normally will be taken as virtually conclusive evidence of equal treatment. However, if proportionality cannot be satisfied, inequality can be justified by showing compliance with one of the other two prongs of the test. Moreover, in assessing whether the interests of the underrepresented gender have been "fully and effectively accommodated," the assumption is that each gender will be treated equally in the absence of justifying reasons for inequality.

Of course, what counts as a justifiable reason for inequality often will be controversial. Does the past success of the men's basketball team at a Division I institution justify them playing a more nationally prominent schedule than the less successful women's team? What if the athletic director promises to upgrade the women's schedule as soon as the team develops sufficiently to compete successfully at that level? Should a 98-pound female gymnast receive the same daily meal allowance as a 275-pound male lineman when the teams are on the road? Would it be an inequity if the lineman were given a greater allowance because he needs more food? Is it an inequity if the basketball coach of the men's team is paid more than the equally experienced and competent coach of the women's team on the grounds that there is more pressure to win and greater chance of being fired after a losing season in the men's program?

Clearly, all of these questions cannot be explored in one paper. In what follows, I will raise some questions about two fundamental parts of the OCR three-pronged test: proportionality and effective accommodation of interests. Because they are fundamental, exploration of these areas may help shed some light on other important issues of gender equity that are likely to arise as well. I will conclude with some brief comments on suggestions for fundamental change in intercollegiate athletics.

Proportionality

The idea that men and women should be represented in an educational institution's athletic program in proportion to their representation in the student body initially sounds plausible. After all, if participation in athletics provides significant benefits and opportunities, and if there is no reason to favor one gender in the distribution of these benefits and opportunities, then one would expect them to be made available to both genders equally. So if 60% of the student body are men and 40% are women, then in the absence of discrimination one would expect to find that about 60% of the institution's athletes are men and about 40% are women.

However, there are a number of problems with this initial expectation. According to the NCAA Gender Equity Task Force, there currently are 3.4 million male and 1.9 million female participants in interscholastic sports at the high school level in the U.S. (4: p. 5). Clearly, there is a significant disproportion in the representation of each gender in sports at the precollege level. Is it reasonable, then, to expect the proportion of women participating at the college level, which is significantly more demanding than the high school level, to suddenly jump? If not, it seems unreasonable to place so much stress on proportional representation in the first place. Where are the additional female athletes needed to achieve proportionality to come from?

In other words, the argument that each gender should be proportionately represented in the university's intercollegiate athletic program presupposes that the members of each gender have an *equal interest* in participating. It is just that presupposition that critics of proportionality call into question.

Many proponents of proportionality do not find this objection persuasive, however. They reply that females in America traditionally have been discouraged from participating in athletics and are only beginning to overcome the kind of socialization that has inhibited participation. Hence, rates of participation are not adequate indicators of true interest. If colleges and universities will provide additional women's sports, the participants eventually will come.

While this rejoinder does have some force, I think it also raises some difficult questions. First, it is important to remember that questions of distributive justice in intercollegiate athletics arise at least at two levels: distribution of resources within the athletic program and distribution within the university generally. Thus, should colleges and universities be required to increase expenditure on athletics at a time when many academic needs are unmet because of lack of funding, simply to generate purely hypothetical interests that some women would have had or might have had if they had been socialized differently?

Perhaps the answer to this rhetorical question is affirmative. After all, if participation in athletics does have important educational, personal, and recreational benefits, why shouldn't women be especially encouraged to participate? Similarly, shouldn't the university take it as part of its mission to expose students to great literature even though they may have no prior expressed interest in it (and may even desire avoiding it)? Moreover, many more women than those who try out for teams may have an interest in participation in athletics, but may not express that interest due to lack of encouragement.

Be that as it may, is *varsity* athletics the place to cultivate such interest? Perhaps what would be more appropriate are more general recreational programs including club sports and intramurals, at a level of lower competitive intensity, designed to involve large numbers of women in sports. The addition of a varsity team or two hardly fulfills such a role and surely is better justified for individuals already strongly interested in participating. Varsity sports demand a high level of commitment, involve a great deal of competitive intensity, and seem most appropriate for those individuals who already have significant interest in participating in athletic competition.

Advocates of proportionality see it as a means for increasing participation in athletics. Moreover, they point out that institutions need not provide proportional participation by gender if they can meet the other OCR criteria. Thus, proportionality is a "goal" and not a "quota."

However, an additional concern about proportionality is that it can function in ways unintended by its supporters, because there are two different ways to remedy disproportional representation of men. The first is to raise the proportion of women participating. The second is to *reduce* the proportion of men participating.

Suppose an institution is 60% male and 40% female. Suppose further that 70% of its 1,000 intercollegiate athletes are men and only 30% of its intercollegiate athletes are women. The school could, of course, try to raise the percentage of female athletes to around 40%, but it may find it very difficult to do so both because of the expense involved and because of the difficulty of finding interested female athletes. Instead, it could cut male teams and reduce the percentage of men playing to, say, under 50% of all athletes. That is, by cutting sports involving 300 male athletes, the school would be left with 700 athletes of whom 400 would be men, and 300 would be women. Men would now only constitute 57% of all athletes and women would constitute 43%. In other words, by cutting men's sports, the institution could achieve proportionality and a "safe harbor" from further legal action *without adding an additional opportunity for even a single female athlete to participate.*

While this is undoubtedly an extreme case, the provision that proportionality is a safe harbor from legal action can act as an incentive to trim men's programs so as to appear to provide equal access to underrepresented women athletes without increasing opportunities for women. In fact, less visible men's sports teams seem to have been cut at a number of institutions, quite possibly in part to achieve a more respectable looking ratio of female to male athletes.

Accordingly, the requirement of proportionality may have the unintended consequence in American colleges and universities of decreasing the total number of slots on athletic teams, quite possibly without significantly increasing opportunities to participate for women.[1] Strictly speaking, the incentive to cut male sports arises not from the proportionality requirement taken alone, satisfaction of which is not necessary for compliance with Title IX, but from the additional suggestion that satisfaction of proportionality is a virtual presumption of immunity from further complaint about gender equity.

Perhaps the problem then is not with the proportionality requirement, conceived of as a long-range goal, but with the additional presumption of virtual immunity. It is hard to understand, in any case, why an athletic program that satisfies proportionality may not be deficient in other serious ways (e.g., women being denied equal access to training facilities). Accordingly, a more sensible policy might be to take proportionality as an ideal to be achieved in the long run, indicate what colleges and universities ought to do in the short run to make modest but significant gains in participation in athletics by females, and drop the idea of a "safe harbor" from examination altogether.

To summarize, the requirement of proportionality raises several issues. First, is it unrealistic and unfair to expect colleges to achieve proportional representation by gender in athletics by increasing the number of female participants, when females are significantly underrepresented in interscholastic athletics at the high school level? (Colleges and universities might still be expected to make genuine efforts to incrementally increase the proportion of women participating in intercollegiate athletics, however, without being expected to achieve proportional representation.) Second, should achievement of proportionality count as a "safe harbor" from either moral or legal scrutiny of an intercollegiate athletics program? This provides an incentive for institutions to achieve proportionality, not by enhancing participation for women, but by eliminating opportunities for men, probably in less visible sports without powerful lobbies to protect them. In addition, it is far from clear that a program that achieves proportionality is equitable in other ways, and so it is far from clear that such programs should receive protection from examination or culpability.

Accordingly, the proportionality test is problematic, whether construed as a legal requirement or as a moral standard that intercollegiate programs can be held culpable for failing to meet.

Interests and Equity

Because few if any intercollegiate athletic programs are likely to achieve proportionality in the next few years, most institutions that wish to demonstrate compliance with Title IX will try to show that they "fully and effectively accommodate" the interests of the underrepresented gender, which typically is women. If we turn to the moral analogue of the OCR test, this means that if men are disproportionately represented in an intercollegiate athletics program, colleges and universities ought to fully satisfy the interests of the gender that is least represented. (The case for full and effective accommodation becomes even stronger if the bulk of funding goes to men, which normally will be the case in athletic programs that include football.) This at least appears to resemble the Rawlsian idea that the group getting the lesser share ought to be made as well off as possible.[2]

Clearly there is a moral case to be made for this kind of approach. Until the passage of Title IX, college athletic programs made little attempt to support the athletic interests of female students, while providing a great deal of support for male athletes. Surely, it is fair and just to require colleges to meet the interests of female athletes, given that so much has been, and is being, done for male athletes.

Nevertheless, the idea that the interests of female student athletes should be "fully and effectively accommodated" raises problems that deserve examination. This is because the accommodation of interests criterion (AIC) is quite strong. In programs that have not achieved proportionality, and in which females are underrepresented when compared to their share of the student body as a whole, the AIC virtually insures that the interests of women athletes will be fully accommodated, even when the same is not true for the interests of men. For example, consider a hypothetical institution in which the student body of 1,000 is 55% male and 45% female. Suppose 200 men and 100 women play in the intercollegiate program. In other words, about

66% of the athletes are men and 33% women. Suppose now that a group of women show an interest in having a varsity crew team, a relatively expensive sport. Under the AIC, the women should get the team and the university is inequitable if it fails to provide it for them. Let us review the case for this conclusion.

Roughly sketched, the argument is that because women have had the lesser opportunity in the past and because men receive the bulk of the benefits provided by participation in intercollegiate athletics, equity requires that the position of women be improved. This case becomes even stronger (perhaps, as Leslie Francis suggests in this issue, it is comparable to the case for some forms of affirmative action) if we assume the past lack of opportunity for women to participate in intercollegiate athletics was a moral *wrong* or has arisen from moral *wrongdoing*.

What problems does this kind of argument face? For one thing, those critics of affirmative action who tend to focus on individuals as the locus of moral analysis will want to raise individual-group concerns. Although women may have been wronged in the past, it is unlikely that those individual women who would now participate in sports if the program were expanded are the very same individuals who have been wronged in the past. A rejoinder to this criticism is that the point of expanding the women's athletic program is not to provide compensation to individuals. Rather, it may be to improve the status of women, provide future opportunities for women, or enhance the overall fairness of the athletic program by providing equal access to each gender. (Indeed, if we add 16 women to the program by making crew a varsity sport, women are still only 37% of the intercollegiate athletes although they constitute 45% of our hypothetical student body.) None of these goals have anything to do with individual compensation, but instead are concerned with moral improvement of the athletic program in the future.

Some would argue that the concerns of the individualist can be laid to rest by such a reply. In any case, the concerns raised by the individualist cover ground familiar to those who have followed the literature on affirmative action (2). Be that as it may, both the individualist criticism and the rejoinder presuppose that women's interests have not been effectively accommodated in the past. This surely is true if we go back to the days before Title IX when women had few opportunities, let alone equal ones, in competitive athletics. But is it necessarily true of our hypothetical student body if crew is not elevated to varsity status?

Suppose the following were the case at our hypothetical university. Although 200 men participate in the intercollegiate program, 300 have tried out for teams. One hundred were cut either because of lack of ability or because the coaching staff could not work effectively with so many players.

Only 15 women who tried out for teams were cut. Thus, 87% of the women who went out for teams secured positions while only 66% of the men who tried out were able to participate.[3] According to a line of argument suggested by these figures, women have had a *greater* chance than men to play varsity sports at our hypothetical institution if we restrict the relevant pool of comparison to those interested enough to try out for teams. In what sense, a skeptic may ask, have women had less opportunity than men to play in the intercollegiate program?

The point here seems to be that in deciding which gender is underrepresented, we need to use the relevant pool of students as our standard of comparison. What is controversial is the specification of the relevant pool. If the relevant pool is not the student body as a whole, but instead it is the students sufficiently committed to try out for teams, it may be debatable whether women are the underrepresented gender. Why then, a critic of the OCR guidelines may ask, should failure to meet the proportionality prong of the OCR test virtually guarantee women that their interests in varsity athletics will be "fully and effectively accommodated"? Their interests already may be accommodated more fully than those of men.

Something like this line of argument was advanced by Brown University when, after attempting to drop two women's and two men's intercollegiate sports, it was sued by the women athletes who wanted their teams protected from cuts. One line of defense advanced by Brown was that "an institution satisfactorily accommodates female athletes if it allocates athletic opportunities to women in accordance with the ratio of interested and able women to interested and able men, regardless of the number of unserved women or the percentage of the student body they comprise" (1: p. 8).

What might be the grounds for rejecting Brown's argument? The U.S. First Circuit Court of Appeals rejected Brown's argument citing a variety of reasons. For one thing, Brown's proposal places a significant administrative burden on the plaintiffs to a suit since they would have to gather evidence as to the number of "interested and able" male and female athletes. Moreover, would the relevant pool be the present student body, the high school pool the university normally recruits from, or an expanded pool it could recruit from if it wanted to attract a larger number of female athletes?

More important, the court believed it proper to assume that, given equal opportunity and encouragement, women will participate in athletics to the same extent as men. Accordingly, that more men show an interest in participation than women under inequitable conditions of opportunity and encouragement must not be taken as determinative. Moreover, the court concluded that even if regulations "create a gender classification slanted somewhat in favor of women, we would find no constitutional infirmity" (1: p. 10).

Convenie...

These kinds of arguments still leave questions unresolved. For example, what is the relevance of appeal to *administrative inconvenience* to claims of *equity* and *fairness?* Surely, the more convenient and less complex policy is not necessarily the more equitable or fair one.[4] After all, plaintiffs in gender equity suits already have the burden of showing that their gender's interests have not been accommodated, yet that is not considered unfair.

The second and more weighty line of argument maintains that because women are currently in a situation that unfairly disadvantages them athletically, their relative lack of current overt expressions of interest cannot be taken at face value. But even here, problems remain. Does the assumption that conditions are not yet fair beg the issue, since the very point at issue is whether or not women's interests are already fairly accommodated.[5] Again, what if the specific institution in question never itself discriminated against or disadvantaged women athletes. (Suppose it were all male until recently going co-educational.) But leaving these points aside, perhaps a more crucial issue is whether *balancing* is permitted at all. That is, in a college or university that has not achieved proportionality as defined by the OCR and that has no recent history of expansion of the women's athletic program, must the interests of any group of women be fully met regardless of other factors that might be relevant? Or, is there simply a weighty presumption in favor of meeting the women's interests, but one which may be overridden if there are sufficiently strong competing considerations on the other side?

In the case involving Brown University, there may have been no such overriding factors. But suppose that in our hypothetical example a very large number of able and interested male students lack the opportunity to play intercollegiate sports and only a small number of able and interested female students lack the same opportunity. Suppose the interested female students want to play an expensive sport (say, ice hockey), but the administration would rather institute a less expensive sport for women (say, soccer) and use the money saved for scholarships for needy students (who may or may not be athletes). Should the administration have the moral (or legal) discretion to decide whether or not to add a women's sport in such a context? If it must add a sport, does it have the discretion to decide which one to add? Or must it add the sport that will satisfy the interested and able students who are petitioning?[6]

Accordingly, we can conclude that just as the requirement of proportional representation of genders in intercollegiate athletic programs raises problems of significance, so too does the requirement that if proportionality is not achieved (and there is no recent history of expansion of the program of the underrepresented gender), then the interests of the underrepresented gender must be "fully and effectively accommodated." What counts as full and effective accommodation, and how is it to be weighed against other factors that are likely to be highly controversial in many contexts? My own suggestion is that some sort of balancing test, in the context of a presumption in favor of the underrepresented gender, is appropriate. But, how strong the presumption should be, or what sort of factors should be allowed to override it, are difficult to decide *a priori* (at least for me) and are probably best left to emerge from case law and consideration of actual and hypothetical examples in moral discourse.

Reform or Revolution

The discussion so far has focused on problems that arise within the existing framework of intercollegiate sport. However, some advocates of gender equity may find that the existing framework is itself the problem. That may be because of the emphasis presently placed on high-visibility men's sports such as basketball and football, or more general doubts about a "male model" of competitive athletics. Proposed remedies may range from the abolition of intercollegiate athletics as we now know them to major changes in the existing framework designed to produce more gender equity. Additional changes may include diverting some of the income presently going to intercollegiate sports to allegedly more central academic purposes.

Of course, the line between reform and revolutionary change is not a sharp one, and some proposals may be hard to categorize. Thus, is the proposal that teams in some noncontact sports, such as tennis and golf, be co-ed, a reform designed to cut costs and minimize gender differences, or is it a revolutionary change in the current gender conscious way we organize sports? While all major proposals for fundamental change in intercollegiate athletics cannot be considered here, some issues deserve attention.

One important set of issues arises from the predominance of high visibility men's sports, such as football and basketball. Where men's and women's sports are parallel, direct comparisons of equity can be made. Is College X spending as much on the women's volleyball team as the men's? Do they play comparable schedules and have similar access to similar practice facilities? Such questions are relatively easy to answer.

What happens, however, when there is no comparable women's sport? Football, in particular, involves large numbers of participants and disproportionately large expenditures. As most campuses, it, along with men's basketball, receives the bulk of the community's and the media's attention. Although women's basketball has been achieving increasing prominence, both in national media coverage and locally on specific campuses, there is little doubt that the bulk of public attention has gone to men's high-visibility sports at the athletically elite colleges and universities. Does the disproportion created in expenditures, participation, and attention by these high-visibility men's sports count as an inequity? If so, what is the appropriate remedy?

Defenders of such programs often argue that men's football and basketball are revenue-producing sports. According to this line of argument, the revenue generated by such programs can be used to support less visible sports teams, including women's teams. Where true, this line of argument would seem to implicitly appeal to something like John Rawls's difference principle that maintains that inequalities are justified insofar as they work to the benefit of the less advantaged group.

However, critics are quick to point out that relatively few football programs, even in Division I, show a profit (8: p. 29). Critics are also skeptical about whether profits there actually are used to support women's athletic programs.

While the critics are right to question whether the major men's sports normally are the giant revenue producers they are claimed to be, the issue of revenue production is itself complex. What counts as revenue? Just gate receipts? While studies fail to show that alumni contribute more to winning than to losing teams, would they contribute as much if men's football and basketball were deemphasized or eliminated entirely? What about the support generated throughout the state for schools like the University of North Carolina? Does it lead to more donations, purchase of university paraphernalia, or even favorable consideration from the state legislature? What about the billions paid to the NCAA by the CBS television network for rights to televise the men's basketball championship? Some of the money is used to pay the expenses of both men's and women's teams to participate in national championships sponsored by the NCAA. This is not to claim that men's visibility sports often are revenue producers after all, but only to point out that the assessment of whether they are or not raises difficult questions about what to include or exclude as profits and losses.

In fact, at many (perhaps most) American colleges and universities, particularly those in Division III of the NCAA (the division with the most members), the point of having sports teams is not to raise revenue or provide entertainment for regional or national audiences, but rather the point is to benefit the student-athletes, the campus, and the local communities. At such institutions, expensive sports like football are funded out of general revenues just like any other program. Are women athletes at such institutions treated inequitably simply because football has a disproportionate amount of participants and expenses?

I suggest not, at least if certain other conditions are satisfied. If women's interests in participating in athletics are effectively and fairly accommodated, it is difficult to see how women athletes lose simply because more is spent on football than other sports. (Do philosophy majors lose if more is spent on physics students, perhaps because of the cost of equipment in physics, or are both kinds of majors treated fairly if they are both enrolled in equally strong programs?) Even in high-visibility programs, difference in spending alone, whether total or per capita, need not necessarily show an unfair inequality, given equal satisfaction of interests.

The problem, of course, is what happens when women's interests are not fairly accommodated? Then, especially where the Rawlsian argument does not apply, it arguably is unfair for so much to be spent on a men's team when some interested and sufficiently talented women are not given an opportunity to play their sport.[7] In the high-visibility programs of Division I, in which over 80 players on a football team may be receiving athletic scholarships, some redistribution to the women's program certainly seems appropriate. (The issue may be complicated, however, if it is true that football players in large Division I programs tend to disproportionately come from less advantaged backgrounds and/or are minority students, while the female athletes are White and come from more advantaged backgrounds.) The issue of redistribution is likely to be very divisive at nonscholarship schools, however, since any transfer will deprive some students who are participating simply for the love of the game of the opportunity to play while providing that opportunity to others. In many contexts, there will be no easy answer as to where opportunities should be cut for some so as to make them more equal for others.

One proposal that deserves attention is to eliminate separate men's and women's teams in parallel sports and have single co-ed teams in each sport. For example, instead of having a men's tennis team and a women's tennis team, have one team with both men and women on it. (Thus, as Francis suggests in this issue, mixed doubles could be made part of intercollegiate tennis.)

While this proposal has promise, it also has problems. Is the idea to cut costs by cutting the number of students participating?[8] If so, significantly fewer students will have a chance to participate. Moreover, it is unclear if financial savings will be significant. Some expenses will be saved on coaching salaries and travel expenses, but there will be fewer alumni of such programs in the future to provide support as well. Because many less visible sports, such as tennis, track, and golf, need not be expensive to begin with, especially at institutions that do not offer athletic scholarships, savings may not be significant either.

Moreover, while there may be benefits other than economic, such as promoting greater cooperation and teamwork between genders, there also may be losses. If men and women compete directly against one another in sports in which there are physiological differences between the sexes, women's skills may be eclipsed by stronger and more powerful men. If contests are arranged so players compete only against opponents of the same gender, it is unclear why the consequences will be as different from those generated by separate men's and women's teams under present arrangements.

Some writers have suggested that we place more emphasis on sports such as gymnastics, in which women are not physiologically disadvantaged, or on other sports in which women might be in a physiologically favored position over men (7: p. 54). While this suggestion has merit, the preferences of most women athletes to play highly popular sports such as basketball, track, tennis, golf, and soccer may not be easy to alter without limiting the athletes' freedom to choose.

Perhaps more important, the suggestion of emphasis placement may presuppose that in sports in which men are physiologically advantaged, the women's game is unlikely to achieve parity of recognition or interest from the general public. I am not sure this is true. It may be far easier to educate sports fans about the nuances of the women's game than radically change the preferences of athletes about what sports to play. Women's tennis has achieved wide fan support, perhaps because the clever volleying game played by women is of greater interest to many spectators than the power game of men. While women's basketball lacks the dunking and highly athletic moves of superstars such as Michael Jordan, it features ball and player movement that also is of great interest. Major contests have filled arenas, and players such as the aptly named Cheryl Swoopes, Dawn Staley, and Jennifer Azzi are wonderful athletes capable of generating plenty of fan support if given sufficient attention in the media. Arguably, the best golf swings in the world are those of female players like Patty Sheehan, who may not drive the ball quite as far as top male players, but who may swing more efficiently. In other words, the assumption that separate women's programs in sports in which men are physiologically favored are of less interest, or that women's games are inferior, is questionable at best.

Why have intercollegiate athletics at all? Wouldn't intramurals be less expensive, involve more students, and serve many of the same social functions? The case for such a view, suggested in Leslie Francis's contribution, is of great interest but also faces problems. Intramural sports, by their very nature, are likely to lack the intensity and levels of skill of intercollegiate sport. For those of us who believe intercollegiate sport should (and often does) have a significant educational component, the intensity of the

intercollegiate contest, and the preparation that goes into it, provide opportunities for gains in self-knowledge, for enhancing developing skills, and for
opportunities to learn to handle pressure. It is doubtful intramurals can
match these benefits.

Perhaps another approach is to move intercollegiate athletics as far as
possible towards the existing model supplied by institutions in Division III
and the Ivy and Patriot Leagues in Division I, in which athletic scholarships
are not awarded, and athletics is conducted within the primary academic
framework of colleges and universities. In such a framework, the intensity
and educational benefits of an intercollegiate athletic program are preserved, although not at the level of the present major Division I programs,
and most major problems are, or can be, eliminated. Such a solution
promotes gender equity as well, because no team is expected to be a revenue
producer, and athletics are funded out of general revenues as are other
components of the institution's educational program. Fairness should be
easier to achieve in such a context because the often pernicious pressures to
win so as to maintain support or enhance revenue can be substantially
reduced or entirely eliminated.

Concluding Comment

In this essay, I have tried to identify and sometimes examine many of the
major issues connected with the search for gender equity in intercollegiate
sports. These issues, as well as others I have not touched upon, are
considered from different perspectives by Leslie Francis and Jan Boxill in
their contributions to this symposium. We hope all three articles show that
the issues of gender equity raised by intercollegiate sport are complex, of
philosophical and ethical interest, and well worth our attention, both as
theorists of sport and out of concern that our educational institutions be fair
and just to all students.

Notes

1. While this result may not be unwelcome to critics of intercollegiate sports,
   it surely is not a desirable way of reducing commitments to intercollegiate
   athletics. It is doubly dishonest, in that it decreases opportunity under the
   guise of equalizing changes for women and avoids the need to debate the case
   for cutbacks or radical reform on the merits.
2. Keep in mind, however, that even if the bulk of funds spent on the athletic
   program go to men's sports, the bulk of participants also may be men.

Whether more is being spent per capita on men than women is a separate question from whether more total funds are being spent on male athletes than on female athletes.

3. This kind of case is not merely hypothetical. At my own institution, which has had outstanding men's and women's basketball teams over the last ten years at the Division III level, the men's program has had to cut sometimes as many as 30 players, even after assignments are made to a junior varsity squad, while the women's program rarely has had to make cuts. The numbers of players trying out for each team are quite different.

4. Perhaps the connection is this. It would be excessive and hence unfair to expect the plaintiffs, who normally would be students, to have the burden of showing a difference in the ratio of interested female to male athletes in the relevant pool, whatever it turns out to be.

5. Thus, in our hypothetical example presented earlier, 87% of the women who went out for teams made them, while only 72% of the men were similarly successful.

6. For a case that has at least some significant resemblances to this example, see *Cook et al. vs. Colgate University* (802 F Supplement 737, N.D.N.Y., 1992) in which a U.S. District Judge upheld the claim of women students that Colgate must elevate the women's ice hockey club to varsity status to accommodate their interests.

7. Again, the issue of gender inequity may be complicated if a significantly greater number of men also are denied the opportunity to participate.

8. In other words, instead of having two tennis teams with 10 men on the men's team and 10 women on the women's team, have 5 men and 5 women participate on one team.

Bibliography

1. *Amy Cohen et al. vs. Brown University.* 1993 WL 111514 (1st circuit, RI) April 16, 1993.
2. Cahn, Steven M. (Ed.). *Affirmative Action and the University.* Philadelphia: Temple University Press, 1993.
3. English, Jane. "Sex Equality in Sports." *Philosophy & Public Affairs,* VII (1978).
4. Gender Equity Task Force of the NCAA. *Final Report of the NCAA Gender Equity Task Force.* Overland Park, KS: National Collegiate Athletic Association, 1993.
5. MacIntyre, Alastair. *After Virtue.* South Bend, IN: University of Notre Dame Press, 1981.
6. Michener, James. *Sports in America.* New York: Random House, 1976.
7. Postow, Betsy. "Women and Masculine Sports." *Journal of the Philosophy of Sport,* VII (1980), 57-58.
8. United States Commission on Civil Rights. *More Hurdles to Clear: Women and Girls in Competitive Athletics.* Clearinghouse Publication No. 63, 1980.

18

CHAPTER

Title IX: Equality for Women's Sports?

Leslie P. Francis

Since their beginnings in 1859 with a crew race between Harvard and Yale, intercollegiate athletics have been central to the mythology of American universities. Varsity football dominates the fall social calendar of student life; "homecoming," timed to coincide with an important football game, evokes alumni nostalgia. Winter is the season for varsity basketball, culminating in the National Collegiate Athletic Association (NCAA) national championship tournaments in early spring. Until quite recently, the participants in intercollegiate varsity sports were nearly all men.

The entry of women competitors into the apparently glorious haze of intercollegiate athletics has been belated and awkward. With the passage of Title IX in 1972, universities were required to provide equal opportunity in all of their federally funded programs. Most moved quickly to establish varsity sports teams for women in numbers roughly equal to their offerings for men. The near similarity in numbers of teams, however, belies important continuing differences. Football remains a major source of attention, revenue, and expenditure. Men's basketball is also a high-profile activity;

Reprinted, by permission, from L.P. Francis, 1995, "Title IX: Equality for women's sports?," *Journal of the Philosophy of Sport, XX-XXI:* 32-47.

women's basketball, particularly with the NCAA tournament and television exposure, recently has taken some steps towards success on the male model. In nonrevenue sports, from skiing and ice hockey to swimming and water polo, although teams are fielded in roughly equal numbers, participation and expenditure rates remain higher for men, in ratios that far exceed the proportions of men in overall enrollments.

The rosy glow of college athletics, perhaps always exaggerated, has been fading of late. Even football is a losing proposition on most campuses. Sperber (27), Thelin (29), and others report mismanagement, overexpenditure, and corruption. The National Collegiate Athletic Association, the private body that regulates intercollegiate athletics, has been criticized for behaving as an economic cartel by Fleisher, Goff, and Tollison (8), Hart-Nibbrig and Cottingham (11), and Lawrence (13), among others. Colleges are rebuked for exploiting, not educating athletes; premier athletes themselves exit early, in increasingly greater numbers, to professional opportunities. Faculties and even university presidents seek, with uneven success, to establish greater control over intercollegiate athletics. As universities confront shrinking academic budgets, athletics expenditures, often more than 5% of the institution's total, are viewed with mounting concern (30). Universities are urged to sell off their money-making sports teams as separate businesses and to abolish the remainder, leaving only intramural activities that all can enjoy. Older and working students may view intercollegiate athletics as part of a romanticized past that never really was and may resent the dedication of large proportions of student fees to their continued support.

Given this critical picture of the current state of intercollegiate competitive sports, there is something of a paradox to women's claims for equal participation. These claims might be viewed as efforts to participate in a practice that is morally problematic on many counts—that is perhaps bad for, and most likely not beneficial for, participants; bad for their fellow students and the universities; and bad for society in general. If intercollegiate athletics in their current state are indeed an activity that universities should discourage, radically alter, or even eliminate, how should claims to equality on behalf of women be evaluated? In this paper, I take women's athletics as a problem about the morality of affirmative action within a social practice that is significantly morally flawed. I argue that within such a context, the case for affirmative action is limited but powerful, at least until there are serious social efforts to improve or eliminate the flawed social practice. I begin with an assessment of the case to be made for the current practice of intercollegiate athletic competition.

I. Why Intercollegiate Athletic Competition?

Since Greek times at least, sports have been thought to be an important part of the process of education. Athletic endeavors, it has been argued, promote discipline and health. They clear the mind for other learning, it is said. For women, athletic participation may also be important in counteracting historical images of weakness and passivity. If this or a similar paean to the educational glory of sports is to be believed, then there are arguments for physical education, health, and intramural sports activities on university campuses. Arguments for the general educational importance of athletics, however, do not necessarily provide support for intercollegiate competition. Indeed, if the development of intercollegiate competition draws money and enthusiasm away from more widespread participation in sports, education and intercollegiate sports may come into conflict. The critical analysis that follows is aimed at intercollegiate sports competition of the kind found in schools offering athletic scholarships, not at the general educational value of sport or at the intramural or club programs open to the entire student body.[1]

Universities typically offer both intrinsic and instrumental arguments for the promotion of intercollegiate varsity competition. Some arguments are based on the value of the activity itself to those involved. Athletics on the competitive level, it is said, develop skills and self-discipline to the highest degree possible for those participating. Team sports encourage cooperation and develop friendships. For many, competitive sports are an enjoyable, even a thrilling, activity. Without further support, however, these arguments do not explain why universities ought to provide such intrinsically valuable activities. Skill development and teamwork surely can be learned outside the university; and there are many valued activities, from good parties to good horse racing, that universities are not generally expected to offer. More complete defenses of intercollegiate competition rely either on the benefits it provides to athletes—benefits which are thought in some way to be relevant to the educational function of the university—or on overall benefits to the university as an institution.

One quite traditional, and perhaps rather quaint, argument for intercollegiate competition is that it develops character traits in athletes—and, by example, in other students—in a way appropriate to the function of the university. The "Battle of Waterloo was won on the playing fields of Eton," the Duke of Wellington once opined.[2] Some recent empirical work by sociologists, however, questions whether the kinds of character traits that are developed in intercollegiate competitive athletes today are appropriate sequelae of a liberal education. Chu (4) and Stevenson (28) report data suggesting that as athletes become more successful, they increasingly value winning rather than fair play, and that coaches tend to model authoritarian rather than autonomous behavior patterns. Both the focus on winning for its own sake, and the authoritarian coaching behavior might seem to be at odds with the values of a liberal education.

An argument that relies heavily on the social role of the modern university is that intercollegiate athletics are a source of upward mobility for otherwise disadvantaged participants. Varsity athletes receive scholarships and academic support that often are not generally available to other students. Premier athletes may parlay their college success into lucrative professional athletic careers. The experience of intercollegiate competition may also prove a useful basis for job opportunities more generally. Unfortunately, the data indicate that these claims are unjustifiably optimistic. Although varsity athletes do receive scholarships and other support, Purdy, Eitzen, and Hufnagel (23) report that graduation rates are low, particularly for minority students in the sports of football and basketball. Women athletes graduate in rates comparable to rates of students overall, but the picture is worsening for women playing basketball as their sport becomes increasingly successful and emulates the model of a male, revenue-earning sport. Dubois's (6) study of post competition occupations of male varsity athletes in comparison to occupations of male students who did not participate in varsity sports shows no advantage for the athletes, whether white or minority. Intercollegiate sports have also been argued to be an important source of opportunities in professional sports. College football and basketball serve to some extent as a farm system for the professional leagues, although professional opportunities are limited. For women, there are few professional sports opportunities, and even fewer lucrative possibilities. If increasing numbers of women are well trained in college competition, however, perhaps they will become a source of pressures for changes in professional sports. Thus the desirability of pressures for increased professional athletic opportunities for women might be an argument for increased opportunities on the university level.

Another argument for varsity competition is the positive contribution it makes to attitudes towards athletes. Successful competition may be a source of self-esteem for the athletes themselves. Competition may also help change attitudes towards historically underappreciated groups. Both university and professional sports have been important forums for the admiration of minority male athletes. Female sports heroes such as Jackie Joyner-Kersee have also emerged from the college ranks into professional and Olympic competition. They are exemplars of achievement and strength, rather than weakness and passivity. If intercollegiate competition contributes to changes in attitudes towards women and minorities, it is arguably linked to the social role of the university in opening opportunities for underrepresented groups in society and should be supported on that ground.

Intercollegiate athletics are also thought to be of significant instrumental benefit for universities. The "big game" is part of the mythology of campus life. Defenders of intercollegiate competition argue that winning sports teams garner respect for the institution, encourage better potential students to apply, and augment alumni donations. One recent survey of the data (30) suggests that this optimism is not borne out. Evidence for the contention that successful teams increase alumni gifts is very mixed. Contributions to booster clubs go to underwrite athletics rather than to bolster academic budgets. In a few cases, the investment in revenue-producing sports is profitable; in most schools, however, even high-profile sports are a losing proposition. In the end, claims that intercollegiate athletics contribute to an overall aura of institutional success are very difficult to pin down.

Finally, defenders of intercollegiate sports competition argue that it fosters university identification and community. Students, who may lead very fragmented and separate lives, come together to cheer on their teams. They are joined by alumni reliving their loyalties to alma mater. Members of the local community may also identify with university sports teams and town-gown conflicts may thus be mitigated (4). Sports are a "safe" vehicle for affiliation, cutting across at least some religious, cultural, racial, and generational lines, and even linking students with alumni and members of the local community. Chu (4: p. 162) has argued that students who attend university athletic events are more likely to be involved with the institution in other ways, although the study does not indicate whether these are dependent or independent variables. Even so, however, overall student community might be fostered more successfully by an intense intramural system such as the one in place at the University of California at Davis. When they attract visitors from afar, university athletic events surely bring money into local businesses; but there may be other, more successful ways for universities to contribute to local economies.

The case for intercollegiate competition on its current scale is thus tenuous. The best case that can be made for the current practice of intercollegiate sports is that they are sought after by their participants and may open opportunities for them, although the empirical evidence in support of this is slim. Varsity competition may also contribute to changed social perceptions of women and minorities, and to an enhanced sense of university community. Many continue to believe that, despite their flaws, university intercollegiate sports make important contributions to institutional glory and community, besides being just plain fun. At the same time, others charge that varsity competition exploits athletes, drains revenue, and detracts from the educational programs of the university. Efforts to remedy discrimination against women and minorities in university athletics thus take place against a background of at best mixed support for the enterprise generally.

II. Title IX and University Athletics

Enacted in 1972, Title IX[3] prohibits discrimination in any educational program or activity receiving federal financial assistance. In part because of debates about Title IX's impact on athletics, universities were given six years from its adoption to develop compliance programs. Despite the phase-in, Title IX was met with resistance from coaches of men's teams, from university athletics directors, and from the National Collegiate Athletic Association. For example, the athletic director of the University of Maryland told a congressional subcommittee in 1975 that his department stood in staunch opposition to women's varsity sports because they did not want to market an inferior product (30). The NCAA lobbied Congress to exempt athletics from Title IX, and, when this effort failed, brought suit challenging the regulations issued by the Department of Health, Education, and Welfare (HEW) to implement Title IX.[4]

At the time Title IX was enacted, university athletic programs were heavily dominated by men's varsity sports. With the impetus of Title IX, many universities moved quickly to add a number of women's varsity teams. By the late 1970s, the typical pattern was for a university to offer roughly equal numbers of men's and women's teams in nonrevenue sports, men's and women's basketball teams, and a football team. Football of course consumed—and, in at least a few cases, produced—immense amounts of revenue. But differences persisted in the patterns of participation in, and support for, other men's and women's varsity teams. In 1985, the percentage of athletic budgets devoted to women's sports in Division I schools offering football was 12%; in nonfootball Division I schools, it was 23% (4: p. 103). Although expenses for women's sports rose after implementation of Title IX, Chu (4) reports that expenses for men's sports also rose by multiples of two to five times as much at different institutions during the same period. As late as 1993, NCAA (19) statistics indicate that only 34.8% of varsity university athletes were women, up from 31.3% in the 1984-85 academic year. In 1992, the NCAA (19) reported that only 30% of athletic scholarship money, 23% of operating dollars, and 17% of recruitment funds went to women. Nationally, the NCAA (19) calculated that the most frequently offered women's sport was basketball (289 schools; 3,873 athletes) and the sport with the most female participants was outdoor track (249 schools; 6,250 athletes). At individual institutions, participation rates over the entire period since the enactment of Title IX have departed noticeably from enrollment rates. At the University of Illinois in the Big Ten Conference, for example, although 56% of the student body was male, over 75% of the varsity athletes (including football players) were male.[5] Pieronek (20) reports that these rates were typical in the Big Ten Conference, which in 1992 proposed to require a proportion of at least 40% female athletes by 1997. At Colorado State University in the Western Athletic Conference, there was a better than 10% disparity in participation rates, a quite low difference by national and Big Ten standards, but insufficient for Title IX.[6] Moreover, with the merger of men's and women's programs at many institutions, Acosta and Carpenter (1) and Lapchick and Slaughter (12) have reported that the number of women coaches and women athletics administrators has dwindled.

By the early 1980s, over 100 Title IX challenges to gender differences in university athletics had been filed with the Office of Civil Rights of the Department of Education (32). In 1984, however, the United States Supreme Court held that Title IX applied only to specific program(s) receiving federal funding, rather than to entire institutions.[7] Because university athletics programs rarely received federal funding on their own, this holding largely deflated the Title IX challenges to them. In 1988, however, the program-specific interpretation of Title IX was superseded by Congress in the Civil Rights Restoration Act.[8]

Since 1988, a new set of Title IX complaints has been brought against university athletics programs, by both male and female athletes. These complaints have forced courts to rule directly on what is meant by nondiscrimination in athletics programs under Title IX and, ultimately, to confront difficult ethical questions about the meaning of equal opportunity in university athletics.

The renewed ability to challenge athletics programs under Title IX coincided with a period of significant retrenchment in university athletics budgets specifically and university budgets more generally. Much of the Title IX litigation was instigated by athletes seeking to block their schools from dropping their chosen sports. Female members of varsity teams objected to cutbacks that eliminated the teams in equal numbers for both sexes. Male members protested cutbacks that were imposed unilaterally on men's teams. In several other cases, women members of club teams sought to compel their university to upgrade their teams to varsity status, a step that the university was unwilling to take for financial reasons.

Judicial analyses of these Title IX claims have followed a pattern set out in the federal regulations and interpretive policy manuals.[9] Athletics programs must not discriminate in awarding financial aid—although they may structure awards differently for separate male and female teams provided that reasonable and proportional aid is available for each.[10] Second, programs must provide equal opportunity in a range of important supportive services: equipment, practice times, travel and per diem allowances, coaching and tutoring, locker rooms, medical and training facilities, housing and dining services, and publicity. Finally, programs must offer a "selection of sports and levels of competition [that] effectively accommodate[s] the interests and abilities of members of both sexes."[11] Relying on a policy interpretation issued by the Office of Civil Rights of the Department of Education,[12] courts have developed a three-prong test for effective accommodation of the interests of a sex that has been underserved historically in an athletic program: universities must offer varsity opportunities in proportion to representation in the student body; or, universities must demonstrate continuing progress in adding opportunities for the underserved sex; or, universities must demonstrate the interests and abilities of the underserved sex are in fact fully met.

This structure of analysis reflects an uneasy compromise between exactly equal levels of participation and the historical differences between men's and women's sports. First, it allows football to remain a sport apart, as long as there is equal opportunity in the program overall, by allowing separate teams in contact sports, along with separate scholarship and revenue functions for those teams. Second, this analysis also permits ongoing, quite large differences between percentages of participation by sex in varsity sports and percentages in the overall student body, that is, if the university can bear the burden of proving that existing interests and abilities are met for the underrepresented sex. This allowance, too, is important to the perpetuation of large football programs.

On the other hand, where there are ongoing disproportionalities between participation rates and the student body, the university will be virtually compelled to accede to demands by women for a sport to be upgraded, or for a sport to be protected from cuts. In the view of the Department of Education (32),

> Institutions where women are currently underrepresented in the athletics program will have a difficult time maintaining compliance with Title IX while eliminating women's teams unless they make comparable cuts, and, in some cases, deeper cuts in the men's program. . . . Institutions that plan to eliminate the same number of sports for men

and women may also have compliance problems if women are already underrepresented in the athletics program.

Women ice hockey players, for example, obtained a court order in line with this analysis, compelling Colgate University to upgrade their club team to varsity status, against a background of differential participation in varsity sports by women and men.[13] Women gymnasts and field hockey players at Indiana University of Pennsylvania successfully fought elimination of their varsity teams (in tandem with the elimination of men's tennis and soccer), despite a university proposal to replace them with women's soccer.[14] At Colorado State University, women blocked the elimination of fast-pitch softball;[15] at Brown University, they fought off cuts in women's gymnastics and volleyball.[16] On the other side, male athletes have not found Title IX a particular ally in their efforts to stall cuts, even when the counterpart women's team was spared. Male swimmers at the University of Illinois, for example, failed in a challenge to their team's elimination despite the continuation of the women's team, because the Illinois athletics programs were predominately (75%) male.[17]

Thus as Title IX is currently implemented, unless a university provides varsity opportunities in proportion to enrollments (which schools fielding football teams are unlikely to do), women's varsity sports are virtually guaranteed protection when women express interest in varsity competition. This bottom line has been characterized by Thro and Snow (31) as a form of affirmative action and criticized as an unfair burden on straitened athletics budgets. A quick but facile reply to this criticism is that universities can do much to end participation rates that are disproportional to enrollments by cutting football rosters.[18] A deeper set of concerns is prompted by the observation that mandated varsity teams may be quite expensive yet benefit only the few athletes who participate in them. Pieronek (20) estimates that in order to achieve proportionality with enrollments but still leave men's varsity sports untouched, universities would need to add on average six sports (and 128 varsity spaces) for women. Is Title IX, as currently interpreted to barter football for women's varsity teams, a desirable model for equality in athletics? Is it an example of affirmative action at all, much less of justifiable affirmative action? Should universities cut football, cut other men's sports, or add women's sports? Should revenues from football, when football is profit-making, be dedicated to football or be used to underwrite the remainder of the academic program?[19] Would models of equality that require major changes in the organization of intercollegiate athletics be morally preferable within the current context?

III. Affirmative Action in University Athletics

The term *affirmative action* encompasses a wide range of positive steps that might be taken in response to discrimination.[20] In university athletics, in addition to the provision of varsity sports opportunities for women, affirmative action might include efforts to evoke women's interest and develop their skills, to encourage intramural participation by more women, to form coeducational teams, and even to reassess the entire way that intercollegiate competition is structured and understood. In comparison, affirmative action in employment has ranged from reassessment of frankly biased selection criteria, to job training and recruitment, to redefinition of entire job categories.

I have argued elsewhere (10) that the case for affirmative action in education can be made on at least three different moral grounds. Affirmative action may be used to compensate identified victims of past injustices; the creation of remedial programs for individuals who have been unjustly denied opportunities is an example. In athletics, Lapchick and Slaughter (12) suggest the example of providing enhanced scholarship opportunities for women who have been discriminatorily denied them. It may serve to correct ongoing discrimination; faculty recruitment or hiring goals may be required when patterns of selection indicate subjective, difficult-to-eradicate bias. An example here might be the recruitment of more women coaches and athletic administrators. A third moral justification for affirmative action is that it may be a method for improving overall distributive justice in society. The United States Supreme Court had held, however, that a concern for social justice is not a legally compelling interest that can justify the state's use of reverse racial preferences in such areas as government contracts.[21] Nonetheless, educational diversity may remain a legally compelling state interest that justifies university consideration of multiple factors, including race, in making admissions decisions.[22] An example from athletics might be increasing participation by women to further the likely development of women's opportunities in professional sports.

These arguments for affirmative action typically are made within contexts in which the activity at issue is thought to be worthwhile both to the individuals seeking increased access and to society more generally. Compensatory affirmative action gives victims something of value, such as a training opportunity. Moral objections to compensatory affirmative action generally rest on the claims of others to the means of compensation, such as admission to a training program, or on whether the source from which compensation is sought is any way responsible for the past victimization, not on whether the means of compensation is itself a good. Corrective affirmative action roots out continuing bias in order, it is hoped, that everyone is treated fairly. Here, the chief moral objection lies not with what is being distributed, but with the risk that affirmative action will introduce new forms of bias. Redistributive affirmative action aims to move society towards more just distribution of the benefits and burdens of social living. Here, too, objections that affirmative action is unjust rest on who wins and loses under the change and why and how they lose, rather than on whether it is a good thing for anyone at all to experience the benefits being redistributed.[23]

What happens to these justifications for affirmative action if an historically disadvantaged group seeks fuller participation in an activity that is socially problematic or that should be reduced or eliminated for good social reasons? If criticisms of the current practice of university athletics are to be believed, this is the problem posed by affirmative action for women in intercollegiate varsity competition. I will argue here that the case for affirmative action is limited, but not entirely vitiated, under such circumstances. Moreover, how the case is changed depends on the nature of the reasons for discouraging the activity; several importantly different reasons are that it is risky to participating individuals, that it is costly but unlikely to yield any benefits to participants, or that it has undesirable consequences for others in society.

First, take activities that are risky to participants. Such risks have been offered as objections to including women in high-injury or high-stress sports.[24] They may be at least part of the explanation for the continued accommodation of separate teams for men and women in contact sports.[25] Risks to participants are, however, unjust reasons for exclusion, so long as the activity is left open to men. Medical experiments with human subjects are an illuminating analogy.[26] Some experiments simply are not permitted by federal regulations because their risks outweigh their potential benefits. Researchers may not enter any subjects in such experiments, even with the subjects' informed consent. In medical research, however, there has been a long-standing practice of routinely excluding women from experiments, allegedly because of the risks of pregnancy or the need for a uniform subject population. This exclusion has been criticized as unwarranted paternalism, because it substitutes the experimenter's risk judgments for the judgments of the excluded group of women subjects, but not for the included men subjects. It thus continues stereotypes of women as less capable of responsible decision-making. Moreover, as Merton (15) and others have argued, the insistence on exclusion to ensure a uniform patient population is misguided because it significantly limits the information that is available about the responses of women to new medical therapies and limits women's access to the therapies themselves in their developmental stages. The

National Institutes of Health (NIH) have recently issued policy guidelines requiring equal participation of women in studies it sponsors and analysis of relevant differences in results by gender, unless there is a compelling justification to the contrary.[27] Thus, in medical research, affirmative action has not been required when experiments are prohibited across the board, but is demanded when a study is open to men but not to women. Applying this analogy to sports, the conclusion would be that universities may decide that some sports are too risky to offer at all, but not that their risks warrant limiting them to men.

A second concern about the assumption that it is desirable to increase opportunities for varsity competition is that there is little evidence that such competition benefits participants with increased educational or job opportunities. This lack of evidence at least undercuts the argument that affirmative action in women's varsity athletics will give more women these benefits and thus increase overall social justice. The fact remains, however, that Title IX only requires a university to protect women's varsity sports when its athletic program is disproportionate, when it has not made continued progress towards improvement, or when there is unmet need among able women competitors. A university can avoid a Title IX order if it can show that there is insufficient interest or ability to field a given women's team. Nonetheless, a university with a problematic history will need to respond to expressions of women's interest despite a lack of evidence that the women will ultimately benefit. Such universities will be ordered to make quite substantial expenditures because a few women want the opportunities. In times of tight budgets, there is something unfortunate about costly expenditures that respond to the desires of a few. This argument could be the basis for the elimination of all varsity sports that respond principally to the interests of their participants—all of what might be called "vanity" sports. The trouble with applying this argument to the present situation, however, is that universities continue to offer at least some low-interest varsity sports for both men and women. As long as universities continue the pattern of funding for "vanity" sports, it is wrong for them to offer this desired benefit disproportionately to men. Title IX's requirements are therefore justified. At the same time, it might be preferable from the point of view of justice to eliminate all "vanity" programs and spend the money saved on more important opportunities for a larger group of students such as intramural sports, an issue to which I shall return in the final section.

Universities opting to eliminate all intercollegiate competition in "vanity" sports, however, would also confront the problem of whether they could choose, legally or ethically, to retain football as a revenue-producing sport.[28] Under current legal standards, they probably could not make this choice;

although Title IX permits differently structured and financed programs, it also requires that there be equal accommodation of the interests of women athletes, including provision of teams at competitive levels and efforts to develop women's teams as revenue-producers on the model of men's teams. It would also be ethically troublesome to retain football while abolishing the remainder of the intercollegiate program for both men and women. This choice would leave the university with a high-profile, highly sought after (albeit most likely not beneficial) showcase for male athletes, with no comparable opportunities for women. An alternative might be to take up the suggestion of critics of university athletics that some allegedly profitable sports enterprises be privatized.

Finally, what are the consequences for affirmative action if the activity to which increased entry is sought is one that there are good social reasons for discouraging entirely? As the initial section of this paper argued, intercollegiate athletic competition might well fall into this category because it is expensive, provides little or no educational benefit, and may foster problematic images of excellence and fair play. If society is genuinely discouraging the activity, then the argument for affirmative action would be undercut. But if society is not working to discourage the activity, the case for affirmative action remains. It is worse from the point of view of justice to continue sponsoring the activity, but leave women out, than to sponsor it without women. It is worse still if one of the concerns about the activity is that it contributes to problematic images of women or other disadvantaged groups. Thus even if it would be best overall to phase out intercollegiate athletic competition, it is better to make serious efforts to include women, even if they increase the resources committed to the enterprise, than to continue it with disproportionate participation by men. In short, universities that stick with football are stuck with Title IX.

There are, to be sure, moral difficulties with phasing out intercollegiate competition, just as there are with phasing out any cherished benefit. Athletes, both male and female, have been recruited with promises of scholarships and competition. They have what I have argued elsewhere (9) might be viewed as legitimate expectations that these opportunities will continue during their time as students; at least, they have been encouraged to form these expectations by those providing the benefits—they have had no reason to believe the assurances were dubious or that they themselves were benefiting as perpetrators of injustice. These expectations might be the basis for constructing a phase-out so as to cushion the impact on present athletes, while not creating a new set of expectations for incoming students. Recruited athletes might, for example, be able to keep their scholarships for four years; or, universities might continue to field competitive teams at least through the junior years of recruited athletes in sports slated for discontinuation.

Phase-outs such as the abolition of all or most "vanity" sports face tremendously difficult issues of coordination, however. Unless all of the schools within a conference—or, perhaps, within a region—adopt similar phase-out strategies, athletes recruited by one school will find themselves left out, while athletes at other schools will continue to compete. They may well believe that they have been treated unfairly by their own schools. While they have no entitlement to continue to compete, and of course are free to transfer, it is true that they are losing a cherished benefit that others just like them continue to enjoy. The situation is perhaps worst when a men's sport is cancelled and women at the same school continue to enjoy the opportunity to compete in that sport.[29] The alternative that avoids the apparent unfairness of differential treatment of athletes with similar expectations is to continue to provide the competitive opportunity until a coordinated system of cuts is in place. Athletes already recruited could continue to enjoy their sport until it was gradually phased down in a coordinated way, and new recruitment efforts would cease. Such coordination strategies are difficult to implement, however, because as Fleisher, Goff, and Tollison (8) argue, individual athletic departments have incentives to keep their budgets as large as possible. Thus the fairest of the likely outcomes is to continue to support men's "vanity" sports, while increasing support for women's sports—an outcome that is expensive and that may lead universities in the long run to reconsider the wisdom of their support for intercollegiate competition.

IV. Beyond the Title IX Model of Equality

The strong protection given women's varsity sports by Title IX is thus justified despite—and perhaps even because of—the flaws of the current system of competition. A better alternative, however, might be to consider ways of radically restructuring intercollegiate athletic competition. In this concluding section, I explore four possibilities for reconstruction and argue that all are preferable, from the point of view of justice, to affirmative action within the current context.[30] None, however, are explicitly supported by the current interpretation of Title IX.

First, universities might increase efforts to encourage women to participate in skills training and sports activities. If women's historical underrepresentation in competitive athletics is in part a result of earlier educational programs and attitudes that discourage them from participating in athletics at all, such efforts are an important form of affirmative action.

Because the aim would be to increase exposure to a real benefit, the focus of such encouragement would be fitness and skills activities that are of lifelong importance and simply not short-term competitive opportunities. An analogy might be the programs at many universities to increase interest and training in science and mathematics among women and minority students. The focus of the Title IX regulations, however, is the provision of levels of competition that "effectively accommodate the interests and abilities of members of both sexes."[31]

A second initiative for universities might be the development of intramural sports programs that expand participation and competition widely throughout the student body. A typical pattern at universities today is the contrast between lavish support for varsity athletics and little support for intramural activities. An alternative would be to improve intramural facilities, to make educational opportunities (such as skills training) available in conjunction with them, and to increase the amenities associated with them. The University of California at Davis is an example of how widespread intramural programs can help to develop a sense of community among students. While Title IX requires the provision of appropriate levels of competition at all levels, including the intramural level, its emphasis, as it has been interpreted in litigation, has been varsity teams, not the overall expansion of athletic participation across the student body.

A more radical option might be the reconsideration of what are considered sports. Sports today emphasize physical characteristics such as bulk (football) and height (basketball)—characteristics that are predominately male—rather than characteristics such as finesse, agility, or endurance. Women athletes confront what Martha Minow (16) has called the "difference dilemma": either they play by historical rules, which fail to acknowledge differences between women and men, or they are stigmatized for calling attention to differences. Women basketball players, for example, have moved into a sport constructed for tall bodies. Although they have in many respects been successful in constructing a different kind of sport—one that emphasizes ball movement, for example—they might have constructed an even more exciting sport had basket height or angle been adjusted. Nonetheless, there have been some encouraging signs in the direction of changed sports emphases. For example, women's soccer has become far more popular, as have endurance track events such as the marathon for women. Gymnastics tests different skills for men and women; women's gymnastics has become a popular sport on some campuses, although sometimes one that advertises based on the sexuality of the women athletes involved. Title IX, as it has been interpreted, however, does not require implementation of new sports for women, except in response to demand; it may even be an obstacle to new sports to the extent that it protects established ones.[32] Moreover, there is no mandate in Title IX for the identification or development of entirely new sports.

Finally, university sports programs might consider the introduction of coeducational teams. Such teams are of course a mainstay of recreational and intramural programs. They emphasize teamwork and complementary skills—both characteristics that are arguably beneficial and useful educationally. Such teamwork opportunities might also be highly useful in acculturating women and men to work together in other contexts, especially if the opportunities are spread widely throughout the student body. Yet no intercollegiate competition today features coeducational teams, although parallel teams are fielded in such sports as tennis, swimming, diving, track, golf, and skiing. Even mixed doubles, a staple of both professional and recreational tennis, is ignored on the college level. Title IX accepts the separation of men's and women's teams outright, with one exception: in noncontact sports in which no team is fielded for the underrepresented sex, members of the excluded sex must be permitted to try out on a skills basis for the team of the other sex.[33]

V. Conclusion

In this article, I have argued that university athletics for women should be treated as a case of affirmative action within a morally flawed practice. So long as the practice continues in its present form, the case for affirmative action remains. But there is a stronger case to be made for radical changes in the current practice. Title IX, the statute requiring equality in federally funded educational programs, does not propose such radical changes and may even in some contexts be a roadblock to them.[34]

Notes

1. As such, my criticism is directed principally at NCAA Division I and Division II schools, which mount large-scale competitive programs. It may not apply to Division III schools, which do not offer athletic scholarships per se, and which adhere to much more stringent limits on funding and other participation in intercollegiate athletics. However, to the extent that Division I practices operate covertly in Division III schools (for example, by using school tours to recruit athletes and suggest the possibility of athletic scholarships), the analysis applies to them also.
2. Quoted in Chu, Segrave, and Becker (5: p. 215); Martin (14) also examines the argument that sports build character.

3. 20 U.S.C. § 1681(a) (1993).
4. *NCAA v. Califano,* 622 F.2d 1382 (10th Cir., 1980).
5. *Kelley v. Board of Trustees of Univ. of Ill.,* 832 F. Supp. 237 (C.D. Ill. 1993).
6. *Kelley v. Board of Trustees of Univ. of Ill.,* 832 F. Supp. 237 (C.D. Ill. 1993); *Roberts v. Colorado State University,* 814 F. Supp. 1507 (D. Colo.), *aff'd* sub nom. *Roberts v. Colorado State Bd. of Agric.,* 993 F.2d 824 (10th Cir.), cert. denied, 114 S.Ct. 580 (1993).
7. *Grove City College v. Bell,* 465 U.S. 555 (1984).
8. 20 U.S.C. § 1687 (1993); P.L. No. 100-259, 102 Stat. 28 (1988).
9. Policy Interpretation, 44 Fed. Reg. 71413 (December 11, 1979; United States Department of Education, 33).
10. 34 C.F.R. § 106.37(c) (1993).
11. 34 C.F.R. § 106.41(c) (1993).
12. 44 Fed. Reg. 71413 (December 11, 1979).
13. *Cook v. Colgate University,* 802 F. Supp. 737 (N.D.N.Y. 1992), vacated and remanded on other grounds, 992 F.2d 17 (2d Cir. 1993). (The other grounds were graduation of the athletes involved in the suit.)
14. *Favia v. Indiana University of Pennsylvania,* 812 F. Supp. 578 (W.D. Pa. 1993), *aff'd* 7 F.3d 332 (3d Cir. 1993). Although the undergraduate population at IUP was 55.6% women, only 38% of the varsity athletic slots and 21% of the athletic scholarships went to women. The court suggested in dicta that Title IX probably not only forbade the cancellation of women's varsity sports when interested athletes were available but also mandated the addition of further women's varsity sports.
15. *Roberts v. Colorado State University,* 814 F. Supp. 1507 (D. Colo.), *aff'd* sub nom. *Roberts v. Colorado State Bd. of Agric.,* 993 F.2d 824 (10th Cir.), cert. denied, 114 S.Ct. 580 (1993).
16. *Cohen v. Brown University,* 809 F. Supp. 978 (D.R.I. 1992), *aff'd,* 991 F.2d 888 (1st Cir. 1993).
17. *Kelley v. Board of Trustees of Univ. of Ill.,* 832 F. Supp. 237 (C.D. Ill. 1993).
18. The NCAA allowed 88 football scholarships in 1993; at many universities, this is equivalent to the total number of scholarships awarded members of women's teams. When nonscholarship players are allowed to join football teams, squad size may balloon to 145. In comparison, National Football League teams are allowed only 45 players. See Pieronek (20).
19. *Blair v. Washington State University,* 740 P.2d 1379 (Wash. 1987) held that the state's equal protection clause and nondiscrimination statute did not require football revenues to be shared within the athletic program; this approach is endorsed by Pieronek (20).
20. The term comes from the remedy section of Title VII of the Civil Rights Act, 42 U.S.C. § 2000e-5 (1993).
21. *City of Richmond v. J.A. Croson Co.,* 488 U.S. 469 (1989).
22. *Regents of the University of California v. Bakke,* 438 U.S. 265 (1978).
23. Where there are no common paradigms of social benefits and burdens, it may be impossible to find agreement on basic principles of justice, much less on when redistribution is justified under conditions of injustice. The theoretical shifts from Rawls (1971) to Rawls (1993) are instructive on this point.

24. An example is the rejection, until quite recently, of the women's marathon in Olympic competition.
25. Or are concerns about sexual contact the real explanation?
26. Another analogy might be inclusion of women in combat positions in the military.
27. "NIH Guidelines on the Inclusion of Women and Minorities as Subjects in Clinical Research," 59 Fed. Reg. 14508 (March 28, 1994).
28. Basketball isn't really an issue here, since women's basketball is so well established and a university could achieve equality by retaining both women's and men's basketball.
29. Cases that are examples are *Kelley v. Board of Trustees of Univ. of Ill.*, 832 F. Supp. 237 (C.D. Ill. 1993), and *Gonyo v. Drake University*, 837 F. Supp. 989 (S.D. Iowa 1993).
30. These possibilities are suggested in English (7), Moulton (18), and Postow (21, 22). They have been criticized by Belliotti (3) and Simon (26).
31. 34 C.F.R. § 106.41(c) (1) (1993).
32. In *Roberts v. Colorado State University*, 814 F. Supp. 1507 (D. Colo.), *aff'd* sub nom. *Roberts v. Colorado State Bd. of Agric.*, 993 F.2d 824 (10th Cir.), cert. denied, 114 S.Ct. 580 (1993), for example, the university sought to substitute women's soccer—a sport that included more athletes and afforded more competitive opportunities—for women's fast-pitch softball. The court refused to allow the substitution and suggested in dicta that CSU might be required to provide both sports for women. If budgets are tight, however, the result might be continued protection of the fast-pitch team, with little development of soccer. For criticism of this outcome, see Chu (4).
33. 34 C.F.R. § 106.41(b) (1993).
34. I am grateful to the University of Utah College of Law for a faculty summer stipend that supported the research on this project. I am also grateful to Peggy Battin, Frances Garrett, and Bob Simon for helpful comments on earlier drafts of this article.

Bibliography

1. Acosta, R.V., and Carpenter, L.J. "Women in Sport." In *Rethinking College Athletics*. Edited by J. Andre and D. James. Philadelphia: Temple University Press, 1991, pp. 313-325.
2. Andre, J., and James, D. (Eds.). *Rethinking College Athletics*. Philadelphia: Temple University Press, 1991.
3. Belliotti, R.A. "Women, Sex, and Sports." *Journal of the Philosophy of Sport*, VI (1979), 67-72.
4. Chu, D. *The Character of American Higher Education and Intercollegiate Sport*. Albany: State University of New York Press, 1989.
5. Chu, D., Segrave, J.O., and Becker, B.J. (Eds.). *Sport and Higher Education*. Champaign, IL: Human Kinetics Publishers, 1985.
6. Dubois, P.E. "The Occupational Attainment of Former College Athletes: A Comparative Study." In *Sport and Higher Education*. Edited by D. Chu, J.O.

Segrave, and B.J. Becker. Champaign, IL: Human Kinetics Publishers, 1985, pp. 235-248.

7. English, J. "Sex Equality in Sports." *Philosophy and Public Affairs,* 7 (1978), 269-277.

8. Fleisher, A.A., Goff, B.L., and Tollison, R.D. *The National Collegiate Athletic Association: A Study in Cartel Behavior.* Chicago: University of Chicago Press, 1992.

9. Francis, L. "Consumer Expectations and Access to Health Care." *University of Pennsylvania Law Review,* 140 (1992), 1881.

10. Francis, L. "In Defense of Affirmative Action." In *Affirmative Action in the University.* Edited by S. Cahn. Philadelphia: Temple University Press, 1993.

11. Hart-Nibbrig, N., and Cottingham, C. *The Political Economy of College Sports.* Lexington, MA: Lexington Books, 1986.

12. Lapchick, R.E., and Slaughter, J.B. *The Rules of the Game: Ethics in College Sport.* New York: American Council on Education, 1989.

13. Lawrence, P.R. *Unsportsmanlike Conduct: The National Collegiate Athletic Association and the Business of College Football.* New York: Praeger, 1987.

14. Martin, W.B. *A College of Character.* San Francisco: Jossey-Bass, 1982.

15. Merton, V. "The Exclusion of Pregnant, Pregnable, and Once-Pregnable People (a.k.a. Women) from Biomedical Research." *American Journal of Law & Medicine,* XIX (1993), 369.

16. Minow, Martha. *Making All the Difference.* Ithaca, NY: Cornell University Press, 1990.

17. Miracle, A.W., Jr., and Rees, C.R. *Lessons of the Locker Room.* Buffalo, NY: Prometheus Books, 1994.

18. Moulton, J. "Why Everyone Deserves a Sporting Chance: Education, Justice, and College Sport." In *Rethinking College Athletics.* Edited by J. Andre and D. James. Philadelphia: Temple University Press, 1991, pp. 210-220.

19. National Collegiate Athletic Association. *Gender Equity Task Force Report.* 1993.

20. Pieronek, C. "A Clash of Titans: College Football v. Title IX." *Journal of College and University Law,* 20 (1994), 351.

21. Postow, B. "Women and Masculine Sports." *Journal of the Philosophy of Sport,* VII (1980), 51-58.

22. Postow, B. (Ed.). *Women, Philosophy, and Sport: A Collection of New Essays.* Metuchen, NJ: Scarecrow Press, 1983.

23. Purdy, D.A., Eitzen, D.S., and Hufnagel, R. "Are Athletes Also Students: The Educational Attainment of College Athletes." In *Sport and Higher Education.* Edited by D. Chu, J.O. Segrave, and B.J. Becker. Champaign, IL: Human Kinetics Publishers, 1985, pp. 221-234.

24. Rawls, J. *A Theory of Justice.* Cambridge, MA: Harvard University Press, 1971.

25. Rawls, J. *Political Liberalism.* New York: Columbia University Press, 1993.

26. Simon, R. *Fair Play: Sports, Values, and Society.* Boulder, CO: Westview Press, 1991.

27. Sperber, M. *College Sports Inc.: The Athletic Department vs. The University.* New York: Henry Holt, 1990.

28. Stevenson, C.L. "College Athletics and 'Character': The Decline and Fall of Socialization Research." In *Sport and Higher Education.* Edited by D. Chu, J.O. Segrave, and B.J. Becker. Champaign, IL: Human Kinetics Publishers, 1985, pp. 249-266.

29. Thelin, J.R. *Games Colleges Play.* Baltimore, MD: Johns Hopkins University Press, 1994.

30. Thelin, J.R., and Wiseman, L.L. *The Old College Try: Balancing Academics and Athletics in Higher Education.* Washington, DC: Clearinghouse on Higher Education, 1989.

31. Thro, W.E., and Snow, B.A. "*Cohen v. Brown University* and the Future of Intercollegiate and Interscholastic Athletics." *Education Law Reporter,* 84 (1993), 611.

32. United States Department of Education. *Technical Assistance Documents for Title IX Intercollegiate Athletics, National Enforcement Strategy.* 1993.

19

CHAPTER

Sports and Male Domination: The Female Athlete As Contested Ideological Terrain

Michael A. Messner

This paper explores the historical and ideological meanings of organized sports for the politics of gender relations. After outlining a theory for building a historically grounded understanding of sport, culture, and ideology, the paper argues that organized sports have come to serve as a primary institutional means for bolstering a challenged and faltering ideology of male superiority in the 20th century. Increasing female athleticism represents a genuine quest by women for equality, control of their own bodies, and self-definition, and as such represents a challenge to the ideological basis of male domination. Yet this quest for equality is not without contradictions and

An earlier version of this paper was delivered at the North American Society for the Sociology of Sport Meetings in Las Vegas, Nevada, October 31, 1986.

The author would like to thank the following people for helpful comments and suggestions on earlier drafts of this paper: Maxine Baca-Zinn, Robert Dunn, Mary Duquin, Juan Gonzales, Pierrette Hondagneu-Sotelo, Michael Kimmel, Don Sabo, Barrie Thorne, and the anonymous reviewers of the *Sociology of Sport Journal*.

Reprinted, by permission, from M.A. Messner, 1988, "Sports and male domination: The female athlete as contested ideological terrain," *Sociology of Sport Journal, 5(3):* 197-211.

ambiguities. The socially constructed meanings surrounding physiological differences between the sexes, the present "male" structure of organized sports, and the media framing of the female athlete all threaten to subvert any counter-hegemonic potential posed by female athletes. In short, the female athlete—and her body—has become a contested ideological terrain.

Women's quest for equality in society has had its counterpart in the sports world. Since the 1972 passage of Title IX, women in the United States have had a legal basis from which to push for greater equity in high school and college athletics. Although equality is still a distant goal in terms of funding, programs, facilities, and media coverage of women's sports, substantial gains have been made by female athletes in the past 10 to 15 years, indicated by increasing numerical participation as well as by expanding peer and self-acceptance of female athleticism (Hogan, 1982; Sabo, 1985; Woodward, 1985). A number of commentators have recently pointed out that the degree of difference between male and female athletic performance—the "muscle gap"—has closed considerably in recent years as female athletes have gained greater access to coaching and training facilities (Crittenden, 1979; Dyer, 1983; Ferris, 1978).

However, optimistic predictions that women's movement into sport signals an imminent demise of inequalities between the sexes are premature. As Willis (1982, p. 120) argues, what matters most is not simply how and why the gap between male and female athletic performance is created, enlarged, or constricted; what is of more fundamental concern is "the manner in which this gap is understood and taken into the popular consciousness of our society." This paper is thus concerned with exploring the historical and ideological meaning of organized sports for the politics of gender relations. After outlining a theory for building an historically grounded understanding of sport, culture, and ideology, I will demonstrate how and why organized sports have come to serve as a primary institutional means for bolstering a challenged and faltering ideology of male superiority in the 20th century.

It will be argued that women's movement into sport represents a genuine quest by women for equality, control of their own bodies, and self-definition, and as such it represents a challenge to the ideological basis of male domination. Yet it will also be demonstrated that this quest for equality is not without contradictions and ambiguities. The social meanings surrounding the physiological differences between the sexes in the male-defined institution of organized sports and the framing of the female athlete by the sports media threaten to subvert any counter-hegemonic potential posed by women athletes. In short, the female athlete—and her body—has become a contested ideological terrain.

Sport, Culture, and Ideology

Most theoretical work on sport has fallen into either of two traps: an idealist notion of sport as a realm of freedom divorced from material and historical constraints, or a materialist analysis that posits sport as a cultural mechanism through which the dominant classes control the unwitting masses. Marxists have correctly criticized idealists and functionalists for failing to understand how sport tends to reflect capitalist relations, thus serving to promote and ideologically legitimize competition, meritocracy, consumerism, militarism, and instrumental rationality, while at the same time providing spectators with escape and compensatory mechanisms for an alienated existence (Brohm, 1978; Hoch, 1972). But Marxist structuralists, with their view of sport as a superstructural expression of ideological control by the capitalist class, have themselves fallen into a simplistic and nondialectical functionalism (Gruneau, 1983; Hargreaves, 1982). Within the deterministic Marxian framework, there is no room for viewing people (athletes, spectators) as anything other than passive objects who are duped into meeting the needs of capitalism.

Neo-Marxists of the 1980s have argued for the necessity of placing an analysis of sport within a more reflexive framework, wherein culture is seen as relatively autonomous from the economy and wherein human subjectivity occurs within historical and structural limits and constraints. This theory puts people back at the center stage of history without falling into an idealistic voluntarism that ignores the importance of historically formed structural conditions, class inequalities, and unequal power relations. Further, it allows for the existence of critical thought, resistance to dominant ideologies, and change. Within a reflexive historical framework, we can begin to understand how sport (and culture in general) is a dynamic social space where dominant (class, ethnic, etc.) ideologies are perpetuated as well as challenged and contested.

Recent critics have called for a recasting of this reflexive theory to include gender as a centrally important process rather than as a simple effect of class dynamics (Critcher, 1986; McKay, 1986). Indeed, sport as an arena of ideological battles over gender relations has been given short shrift throughout the sociology of sport literature. This is due in part to the marginalization of feminist theory within sociology as a discipline (Stacey & Thorne, 1985) and within sport sociology in particular (Birrell, 1984; Hall, 1984). When gender has been examined by sport sociologists, it has usually been within the framework of a sex role paradigm that concerns itself largely with the effects of sport participation on an individual's sex role identity, values, and so on (Lever, 1976; Sabo & Runfola, 1980; Schafer, 1975).[1] Although social-psychological examinations of the sport-gender relationship are important, the sex role paradigm often used by these studies too often

> ignores the extent to which our conceptions of masculinity and femininity—the content of either the male or female sex role—is relational, that is, the product of gender relations which are historically and socially conditioned. . . . The sex role paradigm also minimizes the extent to which gender relations are based on power. Not only do men as a group exert power over women as a group, but the historically derived definitions of masculinity and femininity reproduce those power relations. (Kimmel, 1986, pp. 520-521)

The 20th century has seen two periods of crisis for masculinity—each marked by drastic changes in work and family and accompanied by significant feminist movements (Kimmel, 1987). The first crisis of masculinity stretched from the turn of the century into the 1920s, and the second from the post–World War II years to the present. I will argue here, using a historical/relational conception of gender within a reflexive theory of sport, culture, and ideology, that during these two periods of crisis for masculinity, organized sport has been a crucial arena of struggle over basic social conceptions of masculinity and femininity, and as such has become a fundamental arena of ideological contest in terms of power relations between men and women.

Crises of Masculinity and the Rise of Organized Sports

Reynaud (1981, p. 9) has stated that "The ABC of any patriarchal ideology is precisely to present that division [between the sexes] as being of biological, natural, or divine essence." And, as Clarke and Clarke (1982, p. 63) have argued, because sport "appears as a sphere of activity outside society, and particularly as it appears to involve natural, physical skills and capacities, [it] presents these ideological images *as if they were natural.*" Thus, organized sport is clearly a potentially powerful cultural arena for the perpetuation of the ideology of male superiority and dominance. Yet, it has not always been of such importance.

The First Crisis of Masculinity:1890s Through the 1920s

Sport historians have pointed out that the rapid expansion of organized sport after the turn of the century into widespread "recreation for the masses" represented a cultural means of integrating immigrants and a growing industrial working class into an expanding capitalist order where work was becoming rationalized and leisure time was expanding (Brohm, 1978; Goldman, 1983/1984; Gruneau, 1983; Rigauer, 1981). However, few scholars of sport have examined how this expanding industrial capitalist order was interacting with a relatively autonomous system of gender stratification, and this severely limits their ability to understand the cultural meaning of organized sport. In fact, industrial capitalism both bolstered and undermined traditional forms of male domination.

The creation of separate (public/domestic) and unequal spheres of life for men and women created a new basis for male power and privilege (Hartmann, 1976; Zaretsky, 1973). But in an era of wage labor and increasingly concentrated ownership of productive property, fewer males owned their own businesses and farms or controlled their own labor. The breadwinner role was a more shaky foundation upon which to base male privilege than was the patriarchal legacy of property-ownership passed on from father to son (Tolson, 1977). These changes in work and family, along with the rise of female dominated public schools, urbanization, and the closing of the frontier all led to widespread fears of "social feminization" and a turn-of-the-century crisis of masculinity. Many men compensated with a defensive insecurity that manifested itself in increased preoccupation with physicality and toughness (Wilkenson, 1984), warfare (Filene, 1975), and even the creation of new organizations such as the Boy Scouts of America as a separate cultural sphere of life where "true manliness" could be instilled in boys by men (Hantover, 1978).

Within this context, organized sports became increasingly important as a "primary masculinity-validating experience" (Dubbert, 1979, p. 164). Sport was a male-created homosocial cultural sphere that provided men with psychological separation from the perceived feminization of society while also providing dramatic symbolic proof of the "natural superiority" of men over women.[2]

This era was also characterized by an active and visible feminist movement, which eventually focused itself on the achievement of female suffrage. These feminists challenged entrenched Victorian assumptions and prescriptions concerning femininity, and this was reflected in a first wave of athletic feminism which blossomed in the 1920s, mostly in women's colleges (Twin, 1979). Whereas sports participation for young males tended to confirm masculinity, female athleticism was viewed as conflicting with the conventional ethos of femininity, thus leading to virulent opposition to women's growing athleticism (Lefkowitz-Horowitz, 1986). A survey of physical education instructors in 1923 indicated that 93% were opposed to intercollegiate play for women (Smith, 1970). And the Women's Division of the National Amateur Athletic Foundation, led by Mrs. Herbert Hoover, opposed women's participation in the 1928 Olympics (Lefkowitz-Horowitz, 1986). Those involved in women's athletics responded to this opposition defensively (and perhaps out of a different feminine aesthetic or morality) with the establishment of an anticompetitive "feminine philosophy of sport" (Beck, 1980). This philosophy was at once responsible for the continued survival of women's athletics, as it was successfully marginalized and thus easily "ghettoized" and ignored, and it also ensured that, for the time being, the image of the female athlete would not become a major threat to the hegemonic ideology of male athleticism, virility, strength, and power.

The breakdown of Victorianism in the 1920s had a contradictory effect on the social deployment and uses of women's bodies. On the one hand, the female body became "a marketable item, used to sell numerous products and services" (Twin, 1979, p. xxix). This obviously reflected women's social subordination, but ironically,

> The commercialization of women's bodies provided a cultural opening for competitive athletics, as industry and ambitious individuals used women to sell sports. Leo Seltzer included women in his 1935 invention, roller derby, "with one eye to beauty and the other on gate receipts," according to one writer. While women's physical marketability profited industry, it also allowed females to do more with their bodies than before. (Twin, 1979, p. xxix)

Despite its limits, then, the first wave of athletic feminism, even in its more commercialized manifestations, did provide an initial challenge to men's creation of sport as an uncontested arena of ideological legitimation for male dominance. In forcing an acknowledgment of women's physicality, albeit in a limited way, this first wave of female athletes laid the groundwork for more fundamental challenges. While some cracks had clearly appeared in the patriarchal edifice, it would not be until the 1970s that female athletes would present a more basic challenge to predominant cultural images of women.

The Post–World War II Masculinity Crisis and the Rise of Mass Spectator Sports

Today, according to Naison (1980, p. 36), "The American male spends a far greater portion of his time with sports than he did 40 years ago, but the greatest proportion of that time is spent in front of a television set observing games that he will hardly ever play." How and why have organized sports increasingly become an object of mass spectatorship? Lasch (1979) has argued that the historical transformation from entrepreneurial capitalism to corporate capitalism has seen a concomitant shift from the Protestant work ethic (and industrial production) to the construction of the "docile consumer." Within this context, sport has degenerated into a spectacle, an object of mass consumption. Similarly, Alt (1983) states that the major function of mass-produced sports is to channel the alienated emotional needs of consumers in instrumental ways. Although Lasch and Alt are partly correct in stating that the sport spectacle is largely a manipulation of alienated emotional needs toward the goal of consumption, this explanation fails to account fully for the emotional resonance of the sports spectacle for a largely male audience. I would argue, along with Sabo and Runfola (1980, p. xv) that sports in the postwar era have become increasingly important to males precisely because they link men to a more patriarchal past.

The development of capitalism after World War II saw a continued erosion of traditional means of male expression and identity, due to the continued rationalization and bureaucratization of work, the shift from industrial production and physical labor to a more service-oriented economy, and increasing levels of structural unemployment. These changes, along with women's continued movement into public life, undermined and weakened the already shaky breadwinner role as a major basis for male power in the family (Ehrenreich, 1983; Tolson, 1977). And the declining relevance of physical strength in work and in warfare was not accompanied by a declining psychological need for an ideology of gender difference. Symbolic representations of the male body as a symbol of strength, virility, and power have become increasingly important in popular culture as actual inequalities between the sexes are contested in all arenas of public life (Mishkind et al., 1986). The marriage of television and organized sport—especially the televised spectacle of football—has increasingly played this important ideological role. As Oriard (1981) has stated,

> What football is for the athletes themselves actually has little direct impact on what it means to the rest of America. . . . Football projects a *myth* that speaks meaningfully to a large number of Americans far beneath the level of conscious perception. . . . Football does not create a myth for all Americans; it excludes women in many highly significant ways. (pp. 33-34)

Football's mythology and symbolism are probably meaningful and salient on a number of ideological levels: Patriotism, militarism, violence, and meritocracy are all dominant themes. But I would argue that football's primary ideological salience lies in its ability, in the face of women's challenges to male dominance, to symbolically link men of diverse ages and socioeconomic backgrounds. Consider the words of a 32-year-old white professional male whom I was interviewing:[3] "A woman can do the same job I can do—maybe even be my boss. But I'll be *damned* if she can go out on the field and take a hit from Ronnie Lott."

The fact that this man (and perhaps 99% of all U.S. males) probably could not take a hit from the likes of pro football player Ronnie Lott and live to tell about it is really irrelevant, because football as a televised spectacle is meaningful on a more symbolic level. Here individual males are given the opportunity to identify—generically and abstractly—with all men as a superior and separate caste. Football, based as it is upon the most extreme possibilities of the male body (muscular bulk, explosive power, and aggression) is a world apart from women, who are relegated to the role of cheerleader/sex objects on the sidelines rooting their men on. In contrast to the bare and vulnerable bodies of the cheerleaders, the armored male bodies of football players are elevated to mythical status, and as such give testimony to the undeniable "fact" that there is at least one place where men are clearly superior to women.

Women's Recent Movement Into Sport

By the 1970s, just when symbolic representations of the athletic male body had taken on increasing ideological importance, a second wave of athletic feminism had emerged (Twin, 1979). With women's rapid postwar movement into the labor force and a revived feminist movement, what had been an easily ignorable undercurrent of female athleticism from the 1930s through the 1960s suddenly swelled into a torrent of female sports participation—and demands for equity. In the U.S., Title IX became the legal benchmark for women's push for equity with males. But due to efforts by the athletic establishment to limit the scope of Title IX, the quest for equity remained decentralized and continued to take place in the gymnasiums, athletic departments, and school boards of the nation (Beck, 1980; Hogan, 1979, 1982).

Brownmiller (1984, p. 195) has stated that the modern female athlete has placed herself "on the cutting edge of some of the most perplexing problems of gender-related biology and the feminine ideal," often resulting in the female athlete becoming ambivalent about her own image: *Can* a woman be strong, aggressive, competitive, and still be considered feminine? Rohrbaugh (1979) suggests that female athletes often develop an "apologetic" as a strategy for bridging the gap between cultural expectations of femininity and the very unfeminine requisites for athletic excellence. There has been some disagreement over whether a widespread apologetic actually exists among female athletes. Hart (1979) argues that there has never been an apologetic for black women athletes, suggesting that there are cultural differences in the construction of femininities. And a recent nationwide study indicated that 94% of the 1,682 female athletes surveyed do not regard athletic participation to be threatening to their femininity (Woodward, 1985). Yet, 57% of these same athletes did agree that society still forces a choice between being an athlete and being feminine, suggesting that there is still a dynamic tension between traditional prescriptions for femininity and the image presented by active, strong, even muscular women.

Femininity As Ideologically Contested Terrain

Cultural conceptions of femininity and female beauty have more than aesthetic meanings; these images, and the meanings ascribed to them, inform and legitimize unequal power relations between the sexes (Banner, 1983; Brownmiller, 1984; Lakoff & Scherr, 1984). Attempting to be viewed as feminine involves accepting behavioral and physical restrictions that make it difficult to view one's self, much less to be viewed by others, as equal with men. But if traditional images of femininity have solidified male privilege through constructing and then naturalizing the passivity, weakness, helplessness, and dependency of women, what are we to make of the current fit, athletic, even muscular looks that are increasingly in vogue with many women? Is there a new, counter-hegemonic image of women afoot that challenges traditional conceptions of femininity? A brief examination of female bodybuilding sheds light on these questions.

Lakoff and Scherr (1984, p. 110) state that "female bodybuilding has become the first female-identified standard of beauty." Certainly the image of a muscular—even toned—woman runs counter to traditional prescriptions for female passivity and weakness. But it's not that simple. In the film "Pumping Iron II: The Women," the tension between traditional prescriptions for femininity and the new muscularity of female bodybuilders is the major story line. It is obvious that the new image of women being forged by female bodybuilders is itself fraught with contradiction and ambiguity as women contestants and judges constantly discuss and argue emotionally over the meaning of femininity. Should contestants be judged simply according to how well-muscled they are (as male bodybuilders are judged), or also by a separate and traditionally feminine aesthetic? The consensus among the female bodybuilders, and especially among the predominantly male judges, appears to be the latter. In the words of one judge, "If they go to extremes and start looking like men, that's not what we're looking for in a woman. It's the winner of the contest who will set the standard of femininity." And of course, since this official is judging the contestants according to his own (traditional) standard of femininity, it should come as no surprise that the eventual winners are not the most well-muscled women.

Women's bodybuilding magazines also reflect this ambiguity: "Strong is Sexy," reads the cover of the August 1986 issue of *Shape* magazine, and this caption accompanies a photo of a slightly muscled young bathing-suited woman wielding a seductive smile and a not-too-heavy dumbbell. And the lead editorial in the September 1986 *Muscle and Beauty* magazine reminds readers that "in this post-feminist age of enlightenment . . . each woman must select the degree of muscularity she wants to achieve" (p. 6). The editor skirts the issue of defining femininity by stressing individual choice and self-definition, but she also emphasizes the fact that muscular women can indeed be beautiful and can also "make babies." Clearly, this emergent tendency of women attempting to control and define their own lives and bodies is being shaped within the existing hegemonic definitions of femininity.

And these magazines, full as they are with advertisements for a huge assortment of products for fat reduction, muscle building (e.g., "Anabolic Mega-Paks"), tanning formulas, and so on suggest that even if bodybuilding does represent an attempt by some women to control and define their own bodies, it is also being expressed in a distorted manner that threatens to replicate many of the more commercialized, narcissistic, and physically unhealthy aspects of men's athletics. Hargreaves (1986, p. 117) explains the contradictory meaning of women's movement into athletic activities such as bodybuilding, boxing, rugby, and soccer:

> This trend represents an active threat to popular assumptions about sport and its unifying principle appears as a shift in male hegemony. However, it also shows up the contradiction that women are being incorporated into models of male sports which are characterized by fierce competition and aggression and should, therefore, be resisted. Instead of a redefinition of masculinity occurring, this trend highlights the complex ways male hegemony works in sport and ways in which women actively collude in its reproduction.

It is crucial to examine the role that the mass sports media play in contributing to this shift in male hegemony, and it is to this topic that I will turn my attention next.

Female Athletes and the Sports Media

A person viewing an athletic event on television has the illusory impression of immediacy—of being there as it is happening. But as Clarke and Clarke (1982, p. 73) point out,

> The immediacy is, in fact, *mediated*—between us and the event stand the cameras, camera angles, producers' choice of shots, and commentators' interpretations—the whole invisible apparatus of media presentation. We can never see the whole event, we see those parts which are filtered through this process to us. . . . Rather than immediacy, our real relation to sports on television is one of distance—we are observers, recipients of a media event.

The choices, the filtering, the entire mediation of the sporting event, is based upon invisible, taken-for-granted assumptions and values of dominant social groups, and as such the presentation of the event tends to support corporate, white, and male-dominant ideologies. But as Gitlin (1980) has demonstrated, the media is more than a simple conduit for the transmission of dominant ideologies. If it were simply that, then the propaganda function of television would be transparent for all to see, stripping the medium of its veneer of objectivity and thus reducing its legitimacy. Rather, T.V. provides frameworks of meaning which, in effect, selectively interpret not only the athletic events themselves but also the controversies and problems surrounding the events. Since sport has been a primary arena of ideological legitimation for male superiority, it is crucial to examine the frameworks of meaning that the sports media have employed to portray the emergence of the female athlete.

A potentially counter-hegemonic image can be dealt with in a number of ways by the media. An initial strategy is to marginalize something that is too big to simply ignore. The 1986 Gay Games in the San Francisco Bay Area are a good example of this. The Games explicitly advocate a value system (equality between women and men, for instance) which runs counter to that of the existing sports establishment (Messner, 1984). Despite the fact that the Games were arguably the Bay Area's largest athletic event of the summer, and that several events in the Games were internationally sanctioned, the paltry amount of coverage given to the Games did *not,* for the most part, appear on the sports pages or during the sports segment of the T.V. news. The event was presented in the media not as a legitimate sports event but as a cultural or lifestyle event. The media's framing of the Games invalidated its claim as a sporting event, thus marginalizing any ideological threat that the Games might have posed to the dominant value system.

Until fairly recently, marginalization was the predominant media strategy in portraying female athletes. Graydon (1983) states that 90% of sports reporting still covers male sports. And when female athletes are covered— by a predominantly male media—they are described either in terms of their physical desirability to men ("pert and pretty") or in their domestic roles as wives and mothers. Patronizing or trivializing female athletes is sometimes not enough to marginalize them ideologically: Top-notch female athletes have often been subjected to overt hostility intended to cast doubts upon their true sex. To say "she plays like a man" is a double-edged sword—it is, on the surface, a compliment to an individual woman's skills, but it also suggests that since she is so good, she must not be a true woman after all. The outstanding female athlete is portrayed as an exception that proves the rule, thus reinforcing traditional stereotypes about femininity. Hormonal and chromosomal femininity tests for female (but no masculinity tests for male) athletes are a logical result of these ideological assumptions about male-female biology (Lenskyj, 1986).

I would speculate that we are now moving into an era in which female athletes have worked hard enough to attain a certain level of legitimacy that makes simple media marginalization and trivialization of female athletes appear transparently unfair and prejudicial. The framing of female athletes as sex objects or as sexual deviants is no longer a tenable strategy if the media are to maintain their own legitimacy. As Gitlin (1980) pointed out in reference to the media's treatment of the student antiwar movement in the late 1960s, when a movement's values become entrenched in a large enough proportion of the population, the media maintains its veneer of objectivity and fairness by incorporating a watered-down version of the values of the oppositional group. In so doing, the ideological hegemony of the dominant group shifts but is essentially maintained. I would argue that this is precisely what is happening today with women and sport in the media. Women athletes are increasingly being covered by "objective" reports that do not trivialize their performances, make references to a woman's attractiveness, or posit the superior female athlete as a sex deviant. The attitude now seems to be, "They want to be treated equally with men? Well, let's see what they can do."

What is conveniently ignored by today's sportscasters—and liberal feminists, intent on gaining equal opportunities for female athletes, sometimes collude in this—is that male and female bodies do differ in terms of their potential for physical strength, endurance, agility, and grace. Despite considerable overlap, the average adult male is about 5 inches taller than the average female. Can women really hope to compete at the highest levels with men in basketball or volleyball? The average male has a larger and more powerful body. Males average 40% muscle and 15% body fat, while females average 23% muscle and 25% body fat. Can women possibly compete at the highest levels with men in football, track and field, hockey, or baseball? Women do have some physical differences from men that could be translated into athletic superiority. Different skeletal structures and greater flexibility make for superior performances on a balance beam, for instance. And women's higher body fat ratio gives them greater buoyancy in water and greater insulation from heat loss, which has translated into women's best time in swimming the English Channel both ways being considerably faster than the best times recorded by men. But the fact is, the major sports (especially the "money" sports) are defined largely according to the most extreme possibilities of the male body. If cross-sex competition is truly on the agenda, women are going to be competing at a decided disadvantage, "fighting biology all the way" (Brownmiller, 1984, p. 32), on male-defined turf.

Given these physiological differences between the sexes and the fact that major sports are organized around the most extreme potentialities of the male body, "equal opportunity" as the sports media's dominant framework of meaning for presenting the athletic performances of women athletes is likely to become a new means of solidifying the ideological hegemony of male superiority. With women competing in male-defined sports, the sports media can employ statistics as objective measures of performance. Equal opportunity within this system provides support for the ideology of meritocracy while at the same time offering incontrovertible evidence of the "natural" differences between males and females. And male reporters can simply smile and shrug: "We just call 'em as we see 'em."

Male Responses to Female Athleticism

How people receive and interpret the complex and sometimes contradictory ideological messages they receive through the media is an important issue that deserves more analytic attention than can be offered here (Dunn, 1986). I would like to make a tentative speculation here that the emerging images of femininity being forged by women athletes and framed by the media are grudgingly becoming accepted by the majority of males. Although there is clearly some resistance—even outright hostility—toward female athleticism expressed by a small minority of the men I have interviewed, the following statement by a 33-year-old blue collar man is typical of the majority:

> I really enjoy the progress they [female athletes] are making now, having bobby-sox baseball and flag football for little girls. And in high school they have whole leagues now like for the boys. I think that's

great. You used to watch women's games in the '60s and in the '70s even, and you could watch all these mistakes—errors on routine grounders, things like that. But now they're really sharp—I mean, they can play a man's game as far as mental sharpness. But I think physically they're limited to their own sex. There is still the male part of the game. That is, males have better physical equipment for sports, as for what they can do and what they can't do.

This man's statement expresses many of the basic ambiguities of male consciousness under liberal capitalism in the "postfeminist" 1980s: Imbedded in the liberal ideal of equal opportunity is a strong belief that inequality is part of the natural order. Thus, it's only fair that women get an equal shot to compete, but it's really such a relief to find that, once given the opportunity, they just don't have the "physical equipment" to measure up with men. "They're [still] limited to their own sex."

Conclusion

I have discounted the simplistic notion that women's increasing athleticism unambiguously signals increased freedom and equality for women with the argument that "equal opportunity" for female athletes may actually mark a shift in the ideological hegemony of male dominance and superiority. But it would be a mistake to conclude from this that women's movement into sport is simply having a reactionary effect in terms of the politics of gender relations. It should not be lost on us that the statement made by the above-mentioned man, even as it expresses a continued need to stress the ways that women are different and inferior to men, also involves a historically unprecedented acknowledgment of women's physicality and "mental sharpness."

It has been argued here that gender relations, along with their concomitant images of masculinity and femininity, change and develop historically as a result of interactions between men and women within socially structured limits and constraints. We can see how the first wave of athletic feminism in the 1920s signaled an active challenge to Victorian constraints on women, and we can see that the way this challenge was resisted and eventually marginalized reflected the limits imposed upon women's quest for equality by an emerging industrial capitalism and a crumbling, but still resilient, patriarchy. Similarly, the current wave of women's athleticism expresses a genuine quest by women for equality, control of their own bodies, and self-definition, but within historical limits and constraints imposed by a consumption-oriented corporate capitalism and men's continued attempts

to retain power and privilege over women. As Connell (1987, p. 251) has
pointed out, "In sexual ideology generally, ascendant definitions of reality
must be seen as accomplishments that are always partial and always to some
extent contested. Indeed we must see them as partly defined by the alternatives against which they are asserted."

Organized sport, as a cultural sphere defined largely by patriarchal priorities, will continue to be an important arena in which emerging images of active,
fit, and muscular women are forged, interpreted, contested, and incorporated.
The larger socioeconomic and political context will continue to shape and
constrain the extent to which women can wage fundamental challenges to the
ways that organized sports continue providing ideological legitimation for
male dominance. And the media's framing of male and female athletes will
continue to present major obstacles for any fundamental challenge to the
present commercialized and male-dominant structure of organized athletics. It
remains for a critical feminist theory to recognize the emergent contradictions
in this system in order to inform a liberating social practice.

Notes

1. While this criticism is generally true of U.S. sport sociology, an international
   group of scholars has recently made important strides toward the development of a more critical and reflexive feminist analysis of sport. For an
   excellent collection of articles, see Hall (1987).
2. The discussion here is concerned mainly with sports and the ideology of
   gender relations. It is also important to employ a social-psychological
   perspective to examine the meaning of sports participation in the development of gender identity among female athletes (Duquin, 1984) and male
   athletes (Messner, 1985, 1987).
3. Interviews referred to here were conducted in 1983-84 with 30 male former
   athletes of diverse socioeconomic backgrounds and ages. Since the sample
   does not include nonathletes, the data should be considered suggestive, but
   not representative of a more general male population.

Bibliography

1. Alt, J. (1983). Sport and Cultural Reification: From Ritual to Mass Consumption. *Theory, Culture and Society,* 1(3), 93-107.
2. Banner, L.W. (1983). *American Beauty.* Chicago: University of Chicago
   Press.
3. Beck, B.A. (1980). The Future of Women's Sport: Issues, Insights, and
   Struggle. In D. Sabo & R. Runfola (Eds.), *Jock: Sports and Male Identity* (pp.
   299-314). Englewood Cliffs, NJ: Prentice-Hall.

4. Birrell, S. (1984). Studying Gender in Sport: A Feminist Perspective. In N. Theberge & P. Donnelly (Eds.), *Sport and the Sociological Imagination* (pp. 124-135). Fort Worth: Texas Christian University Press.

5. Brohm, J.M. (1978). *Sport: A Prison of Measured Time.* London: Ink Links.

6. Brownmiller, S. (1984). *Femininity.* New York: Fawcett Columbine.

7. Clarke, A., & Clarke, J. (1982). "Highlights and Action Replays"—Ideology, Sport, and the Media. In J. Hargreaves (Ed.), *Sport, Culture, and Ideology* (pp. 62-87). London: Routledge & Kegan Paul.

8. Connell, R.W. (1987). *Gender and Power.* Stanford, CA: Stanford University Press.

9. Critcher, C. (1986). Radical Theorists of Sport: The State of Play. *Sociology of Sport Journal, 3*, 333-343.

10. Crittenden, A. (1979). Closing the Muscle Gap. In S.L. Twin (Ed.), *Out of the Bleachers: Writings on Women and Sport* (pp. 5-10). Old Westbury, NY: The Feminist Press.

11. Dubbert, J.L. (1979). *A Man's Place: Masculinity in Transition.* Englewood Cliffs, NJ: Prentice-Hall.

12. Dunn, R. (1986). Television, Consumption, and the Commodity Form. *Theory, Culture and Society, 3*(1), pp. 49-64.

13. Duquin, M. (1984). Power and Authority: Moral Consensus and Conformity in Sport. *International Review for Sociology of Sport, 19*(3/4), 295-304.

14. Dyer, K. (1983). *Challenging the Men: The Social Biology of Female Sport Achievement.* St. Lucia: University of Queensland Press.

15. "Editorial." (1986, September). *Muscle and Beauty,* pp. 5-6.

16. Ehrenreich, B. (1983). *The Hearts of Men.* Garden City, NY: Anchor Press/ Doubleday.

17. Ferris, E. (1978). *Sportswomen and Medicine.* Report of the First International Conference on Women and Sport.

18. Filene, P. (1975). *Him/Her/Self: Sex Roles in Modern America.* New York: Harcourt Brace Jovanovich.

19. Gitlin, T. (1980). *The Whole World Is Watching: Mass Media in the Making and Unmaking of the New Left.* Berkeley: University of California Press.

20. Goldman, R. (1983/1984, Winter). We Make Weekends: Leisure and the Commodity Form. *Social Text, 8*, 84-103.

21. Graydon, J. (1983, February). "But It's More Than a Game. It's an Institution." Feminist Perspectives on Sport. *Feminist Review, 13*, 5-16.

22. Gruneau, R. (1983). *Class, Sports, and Social Development.* Amherst: University of Massachusetts Press.

23. Hall, M.A. (1984). Toward a Feminist Analysis of Gender Inequality in Sport. In N. Theberge & P. Donnelly (Eds.), *Sport and the Sociological Imagination* (pp. 82-103). Fort Worth: Texas Christian University Press.

24. Hall, M.A. (Ed.). (1987). The Gendering of Sport, Leisure, and Physical Education. *Women's Studies International Forum, 10*(4).

25. Hantover, J. (1978). The Boy Scouts and the Validation of Masculinity. *Journal of Social Issues,* 34(1), 184-195.
26. Hargreaves, J. (Ed.). (1982). *Sport, Culture, and Ideology.* London: Routledge & Kegan Paul.
27. Hargreaves, J. (1986). Where's the Virtue? Where's the Grace? A Discussion of the Social Production of Gender Through Sport. *Theory, Culture and Society,* 3(1), 109-122.
28. Hart, M.M. (1979). On Being Female in Sport. In S.L. Twin (Ed.), *Out of the Bleachers: Writings on Women and Sport* (pp. 24-34). Old Westbury, NY: The Feminist Press.
29. Hartmann, H. (1976). Capitalism, Patriarchy, and Job Segregation. *Signs,* 1(3), 366-394.
30. Hoch, P. (1972). *Rip Off the Big Game.* Garden City, NY: Doubleday.
31. Hogan, C.L. (1979). Shedding Light on Title IX. In S.L. Twin (Ed.), *Out of the Bleachers: Writings on Women and Sport* (pp. 173-181). Old Westbury, NY: The Feminist Press.
32. Hogan, C.L. (1982, May). Revolutionizing School and Sports: Ten Years of Title IX. *Ms.,* pp. 25-29.
33. Kimmel, M.S. (1986). Toward Men's Studies. *American Behavioral Scientist,* 29(5), 517-530.
34. Kimmel, M.S. (1987). Men's Responses to Feminism at the Turn of the Century. *Gender and Society,* 1(3), 261-283.
35. Lakoff, R.T., & Scherr, R.L. (1984). *Face Value: The Politics of Beauty.* Boston: Routledge & Kegan Paul.
36. Lasch, C. (1979). *The Culture of Narcissism.* New York: Warner.
37. Lefkowitz-Horowitz, H. (1986, April). *Before Title IX.* Presented at Stanford Humanities Center Sport and Culture Meetings.
38. Lenskyi, H. (1986). *Out of Bounds: Women, Sport, and Sexuality.* Toronto: The Women's Press.
39. Lever, J. (1976). Sex Differences in the Games Children Play. *Social Problems,* 23, 478-487.
40. McKay, J. (1986). Marxism as a Way of Seeing: Beyond the Limits of Current "Critical" Approaches to Sport. *Sociology of Sport Journal,* 3, 261-272.
41. Messner, M. (1984). Gay Athletes and the Gay Games: An Interview With Tom Waddell. *M: Gentle Men for Gender Justice,* 13, 22-23.
42. Messner, M. (1985). The Changing Meaning of Male Identity in the Lifecourse of the Athlete. *Arena Review,* 9(2), 31-60.
43. Messner, M. (1987). The Meaning of Success: The Athletic Experience and the Development of Male Identity. In Harry Brod (Ed.), *The Making of Masculinities: The New Men's Studies* (pp. 193-209). Boston: Allen & Unwin.
44. Mishkind, M.E., Rodin, J., Silberstein, L.R., & Striegel-Moore, R.H. (1986, May/June). The Embodiment of Masculinity: Cultural, Psychological, and Behavioral Dimensions. *American Behavioral Scientist,* 29(5), 531-540.

45. Naison, M. (1980). Sports, Women, and the Ideology of Domination. In D. Sabo & R. Runfola (Eds.), *Jock: Sports and Male Identity* (pp. 30-36). Englewood Cliffs, NJ: Prentice-Hall.

46. Oriard, M. (1981). Professional Football as Cultural Myth. *Journal of American Culture,* 4(3), 27-41.

47. Reynaud, E. (1981). *Holy Virility: The Social Construction of Masculinity.* London: Pluto Press.

48. Rigauer, B. (1981). *Sport and Work.* New York: Columbia University Press.

49. Rohrbaugh, J.B. (1979, August). Femininity on the Line. *Psychology Today,* pp. 31-33.

50. Sabo, D. (1985). Sport, Patriarchy, and Male Identity: New Questions About Men and Sport. *Arena Review,* 9(2), 1-30.

51. Sabo, D., & Runfola, R. (Eds.). (1980). *Jock: Sports and Male Identity.* Englewood Cliffs, NJ: Prentice-Hall.

52. Schafer, W.E. (1975, Fall). Sport and Male Sex Role Socialization. *Sport Sociology Bulletin,* 4, 47-54.

53. Smith, R.A. (1970). The Rise of Basketball for Women in Colleges. *Canadian Journal of History of Sport and Physical Education,* 1, 21-23.

54. Stacey, J., & Thorne, B. (1985, April). The Missing Feminist Revolution in Sociology. *Social Problems,* 32(4), 301-316.

55. Tolson, A. (1977). *The Limits of Masculinity: Male Identity and Women's Liberation.* New York: Harper & Row.

56. Twin, S.L. (1979). *Out of the Bleachers: Writings on Women and Sport.* Old Westbury, NY: The Feminist Press.

57. Wilkenson, R. (1984). *American Tough: The Tough Guy Tradition in American Character.* New York: Harper & Row.

58. Willis, P. (1982). Women in Sport in Ideology. In J. Hargreaves (Ed.), *Sport, Culture, and Ideology* (pp. 117-135). London: Routledge & Kegan Paul.

59. Woodward, S. (1985, November 5). "Women Alter Outlook on Sports: Attitude Is Positive in Survey." *USA Today,* p. 1A.

60. Zaretsky, E. (1973). *Capitalism, the Family, and Personal Life.* New York: Harper Colophon Books.

20
CHAPTER

Sexualization and Sexuality in Sport

Paul Davis

Much has been written in recent years about the sexualization of the athlete.[1] I do not wish to rehash it, nor do I wish to quibble with any of it. However, one upshot of the realizations involved in this work is a pervasive distrust of anything that seems to connect sport with the sexual.

I will try to argue that this feeling is exaggerated. This will require the challenging task of attempting to distinguish between sexualization and sexuality. By combining this distinction with ordinary reflections on the essential nature of sport, I will argue that the sport arena is peculiarly unfitted to be unsexual.

I wish first to distinguish two species of athlete sexualization. The first is grounded in sport performance, and the second is not. This distinction matters for two reasons. First, the performance-specific kind serves to confirm that sport as a practice offers unusually generous possibilities of sexualization and will, in turn, vivify the unavoidable phenomenon of sexuality in sport. Second, the other kind more clearly demonstrates the continuity between athlete sexualization and sexualization in general. This should, in turn, improve the prospects of providing a general account of sexualization and of saying why, unlike sexuality, it is objectionable.

The performance-specific species of sexualization is the sexualized imagery of athletic performance commonly found in newspaper and television coverage of sport. Three qualities are (variously) in evidence here:

- The deliberate focus on particular, sexually significant body parts for the purpose of sexual titillation
- The attunement to bodily postures that, through freezing or emphasis, are intended to be sexually titillating
- In the case of photographs in either of the preceding categories, an accompanying, frequently punned caption that confirms the moment as one of sexualized comic relief.[2]

The sport performance is necessary to this sexualization in that it is the movements made and poses struck whilst in the arena that are sexualized.

Sexualization of the athlete not grounded in the sport performance takes diffuse forms. The most familiar, historically, is probably the public observation of the attractiveness of female athletes offered by male journalists and television hosts and commentators. A less banal example is provided by a recent British television talk show hosted by a well-known male soccer player.[3] As the show kicks in, the host is filmed showering and dressing. A camera focused at crotch level highlights sexually significant parts in, arguably, a sexually significant state. It is tempting to conclude that this example is that of a sexualized celebrity who happens to be an athlete, a conclusion made more alluring by the fact that the show is not essentially about sport (the host chats with singers, for instance, without involving sport in the conversation). However, the conclusion is perhaps too abrasive in this case, since some classes of athletes have socially evolved into the intrinsically sexy, grounding context–indifferent sexualization of their members. Some attention has been given in recent years, for instance, to the sexualization of the black male athlete,[4] and it is probably no accident that the host of this show is a black male athlete.

I will not concern myself here with the shady commerce between athlete sexualization and variables such as sex, race, class, and sexual orientation, important though these topics are. This is instead an a priori inquiry into the distinction between sexuality and sexualization and the application of this distinction to the social practice of sport.

Consider another phenomenon, a not uncommon one, that might look at first like another clear case of sexualization: that of swimmers at a club who feel a sexual interest in a locker room photograph of a prolific swimmer in the act of swimming. This case is ambiguous. It would be highly premature to regard it as simply another instance of sexualization. In this context, the photograph is infused with an important generality of meaning. The picture is inscribed with the message that *our sport*—swimming, in this case—is sexy, that swimming is a sexy thing to do. In addition, there is a critical particularity about the photograph and the sexual stimulus elicited. Swimming is something those who enjoy the picture can identify with deeply, something that excites them at a fundamental level and probably has done so since a point in their lives at which talk of *sexual* responses is not an issue. Not just any picture will do, nor is the sexual response of club members an undifferentiated excitation. The sexual response is highly precise and is uniquely caused by the sight of a quality swimmer in the act of swimming.[5]

In addition, qualities of this case sharpen, perhaps in a critical way, the contrast with the preceding cases. Two interrelated features exist here. The first concerns the content of the picture. There is no attempt by the photographer to focus on sexually significant body parts such as the breasts, buttocks, or crotch. The photo does not attempt to reveal a sexually marketable body posture. There is no tawdry caption; all that might appear beneath the photo is the name of the swimmer and the event the photograph is taken from. These qualities distinguish this case sharply from the others, each of which is characterized by at least one of the aforementioned features.

The second feature is that the photograph does not result from an extraneous agenda, nor, relatedly, does it require any contrivance or discordance of content and context. This is in contrast to the performance-specific class of sexualization, in which the shot or photograph is clearly motivated by considerations extraneous to the sport context. The context in the example of the swimming photo is one in which the appropriate considerations are sporting ones, but this is farcically at odds with a shot or photograph that is explicitly shaped to sexually titillate. The appropriate context—if any—for such a shot or photograph is a magazine or video geared toward teenagers. In the case of the television show, similarly, the opening shots are more suited to the beginning of a soft porn video than to the beginning of a talk show. (The aforementioned sexual accolades offered by male journalists and television hosts and commentators are appropriate in—at best—a beauty contest.) Again, none of this grotesquery is present in the case under consideration—a shot of a swimmer swimming, driven by a photographer's ambition, perhaps, of capturing the distinctive character of this particular swimmer or something of the kinesthetic character of high-powered competitive swimming in general. The photograph appears in a swimmers' locker room, and some of the swimmers find it sexually stimulating.

I propose that we consider this instance not sexualization of the athlete but rather unobjectionable sexuality in sport. It also offers an intimation of how sport is particularly unfitted to be unsexual. Clarification of these suggestions requires a brief theoretical detour on the nature of both sport and sexual response.

In his book *Sexual Desire*, Roger Scruton articulates a persuasive case on the essential character of human sexual response.[6] Integral to the phenomenon of sexual desire, he argues, are metaphysical shadows of which we cannot disburden ourselves. Because the "I" seems transparent to itself, the idea irresistibly arises that what I am essentially is "this self-knowing I . . . who lies concealed within, behind or beyond the organism, but who cannot be identical with the organism, for the very reason that the bodily states and the substance of this organism remain obscure to me, while my mental life is thoroughly and completely known."[7] We therefore take ourselves to be "pure, unified individuals, havens of possibility, located outside the limits of natural causality, capable of acting freely and integrally, so as to be responsible for the present action at every future time."[8] This is what it is to be a person. I constantly identify myself without reference to my body and react to you as though you were not identical with your body but operating through it. We are capable of experiencing a quite radical estrangement from our bodies, for example, when examining the state of them, or when considering whether we should lose weight or what we should wear tonight. We can experience even profound alienation from our bodies; when ill or incapacitated, I might think of my body as a prison in which the self is trapped. From the first-person point of view, a person seems essentially a perspective, a willing, experiencing, thinking subject, contingently connected to a body. This theory of the human agent is given considerable and distinguished exposition in the shape of the Cartesian ego, the Leibnizian apperception, the Kantian "transcendental unity of consciousness" and "transcendental self," the Hegelian *Fürsichsein*, and the Sartrean "*pour-soi*." Only when we detach ourselves from the first-person perspective might it seem to rest on an illusion. But we cannot abandon the first-person perspective. We might conclude that we cannot live with it. But neither can we live without it.

If we cannot evade this self-mystification, then neither can we escape its metaphysical counterpoint of embodiment.[9] How can putatively transcendental subjects be individuated except through their bodies? How can I implement my (free) will except through my body (even if this amounts to nothing more than using my voice)? Isn't it true that someone who hits my body has hit *me*? Helmuth Plessner has argued that I stand to my body in a relation that is at once instrumental and constitutive: I *have* my body, but I also *am* my body.[10] Consequently, the relation of self to body has essentially an enigmatic, frequently troubling quality.

In sexual desire, we aspire to suspend this fraught relation of self and body. It is not a body that is desired. The desired is, *qua desired*, a perspectival, freely willing, and responsible being. The desiring wishes his or her own perspective to figure in the perspective of the desired, and wishes himself or herself to be freely desired.[11] At the same time, the aim of desire is the complete embodiment of each point of view. In sexual desire the embodiment of persons is itself the object of our interest. What is desired is the *person as body-subject*. We seek to reveal the life of another in the life of the body, through a largely involuntary gamut of responses such as smiles, stares, blushes, and changes in the sexual organs. We seek to unite the desired with his or her body, and at the ideal limit of sexual response we are profoundly united with our bodies. A critical fact about human sexual response is that the very incitements to desire are often the smiles, the walk, the movements, the expressions, the voice—in short, the *bodily agency*—of the desired, especially when, significantly, it seems not to be self-conscious. In sexual desire we celebrate, perhaps as in no other realm, the fact that our subjecthood is, for all the vaunted glories of free will, responsibility, and the like, a marvelously corporeal phenomenon.[12] This is what gives human sexuality its character as existential triumph. What might be a prison becomes for a time a hospitable home.

Consider sport. Here too the embodiment of the person is the object of our interest. Here too we are, as performer or spectator, interested in neither bodies nor immaterial souls, but the person as body-subject. In its well-documented noninstrumentality, sport is, indeed, a celebration of the body-subject.[13] The athlete is conceived, qua athlete, as a perspectival, freely willing, and responsible being (for that reason, spectators tend to be disappointed by a competitor, and especially a victor, who looks robotic).[14] Again, the athlete seeks the unity of self and body. At the ideal limit of sport, also, a person is profoundly united with his or her body; free will, responsibility, and the rest roundly converge with materiality. Paraphrasing Yeats, we do not know the dancer from the dance.[15] As spectators, we tend to find sport particularly pleasing when, significantly, it manifests a bodily agency that seems not to be self-conscious. (In performance of both sport and sex, indeed, we tend to mess up if we become conscious of our bodies.)[16] The common celebration of the embodied subject makes the idea that sexuality should or could be expunged from sport a singularly fishy one. It is, indeed, the shared centrality of the body that makes sport as a practice particularly vulnerable to performance-specific sexualization. In this respect, sport is distinctive, and the possibilities for sexualization that it offers provide a discontinuity with most of the rest of life. The practice of chess, for instance, is not similarly vulnerable to sexualization. The fact that sport is intrinsically so sexualization-friendly should cast doubt on the ambition of banishing or marginalizing the sexuality that is within it.

The preceding reflections are intended to lend some persuasive force to my suggestion that the phenomenon exemplified in the picture in the locker room is sexuality and not sexualization. In this case, the object of sexual intrigue is the uncompromised, unmediated person as body-subject, manifested in sport. Whatever sexual ramifications the picture has emerge out of the shot of the subject swimming. There is no clash between content and context. There is no decontextualization of this body-subject, because it is the rich and precise character of the movements of a top-level swimmer that the photographer is hoping to capture. It is significant here, as I have already indicated, that those whose enjoyment of the picture has the precise sexual edge I have emphasized have an intimate engagement with the activity of swimming.

Contrast this with the other cases described in this chapter. Imagine a familiar example of an opportunistically captioned tabloid shot of a female tennis player whose lunge with her racquet reveals a little cleavage. This is sexualization, and is objectionable, for two interrelated reasons: it involves an artificial focus on particular, sexually significant body parts, a focus that temporarily detaches the body from the rich and precise bodily agency on display on the tennis court and reconfigures it into something trivially titillating or comic (or both). An observer could experience the intended titillation or amusement without any appreciation of the game of tennis. Conversely, the essentially precise sexual response of the swimmers could not be paralleled with innocuous tennis film or photography if the respondent does not have serious appreciation of tennis.

The talk show example also clearly involves a dramatic rupture of content and context. (And the same is true, again, of the inappropriate comments of male journalists and television commentators and hosts.) The inappropriate footage aggressively detaches the body of the show's host from the context in which his agency is present. In this feature athlete sexualization is continuous with sexualization in general. The critical characteristic is the decontextualization of the body-subject. This provides sexualization, in contradistinction to sexuality. And this is objectionable.

If my argument is sound, then it follows that sexual responses to sport and athletes do not inevitably betoken ideological invasion. Many such responses no doubt do, and those who are sexually titillated by examples such as those presented in this chapter ought not to be, and should retrain their responses.

However, as I have tried to illustrate, a sexual component in the enjoyment of sport needn't always be a guilty secret.

Notes

1. See, for instance, Paul Willis, 1994, "Women in Sport in Ideology," in *Women, Sport, and Culture,* ed. S. Birrell and C. Cole (Champaign, Ill.:

Human Kinetics), 31-45, esp. 35, 41-42; M. MacNeill, "Active Women, Media Representations, and Ideology" (ibid., 273-87); and A. Balsamo, "Feminist Bodybuilding" (ibid., 341-52), esp. 343-45.

2. I borrow this felicitous expression from the essay of M.C. Duncan, M.A. Messner, L. Williams, and K. Jensen, "Gender Stereotyping in Televised Sports," in S. Birrell and C. Cole, 251. The authors apply the description to the use of female spectators in television coverage of sport.

3. "Friday Night's All Wright" (London Weekend Television, 1998).

4. See, for instance, E. Cashmore, 1982, *Black Sportsmen* (London: Routledge) and Pieterse, J.N., 1992, *White on Black: Images of Africa and Blacks in Western Popular Culture* (New Haven: Yale University Press).

5. For powerful criticism of theories of the emotions that reduce emotion to apprehension plus an undifferentiated general excitement, see R.W. Hepburn, "Emotions and Emotional Qualities," 1965, in *Collected Papers on Aesthetics,* ed. C. Barrett, (Oxford: Blackwell), esp. 195. Hepburn's comments are in discussion of emotions evoked by artworks. For a recognition of specificity of affect in discussion of art and sport, see Terence J. Roberts, "Sport, Art, and Particularity: The Best Equivocation," 1995, in *Philosophic Inquiry in Sport,* ed. W.J. Morgan and Klaus V. Meier (Champaign, Ill.:Human Kinetics), esp. 417-18.

6. Roger Scruton, 1986, *Sexual Desire* (London: Weidenfeld and Nicolson), esp. 36-93.

7. Ibid., 56.

8. Ibid., 58. See also Thomas Nagel, 1986, *The View From Nowhere* (New York City: Oxford University Press), 110-26, and also Thomas Nagel, 1979, "Subjective and Objective," in *Mortal Questions* (Cambridge: Cambridge University Press).

9. Kantian philosopher Strawson has stated that persons are essentially the sort of things to which M(material)-predicates and P(psychological)-predicates apply. See P.F. Strawson, 1959, *Individuals* (London: Methuen), 87-116.

10. Helmuth Plessner, 1970, *Laughing and Crying: A Study of the Limits of Human Behaviour,* transl. James Spencer Churchill and Marjorie Grene, Evanston: Northwestern University Press.

11. On the reflective perspectival interplay of sexual response, see Nagel, "Sexual Perversion," in *Mortal Question*.

12. This summation of the nature of persons is that of Michel de Montaigne (*Essays III, viii*). Charles Taylor (1990) quotes it in *The Sources of the Self* (Cambridge: Harvard University Press), 181.

13. See, for instance, Iris Marion Young, "The Exclusion of Women From Sport: Conceptual and Existential Dimensions," reprinted in Morgan and Meier, esp. 263. Also Joseph H. Kupfer, "Sport: The Body Electric," reprinted in Morgan and Meier, esp. 392-93 and 403-4.

14. For endorsement of the notion that sport is properly a competition between persons, see Robert L. Simon, "Good Competition and Drug-Enhanced Performance," in Morgan and Meier, 209-14. For an interesting recent discussion suggesting that our paradigms of freedom and responsibility (and related reactive attitudes such as praise) may be exaggerated in sport as

elsewhere, see David Carr, 1999, "Where's the Merit If the Best Man Wins?" *Journal of the Philosophy of Sport* 26 (1999): 1-9.

15. "O body swayed to music, O brightening glance, / How can we know the dancer from the dance?" W.B. Yeats, "Among School Children," in *Collected Poems* (1982) (London: MacMillan), 242-45.

16. I am indebted to Gunnar Brevik for making this point in his presentation to the 1999 International Association for the Philosophy of Sport conference in Bedford, England ("The Self in Bodily Movement").

IV

PART

ANIMALS AND THEIR USE IN SPORT: WHERE DO WE DRAW THE MORAL LINE?

Are there any limits on the ways that human beings can use animals? Even the way the question is phrased presupposes that it is morally permissible for humans to use other animals in the first place. The real challenge in this section is to explain the moral foundation for any human use of animals for sport. The basic argument is simple. Animals are sentient creatures: they feel pain. It is morally wrong to cause unnecessary pain to any sentient creature. Therefore it is morally wrong to cause unnecessary pain to animals. Almost by definition, the pain animals experience through human use of them in sport is unnecessary. Human survival does not require us to practice sport, in particular sport with animals; such sport is pursued for pleasure. What entitles humans to cause other animals pain for our pleasure?

Any justification of the human use of animals for sport must come to terms with this basic challenge. It is tempting to assume that merely because human beings have the power to cause other animals pain, and just because we always have done so, the current debate is about how much pain we are prepared to tolerate in a civilized society. That was the question posed at the very beginning. We have gradually limited our use of animals for sport. Persian kings of the fifth century B.C. would, for sport, "hunt" lions and tigers that had been captured and released in arenas; the great Roman gladiatorial contests featured contests of humans versus animals; and big-game hunting has been a sport of the well-to-do even into this century. In Britain, fox hunting with hounds still takes place (although in 1999 the government debated banning it, despite the protests of members of the rural community; the ban was not enacted[1]). Are we entitled to use animals for our pleasure, and is the only question the degree to which we are permitted to cause them pain? If so, what ethical principles determine how much pain is permitted? If causing pain for pleasure is ethically permitted at all, how do we stop the slide into allowing humans to do whatever they like to other animals?

The challenges presented in these readings raise issues that extend beyond sport. At stake is the entire ethical relationship between animals and humans. If we are not ethically permitted to use animals for sport, then perhaps we are also not permitted to use them for clothes or food. As you read these articles, try to keep an open mind and be prepared to follow and analyze the arguments—wherever they might lead. These short sections are probably the most ethically challenging ones of the entire book.

Note

1. Fox hunting in Britain is conducted by hounds accompanied by riders on horseback. The specially trained dogs smell out a fox's trail and then chase it across the countryside, catch it, and tear it apart.

21
CHAPTER

The Ethics of Hunting

J. Ortega y Gasset

At this point we arrive at the terminus, the goal of hunting itself. And although this goal or final scene is sometimes the capture of the animal, its most frequent and natural form is the death of the beast. Death, especially "caused" death, murder, is or should be a terrifying thing. The hunter does not just come and go, working hard in valleys and on cliffs, urging on his dogs; rather, in the last analysis, he kills. The hunter is a death dealer.

The mission of thought is to construct archetypes; I mean, to point out from among the infinite figures that reality presents those in which, because of their greater purity, that reality becomes clearer. Once understood in its exemplary form, the reality is also elucidated in its obscure, confused, and deficient forms, and these are the more frequent forms. A person who has never seen a good bullfight cannot understand what the mediocre and awful ones are. This is because bad bullfights, which are almost all of them, exist only at the expense of the good ones, which are very unusual. In the human order at least, the depraved, the stupid, and the trivial are tenacious parasites of perfection. Don't fret about it; the harmful doctor lives thanks to the eminent one, and if there are so many bad writers it is because there have been some good ones.

The exemplary moral spirit of the sporting hunter, that manner of feeling, of taking up and practicing hunting, is a very precise line, below which fall innumerable forms of hunting that are deficient modes of this occupation; deficient in the aspects of dexterity, boldness, and effort, or simply in the moral aspect. Without doubt, above that line there is room for, and there do occur, greater refinements; but if we examine them carefully we will discover that they are mannerisms and excrescences. Hunting, like every human activity, has an ethic which distinguishes virtues from vices. There is such a thing as a rogue hunter, but there is also an affected piety of hunting.

All this leads up to that final scene of the hunt in which the fine skin of the animal appears stained with blood, and that body, once pure agility, lies transformed into the absolute paralysis that is death. Was it all only for this, we ask ourselves. More than once, the sportsman, within shooting range of a splendid animal, hesitates in pulling the trigger. The idea that such a slender life is going to be annulled surprises him for an instant. *Every good hunter is uneasy in the depths of his conscience when faced with the death he is about to inflict on the enchanting animal.* He does not have the final and firm conviction that his conduct is correct. But neither, it should be understood, is he certain of the opposite. Finding himself in an ambivalent situation which he has often wanted to clear up, he thinks about this issue without ever obtaining the sought-after evidence. I believe that this has always happened to man, with varying degrees of intensity according to the nature of the prey—ferocious or harmless—and with one or another variation in the aspect of uneasiness. This says nothing against hunting, but only that the generally problematic, equivocal nature of man's relationship with animals shines through that uneasiness. Nor can it be otherwise, because man has never really known exactly what an animal is. Before and beyond all science, humanity sees itself as something emerging from animality, but it cannot be sure of having transcended that state completely. The animal remains too close for us to not feel mysterious communication with it. The only people to have felt that they had a clear idea about the animal were the Cartesians. The truth is that they believed they had a clear idea about everything. But to achieve that rigorous distinction between man and beast, Descartes had first to convince himself that the animal was a mineral—that is, a mere machine. Fontenelle recounts that in his youth, while he was visiting Malebranche, a pregnant dog came into the room. So that it would not disturb anyone who was present, Malebranche—a very sweet and somewhat sickly priest, whose spine was twisted like a corkscrew—had the dog expelled with blows from a stick. The poor animal ran away howling piteously, while Malebranche, a Cartesian, listened impassively. "It doesn't matter," he said. "It's a machine, it's a machine!"

In a truly exhaustive study of hunting I would feel obliged to delve profoundly into that dimension of its ethics which inflicting death on the animal makes inevitable. But I restrain myself because the theme is enormously difficult. There is, first of all, the unbelievable backwardness and coarseness that characterizes studies of morality. Next to the atrocity of the demagogues, the stupidity of the moralists, or their total absence, is the chief cause of the division that today afflicts the human community. There is greater confusion than ever with regard to the norms which ought to govern the relations between men, to say nothing of those which could orient and regulate our treatment of the other realities present in our environment: the mineral, the vegetable, and the animal. There are people who believe in good faith that we have no obligations toward the rocks and therefore have tolerated advertisers' smearing with pitch or white lead the venerable rocks of the mountain ranges, on which over the millennia the rains have woven prodigious covering of lichens and fungi.

A second difficulty lies in the fact that the ethics of death is the most difficult of all, because death is the least intelligible fact that man stumbles upon. In the morality of hunting, the enigma of death is multiplied by the enigma of the animal.

Finally, a third possibility is contained in the question. Death is enigmatic enough when it comes of itself, through sickness, old age, and debilitation. But it is much more so when it does not come spontaneously but instead is produced by another being. Assassination is the most disconcerting event that exists in the universe, and the assassin is the man that we never understand. Hence his bloody action has always demanded dreadful expiations and he himself has been expelled from the community. There still sound in our ears, perpetuated in the first pages of Genesis, atrocious screams that frighten us, horrible growls of a corraled beast. What we hear is the voice of Cain, the first murderer, the patron of all assassins. He has been condemned, and the God of Adam demands the fulfillment of the tribal law which expels the parricide: "What hast thou done? The voice of thy brother's blood cries unto me from the ground" (Genesis 4:10). Cain foresees the harshness of his future, wandering and without group protection, and he screams to God, crying out: "I shall be a fugitive and a vagabond in the earth, and it shall come to pass that everything that findeth me shall slay me" (Genesis 4:14).

Has anyone noticed the very strange fact that, before and apart from any moral or even simply compassionate reaction, it seems to us that nothing stains as blood does? When two men who have had a fistfight in the street finally separate and we see their bloodstained faces we are always disconcerted. Rather than producing in us the sympathetic response which another's pain generally causes, the sight creates a disgust which is extremely intense and of a very special nature. Not only do those faces seem repugnantly stained, but the filth goes beyond physical limits and becomes, at the same time, moral. The blood has not only stained the faces but it has soiled them—that is to say, it has debased and in a way degraded them. Hunters who read this will remember this primary sensation, so often felt, when at the end of the hunt the dead game lies in a heap on the ground, with dried blood here and there staining plumage and pelt. The reaction, I repeat, is prior to and still deeper than any ethical question, since one notices the degradation that blood produces wherever it falls, on inanimate things as well. The earth that is stained with blood is as damned. A white rag stained with blood is not only repugnant, it seems violated, its humble textile material dishonored.[1] It is the frightening mystery of blood! What can it be? Life is the mysterious reality *par excellence,* not only in the sense that we do not know its secret but also because life is the only reality that has a true "inside"—an *intus* or intimacy. Blood, the liquid that carries and symbolizes life, is meant to flow occultly, secretly, through the interior of the body. When it is spilled and the essential "within" comes outside, a reaction of disgust and terror is produced in all Nature, as if the most radical absurdity had been committed: that which is purely internal made external.[2]

But this is precisely what death is. The cadaver is flesh which has lost its intimacy, flesh whose "interior" has escaped like a bird from a cage, a piece of pure matter in which there is no longer anyone hidden.

Yet after this first bitter impression, if the blood insists on presenting itself, if it flows abundantly, it ends by producing the opposite effect: it intoxicates, excites, maddens both man and beast. The Romans went to the circus as they did to the tavern, and the bullfight public does the same: the blood of the gladiators, the beasts, the bull operates like a stupefying drug. Similarly, war is always an orgy at the time. Blood has an unequaled orgiastic power.

Is the reader beginning to see why it is impossible to go deeply into the ethics of hunting in this essay? When we reach the problem of death we become entangled in more complicated questions and would have to prolong indefinitely an essay of which the exuberance is already too tropical. I have said that the fact of spontaneous death, natural death, is already rather unintelligible in itself. There is, besides, the fact of killing, which multiplies the unintelligibility. But this pyramid of difficulties has yet a third level—namely, *having* to kill. At times killing the enemy, the madman, the criminal is obligatory and unavoidable. And many animal species, man among them, have no other recourse than to kill in order to eat. The result is that we not only have to suffer the presence of death around us, and through imaginative anticipation our own inevitable death, but we also have to produce it and manipulate it. The situation, then, is that when death is said to be horrible, very little has been said about it, because that adjective, like adjectives in general, resolves nothing. Nothing has been said about the fact that the greatest and most moral homage we can pay to certain animals on certain occasions is to kill them with certain means and rituals.

So hunting is counterposed to all that morphology of death as something without equal, since it is the only normal case in which the killing of one creature constitutes the delight of another. This raises to the last paroxysm the difficulties of its ethics.

The English have initiated a form of hunting in which all these conflicts of conscience are cleverly eluded: it is a matter of having the hunt end, not with the capture or death of the animal, but rather with taking the game's picture. What a refinement! Don't you think so? What tenderness of soul these Anglo-Saxons have! One feels ashamed that one day, at siesta time thirty years ago, one killed that overly impertinent fly! Of course the British Empire was not forged with silks and bonbons, but by employing the greatest harshness Western man has ever seen in the face of the suffering of other men.

This reminds me that in the darkest moment of the Spanish civil war an Englishwoman, or a woman raised in England, offered money for ambulances to gather the wounded and to care for them. The offer was accepted, but when it came to carrying out the plan, it turned out that the wounded for whom the woman had intended the ambulances were not men wounded in the war but injured or sick dogs. And the good woman said, "Men who make them are to blame for terrible wars, but dogs are not to blame for the injuries they receive." But how and for what reason was she so sure that men are ultimately to blame for wars? Why does this woman, who manipulates the apothegm like one of Plutarch's philosophers, have enough perceptiveness to discover the blamelessness of the dog and yet be completely blind to the ultimately doggish in man, lost in an existence that he does not dominate and cudgeled from the one side and another by the most impenetrable Destiny? Instead of worrying so much about dogs, she should have tried a little harder to be less sure about things which perhaps one can never be sure about. Under its appearance of ultrasensitive tenderness, that brutal sureness with regard to what is, absolutely or for the present, indiscernible represents a peculiar form of barbarism, nourished at the breasts of stupidity and petulance. I hope the reader will pardon this spontaneous outburst, but nothing in the universe irritates me as much as seeing people feel too sure of things where such sureness is impossible, and when this woman crossed my mind the pure mastiff that I may be ran out to bark at her. Just a few days ago I read in *The Times* news of the skirmish that another woman started in South Africa by suing an insurance company because they refused to guarantee the safety, in wartime, of the goldfish in her pools.

To the real brutality in the treatment of animals which was habitual in some Latin countries some years ago, the Englishman responds with another exaggeration.[3] Photographic hunting is a mannerism and not a refinement; it is an ethical mandarinism no less deplorable than the intellectual pose of the other mandarins. England, like all nations that have enjoyed good fortune for too long, had fallen into intensive mandarinism. The copious admiration that I feel for the strong English people makes me prefer their classic firmness to these recent mannered tendernesses. And such a preference is not purely my whim. In the preoccupation with doing things as they should be done—which is morality—there is a line past which we begin to think that what is purely our whim or mania is necessary. We fall, therefore, into a new immorality, into the worst of all, which is a matter of not knowing those very conditions without which things cannot be. This is man's supreme and devastating pride, which tends not to accept limits on his desires and supposes that reality lacks any structure of its own which may be opposed to his will. This sin is the worst of all, so much so that the question of whether the content of that will is good or bad completely loses importance in the face of it. If you believe that you can do whatever you like—even, for example, the supreme good, then you are, irretrievably, a villain. The preoccupation with what should be is estimable only when the respect for what is has been exhausted.

A good example of this, because of the very insignificance of its substance, is this ridiculousness of photographic hunting. One can refuse to hunt, but if one hunts one has to accept certain ultimate requirements[4] without which the reality "hunting" evaporates. The overpowering of the game, the tactile drama of its actual capture, and usually even more the tragedy of its death nurture the hunter's interest through anticipation and give liveliness and authenticity to all the previous work: the harsh confrontation with the animal's fierceness, the struggle with its energetic defense, the point of orgiastic intoxication aroused by the sight of blood, and even the hint of criminal suspicion which claws the hunter's conscience. Without these ingredients the spirit of the hunt disappears. The animal's behavior is wholly inspired by the conviction that his life is at stake, and if it turns out that this is a complete fiction, that it is only a matter of taking his picture, the hunt becomes a farce and its specific tension evaporates. All of hunting becomes spectral when a photographic image, which is an apparition, is substituted for the prey. The use of a camera is comprehensible when it faces a pretty girl, a Gothic tower, a soccer goalie, or Einstein's hair; it is hopelessly inadequate when it faces the friendly wild boar rooting around in the thicket. The mannerism consists in treating the beast as a complete equal, and it seems to me more authentically refined and more genuine to accept the inevitable inequality which regulates and stylizes the perennial fact of hunting as sport.

One should not look for perfection in the arbitrary, because in that dimension there is no standard of measure; nothing has proportion nor limit, everything becomes infinite, monstrous, and the greatest exaggeration is at once exceeded by another. The Englishman probably believes he has reached the height of tenderness in substituting the camera for the rifle. Consider this, however. Because the waters of India are infectious, he took the filter there to purify them. With surprise he discovered that the Hindu, so remiss in adopting English customs, for once concurred with him and adopted the filter enthusiastically. This is a fine example of how two deeds that are externally identical can have opposite human motivation. While the Englishman used the filter to avoid being killed by microbes in the water, the Hindu, to whom death was unimportant, used it to avoid killing the microbes in the water with his own microbes or gastric juices. The incontinent tenderness of the Englishman is, without further ado, canceled out, but that does not guarantee any authentic superiority on the part of the Hindu. With no standard nothing has merit, and man is capable of using even sublimity to degrade himself.

In situations like the one just mentioned, the Englishman could learn that if he kills a bull his action has a meaning in no way similar to the meaning of killing a bull in a bullfight. Human activities cry out to be looked at from within, and if they almost always go so badly it is because, though they are so precise, we insist on looking at them in such an imprecise way and, when we can, with the naked eye only. If you try to stretch someone's comprehension a bit he will tell you that you are dealing in subtleties, instead of attending only to the question of whether or not the subtleties are true. It will seem a subtlety, that, after I have said I should try to determine here the role that death plays in hunting as sport.

I have indicated that a sport is the effort which is carried out for the pleasure that it gives in itself and not for the transitory result that the effort brings forth. It follows that when an activity becomes a sport, whatever that activity may be, the hierarchy of its values becomes inverted. In utilitarian hunting the true purpose of the hunter, what he seeks and values, is the death of the animal. Everything else that he does before that is merely a means for achieving that end, which is its formal purpose. But in hunting as a sport this order of means to end is reversed. To the sportsman the death of the game is not what interests him; that is not his purpose. What interests him is everything that he had to do to achieve that death—that is, the hunt.

Therefore what was before only a means to an end is now an end in itself. Death is essential because without it there is no authentic hunting: the killing of the animal is the natural end of the hunt and that goal of hunting itself, *not* of the hunter. The hunter seeks this death because it is no less than the sign of reality for the whole hunting process. To sum up, one does not hunt in order to kill; on the contrary, one kills in order to have hunted. If one were to present the sportsman with the death of the animal as a gift he would refuse it. What he is after is having to win it, to conquer the surly brute through his own effort and skill with all the extras that this carries with it: the immersion in the countryside, the healthfulness of the exercise, the distraction from his job, and so on and so forth.

In all of this, the moral problem of hunting has not been resolved, although it must be taken into account. We have not reached ethical perfection in hunting, not in the least. One never achieves perfection in anything, and perhaps it exists precisely so that one can never achieve it, as happens with cardinal points. Its purpose is to orient our conduct and to allow us to measure the progress accomplished. In this sense the advancement achieved in the ethics of hunting is undeniable. Therefore it is necessary to oppose photographic hunting, which is not progress but rather a digression and a prudery of hideous moral style.

Every authentic refinement must leave intact the authenticity of the hunt, its essential structure, which is a matter of a confrontation between two unequal species. The real care that man must exercise is not in pretending to make the beast equal to him, because that is a stupid utopia, a beatific farce, but rather in avoiding more and more the excess of his superiority. Hunting is the free play of an inferior species in the face of a superior species. That is where one must make some refinement. Man must give the animal a "handicap," in order to place him as close as possible to his own level, without pretending an illusory equivalence which, even if it were possible, would annihilate *ipso facto* the very reality of the hunt. Strictly speaking, the essence of sportive hunting is not raising the animal to the level of man, but something much more spiritual than that: a conscious and almost religious humbling of man which limits his superiority and lowers him toward the animal.

I have said "religious," and the word does not seem excessive to me. As I have already pointed out, a fascinating mystery of Nature is manifested in the universal fact of hunting: the inexorable hierarchy among living beings. Every animal is in a relationship of superiority or inferiority with regard to every other.[5] Strict equality is exceedingly improbable and anomalous. Life is a terrible conflict, a grandiose and atrocious confluence. Hunting submerges man deliberately in that formidable mystery and therefore contains something of religious rite and emotion in which homage is paid to what is divine, transcendent, in the laws of Nature.

Notes

1. Once more the etymology corroborates our intuition. The Spanish word *mancillar,* which means "to dishonor," comes from *macellare,* which means "to kill," and especially the activity of the butcher and the slaughterer. *Macellum* is the butchershop and slaughterhouse. Our moral *mancilla* (stain) carries within it nothing other than bloodiness. And the fact is that the Latin word represents an enormous cultural area, because it comes from a Greek word which in turn reproduces a Semitic word.
2. Nevertheless, it is necessary to register with complete honesty the sinuosities and apparent caprices of reality. There is one case in which blood does not produce that disgust: when it spurts from the nape of a bull that has been lanced well (*picado*) and spills down both sides of the animal. In the sun, the crimson of the brilliant liquid takes on a refulgence that turns it into a jewel. This exception, the only one that I know of, is as strange as the rule that it breaks.
3. It is inconceivable that no study from the ethical point of view has ever been made of the Society for the Prevention of Cruelty to Animals, analyzing its standards and actions. I bet one would find that English zoophilia has one of its roots in a certain secret English antipathy toward everything human that is not either English or Ancient Greek!
4. *Requirement* is the name that the philosopher Leibniz gave to the indispensable elements essential to every being.
5. This permits order in the zoological existence. The species form groups in which the hunters and the hunted are articulated. They need each other in order to regulate themselves in the whole. There are no solitary species. More important than the collectivity of individuals is the collectivity of species. Any external intervention, if it is not done carefully, disarranges the marvelous clock of their coexistence. For example; in the game reserves created in Umfolozi, Mkuze, and elsewhere (Zululand), a grave diminishing in number of almost all species for lack of grazing had been observed. This scarcity was due to the fact that the herds of zebras and gnus or jackasses, all great grazers, had grown excessively. But at the same time this abnormal increase in gnus and zebras was due to the fact that hunters had killed too many of the beasts that had previously consumed a suitable number of zebras and gnus.

CHAPTER

Animal Liberation

Peter Singer

I

We are familiar with Black Liberation, Gay Liberation, and a variety of other movements. With Women's Liberation some thought we had come to the end of the road. Discrimination on the basis of sex, it has been said, is the last form of discrimination that is universally accepted and practiced without pretense, even in those liberal circles which have long prided themselves on their freedom from racial discrimination. But one should always be wary of talking of the "the last remaining form of discrimination." If we have learned anything from the liberation movements, we should have learned how difficult it is to be aware of the ways in which we discriminate until they are forcefully pointed out to us. A liberation movement demands an expansion of our moral horizons, so that practices that were previously regarded as natural and inevitable are now seen as intolerable.

Animals, Men and Morals is a manifesto for an Animal Liberation movement. The contributors to the book may not all see the issue this way. They are a varied group. Philosophers, ranging from professors to graduate students, make up the largest contingent. There are five of them, including the three editors, and there is also an extract from the unjustly neglected German philosopher with an English name, Leonard Nelson, who died in 1927. There are essays by two novelist/critics, Brigid Brophy and Maureen Duffy, and another by Muriel the Lady Dowding, widow of Dowding of Battle of Britain fame and the founder of "Beauty Without Cruelty," a movement that campaigns against the use of animals for furs and cosmetics. The other pieces are by a psychologist, a botanist, a sociologist, and Ruth Harrison, who is probably best described as a professional campaigner for animal welfare.

Whether or not these people, as individuals, would all agree that they are launching a liberation movement for animals, the book as a whole amounts to no less. It is a demand for a complete change in our attitudes to nonhumans. It is a demand that we cease to regard the exploitation of other species as natural and inevitable, and that, instead, we see it as a continuing moral outrage. Patrick Corbett, Professor of Philosophy at Sussex University, captures the spirit of the book in his closing words:

> . . . We require now to extend the great principles of liberty, equality and fraternity over the lives of animals. Let animal slavery join human slavery in the graveyard of the past.

The reader is likely to be skeptical. "Animal Liberation" sounds more like a parody of liberation movements than a serious objective. The reader may think: We support the claims of blacks and women for equality because blacks and women really are equal to whites and males—equal in intelligence and in abilities, capacity for leadership, rationality, and so on. Humans and nonhumans obviously are not equal in these respects. Since justice demands only that we treat equals equally, unequal treatment of humans and nonhumans cannot be an injustice.

This is a tempting reply, but a dangerous one. It commits the non-racist and non-sexist to a dogmatic belief that blacks and women really are just as intelligent, able, etc., as whites and males—and no more. Quite possibly this happens to be the case. Certainly attempts to prove that racial or sexual differences in these respects have a genetic origin have not been conclusive. But do we really want to stake our demand for equality on the assumption that there are no genetic differences of this kind between the different races or sexes? Surely the appropriate response to those who claim to have found evidence for sure genetic differences is not to stick to the belief that there are no differences, whatever the evidence to the contrary; rather one should be clear that the claim to equality does not depend on IQ. Moral equality is distinct from factual equality. Otherwise it would be nonsense to talk of the equality of human beings, since humans, as individuals, obviously differ in intelligence and almost any ability one cares to name. If possessing greater intelligence does not entitle one human to exploit another, why should it entitle humans to exploit nonhumans?

Jeremy Bentham expressed the essential basis of equality in his famous formula: "Each to count for one and none for more than one." In other words, the interests of every being that has interests are to be taken into account and treated equally with the like interests of any other being. Other moral philosophers, before and after Bentham, have made the same point in different ways. Our concern for others must not depend on whether they possess certain characteristics, though just what that concern involves may, of course, vary according to such characteristics.

Bentham, incidentally, was well aware that the logic of the demand for racial equality did not stop at the equality of humans. He wrote:

> The day *may* come when the rest of the animal creation may acquire those rights which never could have been withholden from them but by the hand of tyranny. The French have already discovered that the blackness of the skin is no reason why a human being should be abandoned without redress to the caprice of a tormentor. It may one day come to be recognized that the number of the legs, the villosity of the skin, or the termination of the *os sacrum,* are reasons equally insufficient for abandoning a sensitive being to the same rate. What else is it that should trace the insuperable line? Is it the faculty of reason, or perhaps the faculty of discourse? But a full-grown horse or dog is beyond comparison a more rational, as well as a more conversable animal, than an infant of a day, or a week, or even a month, old. But suppose they were otherwise, what would it avail? The question is not, Can they *reason?* nor Can they *talk?* but, Can they *suffer?*[1]

Surely Bentham was right. If a being suffers, there can be no moral justification for refusing to take that suffering into consideration, and, indeed, to count it equally with the like suffering (if rough comparisons can be made) of any other being.

So the only question is: Do animals other than man suffer? Most people agree unhesitatingly that animals like cats and dogs can and do suffer, and this seems also to be assumed by those laws that prohibit wanton cruelty to such animals. Personally, I have no doubt at all about this and find it hard to take seriously the doubts that a few people apparently do have. The editors and contributors of *Animals, Men and Morals* seem to feel the same way, for although the question is raised more than once, doubts are quickly dismissed each time. Nevertheless, because this is such a fundamental point, it is worth asking what grounds we have for attributing suffering to other animals.

It is best to begin by asking what grounds any individual human has for supposing that other humans feel pain. Since pain is a state of consciousness, a "mental event," it can never be directly observed. No observations, whether behavioral signs such as writhing or screaming or physiological or neuro-logical recordings, are observations of pain itself. Pain is something one feels, and one can only infer that others are feeling it from various external indications. The fact that only philosophers are ever skeptical about whether other humans feel pain shows that we regard such inference as justifiable in the case of humans.

Is there any reason why the same inference should be unjustifiable for other animals? Nearly all the external signs which lead us to infer pain in other humans can be seen in other species, especially "higher" animals such as mammals and birds. Behavioral signs—writhing, yelping, or other forms of calling, attempts to avoid the source of pain, and many others—are present. We know, too, that these animals are biologically similar in the relevant respects, having nervous systems like ours which can be observed to function as ours do.

So the grounds for inferring that these animals can feel pain are nearly as good as the ground for inferring other humans do. Only nearly, for there is one behavioral sign that humans have but nonhumans, with the exception of one or two specially raised chimpanzees, do not have. This, of course, is a developed language. As the quotation from Bentham indicates, this has long been regarded as an important distinction between man and other animals. Other animals may communicate with each other, but not in the way we do. Following Chomsky, many people now mark this distinction by saying that only humans communicate in a form that is governed by rules of syntax. (For the purposes of this argument, linguists allow those chimpanzees who have learned a syntactic sign language to rank as honorary humans.) Neverthe-less, as Bentham pointed out, this distinction is not relevant to the question of how animals ought to be treated, unless it can be linked to the issue of whether animals suffer.

This link may be attempted in two ways. First, there is a hazy line of philosophical thought, stemming perhaps from some doctrines associated with Wittgenstein, which maintains that we cannot meaningfully attribute states of consciousness to beings without language. I have not seen this argument made explicit in print, though I have come across it in conversa-tion. This position seems to me very implausible, and I doubt that it would be held at all if it were not thought to be a consequence of a broader view of the significance of language. It may be that the use of a public, rule-governed language is a precondition of conceptual thought. It may even be, although personally I doubt it, that we cannot meaningfully speak of a creature having an intention unless that creature can use a language. But states like pain, surely, are more primitive than either of these, and seem to have nothing to do with language.

Indeed, as Jane Goodall points out in her study of chimpanzees, when it comes to the expression of feelings and emotions, humans tend to fall back on non-linguistic modes of communication which are often found among apes, such as a cheering pat on the back, an exuberant embrace, a clasp of hands, and so on.[2] Michael Peters makes a similar point in his contribution to *Animals, Men and Morals* when he notes that the basic signals we use to convey pain, fear, sexual arousal, and so on are not specific to our species. So there seems to be no reason at all to believe that a creature without language cannot suffer.

The second, and more easily appreciated way of linking language and the existence of pain is to say that the best evidence that we can have that another creature is in pain is when he tells us that he is. This is a distinct line of argument, for it is not being denied that a non-language-user conceivably could suffer, but only that we could know that he is suffering. Still, this line of argument seems to me to fail, and for reasons similar to those just given. "I am in pain" is not the best possible evidence that the speaker is in pain (he might be lying) and it is certainly not the only possible evidence. Behavioral signs and knowledge of the animal's biological similarity to ourselves together provide adequate evidence that animals do suffer. After all, we would not accept linguistic evidence if it contradicted the rest of the evidence. If a man was severely burned, and behaved as if he were in pain, writhing, groaning, being very careful not to let his burned skin touch anything, and so on, but later said he had not been in pain at all, we would be more likely to conclude that he was lying or suffering from amnesia than that he had not been in pain.

Even if there were stronger grounds for refusing to attribute pain to those who do not have a language, the consequences of this refusal might lead us to examine these grounds unusually critically. Human infants, as well as some adults, are unable to use language. Are we to deny that a year-old infant can suffer? If not, how can language be crucial? Of course, most parents can understand the responses of even very young infants better than they understand the responses of other animals, and sometimes infant responses can be understood in the light of later development.

This, however, is just a fact about the relative knowledge we have of our own species and other species, and most of this knowledge is simply derived from closer contact. Those who have studied the behavior of other animals soon learn to understand their responses at least as well as we understand those of an infant. (I am not just referring to Jane Goodall's and other well-known studies of apes. Consider, for example, the degree of understanding achieved by Tinbergen from watching herring gulls.)[3] Just as we can understand infant human behavior in the light of adult human behavior, so we can understand the behavior of other species in the light of our own behavior (and sometimes we can understand our own behavior better in the light of the behavior of other species).

The grounds we have for believing that other mammals and birds suffer are, then, closely analogous to the grounds we have for believing that other humans suffer. It remains to consider how far down the evolutionary scale this analogy holds. Obviously it becomes poorer when we get further away from man. To be more precise would require a detailed examination of all that we know about other forms of life. With fish, reptiles, and other vertebrates the analogy still seems strong, with molluscs like oysters it is much weaker. Insects are more difficult, and it may be that in our present state of knowledge we must be agnostic about whether they are capable of suffering.

If there is no moral justification for ignoring suffering when it occurs, and it does occur in other species, what are we to say of our attitudes toward these other species? Richard Ryder, one of the contributors to *Animals, Men and Morals,* uses the term "speciesism" to describe the belief that we are entitled to treat members of other species in a way in which it would be wrong to treat members of our own species. The term is not euphonious, but it neatly makes the analogy with racism. The nonracist would do well to bear the analogy in mind when he is inclined to defend human behavior toward nonhumans. "Shouldn't we worry about improving the lot of our own species before we concern ourselves with other species?" he may ask. If we substitute "race" for "species" we shall see that the question is better not asked. "Is a vegetarian diet nutritionally adequate?" resembles the slaveowner's claim that he and the whole economy of the South would be ruined without slave labor. There is even a parallel with skeptical doubts about whether animals suffer, for some defenders of slavery professed to doubt whether blacks really suffer in the way that whites do.

I do not want to give the impression, however, that the case for Animal Liberation is based on the analogy with racism and no more. On the contrary, *Animals, Men and Morals* describes the various ways in which humans exploit nonhumans, and several contributors consider the defenses that have been offered, including the defense of meat-eating mentioned in the last paragraph. Sometimes the rebuttals are scornfully dismissive, rather than carefully designed to convince the detached critic. This may be a fault, but it is a fault that is inevitable, given the kind of book this is. The issue is not one on which one can remain detached. As the editors state in their Introduction:

Once the full force of moral assessment has been made explicit there can be no rational excuse left for killing animals, be they killed for food, science, or sheer personal indulgence. We have not assembled this book to provide the reader with yet another manual on how to make brutalities less brutal. Compromise, in the traditional sense of the term, is simply unthinking weakness when one considers the actual reasons for our crude relationships with the other animals.

The point is that on this issue there are few critics who are genuinely detached. People who eat pieces of slaughtered nonhumans every day find it hard to believe that they are doing wrong; and they also find it hard to imagine what else they could eat. So for those who do not place nonhumans beyond the pale of morality, there comes a stage when further argument seems pointless, a stage at which one can only accuse one's opponent of hypocrisy and reach for the sort of sociological account of our practices and the way we defend them that is attempted by David Wood in his contribution to this book. On the other hand, to those unconvinced by the arguments, and unable to accept that they are merely rationalizing their dietary preferences and their fear of being thought peculiar, such sociological explanations can only seem insultingly arrogant.

II

The logic of speciesism is most apparent in the practice of experimenting on nonhumans in order to benefit humans. This is because the issue is rarely obscured by allegations that nonhumans are so different from humans that we cannot know anything about whether they suffer. The defender of vivisection cannot use this argument because he needs to stress the similarities between man and other animals in order to justify the usefulness to the former of experiments on the latter. The researcher who makes rats choose between starvation and electric shocks to see if they develop ulcers (they do) does so because he knows that the rat has a nervous system very similar to man's, and presumably feels an electric shock in a similar way.

Richard Ryder's restrained account of experiments on animals made me angrier with my fellow men than anything else in this book. Ryder, a clinical psychologist by profession, himself experimented on animals before he came to hold the view he puts forward in his essay. Experimenting on animals is now a large industry, both academic and commercial. In 1969, more than 5 million experiments were performed in Britain, the vast majority without anesthetic (though how many of these involved pain is not known). There are no accurate U.S. figures, since there is no federal law on the subject, and in many cases no state law either. Estimates vary from 20 million to 200 million. Ryder suggests that 80 million may be the best guess. We tend to think that this is all for vital medical research, but of course it is not. Huge numbers of animals are used in university departments from Forestry to Psychology, and even more are used for commercial purposes, to test whether cosmetics can cause skin damage, or shampoos eye damage, or to test food additives or laxatives or sleeping pills or anything else.

A standard test for foodstuffs is the "LD50." The object of this test is to find the dosage level at which 50 percent of the test animals will die. This means that nearly all of them will become very sick before finally succumbing or surviving. When the substance is a harmless one, it may be necessary to force huge doses down the animals, until in some cases sheer volume or concentration causes death.

Ryder gives a selection of experiments, taken from recent scientific journals. I will quote two, not for the sake of indulging in gory details, but in order to give an idea of what normal researchers think they may legitimately do to other species. The point is not that the individual researchers are cruel men, but that they are behaving in a way that is allowed by our speciesist attitudes. As Ryder points out, even if only 1 percent of the experiments involve severe pain, that is 50,000 experiments in Britain each year, or nearly 150 every day (and about fifteen times as many in the United States, if Ryder's guess is right). Here then are two experiments:

O.S. Ray and R.J. Barrett of Pittsburg gave electric shocks to the feet of 1,042 mice. They then caused convulsions by giving more intense shocks through cup-shaped electrodes applied to the animal's eyes or through pressure spring clips attached to their ears. Unfortunately some of the mice who "successfully completed Day One training were found sick or dead prior to testing on Day Two." (*Journal of Comparative and Physiological Psychology,* 1969, vol. 67, pp. 110-116)

At the National Institute for Medical Research, Mill Hill, London, W. Feldberg and S.L. Sherwood injected chemicals into the brains of cats—"with a number of widely different substances, recurrent patterns of reaction were obtained. Retching, vomiting, defaecation, increased salivation and greatly accelerated respiration leading to panting were common features."

The injection into the brain of a large dose of Tubocuraine caused the cat to jump "from the table to the floor and then straight into its cage, where it started calling more and more noisily whilst moving about restlessly and jerkily . . . finally the cat fell with legs and neck flexed, jerking in rapid clonic movements, the condition being that of a major (epileptic) convulsion . . . within a few seconds the cat got up, ran for a few yards at high speed and fell in another fit. The whole process was repeated several times within the next ten minutes, during which the cat lost faeces and foamed at the mouth."

This animal finally died thirty-five minutes after the brain injection. (*Journal of Physiology,* 1954, vol. 123, pp. 148-167)

There is nothing secret about these experiments. One has only to open any recent volume of a learned journal, such as the *Journal of Comparative and Physiological Psychology,* to find full descriptions of experiments of this sort, together with the results obtained—results that are frequently trivial and obvious. The experiments are often supported by public funds.

It is a significant indication of the level of acceptability of these practices that, although these experiments are taking place at this moment on university campuses throughout the country, there has, so far as I know, not been the slightest protest from the student movement. Students have been rightly concerned that their universities should not discriminate on grounds of race or sex, and that they should not serve the purposes of the military or big business. Speciesism continues undisturbed, and many students participate in it. There may be a few qualms at first, but since everyone regards it as normal, and it may even be a required part of a course, the student soon becomes hardened and, dismissing his earlier feelings as "mere sentiment," comes to regard animals as statistics rather than sentient beings with interests that warrant consideration.

Argument about vivisection has often missed the point because it has been put in absolutist terms: Would the abolitionist be prepared to let thousands die if they could be saved by experimenting on a single animal? The way to reply to this purely hypothetical question is to pose another: Would the experimenter be prepared to experiment on a human orphan under six months old, if it were the only way to save many lives? (I say "orphan" to avoid the complication of parental feelings, although in doing so I am being overfair to the experimenter, since the nonhuman subjects of experiments are not orphans.) A negative answer to this question indicates that the experimenter's readiness to use nonhumans is simple discrimination, for adult apes, cats, mice, and other mammals are more conscious of what is happening to them, more self-directing, and, so far as we can tell, just as sensitive to pain as a human infant. There is no characteristic that human infants possess that adult mammals do not have to the same or a higher degree.

(It might be possible to hold that what makes it wrong to experiment on a human infant is that the infant will in time develop into more than the nonhuman, but one would then, to be consistent, have to oppose abortion, and perhaps contraception, too, for the fetus and the egg and sperm have the same potential as the infant. Moreover, one would still have no reason for experimenting on a nonhuman rather than a human with brain damage severe enough to make it impossible for him to rise above infant level.)

The experimenter, then, shows a bias for his own species whenever he carries out an experiment on a nonhuman for a purpose that he would not think justified him in using a human being at an equal or lower level of sentience, awareness, ability to be self-directing, etc. No one familiar with the kind of results yielded by these experiments can have the slightest doubt that if this bias were eliminated the number of experiments performed would be zero or very close to it.

III

If it is vivisection that shows the logic of speciesism most clearly, it is the use of other species for food that is at the heart of our attitudes toward them. Most of *Animals, Men and Morals* is an attack on meat-eating—an attack which is based solely on concern for nonhumans, without reference to arguments derived from considerations of ecology, macrobiotics, health, or religion.

The idea that nonhumans are utilities, means to our ends, pervades our thought. Even conservationists who are concerned about the slaughter of wild fowl but not about the vastly greater slaughter of chickens for our tables are thinking in this way—they are worried about what we would lose if there were less wildlife. Stanley Godlovitch, pursuing the Marxist idea that our thinking is formed by the activities we undertake in satisfying our needs, suggests that man's first classification of his environment was into Edibles and Inedibles. Most animals came into the first category, and there they have remained.

Man may always have killed other species for food, but he has never exploited them so ruthlessly as he does today. Farming has succumbed to business methods, the objective being to get the highest possible ratio of output (meat, eggs, milk) to input (fodder, labor costs, etc.). Ruth Harrison's essay "On Factory Farming" gives an account of some aspects of modern methods, and of the unsuccessful British campaign for effective controls, a campaign which was sparked off by her *Animal Machines* (Stuart: London, 1964).

Her article is in no way a substitute for her earlier book. This is a pity since, as she says, "Farm produce is still associated with mental pictures of animals browsing in the fields, . . . of hens having a last forage before going to roost. . . ." Yet neither in her article nor elsewhere in *Animals, Men and Morals* is this false image replaced by a clear idea of the nature and extent of factory farming. We learn of this only indirectly, when we hear of the code of reform proposed by an advisory committee set up by the British government.

Among the proposals, which the government refused to implement on the grounds that they were too idealistic, were: *"Any animal should at least have room to turn around freely."*

Factory farm animals need liberation in the most literal sense. Veal calves are kept in stalls five feet by two feet. They are usually slaughtered when about four months old, and have been too big to turn in their stalls for at least a month. Intensive beef herds, kept in stalls only proportionately larger for much longer periods, account for a growing percentage of beef production. Sows are often similarly confined when pregnant, which, because of artificial methods of increasing fertility, can be most of the time. Animals confined in this way do not waste food by exercising, nor do they develop unpalatable muscle.

"A dry bedded area should be provided for all stock." Intensively kept animals usually have to stand and sleep on slatted floors without straw, because this makes cleaning easier.

"Palatable roughage must be readily available to all calves after one week of age." In order to produce the pale veal housewives are said to prefer, calves are fed on an all-liquid diet until slaughter, even though they are long past the age at which they would normally eat grass. They develop a craving for roughage, evidenced by attempts to gnaw wood from their stalls. (For the same reason, their diet is deficient in iron.)

"Battery cages for poultry should be large enough for a bird to be able to stretch one wing at a time." Under current British practice, a cage for four or five laying hens has a floor area of twenty inches by eighteen inches, scarcely larger than a double page of the *New York Review of Books*. In this space, on a sloping wire floor (sloping so the eggs roll down, wire so the dung drops through) the birds live for a year or eighteen months while artificial lighting and temperature conditions combine with drugs in their food to squeeze the maximum number of eggs out of them. Table birds are also sometimes kept in cages. More often they are reared in sheds, no less crowded. Under these conditions all the birds' natural activities are frustrated, and they develop "vices" such as pecking each other to death. To prevent this, beaks are often cut off, and the sheds kept dark.

How many of those who support factory farming by buying its produce know anything about the way it is produced? How many have heard something about it, but are reluctant to check up for fear that it will make them uncomfortable? To non-speciesists, the typical consumer's mixture of ignorance, reluctance to find out the truth, and vague belief that nothing really bad could be allowed seems analogous to the attitudes of "decent Germans" to the death camps.

There are, of course, some defenders of factory farming. Their arguments are considered, though again rather sketchily, by John Harris. Among the most common: "Since they have never known anything else, they don't suffer." This argument will not be put by anyone who knows anything about animal behavior, since he will know that not all behavior has to be learned. Chickens attempt to stretch wings, walk around, scratch, and even dustbathe or build a nest, even though they have never lived under conditions that allowed these activities. Calves can suffer from maternal deprivation no matter at what age they were taken from their mothers. "We need these intensive methods to provide protein for a growing population." As ecologists and famine relief organizations know, we can produce far more protein per acre if we grow the right vegetable crop, soy beans for instance, than if we use the land to grow crops to be converted into protein by animals who use nearly 90 percent of the protein themselves, even when unable to exercise.

There will be many readers of this book who will agree that factory farming involves an unjustifiable degree of exploitation of sentient creatures, and yet will want to say that there is nothing wrong with rearing animals for food, provided it is done "humanely." These people are saying, in effect, that although we should not cause animals to suffer, there is nothing wrong with killing them.

There are two possible replies to this view. One is to attempt to show that this combination of attitudes is absurd. Roslind Godlovitch takes this course in her essay, which is an examination of some common attitudes to animals. She argues that from the combination of "animal suffering is to be avoided" and "there is nothing wrong with killing animals" it follows that all animal life ought to be exterminated (since all sentient creatures will suffer to some degree at some point in their lives). Euthanasia is a contentious issue only because we place some value on living. If we did not, the least amount of suffering would justify it. Accordingly, if we deny that we have a duty to exterminate all animal life, we must concede that we are placing some value on animal life.

This argument seems to me valid, although one could still reply that the value of animal life is to be derived from the pleasures that life can have for them, so that, provided their lives have a balance of pleasure over pain, we are justified in rearing them. But this would imply that we ought to produce animals and let them live as pleasantly as possible, without suffering.

At this point, one can make the second of the two possible replies to the view that rearing and killing animals for food is all right so long as it is done humanely. This second reply is that so long as we think that a nonhuman may be killed simply so that a human can satisfy his taste for meat, we are still thinking of nonhumans as means rather than as ends in themselves. The factory farm is nothing more than the application of technology to this concept. Even traditional methods involve castration, the separation of mothers and their young, the breaking up of herds, branding or ear-punching, and of course transportation to the abattoirs and the final moments of terror when the animal smells blood and senses danger. If we were to try rearing animals so that they lived and died without suffering, we should find that to do so on anything like the scale of today's meat industry would be a sheer impossibility. Meat would become the prerogative of the rich.

I have been able to discuss only some of the contributions to this book, saying nothing about, for instance, the essays on killing for furs and for sport. Nor have I considered all the detailed questions that need to be asked once we start thinking about other species in the radically different way presented by this book. What, for instance, are we to do about genuine conflicts of interest like rats biting slum children? I am not sure of the answer, but the essential point is just that we *do* see this as a conflict of interests, that we recognize that rats have interests too. Then we may begin to think about other ways of resolving the conflict—perhaps by leaving out rat baits that sterilize the rats instead of killing them.

I have not discussed such problems because they are side issues compared with the exploitation of other species for food and for experimental purposes. On these central matters, I hope that I have said enough to show that this book, despite its flaws, is a challenge to every human to recognize his attitudes to nonhumans as a form of prejudice no less objectionable than racism or sexism. It is a challenge that demands not just a change of attitudes, but a change in our way of life, for it requires us to become vegetarians.

Can a purely moral demand of this kind succeed? The odds are certainly against it. The book holds out no inducements. It does not tell us that we will become healthier, or enjoy life more, if we cease exploiting animals. Animal Liberation will require greater altruism on the part of mankind than any other liberation movement, since animals are incapable of demanding it for themselves, or of protesting against their exploitation by votes, demonstrations, or bombs. Is man capable of such genuine altruism? Who knows? If this book does have a significant effect, however, it will be a vindication of all those who have believed that man has within himself the potential for more than cruelty and selfishness.

Postscript

Since this review is now appearing alongside philosophical discussion of rights and equality, it is worth noting that we can find indications of speciesism even amongst philosophers.

Richard Wasserstrom's "Rights, Human Rights, and Racial Discrimination" serves as an example. Wasserstrom defines "human rights" as those that humans have, and nonhumans do not have. He then argues that there are human rights, in this sense, to well-being and freedom. In defending the idea of a human right to well-being, Wasserstrom says that although we have no means of assessing the comparative worth of different people's enjoyment of, for instance, relief from acute physical pain, we know that denial of the opportunity to experience a good such as this makes it impossible to live a full or satisfying life. Wasserstrom then goes on to say: "In a real sense, the enjoyment of these goods differentiates human from nonhuman entities" (p. 119). But this statement is incredible—for when we look back to find what the expression "these goods" is supposed to refer to, we find that the *only* example we have been given is relief from acute physical pain—and this, surely, is something that nonhumans may appreciate as well as humans.

Later, too, Wasserstrom points out that the grounds for discrimination between blacks and whites that racists sometimes offer are not relevant to the question of capacity for bearing acute pain, and therefore should be disregarded. So again Wasserstrom is taking capacity for perceiving acute pain as crucial. I would want to say that if Wasserstrom's argument is valid against discrimination on the basis of race—and I think it is—then an exactly parallel argument applies against the grounds usually offered for discrimination on the basis of species, since these grounds are also not relevant to the question of ability to bear acute pain. When Ray and Barrett, in the experiment I described in the review, gave electric shocks to over a thousand mice, they must have assumed that the mice *do* feel acute physical pain, since the aim of the experiment was to find out where the mice were most sensitive; and nothing else, surely, is relevant to the question of whether it is legitimate to use mice for this purpose.

I should make it quite clear, of course, that I do not believe Richard Wasserstrom is deliberately endorsing a speciesist position, or in any way condoning the infliction of acute physical pain on nonhumans. I draw attention to the point only in order to show how easy it is, even for a philosopher, to accept unthinkingly a prevailing ideology that places other animals outside the sphere of equal consideration. I would guess that most of Wasserstrom's readers, with similar predispositions, will not have noticed on a first reading that the only basis he offers for "human rights" applies to nonhumans too.

Notes

1. *The Principles of Morals and Legislation,* ch. XVII, sec. I, footnote to paragraph 4. (Italics in original.)
2. Jane van Lawick-Goodall, *In the Shadow of Man* (Houghton Mifflin, 1971), p. 225.
3. N. Tinbergen, *The Herring Gull's World* (Basic Books, 1961).

CHAPTER

Why Hunting and Trapping
Are Wrong

Tom Regan

Since animals can pose innocent threats and because we are sometimes
justified in overriding their rights when they do, one cannot assume that all
hunting or trapping must be wrong. If rabid foxes have bitten some children
and are known to be in the neighboring woods, and if the circumstances of
their lives assure future attacks if nothing is done, then the rights view
sanctions nullifying the threat posed by these animals. When we turn from
cases where we protect ourselves against the innocent threats wild animals
pose, to the activities of hunting and trapping, whether for commercial profit
or "sport," the rights view takes a dim view indeed. Standard justifications
of the "sport" of hunting—that those who engage in it get exercise, take
pleasure in communion with nature, enjoy the camaraderie of their friends,
or take satisfaction in a shot well aimed—are lame, given the rights view. All
these pleasures are obtainable by engaging in activities that do not result in
killing any animal (walking through the woods with friends and a camera
substitutes nicely), and the aggregate of the pleasures hunters derive from
hunting could only override the rights of these animals if we viewed them
as mere receptacles, which, on the rights view, they are not.

Reprinted, by permission, from Tom Regan, 1983, "Why hunting and trapping are
wrong," *The Case for Animal Rights* (Berkeley, CA: University of California Press): 353-
359.

The appeal to tradition—an appeal one finds, for example, in support of fox hunting in Great Britain—has no more force in the case of hunting than it does in the case of any other customary abuse of animals—or humans. All that appeals to tradition signal in this case, and all they signify in related contexts, is that it is traditional to view animals as mere receptacles or as renewable resources. These appeals to tradition, in other words, are themselves symptomatic of an impoverished view of the value animals have in their own right and thus can play no legitimate role in defending a practice that harms them. Such appeals are as deficient in Great Britain, when made in behalf of the "sport" of fox hunting, as they are when made in Japan or Russia in defense of commercial whaling, or in Canada in defense of the annual slaughter of seals. To allow these practices to continue, if certain quotas are not exceeded, is wrong, given the rights view, for reasons that will become clearer as we proceed.

Of course, those who hunt and trap sometimes rest their case on other considerations. It is not *their* pleasure that justifies what they do; rather, it is the humane service they perform for *the animals* that does. The situation, we are enjoined to believe, is this: If a certain number of animals are not hunted or trapped, there will be too many animals belonging to a given species for a given habitat to support. That being so, some of these animals will die of starvation because of their inability to compete successfully with the other animals in the habitat. To cull or harvest a certain number of these animals thus has the humane purpose and achieves the humane goal of sparing these animals the ordeal of death by starvation. How can the rights view, or any other view that is sensitive to the welfare of animals, find fault with that?

The rights view finds fault with this defense of hunting and trapping on several counts. First, the defense assumes that the death endured by hunted and trapped animals is always better (i.e., always involves less suffering) than the death these animals would endure as a result of starvation. This is far from credible. Not all hunters are expert shots, and not all trappers tend their traps responsibly or use traps that exhibit their "humane" concern for animals, the infamous leg-hold trap being perhaps the most notorious example to the contrary. Is it obvious that animals who experience a slow, agonizing death as a result of a hunter's poor shot or a poorly tended trap have a "better death" than those who die from starvation? One looks for an argument here and finds none. Unless or until one does, the defense of hunting and trapping on the grounds that they kill "more humanely" is specious.

Second, appeals to "humane concern" are dramatically at odds with the philosophy of current hunting and trapping practices, as well as with wildlife management generally. This philosophy, or the creed of maximum sustainable yield, applies to hunting and trapping in the following way. Those who hunt and trap are legally permitted, within specified seasons, to "harvest" or "crop" a certain number of wildlife of various species, the quota for that season, both collectively and for each individual hunter, to be fixed by determining whether, together with the best estimates of natural mortality, those who hunt and trap will be able to "harvest" the same number next season, and the next, and so on. In this way the maximum sustainable yield is established. If this philosophy is applied successfully, hunters and trappers will be legally licensed to do the same thing in future seasons as others were licensed to do in the past—namely, kill up to a certain number (a certain quota) of animals. If, that is, restraint is exercised in each season, the *total* number of animals that can be harvested over time will be larger, or, to put the point in its simplest, starkest terms, if fewer animals are killed now, future generations of hunters will be able to kill a larger (aggregate) number of animals in the future, which will be better. This implication of the creed of maximum sustainable yield unmasks the rhetoric about "humane service" to animals. It must be a perverse distortion of the ideal of humane service to accept or engage in practices the explicit goal of which is to insure that there will be a larger, rather than a smaller, number of animals to kill! With "humane friends" like that, wild animals certainly do not need any enemies.

Essentially the same point can be made regarding the aggregate amount of suffering animals will endure if the creed of maximum sustainable yield is successful. If successful, the total number of animals who will die an agonizing death as a result of the poor shooting of hunters, plus those who die in similar agony as a result of poorly tended "humane" traps, plus those who die by natural causes will be larger than if other options were adopted. It is a moral smokescreen, therefore, to defend sport hunting and trapping by appeal to their humane service. The actions allowed by the philosophy of maximum sustainable yield speak louder than the lofty words uttered in its defense. The success of this philosophy would guarantee that more, not fewer, animals will be killed, and that more, not fewer, animals will die horrible deaths, either at the hands of humans or in the course of nature.

But it is not only the inconsistency between what it proclaims and what it implies that marks the undoing of the creed of maximum sustainable yield. That approach to decision making regarding wildlife management policies profoundly fails to recognize or respect the rights of wild animals. No approach to wildlife can be morally acceptable if it assumes that policy decisions should be made on the basis of aggregating harms and benefits. In particular, these decisions should not be made by appeal to the minimize harm principle. That principle sets before us what seems to be a laudatory goal—namely, to minimize the total amount of harm in general and suffering in particular. But that principle lacks the moral wherewithal to place any limits on how this laudatory goal is to be achieved; it lacks the means to assess the means used to achieve this end. If the rights of individuals are violated, that simply does not compute morally, given the minimize harm principle, if violating these rights is instrumental in achieving the goal of minimizing total harm. The rights view categorically denies the propriety of this approach to decision making. Policies that lessen the total amount of harm at the cost of violating the rights of individuals, whether these individuals are moral agents or patients, and, if the latter, human or animal, are wrong. Even if it were true, which it is not, that the philosophy of maximum sustainable yield would lead to a reduction in the total amount of death and suffering for undomesticated animals, it still would not follow that we should accept that philosophy. As it systematically ignores the rights of wild animals, so does it systematically violate them.

The rights view categorically condemns sport hunting and trapping. Though those who participate in it need not be cruel or evil people, what they do is wrong. And what they do is wrong because they are parties to a practice that treats animals as if they were a naturally recurring renewable resource, the value of which is to be measured by, and managed by reference to, human recreational, gustatory, aesthetic, social, and other interests. Animals do renew themselves. Normally, they do not require human assistance to reproduce, any more than do trees, for example; but wild animals are not natural resources *here for us*. They have value apart from human interests, and their value is not reducible to their utility relative to our interests. To make a sport of hunting or trapping them is to do what is wrong because it is to fail to treat them with the respect they are due as a matter of strict justice.

Shorn of their appeal to their "humane concern" for wildlife, defenders of hunting and trapping are likely to protest that what they do is no different in kind from what other animals do in the state of nature. Animals routinely kill members of other (though only infrequently members of their own) species, and the death they suffer at the hands of other animals is gruesome enough to make even the most hardened heart wince. When it comes to interspecies relations, nature is red in tooth and claw. If the rights view professes to condemn sport hunting and trapping, it might be claimed, then it should do the same when it comes to the fatal interaction between animals themselves.

The rights view rejects this argument. Animals are not moral agents and so can have none of the same duties moral agents have, including the duty to respect the rights of other animals. The wolves who eat the caribou do no moral wrong, though the harm they cause is real enough. So it is that, according to the rights view, the overarching goal of wildlife management should not be to insure maximum sustainable yield; it should be to protect wild animals from those who would violate their rights—namely, sport hunters and trappers, commercial developers who destroy or despoil their natural habitat in the name of economic interest, and the like. *It is, in short, human wrongs that need managing, not the "crop" of animals.* Put affirmatively, the goal of wildlife management should be to defend wild animals in the possession of their rights, providing them with the opportunity to live their own life, by their own lights, as best they can, spared that human predation that goes by the name of "sport." We owe this to wild animals, not out of kindness, not because we are against cruelty, but out of respect for their rights. If, in reply, we are told that respecting the rights of animals in the wild in the way the rights view requires does not guarantee that we will minimize the total amount of suffering wild animals will suffer over time, our reply should be that this cannot be the overarching goal of wildlife management, once we take the rights of animals seriously. The total amount of suffering animals cause one another in the wild is not the concern of morally enlightened wildlife management. Being neither the accountants nor managers of felicity in nature, wildlife managers should be principally concerned with *letting animals be,* keeping human predators out of their affairs, allowing these "other nations" to carve out their own destiny.

When we move from sport to the commercial exploitation of wildlife, the moral scene is the same, only worse because the number of animals involved is greater. The rights view condemns the business of killing wild animals. Even if it is true that those whose present quality of life is tied to commerce in wild animals would be made worse-off if their business failed, that is no reason why we should continue to allow it. Like anyone else who enters the world of business, those whose business it is to kill wild animals must understand that they waive their right not to be made worse-off if their business fails. We have no duty to buy their products, and they have no right to require that we keep either their business or their present quality of life afloat. To appeal to the risk of diminished welfare in the case of their dependents is as lame in the present case as it was in the case of animal agriculture, as a defense in support of those whose business it is to kill wild animals. Moreover, while those in this business, like the rest of us, have the right to do what they can to avoid being made worse-off, they, like the rest of us, exceed this right when what they do violates the rights of others. And the commercial exploitation of wildlife does this—with a vengeance. Animals in the wild are treated as renewable resources, as if they had value only relative to the economic interests of those who feed off their dead carcasses. The rights view categorically condemns the commercial harvesting of wild animals, not because those embarked on this business are, or must be, cruel or evil people, but because what they do is wrong. Justice will be done when, and only when, we refuse to allow these commercial ventures to continue.

One can imagine someone accepting the letter but not the spirit of the foregoing. For there are, after all, many nonhumans who are killed, either for sport or commerce, who are not animals in the limited sense in which this word has been used throughout this and earlier chapters—who are not, that is, normal mammalian animals, aged one year or more. A voice might be heard in support of duck hunting, for example, or in defense of the commercial exploitation of baby seals. Because similar protests might be raised in different contexts (for example, one might claim that what one does to nonmammals in science or to poultry in agriculture should not be covered by the same principles that apply to what is done to mammals), a review of this defense of hunting and trapping will be deferred until later.

Here it will suffice to raise a simple question. Let us assume that newly born *wild mammalian animals* (e.g., baby seals) do not yet meet the subject-of-a-life criterion; still, they clearly have the potential to do so. Why, then, should the moral standards that apply to how they may be treated differ in any way from those that apply to how human infants should be? The rights view denies that there is a nonarbitrary difference one could cite to justify treating the two differently. Unless one would be willing to approve of harming human infants in pursuit of sport or profit, one cannot approve of the similar treatment of infant mammalian animals.

No even partial assessment of hunting and trapping could be adequate if it failed to mention the matter of predator control. Sheep farmers in the southwestern United States, for example, are troubled by predatory animals, most notably coyotes, who attack grazing sheep, sometimes killing more than they need to subsist. The economic loss suffered by these farmers occasions their public outcry, and they have taken steps, with the assistance of federal funds and personnel, to control these predators.

Those who accept the rights view must work to bring an end to such predator control programs. The official justification of these programs assumes that the predators cause losses to persons engaged in a justified enterprise—namely, the animal industry. Since the rights view denies that this industry's treatment of animals is morally justified, the harm done to predatory animals in the name of minimizing the financial losses of those engaged in this industry is morally to be condemned. In the struggle between those involved in the animal industry and those predatory animals who inhabit the lands used in the name of this industry, it is the industry, not the predators, that ought to go. And if in response those in this industry appeal to their legal rights to the land and their legal ownership of the animals in their business, those who accept the rights view should reply, first, that the appeal to legal rights by itself never settles any moral question and, second, that the present legal status of farm animals, as owned property, is itself one of the traditions the rights view seeks to change.

24

CHAPTER

Rodeo and Recollection— Applied Ethics and Western Philosophy

Bernard E. Rollin

I

Like many other sports, rodeo can be understood on a variety of different levels. Although professional rodeos (those sanctioned by the Professional Rodeo Cowboy Association) recognize only a limited set of events as part of the sport—bull riding, steerwrestling, saddle bronc riding, bareback bronc riding, calf roping, team roping, and barrel racing—numerous other events are often included. These events are too diverse to list exhaustively but may include goat roping and barrel racing (women's events); wild horse races; wild cow races; chuck wagon races; cowboy bull fighting (in which the animal is not hurt); calf riding for small children; steer riding (less dangerous than bull riding); steer tripping (illegal in most states); rawhide racing; pick-up or rescue races; milk races (where nursing foals are separated from mares, and race back to mama); cow, buffalo, or horse turd throws; greased pig contests; cutting horse exhibitions; competitions involving dressing a wild cow in a negligee. Charro, or Mexican rodeos, which

Reprinted, by permission, from B.E. Rollin, 1996, "Rodeo and recollection-Applied ethics and western philosophy," *Journal of the Philosophy of Sport, XXIII:* 1-9.

have recently garnered much publicity, featured horse tripping, an event now banned legislatively in most states.

The symbolic dimensions of rodeo are quite varied and many have been well-discussed by Elizabeth Lawrence, a veterinarian and anthropologist, in her *Rodeo: An Anthropologist Looks at the Wild and the Tame* (1). In my own experience, rodeos express a broad range of western values relevant to our discussion:

1. Management of Animals: Historically, rodeo evolved from ranch practices that were commonly employed as a normal part of raising cattle under range conditions. Obviously, calves and steers often needed to be roped, horses broken, and steers sometimes were wrestled to the ground or tripped by solitary cowboys in order to be doctored. In justification of rodeo against attacks from people outside of the culture, participants and defenders often invoke the relevance of these practices to the cattle business. I shall discuss this point more fully later.

2. Survival and Success in a Harsh Environment: Western cattle ranching is a hard life, lived in an unforgiving, non "user friendly" environment. Ranchers may control 250,000 or more acres with little help. The nearest neighbors may be 80 miles away. In the New Mexico desert, each cow-calf unit may require 1,000 acres on which to forage; in Colorado or Wyoming this average can drop to between 20 and 50. Under the best of conditions, the land is harsh, subject to climatic variational extremes of over 100 degrees, seriously deficient in water, and intolerant of human errors. Not far from where I live in Northern Colorado, travelers have been known to leave their cars during wind-whipped ground blizzards and freeze to death, unable to find their cars from 20 feet away. In a symbolic sense, rodeo historically trumpeted (and continues to proclaim) ranchers' success despite nature's stacking the deck considerably against them.

3. Demonstration and Extolling of Skills and Traits That Made Survival Possible: Such skills embody primordial masculine virtues—physical strength, courage, quickness, independence (few events involve teams), and self-sufficiency. With the exception of specific women's events, such as barrel racing, rodeo participation is overwhelmingly male.

4. The Uniqueness of Western American Culture and the Pride Taken Therein by Western Americans: It is no secret that the United States has traditionally been politically, socially, and economically dominated by the urban East. In fact, one of the points I make to rancher groups about the need for them to take animal welfare/animal rights social concerns seriously is that "ten square blocks of New York City can outvote all of Wyoming." Westerners—and not just ranchers—feel an element of being neglected, misunderstood, and caricatured stepchildren. A good deal of these feelings are justified (e.g., vide Saul Steinberg's classic cartoon of the New Yorker's conceptual map of the United States, where the entire West, with the exception of California, is represented by a cactus).

Having been so caricatured is an old story, but until recently, the West was at least distorted from a distance. With the recent massive immigration of Easterners, Californians, and Yuppies into ranch states such as Colorado,

Montana, Wyoming, Nevada, New Mexico, and Utah, there is a fear among Westerners of losing their culture—of being "Californicated," as they say. This is compounded by environmentalist attacks on ranching; attempts to raise public land grazing fees or even to remove ranching from public lands; attacks on beef by physicians, feminists, and the Beyond Beef Campaign; attempts at gun control in a culture where gun ownership and handling is traditionally second nature; gobbling up of ranch land by developers; and revisionist accounts of Western American history. Outside attacks on rodeo, often based on urban ignorance, as when cowboys are accused of using leather vises on horses' testicles to make them buck, represent an example directly relevant to the topic at hand.

The result is something of a siege mentality, recently vividly symbolized by the defiant rancher in Nevada who crashed a forest service barrier. And the more they feel besieged, the more Westerners flaunt their uniqueness. Rodeo is probably the strongest symbol of this uniqueness, to no small extent because it is so *prima facie* shocking to the current non-Western, Eastern-urban sensibilities that tend to view nature as good, not adversarial; the pet as the paradigm for all animals; violent sports as abhorrent; and the cowboy as a highly ambivalent figure at best and as an ignorant, know-nothing, brutal redneck shit-kicker at worst.

It is worth pausing here to elaborate on the last point, as it is directly relevant to social ethical concerns about rodeo. There is no cultural icon that is as iridescent as that of the cowboy. On the one hand the cowboy is John Wayne, Gary Cooper, Jimmy Stewart—a gentleman, a protector of widows and orphans, slow to anger, resistant to authority, a loner, and an irresistible force once aroused. On the other hand the cowboy is equally the reckless gunfighter, the outlaw who shoots up a town and makes tenderfeet dance, the lyncher of hippies and the shooter of eagles. (During the Vietnam war, I was frequently told by Europeans that the war reflected Americans' "cowboy mentality.") With the advent of the '80s and '90s, it is the latter take on the cowboy that has tended to predominate, and, while the urban public might thrill at bull-riding and bronc-riding, it is the roping of "cute little calves" that leaves the most indelible and negative imprint and feeds the negative image of the cowboy.

It is not therefore surprising that rodeo is a very plausible target for animal advocates. In the 1970s, a group or over 200 animal welfare/animal rights organizations signed a well-publicized document affirming that rodeo was absolutely unacceptable morally because of the pain and fear engendered in animals. Further, the groups claimed that rodeo could not be fixed or improved, it must be abolished. I was puzzled by this document, for it appeared to me that rodeo was amenable to very plausible modifications that would significantly improve the treatment of rodeo animals. To allay my curiosity, I phoned the vice president of one of the signatory groups, a very powerful organization, and queried him as to the claim that rodeo could not be improved. "Oh that," he said. "That's just fund-raising hype. Of course rodeo can be fixed. But why would we care about fixing it? Rodeo is an insignificant sport, practiced by an insignificant number of people in a few politically insignificant places. If we take a tough line on rodeo, we bring in a lot of contributions, and don't make any powerful enemies!"

II

This, then, is a sketch of the situation I walked into in the 1970s when I first confronted the ethical issues in rodeo as a spin-off from my work in veterinary ethics. My involvement with rodeo issues deepened considerably as I became increasingly occupied with ethical issues in animal agriculture, and particularly with Western ranching. This involvement in turn intensified as I was asked to lecture on the ethics of rodeo to rodeo cowboys, fair and rodeo managers, and others in the rodeo community. In what follows, I hope to show that the issues are far more complex and morally ambiguous than most people realize, and provide some indication of how what is today called "applied ethics" can play a constructive role in social ethics. I speak from a considerable base of experience; between 1980 and the present (1996), I have lectured to somewhere between 5 and 10,000 western ranchers and rodeo people. I have lectured at the Worland Wyoming Bull Test Seminar, the Colorado Cattlemen's Annual Meeting, the Stockmen's Seminar in Kiowa, Colorado, the Houston Livestock show, the Northern Rodeo Association, and dozens of other major and minor forums in Colorado, Wyoming, Montana, New Mexico, Nebraska, Nevada, British Columbia, Alberta, Saskatchewan, Australia, and New Zealand. I have worked closely with the Colorado Cattlemen's Association on successfully eliminating mandated USDA face-branding of Mexican cattle—the first time an agricultural group has taken a pure animal welfare stand against practices allegedly implemented for their benefit. I have taught a course in ethics and animal welfare to ranch kids at Colorado State University since 1980, and lectured to animal science departments all over the West. My work has been written up positively in *Beef Today, Colorado Farmer and Rancher,* and the *Western Livestock Journal.* And, most remarkable to outsiders, I have been able to garner acquiescence to the notion that animals have rights from over 90% of my rancher and rodeo audiences (as opposed to 80% of the general population).

Before discussing my moral-philosophical interactions with members of the Western cattle culture in detail, a basic point about ethical argument needs to be stressed. Plato pointed out long ago that when one is doing ethics with rational adults, one cannot teach, one can only *remind*. In other words, one cannot provide people with a list of ethical answers the way one can teach the state capitals; one can only help them think through ethical issues or their own ethical assumptions in a rational way. (Hence Plato's metaphor of the moral philosopher as midwife.)

An excellent illustration of this point can be found in my veterinary ethics teaching. Like anything else, there are good years and bad years. One particularly bad year, I had spent a great deal of time explaining to the students that I was not there to teach them what was right and wrong—if they didn't know that by the time they reached vet school, they and society were in serious trouble. My job, I insisted, was to teach them how to "think about ethics," how to recognize situations in veterinary medicine in which subtle questions of right and wrong might arise and not be noticed; how to apply their notions of right and wrong to new situations; how to avoid contradicting themselves when doing so, and in short, how to reason about right and wrong. This particular class wouldn't accept this. They wanted me, they said, to tell them exactly what was right and wrong. "We want answers" they whined. "You only give us questions!" Try as I might, I could not get them to see that my job was to help them think about such problems, not to dictate solutions.

One day, I had an inspiration. I came to class early and filled the blackboard with a series of statements: "Never euthanize a healthy animal." "Never crop ears or dock tails." When the students came into class, I pointed to the statements and told them to copy them down and memorize them. "Why?" they asked suspiciously. "Because I'll test you on them," I said. "What are they?" they queried. "These are the answers you've been asking for," I replied. "Who the hell are you to give us answers?" they shouted.

In my own teaching, I employ a different metaphor to make Plato's point. In discussing ethical disagreement, I talk of the need to use judo, not sumo. In other words, one cannot force ethics on someone else—one can only use a person's own ethics to extract the conclusion one wishes. I cannot make you believe what you do not believe, but I can make you realize that what you in fact believe is not what you think you believe. This is equally true whether one is operating on the level of social ethics or personal ethics. To take an example from the former, compare the passage of Prohibition with the passage of the Civil Rights Act. The first was a case of sumo—attempting to force an ethic on people that they did not believe in. The result was a failure; people continued to drink, perhaps even more than they had before.

In contradistinction to that situation, Lyndon Johnson, as a Southerner, realized that all Americans—including segregationists—accepted two premises: All humans should be treated equally, and Blacks are human. The problem was, they had never bothered to draw the conclusion! Johnson guessed correctly that if he "wrote the conclusion large" in law, people would "recollect" it. Had he been wrong, the Civil Rights Act would have been as big a failure as Prohibition!

Despite the evident truth of Plato's assertion, people tend to ignore it. Consider how we attempt to force our views on teenagers, succeeding only in reinforcing their commitment to rejecting them! Consider the animal activists who glumly informed me of their disappointment when, after picketing a medical school for two days while carrying signs reading "Stop the Nazi butchery" and "Research is torture," none of the medical researchers had come out to discuss the issues with them.

Given that sumo doesn't work, and given the siege mentality we discussed earlier, coupled with the fact that this mentality is significantly justified, and given further the independence of cowboys, and the ignorance of both rodeo and ranching displayed by many of their critics, it is not surprising that rodeo and ranch people tend to be defensive. It was thus clear to me that if there was ever a situation for judo and recollection, I was facing it when asked to speak before such audiences.

For recollection to work, there must be something to recollect. If the negative stereotype of the cowboy is correct, and cowboys are insensitive, swaggering, redneck bullies, delighting in frightening and hurting animals, attempting to do Socratic dialogue with rodeo people on the ethics of animal use in rodeo would be as useful an exercise as Allen Ginsberg's attempt to levitate the Pentagon during the Vietnam war by chanting mantras. Happily, such a situation does not obtain, and the truth is very far from the stereotype.

In the first place, cowboys and ranchers, as a group, are the most fair-minded people I have ever dealt with. In my speeches and writings, I have often said that, of the almost 700 groups around the world to whom I have lectured on animal ethics and other bioethical issues, the best audience is one made up of Western ranchers, the worst is MD-PhDs in medical schools. The ranchers will hear what you say, the medical research people will tend to hear what they expect you to say. One *Denver Post* reporter, while commenting in the mid-1980s on my history of effecting change in animal use at Colorado State University, pointed out that I had benefited from CSU's *ethos* as a cowboy institution. "You would never have been able to do this at Harvard," he said, speaking as a graduate of Harvard. "There, they would hang you for what they believed you stand for. At CSU, on the other hand, the Western tradition of 'hear em out before you hang em' is still alive and well."

Second, and the importance of this point cannot be overestimated, ranchers and cowboys are in fact the last bastion of the ethic of animal husbandry, which pervaded animal agriculture for all of human history until the advent of revolutionary changes in agriculture that took place in the mid-twentieth century. For all of human history, agriculture has represented the overwhelmingly predominant use of animals in society. The essence of traditional agriculture was husbandry, which meant first-rate care. (*Hus/band,* etymologically, is "bonded to the house.") Husbandry meant putting the animals one was raising into the most optimal environment possible, the environment in which the animal was best suited to thrive by natural and artificial selection, and augmenting those natural powers with the provision of food during famine, water during drought, protection from predation, medical care, etc. So powerful is the concept of husbandry that it became, for the Psalmist, the metaphor for God's relationships to man: "The Lord is my shepherd, I shall not want. He leadeth me to green pastures, He maketh me to lie down beside still waters, He restoreth my soul."

Husbandry agriculture was therefore about putting square pegs in square holes, round pegs in round holes, and in doing so, creating as little friction as possible. The result of doing this was a win/win situation for both animal producer and animal. This is what Temple Grandin has called the "ancient contract" in which animals were better off in quality of life than they would have been on their own, and humans in turn harvested the animals' products or lives. Any harm done to the animals would as much harm the producer. This is why a minimalistic anticruelty ethic sufficed for thousands of years as the social consensus ethic for animals. Only a sadist or psychopath would hurt an animal intentionally for no good reason. To be sure, this ideal was clouded by relatively short-term insults such as branding, castration, and occasional rough handling, but wise husbandry people knew that "gentling was best." (Gentle handling has been demonstrated to correlate significantly with both milk production in dairy cattle and reproductive success in swine.)

Western ranchers still adhere to the ethic of husbandry, while the rest of agriculture has changed dramatically in the mid-twentieth century. The use of high technology-intensive agriculture (what the vernacular refers to as "factory farming") has broken the fair contract and turned agriculture into a patently exploitative activity, wherein the values of efficiency and productivity have replaced the values of husbandry. We are no longer constrained in our agricultural practices by the animals' biological natures; we have "technological sanders" that allow us to put square pegs in round holes without affecting bottom-line values. Whereas no nineteenth century agriculturalist would have dreamed of crowding thousands of chickens in one building in cages, if only because they would all have died in a month of disease, we now have antibiotics and vaccines that allow us to effect such crowding, yet make a profit. Technology has, in effect, divorced animal productivity from animal happiness.

However, Western ranchers haven't changed their methods of raising animals. They still practice husbandry agriculture that respects the animals' natures. I have only to start the sentence "We take care of the animals . . . ," and my rancher audiences chorus ". . . and they take care of us." My cowboy students invariably tell me the only time they ever "got whipped" by their dad was when they went off to a dance or ball game without taking care of the animals first. No one is likelier to report—and testify against—cruelty and neglect of animals than ranchers. At a closed meeting for agriculturalists in Colorado, the president of the Colorado Cattlemen's Association declared decisively that "If I had to raise animals like those veal people do, I'd get the hell out of the business."

This, then, is the ethic that I can get ranchers to recollect. I go on to explain to them that, contrary to the propaganda they often receive from industry sources, the notion of animals having rights that need to be codified in law now that those rights are no longer guaranteed by a husbandry-based agriculture is a widespread social concern, and a conservative rather than a radical view. In fact, I point out, it is high technology agriculture and the attendant ability to respond to only those aspects of an animal's nature that are relevant to productivity, rather than all of the animal's needs constitutive of its nature, that is radical relative to the history of agriculture. Once I have explained this, over 90% of the ranchers and rodeo people I address affirm that of course animals should have rights that are protected.

III

Since the overwhelming majority of rodeo people come from ranch backgrounds and have thus grown up with the previously described ethic, it is not all that difficult to get them to recollect that ethic, and apply it to rodeo, something they have typically failed to do on their own by compartmentalizing the two domains. Similarly, when I discuss this with ranchers, they often point out that they are reluctant to hire rodeo competitors, whom they see as athletes rather than husbandrymen. As one rancher said to me, "If I need to rope a calf, it is usually because the animal is sick or injured. If that is the case, the last thing I need is some rodeo jock running the animal hell for leather." Indeed I have heard cattlemen seriously discuss the need for distancing beef production from rodeo in the public mind.

In any case, I have enjoyed ample experience using the Socratic recollection approach to get putatively hostile people to begin thinking about the morality of rodeo. One excellent example leaps immediately to mind. Five years ago, I was asked to speak to the Colorado State University Rodeo Club about the new ethic in relation to rodeo. When I entered the room, I found some two dozen cowboys seated as far back as possible, cowboy hats over their eyes, booted feet up, arms folded defiantly, arrogantly smirking at me with what I call the "shit-kicker smirk." With the quick-wittedness for which I am known, I immediately sized up the situation as a hostile one.

"Why am I here?" I began by asking. No response. I repeated the question. "Seriously, Why am I here; I'm not asking you in the metaphysical sense, but rather, what do you expect? You ought to know, you invited me!" One brave soul ventured, "You're here to tell us what is wrong with rodeo."

"Would you listen?" said I. "Hell, no!" they chorused. "Well, in that case I would be stupid to try, and I'm not stupid."

A long silence followed. Finally someone suggested, "Are you here to help us think about rodeo?" "Is that what you want?" I asked. "Yes," they said. "Okay," I replied, "I can do that."

For the next hour, without mentioning rodeo, I discussed many aspects of ethics: the nature of social morality and individual morality, the relationship between law and ethics, the need for an ethic for how we treat animals. I queried them as to their position on the latter question. After some dialogue, they all agreed that, as a minimal ethical principle, one should not hurt animals for trivial reasons. "Okay," I said, "In the face of our discussion, take a fifteen-minute break, go out in the hall, talk among yourselves, and come back and tell me what you guys think is wrong with rodeo from the point of view of animal ethics."

Fifteen minutes later they came back. All took seats in the front, not the back. One man, the president of the club, stood nervously in front of the room, hat in hand. "Well," I said, not knowing what to expect, nor what the change in attitude betokened, "What did you guys agree is wrong with rodeo?" The president looked at me and quietly spoke: "Everything, Doc." "Beg your pardon?" I said. "Everything," he repeated. "When we started to think about it, we realized that what we do violates our own ethic about animals." "Okay," I said, "I've done my job. I can go." "Please don't go," he said. "We want to think this through. Rodeo means a lot to us. Will you help us think through how we can hold on to rodeo and yet not violate our ethic?" To me, that incident represents an archetypal example of successful ethical dialogue, using recollection and judo, not sumo!

Now a cynic might suggest that nothing has changed; that these students went back to competitive rodeo, and soon forgot the concerns I had elicited.

I do not, however, believe that is so. I believe that they were thinking differently about rodeo, and will be instruments of change as they go on through life. Indeed, if I didn't believe this, I would not teach!

For the cynic, I will relate another instance that did immediately result in practical change. When I began teaching ethics in the CSU veterinary school in 1978, the majority of students were from a ranch background. Correlatively, every spring they held a vet school rodeo. A significant minority of the students, usually those not from ranch backgrounds, were opposed to any activity that could or would cause pain, fear, or stress to animals. I realized that Providence had provided me with a perfect "laboratory exercise" for my ethics course. Could the students reconcile their differences and achieve a consensus resolution? To accomplish this, I engaged the entire class in Socratic dialogue, until each could see the others' points. (I got the cowboys' attention by declaring that, to me, veterinarians engaging in rodeo seemed *prima facie* equivalent to orthopedic surgeons picking fights in bars—that metaphor elicited much response!)

In any case, the dialogue persisted over about 3 weeks. Eventually, representatives from the cowboy contingent came to me and said, "We've thought it through. Would it satisfy you if . . ." "Hold on!" I said. "The issue here is not satisfying me. I don't grade you on how you resolve this. I grade you on your knowledge of Kant. You must satisfy yourselves and your peers, not me."

"Okay," they replied. "We've decided to use breakaway ropes in the calf-roping events—that event seems most morally problematic."

"Explain," I said.

"Jerking a calf to a stop at 20 miles per hour when it is roped doesn't seem right. So we will tie the lariat rope to a string, so that when the calf is roped, instead of being jerked, the string will break. We can still demonstrate skill in roping, without hurting the animal." "Sounds good to me," I said.

One woman from a rodeo background lingered after the other students had left. "I don't know if you fully appreciate what these guys have done, Dr. Rollin," she said. "Enlighten me," I said. "I don't think you realize that in the culture they come from, breakaway ropes are used only in women's events," she said quietly. A chill ran up my spine as I realized the profundity of Socratic recollection. Moral reflection in these highly moral men had trumped even their macho cultural attitudes.

It remains to ask where the animal welfare problems with rodeo really lie. And no one knows the answers to that question better than people who rodeo who have been stimulated to reflect on rodeo in terms of their own ethic for animals. The general consensus among such people I have dealt with is that the rough stock riding events—bull riding, saddle and bareback bronc riding—are not terribly problematic, provided that the animals are not hurt by spurring, and the bulls not agitated by electric shock "hot shotting." (This sometimes occurs before a bullride because the rider is judged by how difficult the bull is, and an angry bull is more difficult to ride.) Steer wrestling may cause some neck injury to steers, but that is probably rare and minimal. Calf roping is highly problematic, and that point is, as I suggested above, easily elicited from ranchers. In fact, even some people in the rodeo community have spoken against jerking calves to a stop and flipping them over. While the current PRCA rules mandate fines for jerking calves, that is largely ineffective. As one champion roper said to me: "The fine is $100, the purse is $5,000—you figure it out." A far better approach would be to disqualify any roper that jerked the calf. While it would slow roping times, it would affect everyone equally.

Steer tripping (or steer jerking or steer busting), which involves violently jerking a steer's legs out from under him, is, as mentioned earlier, illegal in all but a few states. In my experience, most rodeo cowboys and managers find it objectionable because of the very real chance of injury to the animals. Very recently, while I was lecturing in Red Deer, Alberta, a group of cowboys, many of them wearing rodeo buckles, approached me to discuss steer tripping. They had attended a rodeo in Oklahoma, one of the few places where steer tripping is still done, and were sickened by a case in which they believed the animal broke its back when it hit the ground. One man told me, "I'll never forget that sound. It was like the crack of a rifle shot." This event should be banned legally, ideally by legislation initiated by the rodeo community.

Many of the non-PRCA-sanctioned events are morally problematic, both because they involve animals getting hurt or stressed (e.g., Chuckwagon races or wild horse races) and because they teach young people to take pleasure in an animal's fear (e.g., greased pig contests). Probably the best way to change these is through recollection.

IV

The difference between urban ethical views of animals and the ethics of rodeo practitioners is usually seen by both sides as unbridgeable, and any attempt to bring them together is seen as impossible. The result is a "showdown mentality," with rodeo people unwilling to budge, and critics of rodeo demanding abolition. I hope I have shown that the tradition of husbandry and concern for animals built into Western ranching is in fact a significant potential bridge. But first, rodeo people must be willing to recollect their moral concern for animals, and critics of rodeo must be willing to acknowledge that moral concern, rather than dismissing rodeo people as a bunch of sadistic, redneck, uncaring moral troglodytes. Again, rodeo people must be willing to acknowledge the rational moral basis of social ethical concern for animals even among urban animal advocates, while urban critics must realize the strong symbolic and cultural dimensions of rodeo, and respect the role it plays in people's minds. Above all, moral dialogue should be seen as a creative challenge to achieving consensus through mutually respectful, rationally based interaction, not, as fruitless quarrels are called in my part of the country, as a "pissing contest."

Bibliography

1. Elizabeth Lawrence. *Rodeo: An Anthropologist Looks at the Wild and the Tame.* Knoxville: University of Tennessee Press, 1982.

V
PART

THE SOCIAL ETHICS OF SPORT: IS SPORT GOOD FOR SOCIETY?

This section introduces some of the major social criticisms of sport. At stake here are fundamental questions about the nature of sport (or in some cases particular sports) and its role in society. With any ethical issue (defined as a morally significant issue that reasonable people might disagree about), the first area of disagreement often concerns definitions and the moral status of the activity under discussion. The two are closely linked. To take just one of the topics in this section, agreement with the statement "Violence in sport is morally bad, and therefore should be avoided" depends on what we mean by violence. Some sports require, as part of their rules, intense physical contact that may cause harm or injury. Are such sports themselves, and here perhaps the best example is boxing, morally objectionable?

The purpose of the articles in this part is to raise the social issues, prompt informed debate, and allow the reader to pursue the topic in more detail.

Violence in Sport and Violent Sport: Definitions

Sports violence is physically assaultive behavior by a player that takes place in a sports context and is intended to incapacitate or cause physical pain or injury to another player (or a fan, coach, game official, police officer, etc.).[1]

Or, alternatively: *Sports violence* is harm-inducing behavior bearing no direct relationship to the competitive goals of sport and relating therefore to incidents of uncontrolled aggression outside of the rules of sport, rather than highly competitive behavior within the rule boundaries.[2]

Violence is often contrasted with *aggression* where aggression is the infliction of an aversive stimulus, either physical, verbal, or gestural on one person by another. Aggression is not an attitude but a behavior, and, most critically, violent aggression is an act committed with the intent to injure.[3]

Assertiveness means the athlete is using legitimate means to achieve his or her goal and has no intention of injuring the opponent.[4]

These definitions have their problems. The definitions hide distinctions that are important to sport and make practical judgments on the acceptability of an action dependent on an assessment of the player's intentions. We will examine these difficulties below.

1. *Intention:* An athlete can cause harm, injury, or even incapacitation to another player without intention and within the rules of the game. Intention is also notoriously difficult to assess, so if the moral status of the act depends on the person's intentions, it may be impossible to determine.
2. *Violence within the rules:* Many sports permit within their rules behavior that may well cause pain to, injure, or incapacitate an opponent. Some games even permit actions intended to cause pain. For instance, the goal of boxing is to incapacitate or hurt the opponent. Wrestling accepts submission as a means of scoring, whereas ice hockey, football, and rugby all permit the physical intimidation of opponents through causing them physical pain. The moral status of an act depends greatly on whether it was performed within or outside of the rules.
3. *The ethos of the game:* The same sport, with the same rules, may be played quite differently at different levels, in different countries or regions, or by men and women. The ethos of a game is the way that game is played in a particular region or at a particular level. Quite high levels of violence—for example, fighting—may occur outside of the rules of the game and yet be expected, or even valued.
4. *Scope:* Discussion of sports violence often includes actions taken by fans or spectators. While these acts take place at sports events, they are not committed by players and are not part of the game itself. There are interesting questions around just why it is that sports events are so often the venue for fan violence, but this is properly an issue for sociological rather than philosophical analysis.

Consent

When assessing the moral status of an action, it is imperative that we examine the issue of consent of the person on whom the action is performed.

For instance, a physician or dentist may cause pain in treating us, but we accept the pain because we have consented to treatment. Any time we play a sport, we consent to the possible harms that we may incur by playing that game within its rules. Because they require physical exertion, most sports carry some risk of harm. In contact sports, that harm may result from the legitimate and permissible actions of an opponent. A crushing but legal tackle may cause catastrophic injury. The tackler may intend to tackle as hard as possible and may even intend to cause pain. (In contact sports the desire to put one's opponent off his or her game by tackling hard and shaking the opponent up may be part of the game.)

Generally, we find morally acceptable those acts that occur within the rules of the game, even if they cause harm. But this observation raises further considerations.

Information

In the medical literature, the doctrine of consent, the requirement that a physician get permission before beginning treatment, is almost always prefaced by the word *informed.* In other words, consent is not valid if the person giving it is not adequately informed of what he or she is consenting to. If playing a game implies a form of presumed consent, and that is the generally accepted view, it is not clear that the players are always informed, that is, that they know just what it is they are consenting to.

Consent and Minors

The doctrine of consent applies to competent adults. It applies less clearly to minors and the incompetent; we do not permit minors to give valid consent to many types of behaviors. Should minors be permitted to consent to the risk of harm that comes from participation in a variety of contact sports?

Consent and the Rules

So far the discussion has focused on actions within the rules. Many sports, however, tacitly accept a certain level of violence outside the rules of the game. *Accept* is a difficult word here, because officials and players may well say that the sport does not tolerate violence outside the rules, but the real test concerns the sort of penalties that are imposed. (As stated earlier, it is important to remember that the same game may be played in different ways in different communities, by different age groups, and by different competitive levels.) For example, in hockey, fighting is an accepted part of the game for many players and in many leagues. The evidence for this statement is that fighting is expected, players who fight are praised and rewarded, and the penalties imposed for fighting are insufficient to deter individuals or to harm teams.

The Causes of Violence

A variety of theories exist as to the causes of violence both in sport and in general.

Biology

One theory suggests that humans are inherently violent. On this account sport offers a relatively safe and controlled way to discharge our aggression.

Psychology

Another theory suggests that violence is caused by frustration as one's efforts to reach a goal are blocked. In sport this frustration could be caused by officials, opponents, and other factors.

Social Learning

The explanation that is currently most generally accepted by researchers is that violence is learned as an accepted method of playing the game. Violence or fighting might be officially condemned and penalized but unofficially praised by coaches, teammates, fans, and the like. The official penalties may be insufficient to deter the behavior.

Sport and Sport Heroes in Popular Culture

Sport is often used as a tool to build nations and demonstrate the superiority of one country or ideology over others. But just what is the price of the use of that tool? Building nations through sport operates by creating an "us against them" scenario, where our country and our athletes are the "good guys" in opposition to the rest of the world. Though this process of creating stories and myths from sporting success builds our personal and national self-image, it does so at the expense of those cast as the "losers."

This same theme of winners versus losers continues in the final two essays, concerning admiration for sports heroes and the issue of disability rights in sport. Images of sports heroes and heroines are images of the strong and powerful, of winners with perfect bodies defeating others. What room exists in sport, then, for those whose bodies do not fit those images of perfection, and what is the effect of celebrating victory and the victorious? Is sport ultimately fascistoid?

Notes

1. *Violence in Canadian Amateur Sport: A Review of Literature* Smith, M.D., Commission for Fair Play, Government of Canada, 1987, p.7.
2. "The Determinants and control of violence in sport," Terry, P.C., and Jackson, J.J., *Quest* 37, 27-37, 1985, p.27.
3. *Sport Psychology: An Introduction,* LeUnes, I.D., and Nation, J.R., Chicago, Nelson-Hall, 1989.
4. "Aggression and Violence in Sport: An ISSP Position Stand." Tenenbaum, G., et al. *The Sport Psychologist* 11, 1-7, 1997, p.1.

CHAPTER

Violence in Sports

Robert L. Simon

The Case Against Boxing

What is the case against boxing? Actually, there are several arguments for the conclusion that boxing ought to be prohibited. A not atypical point of departure for our discussion is the following passage from an editorial in *The New York Times:*

> Some people watch boxing to see skill, others just for the blood. Far worse than the blood is the unseen damage. Retinas are dislodged, kidneys bruised and . . . the cerebral cortex accumulates damage to the higher functions of the brain, leading to loss of memory, shambling walk: the traits of the punch drunk boxer. Can a civilized society plausibly justify the pleasure it may gain from such a sport?[1]

This passage suggests two kinds of reasons for prohibiting boxing. The first is the protection of the boxers themselves. The violence inherent in boxing may make it too dangerous for the participants. In this view, society ought to protect boxers from harm by banning the sport. The passage also suggests a second line of argument. Might we somehow become less civilized, or morally more insensitive, if boxing is permitted to continue?

The question concerning what civilized societies ought to permit implies that the practice of boxing may have social consequences that are harmful, not just to boxers, but to others as well. Do either of these lines of argument justify the prohibition of boxing?

Paternalism and Mill's Harm Principle

There is little question that boxing can be harmful to the participants. Every boxer who enters the ring faces the real possibility of serious injury. Doesn't society have the right as well as the duty to legally prohibit boxing in order to protect boxers themselves from harm and even death?

Before we agree too quickly, however, we should consider the following examples. Should your friends prevent you from ordering ice cream and fatty meats when you go out because such foods contain too much cholesterol? Should your friends prevent you from trying out for the basketball or football team because other sports you might play, such as golf, are much safer? On a broader level, suppose the state passes legislation requiring that reasonably healthy adults who do not exercise for at least thirty minutes a day must pay substantial extra taxes. This legislation is justified as an attempt to save the sedentary from themselves by requiring participation in a healthy life style.

The issue at stake here is one of *paternalism*. Roughly stated, paternalism refers to interference with the liberty of agents for what is believed to be their own good. A major objection to paternalism, however, is that it wrongly disregards the liberty and autonomy of those very agents who are interfered with for their own good.

Perhaps the most influential case against paternalistic interference with the liberty of competent agents was presented by the British philosopher John Stuart Mill (1806-1873) in his eloquent defense of personal freedom, *On Liberty*. Mill himself claimed to be a utilitarian in ethics, committed to the view that the sole criterion of right and wrong is the social utility of acts or practices. At first glance, utilitarianism does not seem to be particularly hostile to paternalism or especially protective of the freedom of the individual. It seems that paternalistic interference with liberty would be justified on utilitarian grounds whenever it produced better consequences for all affected than the available alternatives. Utilitarians might turn out to be interfering busybodies on the individual level and benevolent versions of Big Brother on the state level, interfering with freedom whenever necessary to bring about the best results.

However, in *On Liberty,* Mill advanced important arguments against applying utilitarianism so crudely. Even if, as many suspect, Mill was unable to consistently remain within the utilitarian framework, he did advance important arguments against paternalistic interference with the individual based on respect for the liberty and autonomy of the individual.

In one of the most widely discussed passages of *On Liberty*, Mill declared that

> the sole end for which mankind are warranted individually or collectively in interfering with the liberty of action of any of their number is self protection. . . . The only purpose for which power can be rightfully exercised over any member of a civilized community, against his will, is to prevent harm to others. His own good, either physical or mental, is not a sufficient warrant.[2]

According to Mill, as long as another person's acts are self-regarding, so long as they do not harm or constitute a threat to the welfare of others, interference with them is unjustified.

Why did Mill reject what would seem to be the position most in harmony with utilitarianism, namely, that paternalistic interference with freedom is justified whenever it produces better consequences than alternatives? Perhaps the line of argument Mill advances that is most compatible with his official utilitarianism is one of efficiency. Paternalistic interference is likely to be inefficient. After all, agents generally know their own interests better than others do. Moreover, paternalists may often be influenced by their own values and prejudices or by fear for the safety of others, and so are unlikely to properly calculate the consequences of interfering. As a result, allowing paternalism will create a society of busybodies who, in their efforts to do good, will interfere in the wrong place at the wrong time for the wrong reasons. In a sense, Mill can be read here as advancing a *rule utilitarian* argument. A society following a rule prohibiting paternalistic interference will actually promote utility more efficiently than one adopting a rule allowing it, for in the second society, the good produced by the few cases of justifiable paternalism will be swamped by the harm promoted by unjustifiable paternalistic interferences constantly carried out by utilitarian busybodies.

Although this argument is not implausible, it may not accomplish as much as Mill thinks. After all, wouldn't paternalism still be justified in those few cases where we are convinced it would do more good than harm?

In fact, Mill advanced a second line of argument, not easily reconciled with utilitarianism, which has perhaps been more influential than the approach sketched above. Even if paternalistic interference would produce more good than harm, constant interference with our liberty will stunt our moral and intellectual growth and eventually make us incapable of thinking for ourselves. As Mill maintained, the human faculties of perception, judgment, discrimination, feeling, mental activity, and even moral preference are exercised only in making a choice. . . . The mental and the moral, like the muscular powers, are improved only by being used. . . . He who lets the world . . . choose his plan of life for him, has no need of any other faculty than the ape-like one of imitation.[3]

Here, Mill seems to be appealing more to the value of the idea of autonomy than to social utility understood in the sense of a balance of pleasure or satisfaction over pain or frustration of desires. Arguably, the appeal to autonomy is more fundamental than the appeal to utility, since one must first be autonomous in order to evaluate any moral argument at all, including utilitarian arguments. Autonomy is a fundamental value, it can be argued, precisely because it is presupposed by the practice of moral argument itself.[4]

Finally, one can reinforce Mill's case by arguing that paternalism interferes with the fundamental moral right of individuals to control their own lives. Although moral rights may themselves be sometimes justified by the degree to which they promote utility, or as protections for autonomy, they also can be justified as basic moral commodities which protect individuals from being regarded as mere resources to be used for the good of the greater number. In a sense, rights function as political and social "trumps" which individuals can play to protect themselves from being swallowed up in the pursuit of the social good.[5] Individual rights to liberty protect the ability of persons to live their lives as they choose rather than as someone else, however benevolent, thinks such lives should be led.

Accordingly, supporters of boxing can appeal to the arguments suggested by *On Liberty* to reject the claim that boxing ought to be prohibited. In particular, they can maintain (a) it is unclear whether prohibition really will promote the most utility, (b) even if it does, it prevents both boxers and spectators alike from making the moral choice of whether to engage in and support the sport, and finally (c) it ignores the rights of the boxers and spectators to live their own lives as they themselves see fit. Are such arguments decisive?

Exceptions to the Harm Principle

Is it possible to accept the Harm Principle and still maintain that paternalistic interference with boxing *sometimes* is justified? For one thing, Mill himself acknowledges that the Harm Principle "is meant to apply only to human beings in the maturity of their faculties."[6] Thus, interference with the behavior of children and the mentally incompetent for their own good would be allowed by the Harm Principle. This surely is a plausible restriction because such persons are not in a good position to rationally evaluate their desires so as to determine their real interests, and they are not (yet) capable of making rational and autonomous choices.

However, such a restriction would not allow interference with the behavior of competent adults, some of whom can and do choose to box. Of course, one could argue that the mere fact that some persons choose to box demonstrates their irrationality and lack of competency and thus disqualifies them from protection by the Harm Principle. However, if the only reason for thinking such people are irrational is that they make a choice others of us don't like, such an argument must be rejected. The very point of the Harm Principle is to protect individuals from having the values of others imposed upon them, so we must have independent reason to think that agents are incompetent or immature before we are justified in interfering with their behavior; the mere fact that we don't like their choices is not enough.

A second kind of exception to the Harm Principle might allow interference with the choice of competent adults to participate in boxing. That is, perhaps paternalism is acceptable when its goal is not simply to benefit the people being interfered with but rather is to protect their status as rational and autonomous agents.[7] For example, suppose a person of sound mind and body is about to take a drug which, while causing pleasurable experiences, is highly addictive and will eventually destroy her capacity to reason. Aren't you justified in interfering to remove her supply of the drug, even against her will? After all, your goal is not to impose your conception of happiness upon her but to preserve her capacity to choose her own conception of the good life for herself.

How does this argument apply to the prohibition of boxing? In particular, repeated blows to the head produce brain damage, leading to the symptoms associated with the behavior of the "punch drunk" fighter. Long before those symptoms become evident, however, irreversible brain damage, and gradual diminishment of rational capacities, might have taken place.[8]

Although this sort of argument does provide grounds for interference, whether these grounds are sufficiently strong or weighty to justify interference with liberty is controversial. In particular, unlike the case of a mind-destroying addictive drug, the effects of boxing on mental capacity are long term and uncertain. Moreover, the rewards that some professional fighters can obtain are potentially great. Why is it less justifiable to risk one's capacity for rational choice to secure a great gain than it is, say, to risk shortening one's life span by following an unhealthy but pleasurable diet, or putting oneself under unhealthy stress in order to succeed in business?

Perhaps a third ground for making exceptions to the Harm Principle provides a stronger justification for interference with boxing. We have been assuming that athletes freely and autonomously choose to engage in boxing. But there are grounds for doubting the truth of that assumption.

For one thing, many boxers may be ignorant of the risks of engaging in their sport. Hence, they no more freely consent to run those risks than the person who drives over an unsafe bridge in the mistaken belief that it is safe consents to being thrown into the raging river below.

Of equal importance, many of the participants in professional boxing come from severely disadvantaged backgrounds. These men see boxing as their main chance of escape from the economic and social disadvantages of the ghetto, many of which are due to the injustice of racial discrimination. In this view, the athlete who chooses to box is not responding to an offer or opportunity, i.e., "you can better yourself by becoming a boxer," but rather is reacting to a threat, i.e., "if you don't become a boxer, you will continue to be a victim of social injustice and neglect." Accordingly, since boxers are not autonomous freely choosing agents, but rather are victims of societal coercion, they are not covered by the Harm Principle in the first place.

However, proponents of individual liberty will regard such a view as too extreme. Carried to its logical limits, they will point out, it implies that the poor and deprived should have less liberty to direct their own lives than the rest of us because they are not "truly free" to begin with. In other words, in the name of protecting them from themselves, we would be depriving the disadvantaged of one of the most basic elements of human dignity, the ability to have some control of their own lives. By viewing them only as victims, we would no longer see them as persons in their own right. Would we go so far as to paternalistically deprive them of taking any risks to better themselves since they are, we are told, not able to freely choose to begin with?

This point does have force, but it also must be remembered that poverty and deprivation can lead people to take risks that no one would take unless desperate. The *justice* of a system that presents people with such cruel choices can be called into question. Thus, a proponent of prohibition might agree that the poor and deprived are not mere victims and can make choices but might regard the choice between becoming a boxer and living a life of deprivation as itself unjust. Perhaps a prohibition on boxing could be justified to prevent the imposition of such unjust choices upon the disadvantaged.

The evaluation of this point will depend upon whether one regards the athlete from a disadvantaged and perhaps minority background as having a reasonable set of available choices in our society. If one believes that the alternative to boxing is not starvation, or even welfare, but that educational opportunities are available for those who want to take advantage of them, then one will view the chance to become a boxer as an opportunity. If one regards alternate opportunities as shams, one will be inclined to see boxers as the victim of societal coercion. In any case, to the extent that alternate opportunities are available, it is the responsibility of coaches and parents to inform young athletes of them and of the relatively infinitesimal chances of being successful in professional sports.

Be that as it may, it is doubtful if the current argument supports an across-the-board ban on participation in boxing, even if one makes highly pessimistic assumptions about the range of opportunities available to disadvantaged youth in our society. This is because not everyone who chooses to participate in boxing need be from a disadvantaged background. At most, the argument justifies closing boxing only to certain classes of people, namely, (a) those for whom it is a last resort and who may be "forced" into it because of social or economic pressure, and (b) those who lack the education or have not had the opportunity to fully understand the risks of participation.

We can conclude, then, that although paternalistic arguments in favor of prohibition of boxing are not without force, they are not conclusive either. On the contrary, concern for individual liberty and autonomy justifies us in placing the burden of proof on the paternalist. Although further discussion might warrant us in revising our opinion, it appears from what we have seen that the burden has not yet been met where participation in boxing (and other risky activities) is at issue.

Boxing and the Protection of Society

So far, we have been assuming that the only grounds for prohibition of boxing are paternalistic. But what if the participation in boxing is not simply self-regarding but has harmful effects on others? The Harm Principle permits interference with the individual liberty of some to prevent them from harming others.

But how can boxing harm others? At first glance, it may appear that the only ones boxers can harm are themselves.

However, first glances can be deceiving. To see how boxing can harm society, consider the imaginary sport of Mayhem. The rules of Mayhem are simple. Adult volunteers, who have given their informed consent to participate, are placed in an arena with swords and spears and are divided into two teams. They then fight until only members of one team are left alive. The players on the winning, i.e., surviving, team then get to divide $10,000,000.

Does it follow that if there are no paternalistic reasons strong enough to justify prohibiting Mayhem, there are no reasons at all to justify prohibition?[9]

Isn't it plausible to think that even though there is no direct harm to spectators—the gladiators refrain even from attacking those fans who boo—the indirect harm is substantial. Children might come to idolize (and imitate) trained killers. (Would youngsters collect gladiator bubble gum cards with kill ratio statistics on the back side?) Violence would be glorified and the value of human life inevitably would be cheapened. Such effects may not be inevitable, but the likelihood of eventual harm to others seems sufficient to justify a civilized society in banning Mayhem.

Can't a similar argument be applied to boxing, for as one newspaper editorial exclaimed, "the public celebration of violence cannot be a private matter."[10] After all, although many sports involve the use of force and risk of injury, only boxing has violence in the sense of intentional attempts to injure opponents at its core. Do we want our society to glorify such an activity in the name of sports?

How powerful are these sorts of considerations? In fact, they can be understood as supporting two distinct kinds of arguments. According to the first, public exposure to boxing causes nonparticipants to be influenced adversely and as a result to be more violent or tolerant of violence themselves, thereby increasing the risk for others. In this way, exposure to boxing contributes to the rise of violence throughout society. According to the second kind of argument, adulation of the violence inherent in boxing undermines the standards constituting our community. The public glorification of violence debases our society and changes it into one that is more vulgar and less civilized.

The difference between these two arguments is that the first is more *individualistic,* the second more *communitarian.* That is, the first stresses harm to individuals. The second emphasizes that the social context in which individuals are formed is adversely affected, and so a new and less worthy kind of individual will emerge from the debased social context that results.

The first argument needs to be supported by empirical evidence, which is likely to be inconclusive. In fact, many psychologists have maintained for some time that we can be and often are influenced by models, and, accordingly, if society presents persons engaging in violence as its heroes, toleration of violence and the tendency to commit it will increase.[11] On the other hand, it is unlikely that the normal boxing fan is going to act violently after watching a match. Thus, it is unlikely that any *direct and immediate* tie between boxing and broader social violence exists.

However, conceptual and moral issues are at least as important as empirical ones. Thus, even if participation in or observation of boxing does have subtle long-term effects on the amount of violence committed elsewhere in society, does it *follow* that boxing ought to be prohibited? In answering this question, we must consider its implications for regulation generally if our overall moral view is to be systematically consistent. Suppose, for example, that a book advocates a kind of undisciplined secondary-school education, which, contrary to the author, would actually be educationally harmful to most youngsters. The book's author is highly respected, and it is likely that the book will be widely read and will influence many educators. Are we justified in banning the book because its publication is believed to have harmful effects? On the contrary, it seems that if we prohibit activities like boxing or reading a controversial book because they might have harmful long-term effects, our right to liberty is drastically restricted. We would have ceded to others the ability to make up our own minds for us and to interfere with our lives in a broad range of areas where direct and immediate harm to others is not at issue.

However, to communitarians, advocates of the second argument sketched above, the role of individual liberty has been misrepresented in our whole discussion. We have proceeded, according to this criticism, as if the individual is an autonomous atom who can step back from social institutions and make choices in isolation. It is this individualistic choosing self who is seen as the locus of value, yet, according to the communitarian, such a self is in many ways a fiction. Rather, selves are formed within communities and are constituted or defined by their relationships with others in their social settings. Thus, one is a parent, teacher, coach, member of a religious group, and citizen rather than an isolated individualistic pure agent, allegedly capable of stepping aside from all roles and autonomously evaluating them. What would such an abstract individual be but a mysterious "0" stripped of all distinguishing human characteristics?[12]

What has this roughly sketched communitarian picture of the self have to do with the critique of boxing and with violence in sports? Although the specific implications for policy of theoretical communitarianism are not always clear, the communitarian approach at least emphasizes the need to preserve the common values that bind society together. Boxing and the public celebration of violence undermine the standards of the community and hence transform the kind of individuals it produces. There is no asocial individual who can stand outside his or her community to evaluate boxing. If we tolerate boxing, as well as violence in other areas, we will end up with individuals who no longer share the standards and traditions that lead to the condemnation of violence. Our community will gradually be replaced by one that tolerates and may even welcome behavior that the previous community would have regarded as degrading, threatening, and blatantly immoral.

Although all aspects of the debate between communitarians and what they regard as their liberal individualistic opponents cannot be touched on here, two important points should be kept in mind.[13] First, if the communitarian's major point is that we are so tightly situated within specific communities and traditions that free, rational, and autonomous choice is impossible, we cannot freely, rationally, and autonomously choose to believe communitarianism. That some of us accept a communitarian approach would be just another social fact, to be explained by reference to our social situation, rather than by the truth of communitarianism or the strength of the rational justification for it.

Presumably, the communitarian would not want to accept such a conclusion. But, then, some weight must be given to free, rational, and autonomous choice within communitarianism, even if the account of such choice differs in substantial ways from that of more individualistic approaches to political theory.

However, and this is the second critical point that should be kept in mind, what weight should be given to liberty by communitarians? If their reply is "It's up to the standards of one's community," then they must be reminded that many communities are oppressive, racist, intolerant, and fanatical. On the other hand, if they are to avoid giving weight to the standards implicit in the practices of immoral communities, they seem to be committed to some standard, such as Mill's Harm Principle, or liberal rights to free choice, which is relatively independent of the standards of particular societies. Thus, they cannot settle the issue of whether boxing ought to be prohibited by appealing to the standards of the community, for even assuming there is just one community in our society, the moral question of why its standards *ought* to be obeyed still remains to be answered. (In fact, it can be argued plausibly that many communities in the United States do find the violence in boxing acceptable. Does that settle the moral question of whether it is acceptable?)

Boxing, Morality, and Legality

Our discussion has not provided any conclusive reason for thinking boxing ought to be *legally* prohibited. Paternalistic arguments do not seem strong enough to justify a general prohibition, the link between boxing and individual violence is too tenuous and indirect to support such a general prohibition, and the standards of the community are an insufficient guide to action. On the other hand, while most of us regard individual liberty as of the greatest value, we probably would agree that society does have the right to prohibit such practices as professional gladiatorial contests (such as Mayhem), perhaps on communitarian grounds or perhaps because we doubt that the choice to participate can be truly free or informed. The trouble is that boxing seems to be a borderline case. It is not quite as dangerous as Mayhem, the harm is not as certain or direct, and we can at least begin to understand how a participant can voluntarily accept the risks involved. Thus, the arguments both for and against prohibition seem to be at something of a standoff. Given the dangers of interfering with liberty, perhaps the best policy would be one not of legal interference but of moral sanction and reform.

Thus, whether or not the case for legal prohibition is determinative, many reasons have been given for moral concern about boxing. It is perfectly appropriate for those who share such moral concerns to refuse to support boxing, to urge others to refrain from supporting it, and to advocate strong reforms in the practice of boxing. For example, reformers may want to direct boxing in the direction of becoming an example of the constrained use of force rather than of violence. On this view, boxing as a sport should be distinguished from boxing as a form of violence, just as we now distinguish fencing from actual dueling. Reforms that work in this direction include mandatory use of helmets by fighters, prohibition of blows to the head, and emphasis on scoring points through skill rather than on inflicting damage to opponents. Although boxing probably never will be sedate, it can be modified so it bears a much closer resemblance to fencing than to Mayhem.

To conclude, even if boxing should be immune to legal prohibition on grounds of respect for individual liberty, radical reform of the sport seems to be morally justified. Boxing, as presently constituted, has the goal of infliction of harm by one opponent on another at its core, and so makes violence central. If society should not glorify violence, and if violence in sports might contribute however indirectly to greater tolerance and commission of violence throughout society, or to the erosion of *defensible* community standards, we can be led by such considerations to freely, rationally, and autonomously choose to reduce the level of violence in sports.

Notes

1. *New York Times,* December 14, 1982, p. 30. © *New York Times.* Reprinted by permission.
2. John Stuart Mill, *On Liberty* (1859), edited by Elizabeth Rappaport (Indianapolis: Hackett Publishing Company, 1978), p. 9. Many other editions of *On Liberty* are also in print.
3. *Ibid.,* p. 56.
4. A committed utilitarian might reply, however, that on the contrary, autonomy itself is valuable only because a society of autonomous individuals is likely to generate more utility than one in which the autonomy of individuals is suppressed, perhaps through tyrannical means.

5. The account of individual rights as political trumps has been advanced by Dworkin in *Taking Rights Seriously.*

6. Mill, *On Liberty,* p. 9.

7. For a defense of such a position, see Gerald Dworkin, "Paternalism," in Richard A. Wasserstrom, ed., *Morality and the Law* (Belmont, Calif.: Wadsworth, 1971), pp. 107-126.

8. An accessible discussion of the medical evidence on the effects of boxing, and of the implications of the evidence for policy, can be found in Robert H. Boyle and Wilmer Ames, "Too Many Punches, Too Little Concern," *Sports Illustrated,* April 11, 1983, pp. 42-67.

9. The example of Mayhem is based upon a similar illustration employed by Irving Kristol in his essay, "Pornography, Obscenity, and the Case for Censorship," *New York Times Magazine,* March 28, 1971, reprinted in Joel Feinberg and Hyman Gross, eds., *Philosophy of Law* (Encino, Calif.: Dickenson Publishing Company, Inc., 1975), pp. 165-171.

10. *New York Times,* December 14, 1982, p. 30.

11. An influential account of the role of models in learning is found in Albert Bandura's *Social Learning Theory* (Englewood Cliffs, N. J.: Prentice Hall, 1977).

12. The views presented here represent only a rough sketch of communitarian approaches, but recent communitarian criticisms of liberal individualist approaches to political theory include Alasdair MacIntyre, *After Virtue* (Notre Dame, Ind.: University of Notre Dame Press, 1984) and Michael Sandel, *Liberalism and the Limits of Justice* (New York: Cambridge University Press, 1982).

13. For extended critical discussions of communitarianism, see Amy Gutmann, "Communitarian Critics of Liberalism," *Philosophy and Public Affairs,* Vol. 14 (1983), pp. 308-322; George Sher, "Three Grades of Social Involvement," *Philosophy and Public Affairs,* Vol. 18 (1989), pp. 133-157; Alan E. Buchanan, "Assessing the Communitarian Critique of Liberalism," *Ethics,* Vol. 99 (1989), pp. 852-882; and Patrick Nil and David Paris, "Liberalism and the Communitarian Critique, A Guide for the Perplexed," *Canadian Journal of Political Science,* Vol. 23, No. 3 (1990), pp. 419-439.

26

CHAPTER

Ethics, Sport, and Boxing

Angela Schneider and Robert Butcher

The Sport of Boxing

The first challenge to boxing concerns whether it could even count as a sport. Could an activity that had as its objective the incapacitation of an opponent possibly be a sport? We have to meet that challenge before we can move on to use the principles of sport ethics to evaluate the ethical status of boxing.

Is Boxing a Sport?

Is boxing a sport? There are two approaches to answering this question, one philosophical and the other sociological. The philosophical approach asks if boxing (or whatever activity may be under discussion) fits the logical requirements (meets the necessary conditions) for an activity to be designated a sport. Those requirements are as follows:

- The activity has some identifiable objective or goal.
- Rules exist that make the achievement of the goal more difficult than would otherwise be the case.
- The activity requires physical skill and prowess.

The Canadian Centre for Ethics in Sport supported the research for this paper. The views expressed are those of the authors and should not be construed as the official position of the Centre.

The sociological approach requires that we simply look to see if a sufficient number of people view the activity in question as a sport. (The sociological view also looks for evidence of institutionalization and broadly-based cultural support.)

Either definition is fuzzy at the margins. For instance, whether darts qualifies as a sport depends on the degree of importance you attach to the physical skill of throwing darts (similar questions arise for pistol shooting and motor sports). On the sociological side, there has been a recent push in Canada to declare chess a sport so that it can qualify for Sport Canada funding. It seems odd to conclude that an activity is a sport just because a sufficient number of people say it is.

Neither of these areas of fuzziness applies to boxing. Boxing is a sport. Boxing has an objective and a set of rules, and it clearly requires a great deal of physical skill and prowess. On the sociological side, boxing is typically viewed as a sport, it has an elaborate structure of institutions and regulating bodies, it receives funding from those bodies, and it is featured in the Olympic Games.

Boxing is not only a sport, but it is a sport with a very long history. Homer mentions boxing in his discussion of the funeral games of Patroclus, and it was a sport in the ancient Olympics from 668 B.C. In the modern era, boxing gained popularity in Britain in the late 1700s and made the transition from pugilism—a bare-knuckle brawl with relatively few rules—to boxing with gloves in the late 19th century.[1]

But the question of boxing's status as a sport may represent rather deeper issues than whether the activity merely fits certain definitional criteria. Some cherish the view that an important connection exists between play and sport—that is, the best attitude to hold sport to is one of playfulness. This is not meant to imply a lack of seriousness—a participant may play in complete earnest—but it acknowledges that sport typically stands outside of everyday life and that the activities of sport are freely chosen for their own sake. We have argued elsewhere that this attitude implies a shared set of sporting values and a view of the opponent as a coseeker of the excellent contest.[2] Could a participant hold this view while boxing? Could a fighter genuinely wish for the best person to win? This seems difficult to imagine. Imagine a bar fight or street brawl. Punches are thrown; someone reaches for a bottle or a pool cue. Someone engaged in a fight like this must want to win, regardless of the quality of the process that leads to the outcome. The first goal is victory; the contest itself is of secondary importance. In a fight the winner *is* the best person. Boxing matches are fights. Punches are thrown. Although there are rules, and weapons are not permitted, the pain inflicted is the same as in a bar fight or street brawl. It seems strained to use the language of respect for the game in this context. It is extremely difficult to see how a fighter could honor boxing over his or her personal victory in some actual fight. This may be question-begging; there may be boxers who value the contest over victory, the art of boxing over winning a fight. But the intuitive sense of tension remains. We will examine this issue and the contrast between boxing and fighting later in this chapter.

The force behind the questions here is the evaluative claim that we ought not to sanction an activity as a sport unless it can be played. In other words, we wish to restrict sport to those activities where it is possible to value the process over the outcome.

Amateur and Professional Boxing

It may be important to distinguish between amateur and professional boxing. Throughout boxing's history there has been a division between amateur boxing and professional prizefighting. Professional fights tended to be longer fights to the finish, with the prize being awarded only when one contestant was rendered insensible or indicated surrender. Fights of up to four hours were not uncommon, with contestants continuing to fight despite horrific injuries. A draw was generally not considered a possible outcome. Professional fights now tend to last for 12 rounds.

Professional boxing is a spectacle. Professionals do not wear head protection, have lighter gloves (which increases the possibility of a knock-out), do not wear singlets, sometimes do not have a standing-eight count (standing-eight counts are used in amateur boxing when the boxer is in difficulty—three standing-eight counts in a round or four in a bout end the contest), do not allow injuries to stop the fight unless one boxer is unable to continue (known as a technical knockout, or TKO), and have no formal rule allowing the referee to stop a fight if one boxer is seriously outclassed.

In practice, despite the apparent similarities, a substantial difference exists between a technical knockout (in professional boxing) and referee stops contest (in amateur boxing). Referees are far more likely to stop amateur contests than they are professional bouts. In general, although professional rules allow the referee to stop the fight for injuries, the injuries need to be more severe than those that would cause a referee to stop an amateur fight.

In addition, there are a host of governing bodies for professional boxing, each of which has its own slightly different rules and practices.

In amateur boxing, a structure developed consisting of three rounds of three minutes each. A scoring system rated attack, clean blows to the head or body; and defense, avoiding blows by ducking, countering, and so on. A win on points is the most likely outcome of an amateur boxing match. The referee can also stop the match either by disqualifying a contestant (for breaking the rules in a particularly egregious manner) or because one fighter is deemed too badly hurt to continue (in which case that boxer loses; such a result is recorded RSC, or referee stops contest).

The objective of amateur boxing is the scoring of points. Knockdowns are not scored more highly than other scoring blows. (To score, a blow must connect with the target area of the opponent, must be of sufficient force, and must be delivered with the striking area of the glove, which is designated in white.) Knockouts are not described as an objective. By contrast, the rules of the Canadian Professional Boxing Association say "a clean, forceful hit landed on any vulnerable part of the body above the belt should be credited in proportion to its damaging effect."[3] A knockout (failure to come to scratch, standing ready and able to continue fighting, at the count of 10) or submission is still a definitive method of winning a match in both amateur and professional boxing.

A Moral Evaluation of Boxing

We can now turn to the moral evaluation of this sport. We will first examine the ethical opposition to boxing and then move to arguments designed to show the moral acceptability of boxing.

The Opposition to Boxing

The moral opposition to boxing can focus on two features of the sport: its object and its effects.

The Object of Boxing

The object of boxing is to immobilize or incapacitate the opponent so that he[4] is unable to continue the contest. This goal is achieved by blows with the closed fist encased in an approved glove. In the absence of a knockout or submission, the contest is decided on points, which are awarded for blows most likely to be effective in achieving the goal of incapacitation. It is important to note that a knockout or submission takes precedence over other methods of scoring; that is, even a fighter who was behind on points would still win with a knockout blow.

Could the objective of boxing be described as the scoring of points? Not as the sport is currently practiced. The definitive method of winning is the knockout. The sport could be modified so that a knockout blow is scored in the same way as any other blow. (For instance, scoring blows must be of "sufficient force" to count in amateur boxing, but they are not scored in proportion to their "damaging effect" as in professional boxing. A knockout could end the fight, with the winner being determined by points scored and the final knockout blow scored just like any other blow. We will examine potential modifications to the sport of boxing in more detail later in this chapter.)

Strong moral grounds exist for objecting to the very purpose of boxing. The intention of the sport is to harm or incapacitate the opponent. It is generally wrong to intend to harm or incapacitate another person, so it is wrong to engage in an activity that has that intention as its goal.

This argument retains its force even if very little harm ever actually occurs as a result of boxing. So, even if we could develop gloves and helmets that minimize the risk of harm, one could still object that it is immoral to adopt the stance of intending to incapacitate another human being. (Some exceptions to this general position may arise; later, we will consider whether if one's opponent consents, then one's intentions become permissible.) The attitudes a boxer must adopt toward his opponent require that he view the person as an enemy or adversary who warrants physical incapacitation.

This moral opposition to the very intent of boxing is sometimes expressed quite explicitly. Joseph Boyle, a past president of the American Medical Association, said, "It seems to us an extraordinarily incongruous thing that we have a sport in which two people are literally paid to get into a ring and try to beat one another to death, or at least beat each other into a state of senselessness that will leave them permanently brain-damaged."[5]

Proponents of amateur boxing deny any intent in that sport to incapacitate, declaring that the intention is to win by scoring points. Let us examine this reply.

The Effects of Boxing

The principal arguments against boxing have been grounded in the harm it causes both to participants and to members of societies in which boxing is practiced. The Canadian, British, and American medical associations support a ban on boxing. The British Medical Association (BMA) conducted a review of the evidence for the harm boxing causes in its 1993 publication *The Boxing Debate*.

Death. Between 1945 and 1993, 361 deaths occurred in the ring (worldwide). Most of these deaths were caused by single or repeated concussive blows to the head.[6] Between 1985 and 1993, the BMA identified (from worldwide press reports) eight deaths, three of which involved amateurs. In one instance, a 15-year-old boy died; in another, an 18-year-old amateur died after his first practice fight.

Brain Damage.   There is no safe level for blows to the head. Even when the gloves and helmet are well padded, the brain is shaken in the skull when the head is hit forcibly. A strong punch can carry a thousand pounds of force, the equivalent of being hit by a 12-pound padded wooden mallet traveling at 20 mph.[7] This is bad for you. Even in the absence of a knockout, boxing is harmful. Tearing of the tiny veins and collision of the soft tissue of the brain with the rough internal surface of the skull can cause the subdural hematoma that occasionally leads to death. In addition, the brain has different inertial properties, so when the head is struck, the brain, the skull, and varying parts of the brain all move at different speeds relative to each other. This causes tearing. Brain damage caused by blows to the head is cumulative. The brain has limited regenerative capacities.

Paradoxically, it has been argued that both gloves and head protection increase the risk of brain damage. Gloves protect the fist rather than the head. They therefore allow the contestants to strike much harder without risk of damage to the hand. Bare-knuckle contests, while bloodier, were probably safer, at least in terms of brain injuries.

Head protection reduces cuts around the eyes and almost entirely eliminates damage to the ears. However, both of these injuries are considered relatively minor. Head protection increases the size of the head as a potential target. Blows to the head are therefore more likely. Helmets do not eliminate brain damage.

Eye Damage.   Eye injuries arise from the impact of the glove itself, shock waves caused by blows to the head, and compression and expansion of the fluid-filled elastic sphere that is the eye. Retinal tears and cataracts are the most common eye injuries boxers sustain. Larger gloves and helmets can reduce the risk of impact damage but do not eliminate shock wave and compression and expansion injuries.

Psychological Harm.   "I try to catch my opponent on the tip of his nose because I try to punch the bone into his brain."

"I want to fight, fight, fight and destruct the world."

"I don't want to knock my opponent out. I want to hit him, step away, and watch him hurt. I want his heart."

The first two quotations came from Mike Tyson, the third from Joe Frazier. All are found in Joyce Carol Oates's *On Boxing.*[8] Oates describes boxing as "controlled ferocity." A boxer takes his rage and channels it into a desire to physically conquer and destroy an enemy. It can readily be argued that having those attitudes toward other human beings is psychologically harmful, and any sport that requires or promotes them is doing something harmful.

Harm to Spectators.   One argument against boxing is that it brutalizes its spectators, quite independently of anything that happens to the fighters. When we watch people fight we are descending to our lowest level, a level at which we wish to see battle and blood. We see the victor praised and rewarded for his ability to wreak violence and harm on his opponent. This has the effect of desensitizing us to violence and glorifying a violent response to our problems and those around us. There is some (contested) evidence that rates of violent crime may go up immediately after a highly publicized boxing match.

The Barbarity of Boxing

It is sometimes argued that strong social reasons for banning boxing exist that are independent even of its effects on its participants or spectators. This argument works from the idea that boxing is inherently barbaric or uncivilized. It harks back to a time when male worth was defined in terms of physical prowess and aggression, and when this prowess could not be demonstrated on the battlefield it was demonstrated in the arena. Boxing panders to our baser desires to show self-worth by physically conquering or destroying another person, and to the vicarious pleasure of the spectator who sees such aggression and violence naked and exposed.

So even if no one actually does anything violent as a result of viewing a boxing match, boxing reawakens feelings and emotions that are best left dormant. The argument is that we should be moving on; contemporary society has nonviolence as a goal, and boxing impedes progress toward that goal.

Links to Organized Crime

Critics have argued, particularly in the United States, that boxing should be banned because of its links to organized crime and gambling. This argument applies only to professional boxing and seems backward. If organized crime is a problem, then presumably efforts should be taken to control it rather than boxing.

The Best Defense . . .

In many sports, the best defense is a good offense. The same is often true in ethical analysis. Are there sufficiently good reasons to defend boxing despite the arguments against it?

Freedom, Autonomy, Consent, and Noninterference

What right does the state, or any other entity, for that matter, have to intervene in activities that cause harm to the person concerned? The basic belief of "small 'l' liberalism" (derived from Mill) is that the state is warranted in intervening in a person's behavior only in order to protect others. According to this view, if boxers are competent adults who have consented to fight, the state has no moral right to interfere on the grounds that the activity may do harm to the participants. Those who wish to defend boxing can therefore argue that even if the sport is harmful, no one has the right to interfere in freely chosen activities.

If we accept this principle, then the state ought not to interfere with boxing. In Canada, however (and the law here varies from country to country), this principle is not as clear, or as clearly followed, as some might like. In law, and even in sports law, there has grown a series of limitations on actions to which it is possible to consent. In particular, it is not permissible to consent to have death inflicted on oneself. (For example, there are prohibitions on euthanasia even when the person concerned has given his or her consent. In addition, section 14 of the Canadian Criminal Code explicitly states "No person is entitled to consent to have death inflicted on him. . . .") In case law, in *R. v. Jobidon* the Supreme Court of Canada in 1991 limited the effect of a victim's consent to a fistfight. It ruled that a consent could not exist between adults to "intentionally apply force causing serious hurt or non-trivial bodily harm to each other in the course of a fistfight or brawl." The court reached this decision on the grounds that fistfights were a socially useless activity. The court realized the possible application of its decision to sport and specifically excluded sport, provided the actions taken were within the "customary norms and rules of the game." In explanation, the court stated, "Unlike fistfights, sporting activities and games normally have significant social value; they are worthwhile."[9]

The application to boxing is unclear. If boxing is determined to have significant social value, then actions taken within the rules would be deemed to have consent and would thus be permissible. Actions outside the rules (and norms) of boxing would, however, fall into a different category. If the Tyson ear-biting incident had occurred in Canada, Tyson could have been charged with assault.[10]

This defense merges two of the categories of objection to boxing mentioned earlier. The first, working from the principle of freedom and the value of consent, would exclude state interference from adult boxing (either amateur or professional). Because, however, we live in a society that explicitly limits personal freedoms by reference to the public interest or good, it is possible to argue that boxing should be banned on the basis that it causes harm and that it has no (or insufficient) socially redeeming value. To defend against this charge, boxing would have to demonstrate either that it does not cause harm (or does not cause serious harm) or that its social value outweighs the risk of harm it poses. The no-risk-of-harm argument is implausible. The social value of boxing is also highly questionable.

No Evidence of Harm

The defense here typically takes two forms. The first is to question the evidence of harm, and the second is to argue that boxing actually causes less harm than other permissible sports.

The first move is to distinguish between amateur and professional boxing. Amateur boxing stresses the ways in which it seeks to minimize harm to the boxers by instituting shorter bouts, better safety equipment, better medical supervision, and the focus on scoring points. The argument here centers on whether there is any safe level of blows to the head. Sixteen national medical associations (including Canada's) represented at the 1991 annual meeting of the BMA agreed that "modern medical technology demonstrates beyond doubt that chronic brain damage is caused by the recurrent blows to the head experienced by all boxers, amateur and professional alike. As long as it is legal to hit an opponent above the neck, there are no safety precautions which can be taken to prevent this damage."[11]

The second move argues that although boxing can cause harm, it causes less harm than other permissible activities. For instance, some observers claim that more deaths have occurred from mountain climbing and potholing[12] over the last 50 years than from boxing. Similarly, contact sports such as rugby, football, and hockey all have higher death tolls than boxing. The accusation is that the critics of boxing are inconsistent. The full argument goes like this: Boxing is less harmful than other sports. If boxing is banned on the basis of the harm it causes, all sports that cause equal or greater harm should be banned as well. But that idea is absurd, because it would require banning a large number of high-participation sports. So boxing should not be banned.

This response is somewhat deceptive. First, one needs to look at the relative numbers of participants and the length of time each person plays to assess the risk of death per participant per minute for each sport. Second, this response looks only at death. The brain injuries caused by boxing are chronic and may not show up until many years after the person has stopped boxing. So the comparisons between relative risks of harm from boxing and other sports have not yet been fully made. Finally, it is open to the consistent opponent of boxing to agree that there should be no sports that carry a risk of harm above a certain threshold. If that includes other sports, and if those sports cannot be made safe, then so be it.

The argument that boxing does not cause harm is unpersuasive.

The Value of Boxing

In boxing's favor, proponents argue that the sport builds self-discipline and character, and for a very select few it offers a route out of poverty and despair. The first part of the claim may well be true, but it is no more true of boxing than of many other sports. For example, the explicit mental training that comes with many martial arts provides self-discipline and character more effectively than in boxing. For a very few fighters, amateur boxing may provide a route to a lucrative professional career. It is doubtful that this fact alone is be sufficient to create social value in an activity.

It cannot be denied that boxing has a social value that rests entirely in the fact that it permits people to do something they enjoy. In general, it is socially good that people are able to pursue activities they choose and enjoy. However, this general social good may well be limited on the grounds that what is desired, pursued, or enjoyed is either of no social value or is socially destructive.

Class or Race Struggle

Jim Christy suggests that boxing is the only truly subversive sport. He argues that its practitioners are typically drawn from the ranks of the underprivileged, and its detractors are typically white middle-class liberals.[13] He does not develop this argument, however. The undercurrent is that white middle-class liberals have no business interfering with the actions of any group other than their own. This is a significant issue in a diverse, tolerant, and multicultural society. The difficulty, however, is that this method of conducting the debate leaves no room for assessing the case on its merits. It could be argued that abolitionists insufficiently understand the values of boxing, or that the dangers are overstated. Both approaches would constitute arguments that could be evaluated on their merits. To merely claim that abolitionists are acting as cultural imperialists imposing their view on others is to forgo any chance of debate.

The Special Status of Boxing

It is undeniable that more injuries and deaths occur in other sports than in boxing. It is also undeniable that fighting and other forms of violence occur, and are accepted, in many other sports, hockey being the best example. What makes boxing special is that its roots are in fighting and the desire to physically conquer an opponent. In other sports the fighting and the harm are incidental—that is, the sports could be conducted at the highest possible level without fighting and without injury. It is not clear how boxing could be conducted without fighting and without harm.

A distinction is sometimes made between fighting and boxing. Boxing is the "sweet science," a skillful, almost balletic interplay between two people as they fence for position and advance. According to this view, boxing requires quick eyes and hands, fitness, dexterity, and the ability to move with agility and grace. One needs no special view of one's opponent; one is not intending to inflict harm. Fighting, on the other hand, is physical contest— a test to see which person is the better. A fight might occur on the street, in a bar, on the hockey rink, or in the ring. Fights often occur within a framework of rules. In dueling culture, even fights to the death required that the combatants follow strict codes of behavior. In a fight, one needs a range of physical skills that include strength, endurance, and the ability to fight through pain.

Boxing has a split personality. Boxing as sport—the sort of activity that an athlete can enter into as a straight test of physical skill, boxing without harm or animosity—is a possible future development. Modern fencing developed from an earlier activity that was intended to maim and kill. Boxing could develop in a similar way. If the head were eliminated as a strike zone, boxing could be relatively safe, and athletes could engage in it without feelings of animosity or hatred toward their opponents.

It is an open question, however, whether boxing in this form would allow access to some of the benefits boxing's advocates claim. Boxing of this type would not require particular courage, or the endurance to fight on through pain. It would not require character or "heart," the boxer's term to describe a fighter who struggles on even though he is outclassed and knows that he will get beaten and hurt even more.

Fight fans would also be disappointed. Oates, in *On Boxing,* says that boxing is not a sport; it is not and cannot be playful.[14] It is contest, the naked pitting of man against man to see who survives. A fight requires controlled rage, a fearful channeling of all one's energy and passion into destroying the other. In a fight it is unsurprising that one contestant sometimes steps outside the rules. The rules of boxing give the fight its sporting cloak. But when a cornered animal reacts in anguish and rage to its imminent defeat, it may well lash out against its tormentor in any way that comes to hand. Unsporting? Yes. Surprising? No.

Boxing is special because it tries to turn a fight into a game. The only way that boxing becomes a sport is through the rules that limit the way in which one can inflict damage on one's opponent. Rules are of central importance to all sports. In other sporting activities, however, if a player breaks the rules, his or her actions become merely ludicrous. The absurdity of golf is abundantly apparent if a golfer throws the ball onto the green or drops it into the cup. But in boxing, if you break the rules, what is exposed is a brawl, a fight filled with pain and rage and fear and blood and injury. And, of course, this exposure affects not only those who fight but all of us who watch.

Should Boxing Be Banned?

The debate on boxing takes place in the real world of policy and law. Boxing is banned in some countries, and sometimes philosophical debate moves from the page to the law. The conclusions in this section flow from the preceding discussion. Important principles are at work here. The freedom to choose one's own actions, as far as possible without the interference of others, is a central component of liberal democracy. But we live in communities, and the notion of being a member of a civil society requires that our freedoms can exist only in the context of stable and communal social contexts. Reconciling those competing interests in a way that is principled and fair is the stuff of rational policy making.

All the time that boxing is a form of fighting, it is vulnerable to the criticism that it is barbaric and has no place in contemporary society. If boxing is a form of fight, then it is hard to see how it can escape the charge that it is socially useless and thus not protected as a sport.

But the liberal view of freedom dies hard. We typically resist the dead hand of the state forbidding us from pursuing what we want. However, that view applies only to adults in the fullness of their reflective capacities. Currently in North America, children are allowed to box. The state does have a role in protecting the interests of those who are as yet unable to protect themselves. The authors do not believe that children are in a position to give their valid consent to box. Nor do the authors believe that parents are entitled to give consent for such a risky activity on their children's behalf. We therefore recommend that boxing be banned in Canada for those under the age of 18.

A middle ground for adult boxing also exists. In Canada we accept the view that the state has a role in encouraging certain sorts of activities. This encouragement is accomplished in a variety of ways, often through direct subsidy. We should not encourage boxing. All forms of direct and indirect support should therefore be withdrawn. Boxing should not be featured in provincial or national multisport competitions, and the Canadian Olympic Association should lobby for the removal of boxing from the Olympic Games. Adults should be permitted to box if they wish, but their actions should be neither sanctioned nor encouraged by any publicly funded agency.

Notes

1. Boxing entered the modern Olympic Games in 1906 and gained a worldwide following in the years after World War I. A French variant of boxing was popular in the 18th and 19th centuries. This variation allowed kicking, butting with the head, and wrestling.
2. "Fair Play As Respect for the Game," chapter 2 of this volume.
3. **http://www.canadianboxing.com/new_rules_safety_page.htm**.
4. While acknowledging that women's boxing has been increasing in popularity in recent years, I will use the male pronoun to refer to boxers in this text, as men still constitute the vast majority of both amateur and professional boxers.
5. Quoted in J. Christy, 1990, *Flesh and Blood* (Vancouver: Douglas and McIntyre), 51.
6. British Medical Association, 1993, *The Boxing Debate* (London: British Medical Association), 66.
7. Ibid., 13.
8. J.C. Oates, 1987, *On Boxing* (Garden City, N.Y.: Dolphin/Doubleday).
9. *R. v. Jobidon,* 1991, 2 S.C.R. 714, 766–67.
10. In 1997 in a world heavyweight title fight, Mike Tyson bit off part of the ear of his opponent, Evander Holyfield.
11. British Medical Association, 1993, *The Boxing Debate* (London: British Medical Association), 82.
12. Cave exploring/diving.
13. Christy, 52 ff.
14. J.C. Oates, 1987, *On Boxing* (Garden City, N.Y.: Dolphin/Doubleday), 18.

Patriotic Sports and the Moral Making of Nations

William J. Morgan

"Morality," Oakeshott (23: p. 58) writes, "is neither a system of general principles nor a code of rules, but a vernacular language. General principles and even rules may be elicited from it, but (like other languages) it is not the creation of grammarians [but rather] . . . speakers. What has to be learned in a moral education is not a theorem . . . nor . . . a rule . . . but how to speak the language intelligently." What are we to glean from Oakeshott's conception of morality, and what, if anything, does it have to do with our present topic regarding the connection between sports and nationalism?

To begin with the first question, what we are to understand by Oakeshott's pronouncement that morality is a vernacular language is that moral principles have a point only insofar, Rorty (23: p. 58) writes, "as they incorporate tacit reference to a whole range of institutions, practices, and vocabularies of moral and political deliberation. They are reminders of, abbreviations for, such practices, not justifications for such practices." Accepting this familiar Hegelian line means that we should stop thinking of morality as Kant did, "as the voice of the divine part of ourselves," and think of it instead "as the voice of ourselves as members of a community, speakers of a common language" (23: p. 59)—precisely those community members who under-

Reprinted, by permission, from W.J. Morgan, 1999, "Patriotic sports and the moral making of nations," *Journal of the Philosophy of Sport, XXVI:* 50-67.

write the practices and institutions currently in vogue in society. Herein, then, lies at least in part the answer to our second question. For more often than not, at least in the 20th century, the community we take our moral cues from is the nation. It is from this large and encompassing community that we learn most of our important moral lessons as well as the language to articulate their meaning and force. The patriotic refrain that runs something to the effect, "that's not the way 'we' do things around here," is, therefore, at bottom a moral one, since it stakes out where "we" as a people stand with regard to the good—indicating which desires, values, actions, and forms of life are worthy of "us" as a people and which are unworthy.

Before I try to fit sports into this moral picture, however, I want to first sharpen my claim that nations can, and often do, function as moral communities for their members. I want to sharpen this claim by distinguishing it from Appiah's apparently compatible claim that "nations morally matter, when they do . . . as things desired by autonomous agents, whose autonomous desires we ought to acknowledge . . . even if we cannot always accede to them" (1: p. 28).[1] Appiah's rendering has the virtue of recognizing that the moral standing of nations rises or falls according to the regard in which they are held by their members. But it has the defect of mistaking what that regard consists in. For when nations morally matter, it is not our simple desiring them that confers their moral significance but the fact that they are normative of our desires. That is to say, nations morally matter, when they do, because they belong to the class of what Taylor (26: p. 120) calls strongly valued goods, and it is the mark of such goods that they "are not seen as good by the fact that we desire them, but rather . . . are seen as goods which we ought to desire, even if we do not, goods such that we show ourselves as inferior or bad by our not desiring them." Appiah's account of the moral valence of national communities gets it exactly backward, then, since in reducing patriotism to the desires and preferences of its members it fails to see how as a strongly valued good patriotism belongs rather to the evaluative frameworks by which we assess the moral worth of our desires, not to mention make sense of our moral lives. That is why when love of country and the sense of community it excites assume moral significance for "us," they become so much a part of who "we" are, of our conception of ourselves as moral beings that, as Larmore (10: p. 130) writes, "to imagine them as objects of choice would be to imagine ourselves as without a guiding sense of morality—and so not only ill-equipped to actually choose them, but also lacking the right sort of identification to them."

What role do sports play here? The answer, I contend, is a large and significant one. For if morality is best thought of as a vernacular language, as the common language of the community we identify with, and if the national community is the community that commands our primary loyalty and the one, therefore, by which we set our moral compass, then sports are an important way we learn to speak this national language in morally intelligent terms. That is to say, sports are themselves a kind of language (where language is broadly understood to include not just the words we speak and write but the various gestures, movements, actions, rituals, and symbols we use to communicate with our peers), which, in telegraphing the values and beliefs that are most dear to the (national) communities we belong to, provide us narrative glimpses into the moral character of our communities. They are able to do this by constantly reminding us who we are and who we might yet hope to become by spinning yarns that convey an image of the people we claim to be now and aspire to be in the future.

But I can put this point about the narrative contributions of sports in yet another way that chimes with my claim that nationalism is best thought of as a strongly valued good rather than a simple preference. For it is characteristic of such strongly valued goods, as Taylor (27: p. 91) tells us further, that they "only exist for us through some articulation," only "become available for the people of a given culture through being given expression in some manner." Sports, I want to argue, are an important, perhaps even a paradigmatic, form in which such expression takes place.[2] Their expressive capacity is tied here, as it was above, to their narrative prowess, to the stories they churn out that speak to our cultural values and attachments. And I want to claim that one of the chief narrative roles sports play in the modern era, a role enshrined, for example, in such global sporting events as the Olympic Games, the Commonwealth Games, and the World Cup, is showing how the unfolding stories of the lives of individual people are bound up with the unfolding stories of the different nations and cultures to which they claim allegiance, thereby infusing those lives with a moral sense of purpose and meaning they might otherwise not have.[3]

Are Sports Really Moral Vehicles of Nationalist Sentiment?

I have asserted much and argued little to this point. What is more, my preliminary remarks concerning the narrative potential of sports and their moral meaning for nations are too abstract and fuzzy to be of more than rhetorical use. It is time, therefore, to flesh out these introductory claims, to put some argumentative meat on them, and to clarify their import. I intend to do so by raising and responding to a serious objection that challenges headlong my claim that sports are a morally rich language of nationalism.

That objection claims, contrarily, that sports are more suited for nation-bashing than moral edification since their main story-lines are just too enmeshed in stereotypical tales of cultural superiority to be of any moral consequence. More particularly, it contends that sports are incapable of articulating a compelling moral account of nations because they lack the kind of deep and nuanced expression it would take to convey adequately the force of strongly valued goods like nationalism.

Umberto Eco had something very much like this criticism in mind when he linked the language of sports, which he pejoratively referred to as "sports chatter," to Heidegger's famous (or should I say infamous) notion of "idle talk." Quoting Heidegger directly, Eco (3: pp. 164-165) recounts that "idle talk is the possibility of understanding everything without previously making the thing one's own. . . . Idle talk . . . not only releases one from the task of genuinely understanding but develops an undifferentiated kind of intelligibility for which nothing is closed off any longer." Since sports chatter is for Eco merely a variant of idle talk, it is not difficult to divine what qualifies it for the stereotypical role it is alleged to play in our discoursing about nations. For by inducing people to speak their mind freely about anything and everything—which is what happens when any requirement that they understand just who or what it is they are conversing about is waived, as it apparently is in talk about sports—it opens up a conversational space in which stereotypes can do their best nasty work. Sports are able to do little else, or so Eco argues, because the language they speak is not equipped either for "comprehension" or "discovery." Indeed, all that it is equipped for, and all that it is really interested in, is to make sure "that there is talk." And while Eco acknowledges that even this lowly form of talk plays a salutary role in our conversations with others, what Eco calls a "phatic" one that by keeping the conversation going paves the way for more substantial talk, he denies sports even this faint praise. That is because he can detect in the stories narrated by sports nothing but a "continuous phatic discourse," one that in mistakenly thinking itself to be an end-in-itself never gets beyond its own incessant chatter, never leads to anything more insightful and, hence, more promising, since it is continually caught up in the self-importance of its own talk. What sports offer us as narrative forms, then, comes to precious little, what Eco (3: pp. 64-65) sums up as "contact without any message." This is why he likens sports chatter to "a radio that is turned on but not tuned in, so a background noise and some static inform us that we are, indeed, in a kind of communication with something, but the radio doesn't allow us to know anything."

If Eco is right, then we should expect to find sports literally awash in stereotypes of every conceivable kind, and, of course, of the nationalist kind we are presently considering. And with regard to the latter at least, this is precisely what O'Donnell (17: p. 345) claims to have uncovered in his study of sporting discourse about nations, noting how talk about sports, and in particular sports reporting, in Europe and throughout the world is distinguished in large measure by its "stereotyping of national character to a wide and socially differentiated audience." Whereas at the turn of the 20th century the stereotyping of nations took as its point of departure the absence of (modern) sports in foreign lands, an absence that was construed to be a sign of cultural weakness if not an indication, as Roden (21: p. 511) put it, that these unsporting nations "deserved to be colonized by the bold and athletic," today, argues O'Donnell, this brand of stereotyping takes as its point of departure caricatures of the contrasting styles in which countries engage in sports (sports which, given the remarkable success of Western ludic diffusion, vary hardly at all from one country to the next both with respect to kind and to formal properties such as rules). O'Donnell claims to have discovered in these various athletic styles, then, what amounts to an elaborate athletic taxonomy of national stereotypes. According to the terms of this taxonomy (17: pp. 348-352), athletes from Nordic countries are discursively marked by their "cool," "clinical" approach to sports; those from England by their "no-nonsense, workmanlike, never-say-die" style of play; those from Germany by their "machine-like" efficiency; those from South American and Latin American countries by their "temperamental," "passionate," "hedonistic" flair; and those from African nations by their "magical," "deft" flourishes. Most but not all of these descriptions—a point I will come back to later—are, O'Donnell tells us, imposed in the sense that they neither originated with nor were accepted as adequate or appropriate self-descriptions by the members of these nations. And all of them, he relates further, suggest something unflattering about the nations so characterized. For example, the depiction of Nordic sports as "cool" and "clinical" suggests a certain lack of charisma and dynamism among Nordic peoples, a charisma and dynamism that is held out to be, even if only implicitly, the mark of a more culturally advanced and sophisticated people (17: p. 347).

What is of further interest about O'Donnell's account is that it claims that underlying this athletic schema of national stereotyping is a macro-discourse of sorts, one that connects the global world of sports with the global economy in drawing a boundary between athletically and economically advantaged nations and disadvantaged ones. In European circles, this boundary marks off the "industrious" and prosperous north from the "indolent" and struggling south. Notwithstanding, then, the negative underbelly of the athletic stereotyping of northern European countries, O'Donnell (17: p. 353) thinks the contrast between the "industrious British," the "disciplined Germans," the "cool" and "rational" Swedes, and the "hedonistic," "temperamental," "reckless," and "irrational" manner of Southern European, Latin American, South American, and African athletes, is too obvious to ignore. Moreover, he notes that this macro-discourse gets replayed within nations that are perceived to lie at the periphery of this divide, in which efforts are made to redraw the boundary so as to nullify the stereotype. This would explain, for instance, why soccer fans from northern Italian football clubs often greet rivals from southern clubs with banners referring to them as Africans, and why a leading European newspaper proclaimed that "for many Italians, Africa begins in Catania and Palermo" (17: p. 371).

All told, O'Donnell's empirical evidence and the argument that underlies it appear to strengthen Eco's contention that sporting narratives are more suited for stereotypical than moral expression. Taken together, then, they make for a compelling case against my thesis that sports are a morally rich language of nationalism.

Rejoinders

Or do they? While it would be foolish to dismiss out of hand the force of Eco's argument and O'Donnell's supporting argument and accompanying empirical evidence, it would be equally foolish, I should like to argue, to accede to their main claims. It would be foolish to do so since we have good reason to question their main premise that sports are nothing more than forms of phatic discourse, forms whose stereotypical evocations of chauvinism can be traced to their ingrained inarticulacy.

For starters, we need only revisit Eco's thesis regarding the relation of phatic to substantive discourse to become suspicious of his unsparing criticism of sports. According to that thesis, wherever we find substantive speech of the moral sort that presently concerns us, we should be able to find instances of "idle talk" (and so the likely use of stereotypes) that are said to keep alive the possibility of morally robust speech. So the important question is not why Eco thought discourse about sports would be occasioned by "idle talk," but rather why he thought they would not also be occasioned by substantive moral talk. I can find nothing in his argument to support this conclusion save his dogmatic insistence that it is so. And while I might be prepared on the basis of such insistence (and, no doubt, without it) to accept that there are forms of talk that seem to leave little room for anything else but mindless prating—faculty meetings and receptions come quickly to mind—I am not prepared to do so with regard to sporting narratives.

But my reluctance here has less to do with Eco's apparent violation of his own account of the relation between phatic and substantive speech in his treatment of sports talk, which as we have just seen seems to be based on nothing more than a prejudice against sports, and more to do with his central claim that sports are narratively suspect owing to their inarticulacy, their inability to tell us anything about the national character of the peoples who take them up, that is of any moral consequence. And here O'Donnell's tracking down the source of this inarticulacy to the different styles in which nations engage in (Western) sports that are otherwise identical proves crucial. For it suggests where we need to look to confirm or disconfirm their criticism of sports. Since, however, the premises that drive this criticism of athletic styles are largely unstated, even if the conclusion drawn from them is all too clear, these first need to be laid out. This will require some reconstruction of their main argument.

The key question here is why O'Donnell thought, aside from the evidence he gathered—and, of course, the evidence he chose to ignore—that the different ways in which national teams play sports lend themselves exclusively to stereotypical, rather than moral, expression, one which privileges the nations of the dominant West at the expense of everyone else. I believe the answer, or at least the beginning of such an answer, points us to the Western provenance of these sports. For as we have previously remarked upon, the sports that are the subject of these stylistic experiments are all, or nearly all, Western ones. Not only that, the manner in which these sports are organized, governed, and capitalized is distinctly Western as well.[4] And to show just how deep the Western roots of these sports run, the very notion of using sports as markers of national identity is also a Western one.

Sketched from this angle, the picture we get of Western sports is not a particularly pretty one. For it would appear that the non-dominant nations of the East and West had little choice but to emulate the sporting practices and ways of the dominant West, to seek their athletic fortunes, and the public reputations that follow in their wake, in terms set exclusively by that West. That is not to say that the former nations have not been good pupils, for indeed they have learned the sports of their masters so well that they regularly beat them at their own games (5: p. 179). Nor is it to say that these frequent athletic reversals of fortune did not resonate with subaltern nations, for as Perkins (19: p. 151) tells us, the expatriates and former colonists of, to take but one example, England thought so highly of their athletic triumphs over the mother country that they regarded them as "rites of passage," as proof of their "fitness for home rule." Rather, the point is that the Western-ness of these sports seriously limits their narrative depth and scope because it forecloses alternative forms of expression that address and speak to the sense of belonging, beliefs, and values of non-dominant Eastern and Western peoples.

What is being claimed, then, is that in emulating the sports of the dominant West, dominated nations have lost far more than they have gained. For whatever notoriety they might have gained from their impressive athletic successes and from the artful (stylized) manner in which they were achieved is overshadowed by the fact that what they were emulating was not theirs, was not a reflection or expression of their own cultural sensibilities, attunements, and attachments but of those of their dominant Western neighbors. This is the source of Orlando Patterson's (18: p. 24) plaintive cry that cricket is a game West Indians "have been forced to love" because it is the only real culture they have, but also something they "must despise for what it has done to them." For what it has done to them by supplanting their own indigenous games and sports is deprive them of their own history and public culture. Varying the style in which sports of this Western ilk are played, therefore, counts for little for the same reason that speaking the language of one's oppressors in stylized ways counts for little: Both are forced to make do with basic vocabularies whose criteria of what counts as a rational belief, what counts as a meaningful action, and what counts as a bona fide value, preemptively rules out alternative beliefs as rational ones, alternative actions as meaningful ones, and alternative values as genuine ones. It is thus apparent that not only are Western sports unable to provide different narrative slants on the different nations that engage them because they are unable to articulate the manifold senses in which they see themselves and wish others to see them, but that they cannot but help to subjugate peoples whose beliefs, values, and aspirations do not conform to those of the dominant West. So while modern sports might be a useful tool for drawing attention to the athletic prowess and stylistic ingenuity of *lumpen* nations, they are a self-effacing tool all the same, which makes them an impoverished, not a rich, language of nationalist self-expression.

I have been arguing that the best face we can put on Eco's and O'Donnell's misgivings regarding the narrative promise of sports is precisely the one laid out here, one which takes these sports to task owing to their thorough-going Western-ness. It is the best face we can put on these misgivings because it fleshes out their main argument without setting up a straw man, which, as is true of all straw man arguments, can easily be knocked down. For the criticism as stated constitutes a powerful indictment of the articulative limits of Western sports. If nothing else, it exposes how precious little of the cultural traditions of dominated nations inform the sports played and revered in international circles today, and how in sports, as in seemingly everything else, Westerners have largely had their way with everyone else. But for all its power, it is, I want to argue, a flawed objection in at least two important respects.

First, the case it makes against Western sports—in effect, that they form a seamless monocultural system that crowds out alternative forms of cultural and national expression—is overstated. For although most of the sports that are contested in international athletic circles today are indeed Western ones, there are plenty of such sports to go around to induce, even among quintessential Westerners like Americans, what MacAloon (11: p. 100) aptly refers to as a certain "Babel of tongues." As he argues in this regard, "the average American can make just about as much out of Judo, team handball, or biathlon, as the average Sri Lankan can out of basketball, or the average Kenyan out of gymnastics, ice hockey, or synchronized swimming." Further, other international sports such as foot-racing, throwing and jumping events, and wrestling, notwithstanding the Western imprint of their modernization, resonate just about everywhere because they can be found just about everywhere. This would explain, for example, why the modern sport of boxing flourished in contemporary Africa, given the deep roots of the sport in its ancient warrior traditions.

But the main problem with this rebuff of the articulative prowess of modern sports is the skewed picture of emulation that underpins it. The culprit here is, I believe, an overly robust conception of national identity, a too rigid notion of cultural authenticity, which trades in the specious belief that nations are monolithic, absolutely disjoint communities. It is one thing, in this regard, to claim that, so long as dominated nations judge themselves in all areas by the canons of dominant nations, they will remain in a subordinate position. But it is something else again to claim that dominated nations must divine all of their cultural beliefs and values in isolation from all other nations, that the social construction of nation-ness is somehow vitiated if it incorporates beliefs and values that are not original to these nations. The first claim is surely right if only because a nation that sees itself exclusively in the terms set by other nations is hardly a nation at all, since it lacks an identity of its own, let alone a subordinate one. But the second claim is surely false if only because it willfully disregards the role that cultural borrowing plays in the formation and development of any nation, of how such cultural mongrelization can help shape the life and culture of nations in ways that further, rather than undermine, their sense of themselves as distinctive peoples.[5] In denying this, in insisting that any beliefs, values, and social practices that come from the outside be spurned simply because they come from the outside, it is not hard to see why emulation, no matter the kind, comes to grief on this account, comes off looking like a recipe for cultural ruin. This is, to take but one prominent example, precisely the view that inspired the 19th century French ultra nationalist Jules Michlelet's (30: p. 139) blanket condemnation of would be cultural imitators. "Poor imitators," he sardonically remarked, "take from a neighboring people this or that which among them is a living thing; they appropriate it to themselves . . . in spite of the repugnance of a frame that was not made for it: but it is a foreign body that you are engrafting in your flesh . . . it is death you are adopting."

Of course, the present criticism of athletic emulation does not go quite this far. But it does, I want to argue, work from a not entirely dissimilar strong conception of nation-ness, one that does little to weaken the identification of cultural imitation with cultural degeneracy. And it is this fact, I want to argue, that accounts for its blinkered treatment of emulation, its wholesale dismissal of cultural borrowing. What is blinkered about its treatment is not its suspicion of emulative gestures as such, a suspicion which in certain cases is, no doubt, well founded, but rather its insistence that all such gestures can be lumped under the same family of ingratiating behavior that Veblen (29) famously skewered in his classic treatise *The Theory of the Leisure Class.* According to Veblen, the emulation of the beliefs, values, and practices of others always comes off as ingratiating because it always occurs in the context of the class hierarchical terms that define, better plague, modern society. It is that context, then, that dooms the emulative impulse, since it yokes it to the pathetic and largely futile attempt by social "inferiors" to advance up the rungs of the social ladder by gaining the good graces of their "superiors." Transpose the hierarchical class terms of modern society into the hierarchical nationalist terms of the same, and presto, we get the present criticism of athletic emulation, which reduces it to the same sort of one-sided, inauthentic seeking of the good opinion of dominant nations by dominated ones.

It would be churlish to claim that athletic emulation is immune to this kind of nation-pandering. But it would be equally churlish to claim, as the present criticism does, that it is reducible to such nation-pandering, that all instances of emulation, athletic or otherwise, conform and must conform to this same pattern of ingratiating behavior. For the point is that emulation comes in many different varieties.[6] And at least one variety it comes in, which I want to argue redeems my claim that modern sports qualify as a rich language of nationalist expression, contains none of the offending features noted in this objection. That is because this brand of athletic emulation does inculcate a sense that what nations are emulating is indeed theirs, is an integral part of who they claim to be and where they claim to stand with regard to the good. The sort of self-confirming emulation I have in mind here is exemplified in the dramatic shift apparent between the regard for modern (English) sports shown by 19th century Germans, who initially greeted the introduction of these sports to their native soil with the derisive refrain "Der Sport ist undeutsch," and that shown by their contemporary, 20th century West

German counterparts, who, following the stunning victory of the their national team over the formidable Hungarian team in the 1954 World Cup, triumphantly declared, "Wir sind wieder wer" (We are somebody again).[7] The kind of athletic emulation instanced in the latter self-assertion is, I want to argue, an altogether different animal than the kind lampooned by Veblen and the criticism above, and, therefore, should not be conflated with it.

In order to tease out this alternative sense of athletic emulation, however, it is necessary to cast the emulative successes of dominated nations in a different light. What I have in mind here is anticipated by Walzer's (32: p. 529) claim that "moral makers . . . are like artists or writers who pick up elements of one another's style, or even borrow plots, not for the sake of imitation but in order to strengthen their own work. So we make ourselves better without making ourselves the same." This is a picture of emulation, of cultural borrowing, that goes beyond mere mimicry, since it makes room for the possibility that Western sports and the tropes they generate are capable of a fuller range of expression, one that is not hemmed in by their Western-ness. What is more, this is a picture of emulation that points us back to and enjoins us to take seriously the contrasting styles in which different nations engage in these sports, to consider the possibility that, contra O'Donnell, such variations in style lend themselves to genuine and alternative expressions of moral and cultural meaning rather than to mere stereotypical caricature. For if Walzer is right, then it would be a mistake to treat such stylistic alterations, whether they occur in literature or in sports, as simple reproductions or recapitulations of old, familiar meanings, and better to regard them as possible fertile sites for the articulation of new meanings. Following Walzer's lead in this regard does not require that we deny what we have already conceded: namely, that the menu of Western sports offered at international settings as well as their formal rationality and organizational structure are mostly the same. Rather, it only requires that we deny that the meanings different nations wring from these sports are the same. To put the same point positively, it only requires that we acknowledge the ingenuity of peoples in teasing new meanings out of old, familiar ones, and the textual plasticity (facility for stylistic innovation) of sporting narratives in turning out culturally inflected stories.[8]

The way such stylistic alterations in modern sports lead to the creation of disparate meanings that reflect the manifold senses in which nations see and regard themselves is, then, *pace* Walzer, not unlike the way such stylistic alterations in literary tropes written in modern, "world" languages like English produce much the same result. John Updike's musings on literary stylistic innovations are instructive in this regard precisely because they speak directly to the dilemma faced by authors installed in different parts of the world who write in the "mother tongue." While "most Australians and Americans," he remarks, "write English with no thought of an alternative; others, like certain inhabitants of the Caribbean, Ireland, Anglophone Africa, and India, write it against a background of native tongues or patois that are abandoned or suppressed in the creative effort—an effort that to a degree enlists them in a foreign if not enemy camp, that of the Colonizer" (28: p. 156). Dilemma, yes; insuperable obstacle, no, or so Updike argues. For writing English need not raise the specter of the "Colonizer," he insists, so long as it is sufficiently experimental, so long as it is inclined to stylistic interventions whose point is to transform English into a truly multicultural language, one in which it makes sense to say, with Rushdie (24: p. 54), that "Indian English . . . is not 'English' English . . . any more than Irish or American or Caribbean English is." Surveying some of this "non-English" English work, particularly that produced by Indian writers, Updike details the various stylistic devices they have successfully employed to render English more conducive to their own, unique cultural messages. In particu lar, he cites their use of "compound and coined words, fragmentary sentences, paragraphs a word or a phrase long, whimsical capitalization" (28: p. 156)—all of which, he argues, lend English the eccentric touch it must have if it is to convey the cultural differences these authors wish to get across to their audiences.

The very same, as I noted, can be claimed of modern (Western) sports. Indeed, it can be claimed in even stronger terms here. For the fact is that for most nations of the world today modern sports are played with little or no thought of an alternative.[9] If sports differ at all from their literary counterparts, therefore, it is in the almost universal and self-conscious manner in which the subordinate nations of the world have embraced modern sports over traditional ones, so much so that concerted efforts to forget and (or) suppress the latter figure in this equation hardly at all. What joins (English) literary and (modern) sport practices at the hip, however, is their mutual reliance on stylistic innovations to convey the cultural differences peoples of all stripes seem eager to attribute to and express through them.

Examples of such experimental forms of emulation abound in sports and appear to come in at least three varieties. Enrique Krauze's account of how Mexican soccer players contrived their own way of playing this worldly game against the backdrop of the two prevailing styles of play associated with European and Latin American countries represents one such form and perhaps the standard one. Europeans, remarked Krauze (7: p. 20), play soccer in a manner that is suggestive of "prose," a game that is marked by its "tough, premeditated, systematic, [and] collective" play. By contrast, Latin Americans honed a playing style that is redolent of "poetry," a more fluid

approach to the game that is "ductile, spontaneous, individual, [and] erotic."
In order to put their own national stamp on soccer, therefore, Mexican
players had to devise their own distinctive style, and they did this by mixing
and matching the above styles until they hit on one of their own. They were
thus able to craft a different sort of game, Krauze tells us, one "built on quick
touch, continuous movement, individual brilliance, [and] stoic resistance,"
which better suited, in their eyes, their own self-image as a people.

The Japanese appropriation of American baseball in the late 19th century
suggests a second kind of creative athletic emulation. In this case, what was
appropriated was not just the style but the very content of baseball itself, a
sport whose measured pace and repertoire of skilled movements was
adjudged by Japanese schoolboys of the era to be ideally suited to the
expression of the cultural beliefs and values of the Japanese people. Baseball
was thus singled out because, as Roden (21: p. 520) tells us, "unlike the
mindless tackling and punching . . . sanctioned in American contact sports,"
baseball required "concentration and finesse." In other words, it required a
style of play that cultivated, to their way of thinking, the civic virtues (order,
harmony, and self-restraint) of traditional Japanese society, which would
explain their delight in comparing the "skilled batter" with the "samurai
swordsmen" as well as their fondness for "embellished descriptions of
[baseball sprinkled] with poetic allusions to medieval warrior epics" (21: p.
520). And, of course, they played the game in a manner that capitalized on
these civic virtues. We thus had at the dawn of the 19th century the odd, but
not inchoate, specter of Americans, quite deliberately and resolutely, playing baseball to be more American and the Japanese, equally deliberately and
resolutely, playing baseball to be more Japanese.

The case of Basque soccer provides yet a third example of creative athletic
emulation. It resembles the first, Mexican soccer example insofar as Basque
players also sought to imprint their national identity on the game by
developing their own recognizable brand of play. They succeeded in this
regard by making a name for themselves by their fiery and daring play and
their long-passing game. But what differentiates the Basque appropriation
of soccer was that it was part of a larger self-conscious effort to create a
hybrid national identity for the Basque people, one that was intended to win
them long overdue recognition of their national status in the international
community. For this purpose, the Basque people enlisted both their native
language, the only non-Indo-European tongue left in the continent, and their
trademark soccer sporting culture. By featuring the former, they endeavored
to show themselves as "a very ancient people," a country with deep and
"absolutely distinctive" roots. By featuring the latter, they endeavored to
show themselves at one and the same time as "a very up-to-date" nation, as

modern and as forward-thinking as any of its dominant Western neighbors (13: p. 197). In this complicated mix, then, sports played a modernizing role, but one shorn of its cultural-neutralizing effects.

What distinguishes these creative forms of athletic emulation from their distant stereotypical cousins, which also, as O'Donnell forcefully argued, take their point of departure from contrasting styles of play, is that the stylistic interventions they engineered enabled rather than impeded the collective self-expression of these marginalized nations. This explains why they were able to recognize themselves in the narratives that were the product of these emulative efforts, and why, therefore, they were mostly absent the ingratiating features that bedevil other forms of athletic emulation. In saying this, however, I am not saying that emulative gestures of this creative genre are impervious to stereotypical distortion, that the story-telling they touch off cannot be invidiously redescribed to stoke chauvinist fires. No such immunity can be accorded for the simple reason that no narrative, whatever its emulative pedigree, is safe from the long and menacing arms of the stereotype, that is, can prevent its self-affirming descriptions from being redescribed in self-deprecating ways.

Still, some narrative tellings prove more resistant to such stereotypical mischief and their pernicious effects. And this is the case, I contend, with regard to sporting narratives that owe their voice and authority to the above forms of creative emulation. For when these narratives are allowed to do their work, they function in just the manner we have previously suggested: as rich languages of national self-assertion that help to define the social and moral terms in which disparate peoples make sense of their public, collective lives. To live within the frameworks such narratives stake out, therefore, is to experience the cluster of beliefs, values, and actions that they sanction as more worthy of us as a people than other such clusters of beliefs, values, and actions. That is why the demands these narrative frameworks place on their protagonists have the normative force that they do—that is, are seen by them as commitments to be honored, rather than, as in the case of stereotypes, self-incriminating descriptions to be shunned. Indeed, the normative pull such narratives exert is the very opposite one of that of stereotypes, for the mark of moral success or failure in the case of stereotypes lies in our ability to circumvent the demands they seek to impose, whereas the mark of moral success and failure in the case of these narratives lies in our ability to live up to the demands they set out for us. This explains why the perfectly understandable desire to be free of the baleful influence of stereotypes has no analog in the kinds of narratives we have been discussing, for the desire to live outside any of the frameworks they provide is neither understandable nor desirable, since it is tantamount to wishing to chart a course for our life without a social or moral rudder to guide it.[10] That is why a life lived in the absence of such frameworks, Taylor (27: p. 18) cautions, is a life more likely to be characterized by "a terrifying emptiness," by the sense that "nothing is worth doing" because there is nothing in our life that has any real meaning that might incite us to action.[11]

What, however, of O'Donnell's related claim that the stereotyping of nations is common even among dominant nations? This is a relevant question if only because it points us to a previously unremarked feature of O'Donnell's thesis that claims that sports are stereotypical modes of expression *in extremis*, not just because they taint the poor and the powerless but because they also taint the rich and the powerful. And since our discussion so far has focused only on the first of these, on how poor nations are stereotyped by sports and yet are able to undercut such stereotyping by emulating them in creative ways, we are not out of the woods yet in alleging a more ennobling (moral) role for sporting narratives. We can, of course, safely presume that dominant Western nations are able to avail themselves of the same creative emulative strategies adopted by dominated ones, and do them one better since they have the greater resources and power to enact such strategies. But we cannot simply presume that doing so will rid the sports they play of their stereotypical taint unless we know something more about this sort of athletic stereotyping. At the very least, then, we need to explain this form of athletic stereotyping before we consider how it might be effectively countered.

To begin with the explanation, there are a variety of ways to account for such stereotyping, some of which are compatible with O'Donnell's thesis and at least one of which is not. With regard to the compatible ones, it could be argued, simply, that dominant nations are all sufficiently powerful and resourceful enough to tweak one another in sports and, certainly, outside them. It could be argued further, as O'Donnell himself in this case did argue, that there are stereotypes and there are stereotypes, and that some are more benign in their effects than others. Among examples of the benign sort are stereotypes that besmirch the name of dominant nations in ways that not only do not challenge their dominance but, in fact, help to solidify it. (O'Donnell's examples included, as noted previously, the "industrious British," the "disciplined Germans," and the "cool and rational Swedes.") And it could be argued further in this vein, and for my purposes finally, that even dominated nations have the wherewithal on occasion to tweak their dominant counterparts, and that perhaps, in light of their athletic successes, sports afford such nations the greatest opportunity to do so.

As I said, I find all three of these explanations plausible. But I do not find them fully persuasive because there is an even more plausible explanation for O'Donnell's claim that stereotyping is rife even in the athletic discourse of dominant nations. And that is that he is confused about what counts as a stereotype and what does not. I want to pursue this explanation, however, not just because I find it the most plausible one, but because it provides an answer to my second question as well, one that suggests that sports are not exclusively or foremost stereotypical instruments. For on all of the above explanations, sports come off as just such one-dimensional stereotypical devices, no matter whether they are deployed by the rich or the poor.

O'Donnell's treatment of the national stereotyping of English sports, their "never-say-die" temperament and style of play, best exemplifies the confusion of which I speak here. For if this characterization is indeed a national stereotype, then we would expect to find, first, that the English would chafe at what it has to say about them, since they would not regard it as a fitting description of their national character, and, second, that they would instinctively shirk the demands and claims it imposes on them, since they would regard those demands and claims as alien to their national character. This holds, as I argued previously, even for those who "act out" their stereotypes because they are unable, for whatever reason, to break their grip. For "acting out" a stereotype counts neither as acceptance of it nor as striving to "live up" to its accords.

According to O'Donnell's own account, however, neither of these conditions obtained in the English case. To begin with, says O'Donnell (17: p. 359), the English did not reject but heartily embraced this "never-say-die" description as a true characterization of their indomitable athletic spirit, of their refusal to give up no matter how desperate their plight. They were readily able to accept this athletic rendering of their national character, and lay claim to authorship of it, precisely because this is how they saw and regarded themselves in sporting terms. Secondly, and even more significantly to my mind, O'Donnell (17: p. 359) notes that the reason why the "rejection of the 'national' stereotype [was] least in evidence" in the English case was because failure was "explained not by shortcomings suggested by the stereotype but by the inability *to live up to* the positive aspects of the stereotype itself" (my emphasis). But if O'Donnell is right about this as well, then what we have here is not, properly understood, a stereotype at all, but a narrative framework of the sort previously discussed. For as we have said, it is characteristic of such frameworks, but not of stereotypes, that the claims they make upon us are regarded as normative ideals we are obliged to realize, not self-incriminating descriptions we are obliged to resist. To sum up then, if O'Donnell is right that the English endorsed this athletic description of their national mettle and sought to live up to the ideal it embodied, then he erred in calling it a stereotype.

The moral to be drawn from O'Donnell's apparent error here is not that dominant nations are, in fact, impervious to athletic stereotyping, for they are clearly not, but rather that such stereotyping does not differ in kind from that of dominated nations, even if the power vectors are not the same. And if that is so, then it means that this brand of athletic stereotyping can be narratively upended in much the same experimental (stylistic) ways we noted of dominated nations.

Conclusion

I have argued that one of the chief narrative roles international sports play in the modern world today is to articulate the distinctive moral identities, beliefs, and values of the nations that make it up. In doing so, I have challenged Eco's and O'Donnell's contrary contention that there is little more to such sports than the swapping of stereotypical tales of national superiority. But in trying to make my case I have tried to meet their counterargument, as well as the empirical evidence that supports it, halfway, for it must be conceded that national stereotyping is part of the lexicon of sports. That is why in pressing my thesis that sports are a morally rich language of nationalist expression I have not asked my readers to play the part of the proverbial "ostrich," and simply bury their head in the sand and ignore any claim or evidence to the contrary, but only the part of the proverbial critic, and ask whether there is more to sports and the yarns they spin than what Eco and O'Donnell allow. Answering this question, I am convinced, shows that what they have to say regarding the athletic stereotyping of nations is only part of the story, and not the most interesting or compelling part.

A final doubt. It might be rejoined that even if I have succeeded in showing that sports do indeed play a moral role in articulating the moral identities of diverse peoples, that they are more than stereotypical instruments, I have made much too much of their moral significance. It might be so rejoined because their narrative contributions have come largely in the form of recognition-gains, and while the achievement of national recognition is not without moral significance, it does not rank up there, for example, with distributive justice (that is, with the equitable distribution of such things as income and property across nations). To make matters worse, it is not just that recognition-gains pale in comparison to those of distributive justice, but that the former seems to have nothing much to do with the latter. For as the recognition of previously unrecognized and misrecognized nations has proceeded apace, thanks in no small measure to international sports, so too have the gross inequalities in income and property that distinguish the haves from the have-nots. This makes it even more difficult to regard the recognition-gains that are attributable to sports as anything more than hollow moral triumphs.

It is important, first, to understand what this criticism is not. It is not an attack on the moral salience of recognition itself, such as one finds in the Stoic counsel to disregard the opinion of others in matters of self-respect. Since for the Stoics, self-respect is something one bestows on oneself by virtue of one's humanity, it is not something that can be taken away or diminished by how one is viewed by others. And those that mistakenly think otherwise are, as Epictetus says, merely "a corpse and a gallon of blood" (15: p. 24).[12] But the moral counsel that informs the present objection is not that recognition is nothing, that seeking a public reputation is on its face wrongheaded, rather only nothing special. So what we need to defend here is not the morality of recognition as such but its moral significance.

The place to begin such a defense, and that is all that can reasonably be attempted presently, is to argue that the idea that the achievement of national recognition is not a big deal, morally speaking, is a prejudice of the dominant West. As George Bernard Shaw once said, "A healthy nation is as unconscious of its nationality as a healthy man of his bones. But if you break a nation's nationality, it will think of nothing else but getting it set again" (9: p. 68). Those of us fortunate enough to live in the prosperous West are able to take our national standing as well as the cultural security it provides us for granted precisely because it is not broken and has seldom been challenged.[13] Were this not the case, and there is no guarantee that it will remain the case, we would not be so casually disposed toward our own nationality. For those not so fortunate, however, and the subaltern peoples we spoke of earlier fall into this category, such complacency is out of the question since their nationality has frequently been broken, and seldom healthy. When viewed with our Western blinders off, then, the achievement of national recognition and the narrative accomplishments of sports in its name hardly come off as morally innocuous.[14]

The second, and for my purposes final, reason we should not be so quick to discount the moral importance of national recognition is that its attainment is, after all, crucial to the cause of distributive justice. For if the historical record tells us anything it tells us that if there is ever to be anything like distributive justice on a world scale, then those whom have been summarily denied it will have to speak up for themselves rather than be spoken for by their powerful neighbors—that is, will have to stake out their own case as to why they are the rightful beneficiaries of the resources and opportunities that are the mark of such justice. In other words, if they ever expect to be considered candidates for distributive justice, they must first be considered legitimate moral claimants, and in order to be considered legitimate moral claimants in the world today, such as it is, they will have to be first recognized and accepted as bona fide nations rather than, for example, lawless tribes. And here is where sports of the international kind, I have been arguing, do their best and most effective work. That is why I regard MacAloon's (12: p. 42) claim that "to be a nation recognized by others . . . a people must march in the Olympic Games opening ceremonies," as no idle boast, but rather as an important clue as to the true moral significance of sports and the stories they tell. For to the extent that those sports and the tales they spin have helped fledgling nations forge a name and carve out a place for themselves in the international arena, the arena in which what counts as distributive justice and how it is to be meted out gets decided, is the extent to which we should view the narrative work they do as legitimate and important moral work.

Notes

1. Two further points warrant mention here. First, the alert reader will have already noticed that I have used the notions of nationalism and patriotism interchangeably. I have done so because I regard patriotism, love of and devotion to the best traditions of one's country, to be one important strand of nationalism. Efforts to distinguish these two notions, such as that commonplace patriotism stands for love of country and nationalism for hatred of others, strike me as stipulative at best, and so as subject to the usual reproof of factual incorrectness. Second, while I reject Appiah's moral account of patriotism, I think his moral account of the state is on the mark. As he writes, "States . . . matter morally . . . because they regulate our lives through forms of coercion that will always require moral justification" (1: p. 28). I find this completely persuasive because states are foremost regulatory institutions that govern the lives of the people who inhabit them by claiming a monopoly on the "legitimate" force that may be exercised within their precincts. Since, however, my present interest is in nations, I will have nothing further to say about states, notwithstanding the complex and often deep relations that bind the two together.

2. This is my response to Rorty's (22 : p. 4) other point that "the only version of national pride encouraged by American popular culture is a simpleminded militaristic chauvinism," and to his larger point that there is a "widespread sense that [expressions of] national pride [are] no longer appropriate" in America and perhaps in the other rich Atlantic nations. I think sports are a telling exception on both counts, since I will argue that they often furnish a less chauvinistic and more positive and nuanced image of national life, to include American national life, and since many people regard them as appropriate expressions of national pride. This is not to deny that belief in things like

national pride is indeed waning. But I believe that has more to do with the fact that less and less things in our culture offer themselves up for such national expression. As Kaplan (6: p. 12) has argued, for instance, contemporary wars and military operations, unlike the two World Wars of this century, "will have increasingly little meaning for the nation," since they will assume mainly the form of small "rescue details." And as Miller (16: p. 170) has further observed, while the English used to point, justifiably so, to their constitutional democratic arrangements as proof of their national distinctiveness, today they are no longer able to do so, since those democratic arrangements have become the rule rather than the exception in most of the world.

3. In arguing that one of the chief narrative roles sports play today is to showcase the national identities of its members I am not claiming that this is its exclusive or even its primary role. It is plainly evident, for instance, that sports also express sub-national (of an ethnic, civic, and religious sort) and, less often, supra-national identities (of a cosmopolitan sort). My present emphasis on nationality, then, has only to do with my interest in international sports in which, I argue, issues of national identity are paramount.

4. Which is why Judo, the lone Olympic sport whose roots are not Western, is not a true exception, since the manner in which it is presently played and organized is decidedly Western.

5. As Walzer (31: p. 69) notes, even those nations most sure of their singular identities and cultures (the Poles and Armenians, for instance) are revealed, in fact, to be "historical composites" once their pasts are sufficiently scrutinized.

6. Guttmann gives a nice sampling of some of these other forms of athletic emulation. He cites in this regard, "the desire of anglophile Indians to adopt the costumes and the mannerisms of the elegant, self-assured cricketers they had known while at Oxford, the rush of thuggish soccer fans in Cologne to ape the violent behavior of Liverpuddlian 'football hooligans,' the urge of Trinidadian basketball players to mimic the moves of Michael Jordan, and the eagerness of young Parisians to imitate the insouciance of Californian surfers" (5: p. 177). At least some of these examples of athletic emulation are ingratiating in the sense sketched by Veblen (to include even the aping of English soccer hooligans by Germans, which constitutes something of an innovation insofar as it is, apparently, motivated by a desire to move down rather than up the social hierarchy).

7. It should be noted that the exuberance the West Germans displayed over the success of their national team was owed to two further factors. First, this was the first World Cup competition following World War II in which a German team was allowed to participate. And second, this was the initial period of the "Cold War," which meant that the victory over the Hungarians was viewed, as well, as a victory for the capitalist, free West. Indeed, in Hungary the loss sparked a near anti-Communist revolt causing much consternation among East Germany's party leaders (see 2: p. 21).

8. It should be noted here that the narrative facility claimed of Western sports in this regard, their ability to turn out culturally inflected stories that speak to the particular aims and aspirations of particular peoples, is owed in part to a universal feature of these sports. I am referring here to what Guttmann (5: p. 188) calls the "standardized universality" of Western sports, a universality

that makes it possible, he further notes, for "everyone to play the game." And a feature, I add, that makes it possible for each participating nation to play these games in their own self-styled ways. This encompassing feature of Western sports also explains in part the previously observed successes dominated nations have had in defeating dominant nations at their own games.

9. That there has been scarcely little resistance for some time now to Western sports by dominated nations is, I should note, part of my answer to the charge of coercion leveled in Orlando Patterson's previously cited claim that cricket is a game West Indians "have been forced to love." This holds true for much of the Islamic world as well, which has been much less hostile to Western sports than it has been to almost everything else Western. As Finnegan (4: p. 56) has recently observed, the embassy of the Islamic Republic of Iran in Sarajevo has prominently displayed on its front wall a glass case filled with brochures extolling the virtues of "skiing, chess, fencing, judo, squash, and handball" for fulfilling the "holy motherhood duties" of Islamic women. The second and last part of my answer to Patterson's charge is to echo Guttmann's (5: p. 179) important reminder that in the period when Western sports were forcibly imposed on dominated peoples by dominant ones, this was only half the story. As Guttmann points out, "Culturally dominated groups have often had sports imposed upon them; they have also—perhaps just as often—forced their unwelcome way into sports from which the dominant group desired to exclude them."

10. Nothing in my argument, however, suggests that people do not act out their stereotypes, nor that they even seem to do so at times willfully (though some special confusion on their part would have to obtain in this instance). Rather, what my argument rules out as incoherent is that people can be said to "live up" to (in the sense of try to fulfill) their stereotypes. Claims of this sort, I want to insist, rest on a confusion about the character of stereotypes—that is, a confusion about what such stereotypes amount to and about what sort of response is warranted from those whom they target.

11. My argument that sports are a rich language of nationalist expression does not pretend that the linguistic mileage dominated nations, at least, are able to get out of sports does not involve some sense of social loss on their part. That is because no single kind of sport, no matter how impressive its reach, can include within itself all other kinds and the different and often conflicting values associated with them. So a culture whose indigenous sports stress out-of-doors group problem-solving activities could legitimately claim to have lost something of special value to them, as an astute reviewer pointed out to me, if it found it necessary to abandon these sports for the comparative-competitive sports of the West in order to be recognized as a legitimate nation—even if they successfully managed to avoid being stereotyped in the process. There is, I think, no denying such social loss. What is open to question, however, is what to make of it. For the loss of certain valued ways of life is sometimes offset by what takes its place. How to know what counts as a net loss or gain in such instances is, of course, no easy or trifling matter, and can only be determined by muddling through, by playing off the old and new forms against one another. We can do little else in the present case of sports. But even if we come to be persuaded that Western sports constitute an

advance over traditional ones in certain key respects, social loss of one form or another will always have to be acknowledged and reckoned with in making these judgments.

12. A further reason to be suspicious of this Stoic counsel is that it is merely a variant of the previously discussed and rejected Kantian notion that morality has to do with "the voice of the divine part of ourselves"—in this case that part that determines our self-respect. The best reason for holding that there is no such divine part of ourselves is of the same kind, as MacIntyre (14: p. 69) put it, as the best reason we have for holding that there are no witches or unicorns: Every attempt to come up with such reasons has failed.

13. That is not to say that all is well with Western nations, that they are healthy in every respect. For as a reviewer insightfully observed, while the prosperity and recognition of these nations is as strong as ever, that does not mean that they are not broken in some other sense. And I am persuaded that this is right, that, for example, the decline in civic virtues and the manifest weakness of associational life in these countries has seriously weakened their national identity and sense of belonging.

14. There is one important exception to this alleged Western bias, and that is so-called liberal nationalist theorists like Kymlicka (8) and Tamir (25) who have persuasively argued that membership in a stable and secure national community is what ensures that the choices and life-plans we enact as individuals are valued and meaningful ones. That is why they regard such membership as a "primary" good in Rawls (20: p. 188) sense—that is, as something we need in order to accomplish whatever else we may want.

Bibliography

1. Appiah, K. "Cosmopolitan Patriots." In: *For Love of Country*, J. Cohen (Ed.). Boston: Beacon Press, 1996.
2. Delius, F. "In Germany, Even Soccer Is Serious." *The New Republic*. July 4:20-22, 1994.
3. Eco, U. *Travels in Hyper-Reality*. London: Pan Books, 1987.
4. Finnegan, W. "Forget About Shirts and Skins." *The New Yorker*. February 26 and March 4:56, 1996.
5. Guttmann, A. *Games and Empires*. New York: Columbia University Press, 1994.
6. Kaplan, R. *An Empire Wilderness*. New York: Random House, 1998.
7. Krauze, E. "Pri-Game, in Mexico, Soccer as Politics; Politics as Soccer." *The New Republic*. July 4:16-18, 20, 1994.
8. Kymlicka, W. *Multicultural Citizenship*. Oxford, UK: Clarendon Press, 1995.
9. Kymlicka, W. "The Sources of Nationalism." In: *The Morality of Nationalism*, R. McKim and J. McMahan (Eds.). New York: Oxford University Press, 1997.
10. Larmore, C. *The Morals of Modernity*. Cambridge, UK: Cambridge University Press, 1996.

11. MacAloon, J. "Double Visions: Olympic Games and American Culture." *Kenyon Review*. Winter:98-112, 1982.
12. MacAloon, J. "The Turn of Two Centuries: Sports and the Politics of Intercultural Relations." In: *Sport: The Third Millenium*, F. Landry, M. Landry, and M. Yerles (Eds.). Saint-Foy, France: Les Presses De L'Université Laval, 1991.
13. MacClancy, J. "Nationalism at Play: The Basques of Vizcaya and Athletic Bilbao." In: *Sport, Identity, and Ethnicity*, J. MacClancy (Ed.). New York: New York University Press, 1996.
14. MacIntyre, A. *After Virtue*. Notre Dame, IN: University of Notre Dame Press, 1984.
15. Margalit, A. *The Decent Society*. Cambridge, MA: Harvard University Press, 1996.
16. Miller, D. *On Nationality*. Oxford, UK: Clarendon Press, 1995.
17. O'Donnell, H. "Mapping the Mythical: A Geopolitics of National Sporting Stereotypes." *Discourse and Society*. 5:345-380, 1994.
18. Patterson, O. "The Ritual of Cricket." *Jamica Journal*. 3:24, 1969.
19. Perkins, H. "Teaching Nations How to Play: Sport and Society in the British Empire and Commonwealth." *International Journal of the History of Sport*. 6:145-155, 1989.
20. Rawls, J. *Political Liberalism*. New York: Columbia University Press, 1993.
21. Roden, D. "Baseball and the Quest for National Dignity in Meiji Japan." *American Historical Review*. 85:511-534, 1980.
22. Rorty, R. *Achieving Our Country*. Cambridge, MA: Harvard University Press, 1998.
23. Rorty, R. *Contingency, Irony, and Solidarity*. Cambridge, UK: Cambridge University Press, 1989.
24. Rushdie, S. "Damme, This Is the Oriental Scene for You." *The New Yorker*. June 23 and 30:50-54, 1997.
25. Tamir, Y. *Liberal Nationalism*. Princeton, NJ: Princeton University Press, 1993.
26. Taylor, C. *Philosophy and the Human Sciences, Philosophical Papers II*. Cambridge, UK: Cambridge University Press, 1985.
27. Taylor, C. *Sources of the Self: The Making of the Modern Identity*. Cambridge, UK: Cambridge University Press, 1989.
28. Updike, J. "The God of Small Things, 'BeachBoy'." *The New Yorker*. June 23 and 30:156-161, 1997.
29. Veblen, T. *The Theory of the Leisure Class*. New York: Mentor Books, 1953.
30. Viroli, M. *For Love of Country*. Oxford, UK: Clarendon Press, 1995.
31. Walzer, M. *Thick and Thin: Moral Argument at Home and Abroad*. Notre Dame, IN: University of Notre Dame Press, 1994.
32. Walzer, M. "Two Kinds of Universalism." In: *The Tanner Lectures on Human Values*. Salt Lake City: University of Utah Press, 1990.

CHAPTER

Is Our Admiration for Sports Heroes Fascistoid?

Torbjörn Tännsjö

Introduction

Already looking forward to the Olympic Games in Sydney at the turn of the millennium, I try to recollect what happened last time in Atlanta. How did I react? I realize that once again I was swept away with enthusiasm and admiration for those heroic athletes who had stretched the limits of what is physically possible for humans to achieve. Some have run faster than anyone has done before. This is true of Michael Johnson. Others have excelled and shown that, contrary to what should have been expected, they are—still—invincible. This is true of the greatest of them all, Carl Lewis. My query is: Is my enthusiasm for Johnson, Lewis, and all the other athletic heroes, respectable? Upon closer examination, my answer is *no*. My enthusiasm is not respectable. On the contrary, it is of a fascistoid[1] nature. So the problem is really what to do about it. The problem is pressing, for my attitude toward the Games is not exceptional. I share it with a great many other people who walk this planet. This is why the games were so widely broadcast.

Many people have pointed out that there is something unhealthy in much of the public interest in team sports on an elitist level. There was a time in

Reprinted, by permission, from T. Tännsjö, 1998, "Is our admiration for sports heroes fascistoid?," *Journal of the Philosophy of Sport, XXV:* 23-34.

many European countries when the Workers' Movement fought actively against the growing interest in sports. This concern has withered, but the rationale behind it remains relevant. As a matter of fact, team sports have often been used by nationalist governments to create a chauvinist zeal in their own populations. This zeal has rendered easier the formation of totalitarian government, oppression of minorities at home, and imperialist adventures abroad. National sports teams have become emblems of their respective nations. These facts are rather obvious. It is also obvious that some of the interest that most people take in elitist sports events is nourished by these kinds of nationalistic sentiments. The interest as such reinforces the nationalism. This is indeed a vicious circle. But what about the public interest in the individual athletes in the Olympics? Should it be condemned because it reinforces an unhealthy nationalism?

To some extent it certainly does. Even individual athletes may become the target of these kinds of sentiments. Johnson and Lewis have reinforced U.S. nationalist sentiments. I am, on my part, more interested when a Swede succeeds in the Olympics, than when someone else does. But this cannot be the only source of my interest in the Olympic games. For my main interest is in the achievements of people like Johnson and Lewis. So perhaps much (the main part) of my admiration for their achievements is, after all, respectable? Perhaps much of the general interest taken in the games is respectable?

If this were the case, there would be room for optimism. For it seems to be part of the received wisdom that nationalism within sports withers. When big business in the form of international enterprises enter the arena, in the manner of sponsoring, advertising, and selling and buying television rights, national governments have to go. Often, the foreign NHL professionals do not bother to take part with their respective national teams. Instead of nationalism and interest on the part of the public in one's "own" team, admiration comes for the achievement of the outstanding individual. Local teams turn into corporations. And these corporations are seen as places where the outstanding individual can excel. However, this interest in the achievement of the outstanding individual is really no better than our (perhaps outmoded) nationalistic interest in the fate of "our" own team. Or so I will argue in this paper.

My thesis is that our admiration for the achievements of the great sports heroes, such as the athletes that triumph at the Olympics, reflects a fascistoid ideology. While nationalism may be dangerous and has often been associated with fascism, what is going on in our enthusiasm for individual athletic heroes is even worse. Our enthusiasm springs from the very core of fascist ideology.

Note that my thesis is not that there is anything fishy about the motives of the athletes themselves. I say nothing about this. Nor do I condemn those who organize sports events, those who train young people to become members of the athletic elite, or those who profit from the games, and so forth. In the present context, the *exclusive* target of my criticism is what goes on within the enormous, world-wide public, watching sports, usually through television. My interest is in the values entertained by you and me, we who tend, over and over again, to get carried away by such events as the Olympic Games.

Traditional Team Sports on an Elitist Level

Before developing my main argument, let me briefly comment on why it is a bad thing to have nationalistic values expressed and reinforced by publicly broadcast sports events. If this is a kind of danger in relation to elite sports that is becoming outmoded, and so it seems to be, it might be interesting to reflect on what it is we are getting rid of. When we see this more clearly, we are on firmer ground in our investigation of the new kind of danger we exchanged for the old one.

The main problem with nationalism is its orientation towards abstract symbols: the flag, the team (seen as an emblem), and yes, even the nation conceived of abstractly. When such entities are celebrated, the individual tends to become replaceable. The nation can get strong, it can be successful, even if each and every one of its citizens suffers. This individual suffering need not matter in the very least to the nationalistic ideology. In a similar vein, when the team becomes a representative of the nation, *its* individual members tend to become replaceable. When our football or soccer heroes are successful, we cheer for them. When they fail "us," we despise them.

This way of regarding our sports stars as representatives of our country, conceived of abstractly, fits with a common view of the military force. It may easily spread and permeate all the relations between people in a country. Young women are treated as potential instruments that shall safeguard the strength and survival of the nation; young men are viewed merely as potential soldiers, and so forth.

One might object that this is only a description. What is actually *wrong* with celebrating abstract symbols? Why not stress the interests of the nation rather than the interests of individual beings? Why not stress the survival of a race or species rather than of individuals making it up?

The answer is, as far as I can see, that abstract entities as such are of no value. What matters, ultimately, from a moral point of view, is what happens to individuals capable (at least) of feeling pleasure and pain. Only *individual* values are genuine. In order to be good absolutely, something must be good *for* an individual, capable of feeling (at least) pleasure and pain.

This is not to say that there exist no positive examples of nationalism. The U.S. struggle, say, for national independence was a worthy aim. But in those times, nationalism had a content. It was possible to see over and above the flags and the marches a point to the struggle, a point relating, in the final analysis, to respectable individual interests (in avoiding oppression, of various kinds). Even so, the flags and the marches are dangerous things. When the struggle is over, they tend to stay with us and live their own lives in the form of fetishes.

I will not try to argue the point in the present context that all respectable values are individual. I have discussed it in detail in *Hedonistic Utilitarianism* (2). It is here simply taken for granted. This means that if someone claims that the strength of his or her nation is of value in itself, he or she makes a value mistake. This mistake is dangerous if it leads to actions where individual interests actually get sacrificed for the sake of abstract, symbolic values. And this kind of sacrifice is the rule rather than the exception when a nationalistic ideology gets a firm hold of the members of a nation—in particular, if the nation in question does not face the least *threat* from any other nation.

Even if this be conceded, it might perhaps be argued that the kind of nationalism fostered by the public interest in team sports events is innocent. It might even be argued that nationalism in relation to sports is a good replacement for political nationalism (i.e., the kind of nationalism that is truly dangerous). It is better if people live out their nationalism in front of their television sets or on the seats around the sports arenas, than if they channel their nationalism through political parties and movements. Only in the latter case does their nationalism pose a real threat to important values.

I do not believe that this argument is tenable. The nationalism fostered by our interest for our "own" national team, and the nationalism we exhibit on the political arena, tend to reinforce each other. In particular, in periods where political nationalism is strong, what happens on the sports arenas tend to become politically important. There is only a small step from being a soccer hooligan to joining a fascist organization modeled on the Hitler Jugend. I will not develop this line of thought, however. The reason for not developing it has already been adumbrated. I think the common observation, that nationalism is becoming less and less important in relation to sports, is correct.

Why is nationalism within sports becoming less important? This has to do with commercialization and internationalization. The best sportsmen and the best teams earn enormous amounts of money. They can afford to allow themselves a considerable independence from political authorities and interests. They can take liberties with their own sports organizations. They rely rather on their own impresarios than on elected authorities of the Olympic Committee. However, when the old nationalism gives way, it gives way to something no less problematic. Let me now develop this main theme of my paper.

Contempt for Weakness

Nationalism, or chauvinism, has sometimes been thought to be a defining trait of nazism. However, in his seminal book, *Our Contempt for Weakness*, Harald Ofstad has argued, convincingly it seems to me, that the nationalism of the Nazis was only a contingent fact. To be sure, Hitler put the German nation before all other nations. And he put the so-called Aryan race before all other races. However, the hard core of nazism was different. The hard core of nazism was a contempt for weakness. This is shown by Hitler's reaction when the Third Reich broke down. In Hitler's own opinion, the defeat showed, not that there was something basically wrong with the Nazi ideology, but that there was something basically wrong with the German Nation. The German Nation had proved to be weak rather than strong. So eventually Hitler came to feel contempt for it (1: p. 24).

My thesis is: When we give up nationalism as a source of our interest in elite sports activities, when we give up our view of individual sportsmen and teams as representatives of "our" nation, when we base our interest in sports on a more direct fascination for the individual winners of these events—we move from something that is only contingently associated with nazism (nationalism) to something that is really at the core of nazism (a contempt for weakness).

Obviously, in my argument, a premise is missing. It is one thing to admire the person who wins the victory, who shows off as the strongest, but another thing to feel contempt for those who do not win (and turn out to be weak). I believe, however, that in doing the one thing, we cannot help but do the other. When we celebrate the winner, we cannot help but feel contempt for those who do not win. Admiration for the winner and contempt for the loser are only two sides of the same Olympic medal.

This is not to say that those who win the contest feel contempt for those who don't. It is one thing to compete and to want to win and quite a different thing to admire, as a third party, the winner. My argument relates to those who view sports, not to those who perform. Those who perform may well look upon each other as colleagues. They may feel that they are doing their job, and that is all. The winner may well feel respect for the loser. Or the winner may entertain any other feelings. It is not part of my project to speculate about this at all. My argument does not relate to the responses of the athletes; it relates to *our* responses to what they are doing. We, who comprise the public *viewing* the sports events, are the ones who admire the winner and feel contempt for the loser. If we are sincere in our admiration, and we often are, we cannot *help* but feel contempt for the losers. We would be *inconsistent* if we did not feel any kind of contempt for the losers, once we sincerely admire the winner.

To see why this is so we ought to think critically about *why* we admire those who excel in the Olympics. Our feeling is based on a value judgment. Those who win the game, if the competition is fair, are *excellent*, and their excellence makes them *valuable*; that is why we admire them. Their excellence is, in an obvious manner, based on the strength they exhibited in the competition. And the strength they exhibit is "strength" in a very literal sense of the word.

But our value terms are comparative. So if we see a person as especially valuable, because of his excellence, and if the excellence is a manifestation of strength (in a very literal sense), then this must mean that other people, who do not win the fair competition, those who are comparatively weak, are *less* valuable. The most natural feeling associated with *this* value judgement is—contempt. It is expressed in the popular saying: Being second is being the first one among the losers.

Contempt can take very different forms, of course. It may be of some interest in the present context to distinguish between three forms of contempt. First, contempt can take an aggressive form, as was the case with the Nazis. They wanted to exterminate weakness (by exterminating those who were weak). Second, contempt can take a negligent form. We try not to think at all about those for whom we feel contempt. We "think them away." We treat them as nonexistent. We do not care about them at all. Third, contempt can assume a paternalistic form. We want to "take care" of those "poor creatures" for whom we feel contempt. Common to all these reactions (all based on the idea that some individuals are of less value than others) is a tendency not to treat those who are considered less valuable with respect. They are not treated as full persons.

The surer we are that "we" are among the strong ones, among those who are valuable, the more prepared we are, I conjecture, to adopt the paternalistic reaction to those whom we consider weak. The more we fear that we might really belong to the weak ones, I also conjecture, the stronger our inclination to treat the weak ones negligently, as nonexistent—or even aggressively, with hatred: We want to exterminate them (i.e., *make* them nonexistent).

This is what is going on when enthusiastically we stay up half the night watching the athletes compete. To be sure, to some extent what takes place does so only in a symbolic way. We admire Carl Lewis for his excellence, and we feel some contempt for those who fall behind. However, we know that we would never stand a chance of beating Carl Lewis. Does this mean that we realize we are among those who are weak? It means, probably, that we fear this. But many of us believe we have other skills that compensate for those Carl Lewis possesses. Even if we are not physically as strong as he is, we may possess other kinds of strength. We may excel in respects that are (in our own opinions) more valuable than "strength" in the literal sense of the word.

But what if we do not? I believe that some of us may fear that we might fail on *all* relevant accounts. Those of us who do, I conjecture, are those who cheer most loudly for people like Carl Lewis.

What respects are relevant? This question is not possible to answer in a general manner. The Nazis had one (rather vague) notion about what kind of strength was important. We may have a differing view. As a matter of fact, each person may have his or her own opinion about this. But there is really no *need* to give a general answer to the question: What kind of strength is important to exhibit? As soon as we hold one opinion or another about it, we are vulnerable to the kind of argument I want to level in the present paper. Any person who is eager to be strong, who is prepared to feel contempt for those who are weak, and who fears that he or she may belong to those who are weak—any person who feels that those who are in any sense "strong" are better than those who are "weak"—are open to the criticism that he or she has fallen pray to the core of Nazi ideology.

There is a kind of betterness that is moral. A person, S, is (morally) better than another person, P, if and only if S is more praiseworthy, admirable, or deserving of the good things in life than is P. This notion is given a fascistoid twist when moral betterness is conceived of in terms of *strength*.

But must we feel contempt for those who are less successful (valuable)? Can we not just admire them less? I think not. For there are normative aspects of the notion as well. Those who are less valuable have to stand back when some goods (and evils) are to be distributed. And when resources are scarce, treating one person well is tantamount to treating another person badly. In a sports situation, this is clearly the fact. The setting is competitive. Olympic medals (and the money and reputation that go with them) are a scarce resource.

If we want to be sure that we do not get carried away by our admiration for winners, we ought to resist the very idea of moral excellence and betterness. In particular, we ought to resist the idea that moral excellence consists of *strength*.

To be sure, the idea of moral excellence in general and of moral excellence as (at least partly) a matter of strength of some kind, is an idea with deep roots in the history of philosophy, playing a crucial role for example in the ethical thinking of Aristotle. Yet an ethical theory can be constructed without having recourse to it. The utilitarian tradition, for example, bears witness to this.

Of course, even a utilitarian must concede that a life can be better or worse, for the person who lives it, depending on the content of the life, as experienced "from inside"; but this does not mean that a *person* can, as such, be (morally) better or worse. A certain kind of character can be more conducive to happiness than another kind of character, and should for this reason be encouraged; however, this has nothing to do with moral worth. In particular, it has nothing to do with strength of any kind. And the idea that strength is a proper grounds for admiration, the idea that underlies our fascination for the winners of sports events, is one that we ought to resist.

Objection: Similarities in the Arts and Science

Those who are prepared to concede that there is something to the argument stated above may still want to protest. They may want to argue like this. Even if there is something fishy about the reaction of the sports public to athletic achievements, it is unfair to single out sports for exclusive concern. After all, even within science and the arts we meet with the same phenomenon. Some people exhibit an unusual scientific or creative skill (strength). They make important contributions to science or create valuable pieces of art. They are then met with admiration. Does that not mean we value these persons in a manner similar to the way we value successful athletes? And if we do, does this not mean we think of those who are less successful in these areas as less valuable? Do we not exhibit contempt for weakness, then, when, for example, we give Nobel Prizes and the like to some "outstanding" persons?

At least to some extent I think this argument sound. And to the extent that it is sound, we ought to be ashamed of ourselves. But I think it sound only to some extent. For, to be sure, when we become enthusiastic about scientific and cultural achievements, we *need* not have scientists or artists as the focus of our attention. We can admire Frege's theories and Mozart's operas without feeling that Frege and Mozart are valuable persons. We can value the *products* of their ingenuity, not their genius itself. We can say truthfully that what they produced is of the utmost value but still retain the view that *they* are not more valuable than anyone else. They are merely *instrumental* to things of importance in themselves.

To be sure, even within science and the arts there are ugly manifestations of the phenomenon I have criticized within sports. Some people tend to get carried away with their admiration for lonely, heroic "geniuses" in the development of human science and art. Philosophy is not free of this phenomenon. There are people who speak with admiration of philosophers such as Nietzsche, Heidegger, and Wittgenstein, not because of any clear thoughts they have absorbed from the writings of these philosophers, but because they feel confident that these philosophers are especially "deep" and "inspired" thinkers. All this, like the actual Nazi ideology, is part of the legacy of the romanticism of the 19th century. However, while this phenomenon within science and the arts may be seen as a kind of corruption, it belongs in a more essential way to sports.

We can and we ought to admire the *products* of skillful scientists and artists, not these persons themselves, at least not because of their skill. (Perhaps some of them deserve our admiration because of their moral qualities, but Frege is not among those.) However, we cannot but admire the winning athletes themselves or else give up our interest in watching sport. Or can we? Why not consider the sports as simply a (very popular) part of human culture, where the results (products) of the individual achievements are what count?

Objection: We Admire Results, Not Athletes

I believe that there may be something to the objection that sport is not very different from art. In both cases there is excitement over the results of people's strivings. However, while the results are often, and should always be, the main focus of our attention within the arts, sports are different. There is an aesthetic aspect even to sport, to be sure. Some people are met with admiration not only because of their strength, but also because of the beauty with which they perform. Juantorena ran more beautifully than anyone before him. Why not say that it is the beauty of his running we admire, not himself? We admire the beauty in his running in the same way that we admire the beauty in a piano concerto by Mozart.

This line of argument is tenable to some extent. The Juantorena example is not a very good one, however. Had Juantorena not also been, for the time being, the fastest, we would not have remembered him for the beauty in his way of running. In the final analysis, what counts is who breaks the tape. But in some team sports, such as soccer, the aesthetic dimension may be considered more important. I believe that it might be of considerable importance, particularly among skilled audience members. After a match, they can discuss for hours the beauty in a single rush, irrespective of the outcome of the match where it took place. However, even *their* interest in the aesthetics of the play tend to be secondary, in the final analysis, to the outcome of the match. Remember that during the Chinese Cultural Revolution, there was a period when soccer competitions were reviewed with no mention of the outcome. At least among the majority of the sports public, this policy met with little approval and soon had to be changed.

As a rough approximation, then, we may say that, though there is room in science and the arts for admiration both of scientists and artists for their skill (their metaphorical "strength") and for their results, within sports there is room only for admiration of performers. The "results" they produce are not genuine; they are mainly results of measurements, measurements intended, first of all, to establish who won. But winning (a fair competition) is only a means. It is a means to prove excellence. So what we admire in sports is really the excellence shown by the winner.

Take away our admiration for the winner of the genetic lottery, who has proved his superiority in a big sports manifestation, and you take away most of our interest in the manifestation. This is true in particular for those of us who are not experts in the field and who tend to get carried away only now and then when we are informed by media that something remarkable is going on in a sports arena (like the Olympics).

But could it not be argued that what we admire is not really the *excellence* of the winner but what the winner has achieved *given* his natural endowments? And would not this kind of reaction on our part be morally more acceptable?

There is a grain of truth in this objection. And this grain of truth explains that there is a public interest in such things as female competition, competition between seniors, competition between handicapped persons, and so forth. When someone wins the Olympics for handicapped persons and we admire him or her for winning, we admire the achievement (given the constraints). In spite of the obstacles, this person made quite an achievement, we concede. However, the relatively weak public interest in such competitions, as compared to the interest in competitions of the absolute elite, shows that this kind of public interest in sports is of minor importance.

As a matter of fact, I suspect that there is even an element of contempt for weakness underlying many people's interest in this kind of handicap sport—but that it takes a paternalistic form. We do not take those who perform in handicap competitions seriously. We encourage them to go on but only in order that they develop into something less worthy of our contempt. In any case, if we are forced to choose, what we, the vast majority of us, want most to watch are competitions involving the *absolute* elite, not the Olympics for handicapped people.

Moreover, even if we are prepared to admire people who have worked hard, at least if they succeed in the competition (and the ability to work hard need not be anything that must be explained with reference to genes), I believe we will admire even more a person who excels *without* having worked hard for it. If a middle-aged member of the audience who never exercised unexpectedly walked down from the stadium and joined the Olympic 10,000-meter race and, because of superior natural talent, defeated all the finalists, the success would be formidable. Our admiration for this person would be unlimited. It is talent (which can be genetically explained), not achievement, we admire most. The point of the contest is to show who has the most superior talent.

This elitism of ours is also revealed by our way of reacting to doping. We want the competition to be fair. We are not prepared to admire Ben Johnson only because he has run 100 meters faster than anyone before or after him. Why? We suspect that Carl Lewis is genetically more fit than Ben Johnson. This is why we condemn Ben Johnson. He cheated.

But how do we know that Carl Lewis did not cheat too? Perhaps he was only more clever and got away with it. If doping were allowed, we would avoid *this* problem. We would not need to fear that the winner was not the strongest individual. If everybody were free to use whatever drugs they find helpful, then the crucial test, the competition, would show who is most fit. The competition is then fair.

For this reason, it is not at all implausible that doping, the deliberate use of drugs intended to enhance our strength, will rather soon be permitted. At least it is plausible to assume that drugs that do not pose any threat to the health of those who use them will be allowed. This seems only an extrapolation of a development that has already taken place. After all, there was a time when training was looked upon with suspicion. No one questions training today, and all athletes engage in it. Then came a time when *massive* training, on a professional basis, was condemned; I can vividly recollect the disdain with which swimmers from Eastern Germany were regarded by Western media during the 1960s. These days are also gone. Today, all successful athletes train on a professional and scientific basis. To the extent that all have the same resources at their disposal (an ideal we are far from having realized, of course, because of social differences and differences between nations), the competitions remain fair. But if training, even on a professional and scientific basis is all right, then why not accept doping as well, at least so long as the drugs used are not especially dangerous to the user?

If we were to permit such performance-enhancing drugs, we would no longer need to entertain the uneasy suspicion that the winner used prohibited drugs and managed to get away with it. We could then watch the games in a more relaxed manner.

A special problem, of course, is posed by the possibility of genetic engineering. What if those who win the Olympic Games in some not too distant future are not winners in a natural genetic lottery but genetically *designed* to do what they do? Would we still be prepared to stay up half the night to watch them perform? Would we still be prepared to admire those who make the greatest achievements? Would we still be prepared to cheer for the winners?

My conjecture is that we would not. Interestingly enough, then, genetic engineering may come to pose a threat not only to elitist sport but to the fascist ideology I claim underlies our interest in such sports.

Objection: Contempt for Weakness Is Human Nature

A fourth objection to my thesis that our admiration for sports heroes is at its core fascist needs to be addressed. Is not our admiration for strength, and a corresponding contempt for weakness, only natural? Are these feelings, moreover, not natural as well? Hence, is not a criticism of them misplaced? Since our nature is given to us by evolution, and since that nature dictates that we admire strength and feel a contempt for weakness, it hardly seems fair to criticize the possession and expression of these kinds of feelings.

This objection is flawed, but it renders necessary some important distinctions. It may be true that most of us are, by nature, competitive. We compete with each other, and we enjoy doing so. But there is nothing wrong in this, or at least, this competitiveness is not the target of my criticism. The competitiveness might go to an unsound extreme in certain circumstances, of course, but I do not intend to say that our competitiveness, as such, is immoral. Our competitiveness engenders important achievements, and it is a source of excitement and joy. It is also, of course, a source of disappointment and dissatisfaction. However, this is only as it should be; without *some* disappointment and dissatisfaction our lives would feel rather empty. I can readily concede this, for my criticism, in the present context, is not directed against competitiveness as such, nor to competitiveness in sports. I accept that scientists compete in a struggle to be the first to solve a certain problem, and I accept that athletes compete to win an important race. What I protest against is the admiration we show for the winner, be they scientists or sports heroes—and the corresponding contempt we feel for the losers. This reaction of *ours,* not the natural pride felt by *the winner himself,* is immoral. And the stronger our enthusiasm for the winner (and the stronger our corresponding contempt for the losers), the more immoral our reaction.

However, is not also this admiration for the winner, and the corresponding contempt for the loser, only natural? Well, this may depend on what we mean by calling a disposition "natural." Here we need another distinction.

One way of talking about "natural" dispositions is as follows. A certain disposition is "natural" if nature (evolution) has provided a species with it in the form of a blind *instinct*. If this is how the disposition is given to the species, then there is no room for blame when individual members of the species act on it. There is no point in blaming the lion for preying on the antelope. Under the circumstances, the lion can't help doing what it does. And it cannot help finding itself under the circumstances, either.

Another way of taking the idea that a certain disposition is "natural" is as follows. Evolution has provided the species with the disposition, but not as a blind instinct. Individual members of the species tend to act on it to be sure. And there exists a good evolutionary explanation *why* they do. However, sometimes they do not. When they don't, we need an explanation for this fact, an explanation cast, not in terms of evolutionary biology, but rather in cultural or psychological terms.

It seems highly implausible that our admiration for strength and contempt for weakness is natural in the former sense. Human beings are not driven by instinct when they cheer for the winners of the Olympics. If people choose not to do so, then they often succeed. Some people do choose, for one reason or another, not to join in, when the public hysteria is raised by main sports events. And they succeed in not joining in. So this is a possible course of action.

However, it might well be that we need an explanation why they do not join in, and the explanation may have to be cast in psychological or cultural terms. For snobbish reasons, say, they do not want to go with the crowd. Be that as it may, they *can* stay out of the events and they *do*.

So it might well be that our admiration for strength and our contempt for weakness, exhibited most prominently in our reaction to sports, is natural in the sense that is has been given to us by evolution: It takes education of some kind to avoid developing it. From an evolutionary perspective, it might have been advantageous to show contempt for weak individuals. It might have been advantageous to cheer for those who are skilled in aspects that relate to human survival. To borrow a phrase, if you can't beat them, join them. In particular, it might have been advantageous, alas, to despise handicapped children, not to feed them—and even to kill them, rather than to raise and nurture them.

This does not show, however, that such admiration for strength and contempt for weakness is morally acceptable. On the contrary, such kinds of contempt are *not* acceptable. They are morally evil. And to the extent we can through education counteract the influence of them, we ought to do so.

This raises an important and strongly contested question. If contempt for weakness is immoral, in particular when it is directed against individuals who are "weak" in a very literal sense of the word (people who are physically or mentally handicapped), does this mean that selective abortion (of fetuses with defective genes) is not acceptable?

It does not. It does mean, however, that some grounds for selective abortion are not respectable. It is not respectable to abort a fetus because one feels a "natural" contempt for the kind of handicap one knows it will be born with. Instead, one ought to convince oneself to accept and treat with respect individuals with this handicap. However, in rare circumstances, it can be obligatory to abort a fetus selectively, because one knows that the child it will develop into, if carried to term, will lead a miserable life, one filled with pain and devoid of pleasure. But then the abortion should not be carried out because of contempt for this (possible) child but, rather, out of compassion.

There may also exist selective abortions that are morally legitimate on the account that they save the family from unnecessary burdens, or, simply, because it allows a healthy child to be born rather than a handicapped one.

However, in all these kinds of selective abortions, as has been repeatedly and correctly noted by representatives of the handicapped people's movement, there is a risk that we might well be acting on an immoral contempt for weakness, rather than on a morally admirable compassion. Selective abortions provide much room for rationalization and wishful thinking. This is something we should always keep in mind.

Conclusion

I conclude, then, that our enthusiasm for our sports heroes is fascistoid in nature. It is not respectable. Our admiration for strength carries with it a fascistoid contempt for weakness. There are relatively innocent (paternalistic) forms of this contempt, but there is always a risk that they might develop into more morally problematic kinds, where we choose not to acknowledge those who are weak, or to reject them as unworthy of our respect, or worse yet, to seek their extermination (as did the Nazis).

It is true that sports are not the only place where this admiration for strength and a corresponding contempt for weakness is exhibited. We see the same phenomenon in the sciences and the arts as well. And when we do, what we see is no less morally depraved than what is exhibited in our enthusiasm for the winners of the Olympics. However, there is a rough but crucial difference between sports, on the one hand, and science and the arts, on the other. In sports, admiration of the winner is essential. If we do not admire the winners, and admire them *qua* winners of a genetic lottery, there is no reason to watch the games at all. For the aesthetic dimension of sports, however important it might be as an additional value, commands very little interest of its own. If our admiration for strength and contempt for weakness were somehow purged from sports, there would, I contend, be little reason to watch them. There will be little reason to watch sports competitions.

This is not to say, of course, that there will be little reason to take part in sports. We can all take joy in the exercise and excitement they provide. There is always someone to compete with. (If with no one else, one can always compete against oneself.) But if we get rid of our unhealthy enthusiasm for strength and corresponding contempt for weakness, no one will be able to arrange the kind of Summer Olympic Games that we witnessed in Atlanta in 1996.

Recommendation for the Future

Suppose we are now convinced that there is something wrong with our enthusiasm for sports heroes like Carl Lewis and Michael Johnson—what should we do about it?

Well, our enthusiasm for sports is much like an addiction. How do we defeat addictions? There is little help in imposing sanctions and using force. We cannot compel a person not to smoke, at least not if there remains a physical possibility for him or her to continue the habit. The only way to make someone give up a bad habit is to *convince* the person in question that the habit *is* bad. Then a possibility opens up that this person might, himself or herself, overcome the habit. This may take a lot of strength, skill, time, control, and cunning. However, eventually many people succeed in giving up even deeply entrenched bad habits. I suppose that something of the kind is what we ought to do with regards to our enthusiasm for sports heroes.

In sum, we ought to realize that our enthusiasm for sports heroes is fascistoid in nature. That is why it is no exaggeration to say, in closing, that if we are to grow as moral agents, we need to cultivate a distaste for our present interest in and admiration for sports.

Note

1. My neologism *fascistoid* should be understood in analogy with the word *schizoid*. Just as something schizoid tends to or resembles schizophrenia, something fascistoid tends to or resembles fascism.

Bibliography

1. Ofstad, H. *Our Contempt for Weakness. Nazi Norms and Values—And Our Own.* Stockholm, Sweden: Almqvist and Wiksell, 1998.
2. Tannsjo, T. *Hedonistic Utilitarianism.* Edinburgh, Scotland: Edinburgh University Press, 1998.

CHAPTER

Convention and Competence: Disability Rights in Sports and Education

Anita Silvers and David Wasserman

In the last six months, federal district courts have issued decisions in two highly publicized cases alleging discrimination on the basis of disability. In one, the Professional Golfers Association (PGA) was ordered to allow Casey Martin, a talented contender with a serious leg impairment, to use a golf cart in its championship tournaments, in contravention of its existing rules. In the other, Boston University (BU) was permitted to maintain its foreign language requirement without exceptions for learning-disabled students after a court-mandated faculty committee determined that the requirement was "fundamental to the nature of a liberal arts degree" at that university.

Both cases were brought under Title III of the Americans with Disabilities Act (ADA), which prohibits discrimination in "public accommodations," a term which covers a wide range of facilities, institutions, and organized activities. Both addressed the same issue under Title III: Was the proposed exception a "reasonable modification," or would it "fundamentally alter the nature" of the good, service, or activity in question?

Reprinted, by permission, from A. Silvers and D. Wasserman, 1998, "Convention and competence: Disability rights in sports and education." Report from the Institute for Philosophy and Public Policy, Volume 18, No. 4, pp. 1-7.

The drafters of the ADA expected the meaning of "reasonable modification" to be fleshed out in the courts, and the two rulings were made in the context of the distinct bodies of case law governing organized sports and higher education. Still, the cases *look* similar, at least from the distance of a newspaper report, and so it may seem puzzling that they were resolved differently. Why should the PGA not be allowed to decide that walking is fundamental to tournament play, if BU is allowed to decide that a foreign language requirement is fundamental to its liberal arts program?

Several explanations suggest themselves. The courts may be more deferential to the judgment of faculty committees, given the greater prestige of academics and the long tradition of university self-government, than to professional athletic associations. The nature of Casey Martin's disability was clear and undisputed while the diagnosis of "learning disability" on which the BU students' ADA claim rested remains deeply controversial. Finally, the opportunities available to the plaintiffs in the two cases were strikingly different. While there is only one PGA Tour (the most prestigious of the four tours offered by the PGA, and arguably the most prestigious in golf), there are lots of places to obtain a liberal arts degree—some more prestigious than BU, and many not requiring two years of a foreign language. For these reasons, the courts may have been more inclined to require inclusiveness and accommodation on the part of the PGA, while holding BU to a less demanding standard.

Ultimately, however, we cannot explain the appearance of inconsistency, or assess the merits of these decisions, without some understanding of how the ADA defines discrimination and what it requires for its redress.

What the ADA Demands

In enacting the ADA, Congress found that people with disabilities had been systematically denied "the opportunity to compete on an equal basis" by pervasive discrimination, involving not only "outright intentional exclusion" but also "architectural, transportation, and communication barriers," "exclusionary qualification standards and criteria," and the "failure to make modifications to existing facilities and practices." The ADA thus treats discrimination against people with disabilities as, in part, a sin of commission—the imposition of exclusionary practices and standards—and, in part, a sin of omission—the failure to remove barriers and to make reasonable modifications. This understanding of discrimination reflects a recognition that our society has deliberately or negligently excluded its disabled members from a wide range of activities by structuring those activities in a way that makes them needlessly inaccessible.

Eliminating such structural discrimination often requires significant changes in the physical and social environment. The most visible accommodations required by the ADA are the design features that ensure access for people in wheelchairs or people who are blind: curb-cuts, ramps, accessible entrances and bathrooms, braille signs, and computers that read their own screens aloud. But the ADA also requires less tangible accommodation, in the "design" of jobs, tasks, and activities. As one recent law review article observes, "By contrast to earlier prohibitions against discrimination, the ADA incorporates a more explicit understanding of the contingency of existing job configurations: that they need not be structured the way that they are. Rather than taking job descriptions as a given, reasonable accommodation doctrine asks how the job might be modified to enable more individuals to perform it."

The demand for restructuring may make the ADA look more "affirmative" than other civil rights laws; the measures required to accommodate people with disabilities appear more extensive, and less directly linked to the redress of prior intentional discrimination, than those required to protect the rights of women and minorities. But in fact, the changes mandated by the ADA are more circumscribed than those mandated by other civil rights legislation. For example, the ADA requires job restructuring only for those disabled individuals "otherwise qualified" to perform the job's "essential functions." Moreover, it requires modifications only if they are "reasonable," if they do not impose an "undue burden," and, to bring us back to the present cases, if they do not "fundamentally alter the nature" of the activity, good, or service being offered.

These exceptions make the antidiscrimination mandate of the ADA a good deal more conservative than it initially appears, but they still demand a bracing exercise in institutional self-examination. They require employers, public and private service providers, and, ultimately, the courts to decide what constitutes the essential functions of a job or the fundamental nature of an activity, good, or service. Because the functions of a job, the requirements for a degree, the rules of a game or social practice depend to a large extent on convention, habit, and the practical imperatives of bygone eras, it will often be difficult to say whether they are essential, or why. And because the ADA places the burden of proof on those who seek to maintain exclusionary practices, the difficulty of establishing that such practices are essential will often work to the benefit of those demanding accommodation.

Demonstrating Competence

If the implementation of the ADA has been complicated by uncertainty about the essential nature of various activities, goods, or services, it has also been complicated by uncertainty over what constitutes competence or qualification in those persons who are excluded from them. Formally, the second concern might not appear independent of the first: the competence or qualification of a person with a disability would seem to depend on the essential requirements of the job or the fundamental nature of the activity. But competence is not always assessed with reference to the requirements of a particular task or job. We will sometimes be more certain about a person's talent for achieving the outcomes associated with an activity than about the activity's fundamental nature; even those who claimed that walking was fundamental to the PGA Tour conceded that Casey Martin had already shown himself to be a formidable golfer. It may also be that our understanding of an activity's fundamental nature will be decisively *shaped* by our convictions about an individual's achievement. If we are more certain of the consummate skill that Casey Martin displays in playing golf than we are about the specific skills which golf requires, we may deny that the highest-level professional golf could possibly require any skill that Martin lacks. Along with his defenders, we may conclude that the PGA Tour is essentially a shotmaking competition.

There is a second reason why the assessment of competence is so uncertain: competence is more likely to have been attained and exhibited in some domains than in others. This may be the most striking contrast between the PGA and BU cases. Golfers who seek to compete in the PGA Tour will have had abundant opportunity to demonstrate their talent in other tournaments, while students at a liberal arts college most likely have promise rather than actual accomplishments to show. Admittedly, some college students can boast a Westinghouse Science Prize or a poem published in the *New Yorker*. But they are the exception. A liberal arts education offers few venues for precocious achievement, and talent in its specific domains may simply take longer to cultivate and display. The PGA case thus appears closer than the BU case to the ADA's paradigm injustice of a talented person with a disability denied an opportunity to "participate in, and contribute to, society."

In saying this, we do not mean to suggest that the ADA requires plaintiffs to display competence as clearly as Casey Martin did. Indeed, most people who claim discrimination based on disability will probably fall somewhere between Martin and the BU students, with achievements more concrete than the students' but less compelling than Martin's. Our suggestion is simply that in close or disputed cases—particularly cases where the fundamental nature of the activity is at all uncertain—plaintiffs are more likely to prevail if they can clearly display competence or qualification in the activities from which they have been excluded.

The "Fundamental Nature" Test

However unfair Casey Martin's exclusion from the PGA Tour might have appeared, it might not have been illegal if walking were indeed fundamental to the highest-level professional play. On this point, there was conflicting and ambiguous evidence. The PGA rules clearly stated that contestants were to walk the course, and some players regarded that as a formidable challenge in hot, humid weather and difficult terrain. But walking was not (otherwise) part of the competition: players did not get lower scores for faster walking, and no minimum pace or time was specified. Moreover, many players felt that walking was actually advantageous, giving them a feel for the course they would lack if they rode in a cart. Finally, the fact that other tournaments permit carts did not settle the issue of how to regard the walking requirement in the PGA Tour. That requirement may be seen as gratuitous, since walking is deemed essential in no other tournament, or, no less plausibly, as a defining requirement of the PGA Tour, distinguishing it from other tournaments.

Behind this specific clash of interpretations lies the more general question of how the courts could ascertain the fundamental nature of a conventional activity like PGA Tour golfing. This question invites comparison with the inquiry mandated under Title I of the ADA as to whether a given requirement is an "essential function" of a job. Title I prohibits employers from refusing to hire or retain "otherwise qualified" individuals on the basis of their disabilities; an individual is otherwise qualified if she can perform the "essential functions" of the job with reasonable accommodation. If the person with a disability cannot perform an essential function even with accommodation (such as the provision of assistive technology), the individual is not qualified.

Though many of the functions that people with disabilities cannot perform are clearly incidental to the jobs they seek to do, such as walking up a flight of stairs to work as a computer programmer, there is often disagreement about whether a particular function is incidental or essential (e.g., is the ability to quickly analyze a fact pattern and apply complex rules essential to lawyering, or is speed incidental, and extra time on bar examinations therefore a reasonable accommodation for applicants with learning disabilities?). Such questions—which were rarely asked before civil rights laws forced employers to address them—will sometimes be difficult to answer. But generally they can be resolved by examining a company's past practice, its productive and financial goals and constraints, and the practice of similar organizations: Does the employer really need this employee to perform this function in order to maintain its productivity or market share, comply with OSHA or EPA standards, or increase its dividends?

The inquiry may be less straightforward when a person with a disability seeks access to an activity, good, or service rather than a job. Formally, the language of Title I (regarding employment) and Title III (regarding public accommodations) is quite similar. Where the former requires "reasonable accommodation," the latter requires "reasonable modification"; both make an exception for undue burdens. And much as an employer is not required to accommodate a person with a disability who cannot perform the essential functions of the job, an organization is not required to modify the activity, good, or service it offers if that change would "fundamentally alter [its] nature." If walking indisputably had as incidental a role in golfing as it has in computer programming, the Casey Martin case would be an easy one under either section of the ADA.

The demand for reasonable modification suggests that the ADA recognize the same contingency in the "existing configurations" of activities like sports and education as it does in employment. But the contingency in such activities is different from that found in jobs. Sports are conventional in a way that jobs are not (or are not generally thought to be). Their features are not dictated by the external objective of making a product or a profit, but are shaped by tacit consensus and informal practice of the participants themselves. Education falls somewhere in the middle: closer to employment if we see it in more instrumental terms as job training; closer to sports if we see it as a constituent of a good, cultured, or civilized life, e.g., "Part of being an informed and cultured member of our society is having learned (or at least having been exposed to) a foreign language or the Classics of Western Civilization."

The more conventional character of sports, and arguably of education, may appear to make them more flexible, more amenable to modification, than the production- or profit-driven operations of a business. But their conventional nature is double-edged. The rules and practices that define a sport or a liberal arts education may be in some sense arbitrary, but they may also acquire a non-instrumental value that few job descriptions possess. The ADA's exemption for modifications that fundamentally alter the nature of an activity, good, or service can be seen as protecting, perhaps too categorically, the attachments and expectations that develop around conventional activities.

In the BU case, the court deferred to the considered judgment of a faculty committee that the foreign language requirement was essential to a liberal arts education at Boston University. There was ample precedent for this deference in other cases addressing the fundamental nature of an academic or professional program, based in part on the tradition of academic autonomy. (Indeed, that deference might have been greater if the BU president had not provoked the controversy with a wholesale attack on his school's program for students with learning disabilities and on the very idea of accommodating such disabilities.) Such deference may look elitist if we see the nature of a liberal arts degree as no less conventional than a golf tournament—why should academics be allowed to judge which of their conventions are fundamental while sports organizers must yield to the court's judgment? It will look a little less elitist if we see the requirements for a liberal arts degree as instrumental—developing the skills needed to succeed in civic or commercial life outside the academy (or within it, as professors). But the university might be reluctant to justify its foreign language requirement in instrumental terms. If the question is whether students perform better at various life pursuits with the minimal proficiency that two years of a foreign language confer, the BU faculty has no more expertise than other educators in providing an answer. Rather, the university may see the foreign language requirement as an essential constituent of a liberal education *as BU defines it.* In that case, its authority to impose the requirement is a matter of prerogative, not expertise.

Protected Values

We would like to conclude with some reflections on the values that may be protected by the "fundamental nature" exception of Title III. If the law were simply concerned with equitably distributing the costs of reasonable accommodation and modification among people with disabilities, employers, public accommodations, and the larger society, it is not clear why it would need such an exception in addition to that for "undue burden," as well as the overall requirement of reasonableness. If a public accommodation can modify its activity, service, or good without undue burden, what does it matter that the modification alters its fundamental nature?

This impatience with convention is found in some feminist writing on sports, which challenges the need for rules that limit the participation and success of women. Thus, Janice Moulton maintains:

> As it is now, athletes are used to adjusting their play to rule changes, and systems of scoring now exist to allow players at different levels to compete together. Informal games of many kinds are played with whoever shows up, and every school athlete has played in such games. The rules are freely revised to take into account the number of players, the playing field . . . , the level of skill, and anything else considered important. People who object to making changes in the standard rules may not realize how very often such rules are altered in practice.

As anyone who has followed the protracted controversies about rule changes in many sports will appreciate, however, players and spectators are often fiercely attached to the status quo, and regard even minor changes as threats to the integrity of the sport. Changes far subtler than those needed for the inclusion of people with various disabilities might well alter the style of play and the character of the game. The point is not that such changes would make the sport intrinsically better or worse, or would impose any tangible burden on the players, spectators, or organizers, but that they would alter familiar and cherished conventions. Moulton recognizes how sports talk pervades our social lives and civilization, but fails to recognize how much of that talk concerns the very details she would so readily alter in the interest of greater inclusiveness. It is not the improvised pick-up games that are debated in the barbershops and the tabloids; it is organized sports with highly specific rules and other conventions, a knowledge and acceptance of which is presupposed in the spirited discourse Moulton observes. This hardly renders those conventions sacrosanct, but it does suggest that changes can be wrenching and disruptive.

Moreover, one does not have to be a fetishist about existing conventions to worry about the broad postwar trend, in work, school, and sports, toward specialization. American sports used to place a premium on endurance and versatility, just as American universities once imposed a comprehensive liberal arts curriculum. A football career required a full 60 minutes on the gridiron, on defense and offense; a B.A. once required not only proficiency in Latin and Greek, and a familiarity with the classics of Western Civilization, but also an ability to swim several laps in an Olympic-size pool. The specialization that has overtaken many domains may be a welcome trend for those with finely honed but narrow talents and capabilities. But in these domains, many well-intentioned people fight to preserve an emphasis on versatility or well-roundedness, lest the participants become technicians instead of scholars or athletes. And even those not disposed to rearguard actions may feel some sense of loss when excellence in golf is confined to shotmaking or when pitchers no longer have to come to the plate to face their opposite numbers on the mound, leaving that task to designated hitters. Whether or not we believe that the law should attempt to take cognizance of such costs, it must recognize the danger of deforming a practice so extensively that it is no longer one in which previously excluded or included people wish to participate. At that point, the attempt to reshape the practice becomes self-defeating. If the ADA does give weight to convention in exempting public accommodations from changes that would fundamentally alter the nature of their activities, goods, and services, this is consistent with the generally conservative and incremental character of that statute. The ADA is committed to opening up existing employment, facilities, activities, goods, and services to people with disabilities, but it was not designed to equalize opportunities in more radical ways. While the interests of people with specific disabilities might be well served by the creation of new sports emphasizing skills in which they were likely to have developed compensatory superiority—the rough analogue of a proposal made by Jane English for reducing sex inequality in sports—or of more universities like Gallaudet, the ADA requires nothing of the sort. Rather, it calls for the maximum feasible integration, and leaves it to the courts to decide whether what is of distinctive value in an enterprise can be preserved by changes that permit people with a given disability to participate, and even to compete and win. Will the singular virtues of the highest-level professional golf be compromised if players use carts to go from hole to hole? Would a BU liberal arts degree lose its special character if it were conferred without two years of a foreign language? Such questions will often be difficult ones, both for disabled individuals who seek inclusion and for institutions which are pressed to change. Nevertheless, they provoke a valuable exercise in institutional appraisal.

Making Exceptions

One issue close to the surface but rarely discussed in cases like these is why we should have to choose between excluding people with disabilities from an activity, or altering its rules and conventions for everyone so that people with disabilities can be included. Why not simply make an exception to those rules or conventions for participants with disabilities? What does it matter if a few people are allowed to depart from the conventions that govern a sport or an academic program?

The most obvious concern is that exceptions would give some participants an unfair advantage, thereby imposing an undue burden on the others. Suppose that Casey Martin won a game on the PGA Tour by one stroke, pulling ahead on the final hole to beat a player exhausted by walking a long course on a hot, humid day. Or suppose that the two top seniors at BU had equal GPAs, but that one was a learning-disabled student who had gotten A's in foreign culture but would probably have gotten C's or D's in a foreign language, the other a non-LD student who had gotten B's in a foreign language, but would probably have gotten A's in foreign culture. Would it be fair to award Casey Martin the trophy, and to make the learning-disabled student valedictorian?

A second concern is that exceptions would alter the fundamental nature of an activity. Clearly, this could happen if an "exception" were available to all—and if there were some advantage to non-disabled participants in the alternative way of engaging in the activity. But it could also happen even if the exception were limited to disabled participants, since our notion of what constitutes achievement in that activity would be affected by their success. BU, for instance, would be hard-pressed to claim that two years of a foreign language were integral to its conception of liberal arts education if several of its recent valedictorians were learning-disabled students who lacked that coursework.

Operating in a legal framework somewhat different from the ADA, the Ontario court faced both of these concerns when it was asked to decide whether the province's Youth Bowling Council could exclude Tammy McLeod, a girl with cerebral palsy, from tournament play. Tammy aimed and released the ball down a ramp rather than holding it in her hand. The judge concluded that the girl was "not able, because of handicap, to perform the essential act of bowling—manual control and release of the ball." Under the ADA, such a finding would have settled the matter. By analogy with Title I, the employment section, the bowling council would not be required to include Tammy if she was unable, even with accommodation, to perform the essential functions of the sport. But under the Ontario Human Rights Code, as the judge interpreted it, the bowling council *was* required to include her. A person with a disability is entitled to accommodation whether or not she can perform the essential functions of an activity, so long as the accommodation does not impose a hardship on the organizers or on other participants. In this case, the judge ruled that there was no hardship: Tammy's device gave her "no competitive advantage over others" (since it did not allow her to impart speed or spin to the ball), and her use of it did not require other bowlers to alter their manner of play in the slightest.

The judge went on to say, however, that if use of the ramp *had* given Tammy a competitive advantage, or if she were to adopt a more sophisticated device, the bowling council might well be allowed to exclude her. In effect, he ruled that Tammy could participate as long as she was not competitive. He gave her permission only to engage in a loosely parallel activity alongside real bowlers, in which she was unlikely to obtain a higher score than the real bowlers, and unlikely to be regarded as having won a bowling game even if she did. Though she could be a participant in some attenuated sense, she could never be a contender. This resolution is ironic in a case where the judge emphasized the inherently competitive nature of sports: "All sport at all levels involves competition; all participants strive to win." It may have been a fair resolution for a youth tournament, where winning is not the only thing, but if so, the decision was fair for reasons that belied its stated rationale.

It will, of course, be as difficult to say when an alternative way of performing an activity confers an unfair advantage as it is to say whether it departs from the fundamental nature of that activity. From the moment he began to dance around Sonny Liston in Las Vegas, to the moment he had the ropes loosened in the Kinshasa ring to defeat George Foreman with his rope-a-dope, Muhammed Ali was accused of gaining unfair advantage or threatening the fundamental nature of heavyweight boxing; he is now almost universally regarded as having improved it. A cart on a PGA Tour golf course is surely closer to looser ropes in a boxing ring than to ramps in a bowling alley. But closer cases and difficult judgment calls will inevitably attend the integration of people with disabilities.

Bibliography

1. Pamela S. Karlan and George Rutherglen, "Disabilities, Discrimination, and Reasonable Accomodation," *Duke Law Journal*, vol. 46. no. 1 (October 1996).
2. Ruth Shalit, "Defining Disability Down," *New Republic* (August 25, 1997).
3. Michael Grunwald, "U.S. Launches Drive for Disabled Golfer: Justice Dept. Invokes ADA in Martin Case," *Washington Post* (August 24, 1998).
4. Janice Moulton, "Why Everyone Deserves a Sporting Chance: Education, Justice, and College Sport," in *Rethinking College Athletics,* edited by Judith Andre and David N. James (Temple University Press, 1991).
5. Jane English, "Sex Equality in Sports," *Philosophy and Public Affairs,* vol. 7 (Sprint 1978).
6. *Youth Bowling Council of Ontario v. McLeod, 75 Ontario Reports* (2d).

Index

About the Editors

William J. Morgan, PhD, is a professor of cultural studies at the University of Tennessee in Knoxville.

Morgan has served as editor and has published extensively in the *Journal of the Philosophy of Sport*. He has presented numerous papers on the topic of ethics in sport throughout the world and has written several books on the topic: *Philosophic Inquiry in Sport*; *Leftist Theories of Sport: A Critique and Reconstruction; Sport and the Humanities: A Collection of Original Essays;* and *Sport and the Body: A Philosophical Symposium.*

Morgan is former president of the International Association for the Philosophy of Sport and in 1995, received the association's Distinguished Scholar Award. In the same year, he was elected an active fellow of the American Academy of Kinesiology and Physical Education. He and his wife, Susan, reside in Knoxville, Tennessee. He enjoys running, rowing, and cycling.

Klaus V. Meier, PhD, is a professor at the University of Western Ontario. An influential figure within and a major contributor to the field of philosophy of sport, he served as editor of the *Journal of the Philosophy of Sport* from 1977 to 1994 and has been coeditor of *Olympika: The International Journal of Olympic Studies* since 1992.

Meier was president of Philosophic Society for the Study of Sport from 1984 to 1985 and has been a member of the society's executive council since 1977. In 1991, he was elected International Fellow in the American Academy of Kinesiology and Physical Education.

Angela J. Schneider, PhD, is the assistant dean of ethics and equity for the faculty of health science at the University of Western Ontario. She is current president of the International Association for the Philosophy of Sport, and she also serves as vice-chairperson of the World Anti-Doping Agency's Ethics and Education Committee and chairperson of the Expert Advisory Committee on Education for the Canadian Centre for Ethics in Sport. Schneider has consulted on numerous Canadian sport education television programs and international radio programs. She lectures throughout the world on the subjects of ethics in sport, performance-enhancing drugs in sport, and Olympic education.

Schneider won an Olympic silver medal in rowing at the 1984 Summer Olympic Games in Los Angeles. She serves as an executive member of Women's Sport International. She has also received the distinguished Canadian Olympic Gala Award for Olympians who have made significant contributions in the arts. She lives in Ilderton, Ontario, where she enjoys rowing, coaching, and family life with her partner and three sons.